MW00462333

+495
11 20

**MACROECONOMIC
THEORY**

ECONOMICS HANDBOOK SERIES

Seymour E. Harris, Editor

Burns: Social Security and Public Policy
Carlson: Economic Security in the United States
Fisher: The Identification Problem in Econometrics
Hansen: A Guide to Keynes
Hansen: A Survey of General Equilibrium Systems
Hansen: The American Economy
Hansen: Monetary Theory and Fiscal Policy
Harris: The Economics of Harvard
Harrod: The British Economy
Henderson and Quandt: Microeconomic Theory
Hirsch: The Economics of State and Local Government
Hirsch: Urban Economic Analysis
Hoover: The Location of Economic Activity
Johnston: Statistical Cost Analysis
Kindleberger: Economic Development
Lebergott: Manpower in Economic Growth
McKean: Public Spending
Nourse: Regional Economics
Ott, Ott, and Yoo: Macroeconomic Theory
Phelps: Fiscal Neutrality Toward Economic Growth
Quirk and Saposnik: Introduction to General Equilibrium Theory and Welfare Economics
Taylor: A History of Economic Thought
Theil, Boot, and Kloek: Operations Research and Quantitative Economics
Tinbergen and Bos: Mathematical Models of Economic Growth
Vickers: The Theory of the Firm: Production, Capital, and Finance
Walton and McKersie: A Behavioral Theory of Labor Negotiations

**McGRAW-HILL
BOOK COMPANY**
New York
St. Louis
San Francisco
Auckland
Düsseldorf
Johannesburg
Kuala Lumpur
London
Mexico
Montreal
New Delhi
Panama
Paris
São Paulo
Singapore
Sydney
Tokyo
Toronto

DAVID J. OTT

Professor of Economics
Clark University

ATTIAT F. OTT

Professor of Economics
Clark University

JANG H. YOO

Assistant Professor of Economics
Clark University

Macroeconomic Theory

This book was set in Times New Roman.
The editors were J. S. Dietrich and Claudia A. Hepburn;
the production supervisor was Dennis J. Conroy.
The drawings were done by Oxford Illustrators Limited.
Kingsport Press, Inc., was printer and binder.

Library of Congress Cataloging in Publication Data

Ott, David J
    Macroeconomic theory.

    1. Macroeconomics—Mathematical models. I. Ott,
Attiat F., joint author. II. Yoo, Jang H., joint
author. III. Title.
HB171.5.088   339   74-19014
ISBN 0-07-047918-6

MACROECONOMIC
THEORY

1 2 3 4 5 6 7 8 9 0 K P K P 7 9 8 7 6 5

To DANA and CHONG

CONTENTS

Preface   ix

Part 1 Basic Macroeconomics

  1 Introduction   3
  2 Output, Prices, and Employment: Concepts and Measurement   8
  3 Basic Macroeconomic Models: A Review and Critique   26

Part 2 Refinements and Extensions of the Basic Equilibrium Model

  4 Consumption   59
  5 Business Fixed Investment   93
  6 Investment in Residential Construction   119
  7 Inventory Investment   130
  8 The Foreign Sector   140
  9 The Demand for Money and Other Financial Assets   159
10 The Supply of Money and the Financial Sector Equilibrium   195
11 The Government Sector: The Budget Constraint   212
12 Production Functions, the Labor Market, and Aggregate Supply   219
13 A Summary of the Expanded Model   233

Part 3 Economic Growth

14 Inflation, Productivity, and the Phillips Curve   247
15 Equilibrium Growth Models without Money   264
16 Money and Growth   298

Part 4 Disequilibrium Macrotheory

17 Limitations of Equilibrium Macromodels   323
18 Keynes's Disequilibrium Model: The Two-Market Case   331
19 Distribution and Spillover Effects   345
20 Money and Disequilibrium   364

Indexes   383

   Name Index
   Subject Index

PREFACE

The purpose of this book is to provide a clear, rigorous, and structured presentation of macroeconomic theory for the use of graduate students in economics and to serve as a reference book for advanced undergraduate students. It is the product of over a decade of teaching a two-course sequence in macroeconomic theory for beginning graduate students who have a background in both intermediate macrotheory and microtheory and are familiar with the basic mathematical tools used in the professional journals that graduate students are expected to be able to read.

We have structured the book into four parts. Part 1, "Basic Macroeconomics," provides a brief discussion of some of the basic concepts used throughout the book (types of equations, variables, etc.), a quick review of the basic data important to macroeconomics (the national income accounts, prices, employment, etc.), and a concise, rather "tight" survey of the basic *equilibrium* macromodels which are covered, with less rigor, in most intermediate macrotheory courses. Part 2 expands on this base, dipping into more recent literature to survey theories and empirical estimates of the components of planned spending (consumption, investment, the foreign sector, the demand for and supply of money, and government budget policy) and the determinants of aggregate supply (the production function and the demand for labor and the supply of labor). Throughout Part 2, an attempt is made to give the student a "feel" for the empirical work done in each area. The empirical findings cited are pulled together in a summary of the revised equilibrium macromodel with the values of the fiscal and monetary multipliers calculated from the empirical studies cited in the preceding chapters.

Part 3 moves on to dynamic equilibrium macromodels. The dynamics of the "Phillips curve" literature is used to introduce this section, and this is followed by an extensive survey of equilibrium growth models, including growth models with a monetary sector.

The final section of the book, Part 4, is unique (as of this writing) to macroeconomics texts. The student is given an extensive introduction to the "new macroeconomics" of *disequilibrium* models. Students using this book will thus be versed in concepts increasingly important in the literature—spillover and distribution effects, price and wage "stickiness," etc.

Three themes are carried throughout the book. First, we emphasize the *microfoundations* of macroeconomic theory. Second, we attempt at least to acquaint the reader with some of the empirical evidence about the value of critical parameters. Third, we believe in, and stress, the usefulness of mathematics as an efficient device for understanding, and, indeed, simplifying, the intricacies of modern macroeconomic theory.

Since there are three coauthors of this book, the intellectual debts are necessarily substantial. Without attempting to identify the line of debt for each of us separately, we would like to thank the following persons who at one time or another were our teachers: Dudley Dillard, John G. Gurley, Daniel Hamberg, Gardner Ackley, Morris Bornstein, Richard Musgrave, Wahib Massiha, Thomas Saving, W. Phil Gramm, and C. E. Ferguson. Special thanks are due the readers of the manuscript —Michael Klein, Eugene Brady, Stephen Goldfeld, and Barry N. Siegal. Their comments and suggestions were invaluable in improving the final product, although they bear no responsibility for it. Finally, we wish to thank Jack Crutchfield for pushing us to finish the book in its critical stages, and J. S. Dietrich, the Economics Editor, for expediting the publication process.

Perhaps those most directly entitled to our gratitude are the graduate students who, both at Southern Methodist University and at Clark University, suffered through successive editions of the manuscript, and repaid us by their diligence in pointing out errors and mistakes.

We also wish to acknowledge the clerical and typing assistance of Maureen Baril, Bobbi Karman, and Susan Chin.

DAVID J. OTT

ATTIAT F. OTT

JANG H. YOO

**MACROECONOMIC
THEORY**

PART ONE

Basic Macroeconomics

1

INTRODUCTION

By the early 1960s, some twenty-five years after the publication of J. M. Keynes's *The General Theory of Employment, Interest and Money*, macroeconomic theory seemed to have settled into a somewhat comfortable rut. The interpreters of Keynes had refined and polished the basic "Keynesian" models into a generally accepted mold, and economists of widely varying political and philosophical persuasion found themselves falling back on this burnished Keynesian framework to provide answers to the basic issues of public policy—providing high employment, containing inflation, and finding methods to achieve balance of payments equilibrium.

A decade later, the policy problems are the same, but the theoretical structure of macroeconomics is in the process of rapid change. This change is occurring in two directions: First, there has been a remarriage, of sorts, between microeconomic and macroeconomic theory. Many of the basic equations in the standard Keynesian model—e.g., the consumption and investment functions—have been more firmly grounded in the theory of the firm and the household. Second, and perhaps more fundamental, the basic foundation of the Keynesian model—that the economy can be examined with a general equilibrium model—is being questioned. The "new macroeconomics" concentrates on models of *disequilibrium* in the economy (and, to come full circle, the source of inspiration for these models is Keynes's *General Theory*).

In this book, we attempt to provide a survey of macroeconomics, beginning with the standard Keynesian framework, then proceding to the major refinements made in this model, and, finally, introducing the new area of disequilibrium models. Before beginning the survey, however, we review some basic concepts in this chapter, and in Chapter 2 we review the problems of measurement of the key macroeconomic variables: output, prices, and employment.

BASIC CONCEPTS

Macroeconomic theory, like microeconomic theory, involves the construction of *models* of the behavior of certain economic variables of interest or concern. The differences between macroeconomics and microeconomics are thus the variables of concern. Macroeconomics is concerned with economics "in the large" (Ackley, 1961), that is, with the behavior of the most aggregative variables such as a nation's output, the general price level, and the overall unemployment rate. Microeconomics, on the other hand, concerns itself with similar variables at a lower level of aggregation. For example, it deals with output and prices for an industry rather than for the economy as a whole.

Thus we cannot separate economic *theory* neatly into two boxes labeled "macroeconomics" and "microeconomics." Consistency requires that the microeconomic propositions about individual and firm behavior be reflected in the behavior of macroeconomic aggregates. At the same time, the subject matter to which theory is applied —the questions we seek to answer—does make the division meaningful and efficient.

Let us consider some of the basic concepts used in constructing theoretical macromodels (or micromodels).

Variables and Types of Variables

The concept of a variable is straightforward: it is a magnitude which is measurable and takes on different values. The variables of interest to us will be developed as we go along, and in any case listing them at this point would not be very informative since their importance only becomes obvious within the theoretical framework used. At the same time, it is useful here to list some of the more important ways variables are classified.

First, variables are either *exogenous* or *endogenous*. Exogenous variables are those determined "outside the system." For example, most macromodels treat *population* as an exogenous variable since it is explained by all the forces determining the birthrate and deathrate, most of which are possibly noneconomic in nature. An endogenous variable is one which is explained within the model being used. In macromodels, aggregate consumption is commonly one variable of this type.

Second, a variable may be either a *flow variable* or a *stock variable*. A flow variable has a time dimension; a stock variable does not. For example, when we speak of a nation's output, it is per unit of time, usually a year. On the other hand, when we speak of a society's stock of capital, it is dimensioned at *a point in time*, for example, at the end of some year. Yet flow and stock variables are related. If we are discussing a nation's stock of capital K (measured in physical units), then the rate of change of the stock variable—dK/dt—is a flow variable, the rate of investment per period. In fact, as we shall see repeatedly later on, this relationship is a critical one in macroeconomics. Since a positive amount of net investment represents the rate of change of society's physical capital, stocks cannot be assumed constant (over any appreciable period) unless the value of the flow variable to which they are related is zero in each case. So, if stocks determine behavior—for example, if wealth affects consumption—then positive flows affecting wealth will in turn affect consumption as stocks change.

Finally, consider the nature of *prices* as variables. They are not flows or stocks. Rather they are the *ratio* of two flows. For example, the price of cars is the ratio of the flow of expenditures on cars to the flow of cars sold during a particular period. Since both flows have a time dimension, this cancels out.

Equations and Types of Equations

Equations portray the relation between specific variables. For example, we may say that total consumption C is a function of total income or output Y,

$$C = \bar{C} + cY$$

or

$$C = 100 + 0.6Y \qquad (1\text{-}1)$$

for $\bar{C} = 100$ and $c = 0.6$. In this case, the relationship has a *specific form*; namely, we have made C a linear function of Y. We could have written (not knowing or needing to know the specific form)

$$C = C(Y) \qquad \frac{dC}{dY} > 0 \qquad (1\text{-}2)$$

which is a *general form* of the equation constrained so that when Y rises so does C.

Besides illustrating the difference between general and specific forms, Eqs. (1-1) and (1-2) are examples of a type of equation—a *behavioral equation*. Behavioral equations specify the relation between certain variables based on the behavioral assumptions made about households or firms. These equations are the meat of macromodels and occupy most of the macrotheorists' time. A behavioral equation should explicitly account for the microfoundations of macroeconomics; to accurately specify the consumption function, we should have a well-founded theory of household consumption behavior.

Another type of equation is one specifying an *institutional* or *technological* relationship. For example, if banks are required by law to hold a fraction r of their deposits D as required reserves R^r, then

$$R^r = rD \qquad (1\text{-}3)$$

specifies this institutional equation. Or if, given the state of technology and the capital stock, the supply of output in the economy Y_s is positively related to the input of the services of labor N, we may write

$$Y_s = F(N) \qquad (1\text{-}4)$$

as the *production function* which specifies (in general form) this technological relationship.

In any macromodel we use a number of *definitional equations*. For example, if aggregate demand is the sum of consumption plus investment demand I, we have

$$Y_d = C + I \qquad (1\text{-}5)$$

as a definitional equation.

Finally, there are *equilibrium equations*. These specify the condition under which a given market is cleared. For example, if the demand for output is defined to be consumption (1-2) plus investment (assumed to be exogenous) and if the supply of output is determined by the production function (1-4), we have, as an equilibrium condition,

$$Y_d = Y_s \qquad (1\text{-}6)$$

or

$$C(Y) + I = F(N)$$

Economic Models

An economic model simply represents putting together the various equations describing the behavioral relationships, institutional or technological conditions, definitions, and equilibrium conditions for the economy. As an example, consider the familar textbook income-determination model (with no government sector):

(Consumption function)	$C = 100 + 0.6Y$	(1-1)
(Investment function)	$I = \bar{I} = 50$	(1-7)
(Production function)	$Y_s = Y$	(1-4a)
(Aggregate demand)	$Y_d = C + I$	(1-5)
(Equilibrium condition)	$Y_s = Y_d$	(1-6)

We have made use of all the types of equations discussed above. Equation (1-4a) departs from (1-4) in that it assumes that aggregate supply is perfectly elastic in response to changes in aggregate demand, but this too involves an assumption about the production function, and so it is still a technological type of equation. However, the variables used are all flow variables; we have avoided the complexity introduced by price and stock variables to simplify the exposition.

Thus, we have a model which has two behavioral equations—the consumption function and the investment function (where investment is treated as exogenous, as denoted here and throughout the book by a "bar" over the variable); one technological equation (the production function); a definitional equation for aggregate demand; and an equilibrium condition. These equations are *structural equations*; they define the structure of the model. Solving the model produces the equilibrium values for the endogenous variables C, Y_d, Y_s, and Y, and for the exogenous variable I, since the number of independent equations equals the number of unknowns.

Combining the structural equations yields yet another type of equation—the *reduced-form equation*. If we solve the model for Y by substituting (1-1) and (1-7) into (1-5) and then substituting (1-5) and (1-4a) into (1-6), we get

$$Y = 100 + 0.6Y + 50$$

$$Y = \frac{150}{0.4} = 375$$

$$Y = \frac{\bar{C} + \bar{I}}{1 - c} \tag{1-8}$$

where c is the coefficient of Y in Equation (1-1).

Equation (1-8) is the reduced-form equation for Y which relates Y to all the exogenous or predetermined variables in the model consistent with the structural specification of the model.

Statics and Dynamics

Macroeconomic models (like microeconomic models) may be framed in static or dynamic terms. In Chapters 3 to 13, we deal mostly with *comparative statics*. For example, the model described above is solved for the reduced-form equation for Y, and we investigate the change in Y from one equilibrium solution to another. A change in $\bar{C}$, from 100 to (say) 150, would produce the change in Y

$$\Delta Y = \frac{\Delta \bar{C}}{1 - c} = \frac{50}{0.4} = 125$$

This mode of analysis, which is still the dominant pedagogical device in economic theory, is deficient in that it takes no account of time. The consumption and investment functions and other behavioral equations may be shifting constantly, so that investigating a "once and for all" change in Y may not be very informative. The province of *dynamic* analysis is thus the movement of the variables over time. Most often this takes the form of constructing moving *equilibrium* models of growth. These we examine in Part 3.

Another objection to both comparative-statics and equilibrium growth models is that they assume the economy is in fact in equilibrium. However, the real world may be more often (if not continuously) in *disequilibrium* than in equilibrium, and this requires a different type of model than the comparative-statics or equilibrium growth models. Some developments in this area are discussed in Part 4.

READINGS FOR CHAPTER 1

ACKLEY, G.: *Macroeconomic Theory* (New York: Macmillan, 1961), chap. 1.
ALLEN, R. G. D.: *Macro-Economic Theory* (New York: St. Martin's, 1967), chap. 1.

2

OUTPUT, PRICES, AND EMPLOYMENT: CONCEPTS AND MEASUREMENT

To understand the forces that cause output, employment, and prices to vary, we must understand how economists define and measure these concepts. In this chapter we discuss available concepts and measures of national output and income, prices, and employment and unemployment.

THE CONCEPTS OF INCOME AND OUTPUT

Whatever is produced in any period accrues to someone; measured income and production in any period are identical. We may thus approach the problem of how to properly define income and product from the point of view of either production or income. To measure a nation's output or income, we must begin by deciding on an economically meaningful concept of income or product.

Let us begin by looking at the income side. *The economically meaningful concept of income is that amount an economic unit can consume during a specific period without reducing its income potential, or wealth,* or its *receipts* adjusted to allow maintenance of its income potential, or wealth.

To clarify this definition, suppose we have a household with a two-period horizon. We assume its wealth V is measured at the beginning of the period and spending occurs at the end of each period. Then the household's wealth, or *income potential*, at the beginning of period 1 is

$$V_1 = R_1 + \frac{R_2}{1 + i}$$

where R_1 and R_2 are receipts in periods 1 and 2 *net of expenses* required for their receipt and i is the relevant discount rate. It follows at the end of period 1 (the beginning of period 2) *before* any income is spent on consumer goods or investment goods, the household's wealth is

$$V_2 = R_1(1 + i) + R_2$$

By our definition, the household's *net income* Y_1 (at the end of period 1) is that amount it can dispose of without reducing its income potential, or the excess of V_2 over V_1 which can be consumed and still leave $V_2 = V_1$.

$$Y_1 = V_2 - V_1$$

$$= R_1(1 + i) + R_2 - R_1 - \frac{R_2}{1 + i}$$

$$= iR_1 + \frac{iR_2}{1 + i}$$

$$= iV_1$$

If $iV_1 > R_1$, the household can spend more than its current receipts by borrowing and still maintain its capital. If $iV_1 < R_1$, some of R_1 must be set aside to maintain income potential. Income defined as iV is also called *permanent income*, a concept currently used extensively in economic theory, and one we return to when we discuss consumption theory in Chapter 4.

However, income is not defined in the national income accounts as permanent income, for obvious reasons—future receipts are uncertain and hence basically non-measurable. Instead, the national accounts use essentially current receipts (our R_1, which excludes expenses involved in earning the income) less an arbitrary depreciation entry for nonhuman capital. *Thus we must begin our discussion of the national accounts by recognizing that the income concept used is not the proper one from the point of view of economic theory*, however valid the reasons which may force this choice on the account builders.

Furthermore, the problems only begin here. Since receipts are generated in production, a decision must be made about *which* output (and the resulting income) will be included. The national income accounts for the United States (toward which our discussion is oriented) basically begin with the notion of national output as a welfare concept—only that output which adds directly to the utility of consumers or is produced via derived demand to *in turn* produce goods and services which give utility to consumers (as in the case of capital goods) should be counted in measuring output and income. In short, *the national income accounts begin with the notion of measuring production of and income from production of economic goods*—goods and services which are relatively scarce and thus command a price in the marketplace, or *would* command a price if they were to pass through the marketplace. But *even this criterion is not adhered to, for the income from production of many economic goods is so difficult to measure*—the act of shaving, the work of the housewife, and the myriad ways individuals use their leisure time all represent "production" of and income from economic goods, in the sense that when traded on the market these goods and services command a price—that it is excluded from national income or product.

In the national accounts the *basic working definition* used is that all goods and services passing through the marketplace are economic goods, whereas if a good or service does not pass through the marketplace, a transaction *generally* will not be reflected in national income or output, which thus excludes the nonmarket activities of households. However, a number of exceptions are made to this rule. Some activities *not* passing through the marketplace are included in national income or output, while some activities that do pass through the marketplace are excluded.

In general, *imputed* income for nonmarket activities is included where it is considered feasible. The major cases where imputed income from nonmarket activity is estimated and included in national income or output are:

1 Wages in kind (uniforms, meals, etc.)
2 Agricultural income in kind (livestock and crops consumed on the farm)
3 Rent from owner-occupied housing
4 Interest from financial intermediaries

On the other hand several types of income arise out of market transactions which are *not* included in national income. These are:

1 Income from illegal activities
2 Capital gains and losses
3 Transfer payment income
4 Interest payments by the federal government and by consumers

The exclusion of income from illegal activity is a reflection of the national welfare orientation of the accounts. Even though activities such as gambling (where illegal), prostitution (where illegal), and narcotics sales in a sense pass through the marketplace, command a price, and presumably provide satisfaction to consumers, they are excluded from measures of national income or output because these have been defined by society, through its laws, as socially unproductive activities. Thus liquor consumption would presumably not be included in income and output for the period where national prohibition was in effect in the United States, but would be before and after this period.

Transfer payments are payments of income that do not reflect current production. Most transfer payments are made by governments—federal, state, and local—for income maintenance or redistribution purposes. Examples are social security benefits, G.I. benefits, unemployment compensation, and relief. In each of these cases no current production activity is rendered in connection with the payment, and since national income is a measure of income from current *production*, transfer payments must be excluded. Capital gains and losses are excluded for the same reason. When investors realize gains or losses from security transactions, or when business firms receive income from selling physical assets in periods where inflation causes their prices to rise, no *production* is reflected in the income received, and it is thus excluded from measures of output and/or income.

The reasons for excluding interest paid by the federal government and by consumers from national output and income are not as obvious as in the previous cases. The basic reason is that the bulk of these interest payments are not considered to be a return on (or payment for) the services of a factor of production. In the case of the federal government, the debt arose largely as the result of wartime expenditures, and does not correspond to a stock of government-owned physical assets which generate a stream of returns which would be measured by government interest payments. The 1964 revision of the United States income and product accounts puts consumer interest payments on the same basis, on essentially the same grounds.

Once the output and income to be included in national income or product is decided upon, the next problem to be faced is *what allowance to make for the direct expenses involved in obtaining that output or income, as these must be deducted to obtain net income or product.* Looked at from the output side, this problem is one of deciding what constitutes *final product* and what constitutes *intermediate product*. Total output *minus* intermediate product (the expenses involved or goods and services used up in getting final product) equals final product.

The United States income and product accounts treat as final product all goods and services purchased *but not resold* during the period under study. All goods and services *resold* during a period are classed as intermediate product. *While this may provide a convenient working definition of final and intermediate product, its main effect is to count as final product some product which is really intermediate, even though it is not resold during the period.* In all the cases discussed earlier where output of and income from economic goods and services are excluded because the goods and services do not pass through the marketplace, purchases of goods and services used to "produce" the nontraded final product (such as leisure) will be treated as *final* product, when really they are intermediate to the production of the (excluded) final product. This shows up mainly in the case of households, where purchases of food, recreational equipment, etc., are treated as final product when really they are "used up" in producing a nonmarket final product. In general, less allowance is made for household expenses in production than for firms. The time and cost of commuting to work are not considered as a cost of getting output (an intermediate product); yet the purchases of gasoline and oil, car maintenance, etc., that this gives rise to are treated as final product, and no allowance is made for the leisure time thus lost.

An even more obvious case where the working definition departs from a meaningful economic one is government purchases of goods and services. All government purchases of goods and services, whether from private business or in the form of the services of government employees, are treated as *final* product, which is consistent with the working definition in that none of the goods and services is resold during the period. Clearly, however, much of what the various levels of government buy is essentially intermediate product—it is an input to the production of other (final) goods and services. As examples, government services such as police protection, national defense, highway construction, and the courts all essentially involve provision of intermediate product that makes production of final product possible. However, since no generally accepted dividing line between final product purchased by government and intermediate product purchased by government exists, it is all treated as final product under the working definition based on resale.

The final problem we will mention concerns the *depreciation entry* used in the national accounts. As we saw earlier, the depreciation of income potential when income is defined as permanent income can be positive or negative; it depends on the relation between current receipts R_1 and permanent income iV. The first point to be made is that in the national income and product accounts no attempt is made to employ this economically meaningful concept of depreciation. The depreciation data are basically those used by firms, with an original cost basis, and using straight-line, declining balance, or sum-of-the-digits depreciation formulas. Furthermore, no such allowance is made for households or government, as would be the case were the permanent-income approach to be used. The allowance is restricted to business firms and applied only to their physical capital.[1]

MEASURING OUTPUT AND INCOME

Now that we have some idea of the concepts of income and output used in our national income and output accounts, we will briefly survey the structure of the accounts. To measure output and income for the economy, economists use a system of dual-entry accounts, commonly called the "national income accounts." Out of this system of accounts we get a number of measures, the most important of which (and the one we discuss first) is a measure of the nation's gross output, or *gross national product* (GNP), which is defined as *the sum of the market value of all currently produced final goods and services in the economy for some particular period.* In short, we estimate how much of each and every "final" good or service is produced in a period, multiply this amount by the *market price* of each good to get the *value*, and sum to get the total value of current goods and services produced.

The Production Statement for the Economy

To measure a nation's output, it is logical to begin with the statements of a business firm since most economic activity takes place in business firms in our economy. We want to know the total value of production in the economy. With a statement of

---

[1] For a more complete discussion of the treatment of depreciation, see Bailey (1962, pp. 279–280).

each firm's production, we can add up the production of all firms and be very close to describing the nation's total output.

Table 2-1 shows a "production statement" for some hypothetical firm we shall call "The Big Deal Corporation." The statement is basically just a rearrangement of the more familiar "income and expense statement." On the right side, the value of production is measured, whether that production was sold to consumers, government, or other firms or whether it went into inventory.[2] On the left side are the expenses connected with producing the output and gross profits.

The only items deserving special attention are "Retained earnings and inventory valuation adjustment," "Net increase in inventories," and "Less: government subsidies." If we simply took the change in the firm's inventories at *book value* from its accounts, the result might distort our measure of the firm's *production* or output. The net change in the firm's inventories *at book value* during period 1 (from the end of period 0 to the end of period 1) is

$$p_1 K_{I_1} - p_0 K_{I_0}$$

where p_1 is the average price of goods in stock at the end of period 1, p_0 is the average price of goods in stock at the end of period 0, and K_{I_1} and K_{I_0} are the physical quantities of inventories at the end of periods 1 and 0, respectively. What we want to measure though is $p_A(K_{I_1} - K_{I_0}) = p_A \Delta K_I$, the value, *at average prices over the period*, of the *change in the physical volume of inventories*. The inventory valuation

Table 2-1   BIG DEAL CORPORATION PRODUCTION STATEMENT
(Millions of dollars)

Materials purchased	450	Net sales:	
Wages and salaries	300	To Company A	400
Employer's social security contributions	10	To Company B	250
Rent	150	To government	500
Interest	150	To individuals	300
Gross profits	350	To foreigners	200
Corporate income taxes	(175)	Net increase in inventories	100
Dividends paid out	(50)		
Retained earnings and inventory valuation adjustment	(125)		
Depreciation	190		
Property taxes	100		
Less: government subsidies	50		
Charges against production	1,750	Total production	1,750

To avoid double counting, the items in parentheses are not added to the totals. The two sides of the production statement must balance, since in producing output the firm's receipts must equal costs.

[2] A basic accounting identity is that production equals sales *plus* inventory increase (less inventory decrease). Production exceeds sales when part of production goes into inventory. Production is less than sales when part of sales is made by reducing inventory.

adjustment (IVA) is a technique to adjust the change in the book value of inventories for price changes so that it approximates the value of the physical change in inventories. Since IVA changes the right-hand side of the production statement, the left side must be changed also, and the item changed is profits.

The deduction of government subsidies from the left-hand side is the counterpart to its deduction from the right-hand side in converting the income and expense statement of the firm to the production statement of Table 2-1. The firm's *income* on the right side would include government subsidies, but in measuring *production* we want to exclude income that does *not* arise from production, and so government subsidies are subtracted from *both* sides.

Now if we picture the same type of statement for *all* firms in the economy, it appears as in Table 2-2.[3] The same items generally appear on both sides of the production statement. Two new entries on the left—"Proprietor's income" and "Surplus of government enterprise less subsidies"—account for noncorporate firms (partnerships and proprietorships) and government-owned businesses, respectively. These noncorporate private and government enterprises make sales and incur expenses, but the difference is not called profit as in the case of corporations, and so special

Table 2-2 PRODUCTION STATEMENT OF ALL FIRMS IN THE ECONOMY
(Billions of dollars)

Wages and salaries	260	Sales:	
Employer's social security contributions	8	To consumers	302
Rental income of persons	13	To government	90
Interest	18	To domestic firms:	
Depreciation	40	intermediate products	(218)
Indirect business taxes	42	Capital products	50
Proprietor's income	11	To foreigners (net)	20
Gross profits	63	Plus: net increase in	
Dividends	(16)	inventories	3
Taxes	(34)		
Undistributed profits and IVA	(13)		
Surplus of government enterprise less subsidies	10		
Intermediate product (material) purchases	(218)		
Total	465		465

SOURCE: Hypothetical data.

[3] For national income accounting purposes, owners that occupy their houses are treated as fictitious "firms." The reason is that the services they receive from their houses is properly income to them and part of the GNP. The value of these services is included on the right side in "sales to consumers." On the left side wages, materials purchased, etc., incurred in maintaining the houses are entered under the respective headings, while the difference is entered under "Rental income of persons." Recall also that imputations are made for wages in kind and agricultural income in kind. These are entered in "Wages and salaries" on the left side and "sales to consumers" on the right side.

entries have to be made on the left for these items when the sales of such firms are counted on the right side.[4] In addition, a separate category, "Intermediate product purchases (sales)," has been entered on both sides of the production statement. This category represents purchases of raw materials and other inputs to be used by firms in producing final product. Purchases of intermediate product must equal sales, and since we are interested in measuring the output of final product, we can subtract this item from both sides of the production statement. This leaves us with 465 as the measure of final product produced by all firms in this period, and, of course, 465 as income generated in producing final product.

One final adjustment must be made to GNP. Note that on the right side we have included sales by business firms to government, or, looking at it another way, we have included government purchases of goods and services from private business. However, federal, state, and local governments not only buy goods and services from private business, but also hire the services of their own employees. We add, then, the total of government payments of wages and salaries to its employees (assumed to be 40 in Table 2-3) to both sides of the production statement, combining it with government purchases from business to get government purchases of goods and services (G) on the right side, and adding 40 to wages and salaries on the left side.[5] The total of either side is the GNP.

The final production statement or national income account for our hypothetical economy is shown in Table 2-3. On the right side, we have combined government wage and salary payments with government purchases of goods and services from

Table 2-3 **GROSS NATIONAL PRODUCT**
(Billions of dollars)

Charges against GNP		Expenditures	
Wages and salaries	300	Government purchases of	
Private	260	goods and services (G)	130
Government	40	Personal consumption	
Employer's social security contributions	8	expenditures (C)	302
Rental income	13	Gross private domestic	
Interest	18	Investment (I)	53
Proprietor's income	11	Net exports (X-IM)	20
Depreciation	40		
Indirect business taxes	42		
Surplus of government enterprise less			
subsidies	10		
Gross profits	63		
	505		505

SOURCE: Data are not *actual* data but are hypothetical data used to illustrate principles involved.

[4] The entry for government enterprises is a *net* figure, combining the "profitable" government-owned firms with the "unprofitable" ones.
[5] Recall that net interest on the federal debt and government transfer payments are *not* included in production or G.

private firms to get "Government purchases of goods and services (*G*)." We have combined the figures for "Net increase in inventories" and "Sales of capital goods" into "Gross private domestic investment (*I*)." Business sales of goods to consumers are called "Personal consumption expenditures (*C*)." Net sales to foreigners are "Net exports (X-IM)." Thus GNP from the expenditures side is

$$C + I + G + \text{(X-IM)}$$

or the sum of spending on United States-produced final goods and services and on imports by consumers, government, business, and foreigners. The left side of the production statement is the income generated, or payments made, in producing GNP, which is often called *gross national income*, or GNY.

If imports of goods and services IM are split into imports of consumption goods IM_C, investment goods IM_I, and goods imported for use by the government sector IM_G, then the expression above is more easily seen as a measure of total expenditures for U.S.-produced output:

$$\text{GNP} = (C - \text{IM}_C) + (I - \text{IM}_I) + (G - \text{IM}_G) + X$$

The terms in parentheses represent, respectively, consumption, investment, and government spending on *domestic* output, i.e., total spending (of each type) *less* the portion spent on imported goods.

Table 2-4   PRODUCTION STATEMENT FOR THE UNITED STATES, 1972
(Billions of dollars)

Wages and salaries	627.3	Personal consumption expenditures (*C*)	726.5
Other labor income	40.7	Gross private domestic investment (*I*)	178.3
Employer social security contributions	39.0	Net exports (X-IM)	−4.6
Proprietor's income	74.2	Exports	73.5
		Less: imports	78.1
Rental income of persons	24.1	Government purchases of	
Corporate profits plus IVA	91.1	goods (*G*)	255.0
Corporate taxes	(42.7)		
Dividends	(26.0)		
Undistributed profits	(29.3)		
IVA	(−6.9)		
Net interest	45.2		
Business transfer payments	4.6		
Indirect business taxes	109.5		
Surpluses of government enterprises less government subsidies	1.7		
Capital consumption allowances	102.4		
Statistical discrepancy	−1.5		
GNP	1,155.2	GNP	1,155.2

SOURCE: U.S. Department of Commerce, Office of Business Economics *Survey of Current Business* (June 1973), p. 16.

In one respect it may seem that we have violated our definition of gross national product. On the right side of Table 2-3 we have counted production of new capital goods ("Gross private domestic investment") as a part of GNP, and the incomes generated in producing new capital goods are counted in on the left side. Capital goods would seem to be as much as intermediate product as flour, wheat, steel, and all others so classified. When a firm buys a machine, the machine yields a stream of services over time that shows up in increased output. Capital goods are an *input* in the production process—not final output. Yet this is perfectly consistent with the concept of income or output. The capacity used to produce capital goods *could* be used for consumption or government purchases if there were no investment. In a sense we measure *possible* final product by including capital goods output in GNP. On the other hand the production we *do* classify as intermediate product *must* be available to obtain final product—we cannot divert that capacity. In this sense there is a difference, in the short run, between investment and other intermediate goods.

Table 2-4 presents the actual production statement for the United States for 1972, taken from the United States national income accounts. The entries (but not the dollar amounts) are virtually the same as in Table 2-3, except for minor name changes and a few added items on the left side:

1 "Capital consumption allowances" is basically the "Depreciation" item in Table 2-3. However, it includes charges in addition to depreciation, e.g., accidental damage to fixed capital.

2 "Business transfer payments" represents payments by firms not in connection with production. The major part of this is bad debts written off.

3 "Statistical discrepancy" is a balancing entry. Since the items on the two sides are estimated from different sources, there is always some error. The left side is thus adjusted with this entry to equal the sum of the items on the right side.

NET NATIONAL PRODUCT, NATIONAL INCOME, AND PERSONAL INCOME

Other useful measures may be obtained from the production statement. One such measure is *net national product* (NNP). Gross private domestic investment represents total output of capital goods in the period. Part of the new machines, plant, and other facilities may be used to replace capital that has worn out, has become obsolete, or has been damaged accidentally. *Net investment* is investment in excess of the amount needed to replace those capital goods that have become worn out, damaged, or obsolete during the period—it equals *gross investment* less capital consumption allowances (CCA):

$$I_n = I - \text{CCA}$$

Net national product is that part of the nation's output that is available for other uses *after* provision for capital consumption allowances:

$$NNP = GNP - CCA$$
$$= C + I + \text{X-IM} + G - CCA$$
$$= C + I_n + \text{X-IM} + G$$

In Table 2-4, we obtain NNP as

$$NNP = GNP - CCA = 1155.2 - 102.4 = 1052.8$$

NNP provides a better picture of the nation's economic progress than GNP since it measures the amount of output that is "left" *after* society provides for maintaining its capital stock. However, in practice it is not used extensively, primarily because the depreciation component of capital consumption allowances is somewhat arbitrary and unreliable.

Another measure of national product or income is *national income* (NY). This measures the results of productive activity in terms of the earnings of the "factors of production" (labor, capital, and natural resources) that are used in production. To obtain NY from GNP, we take the left side of the production statement and make the following adjustments:

$NY = GNP -$ business transfer payments $-$ indirect business taxes $-$ net surpluses of government enterprises $- CCA -$ statistical discrepancy

In short, we subtract from GNP all charges which do not represent factor-of-production incomes. None of the items subtracted accrue as income to labor, capital, or owners of natural resources. Alternatively, we may write NY as being equal to NNP less all the items above except CCA (since they are already taken out of NNP).

Finally, we can obtain *personal income*, a very important measure of the incomes *earned* by persons (though they may not receive it) during the period. The details of deriving this measure may be postponed for a moment, but it should be noted that this measure is the only item from the national income accounts available on a monthly basis. For this reason alone it is important to understand.

CLASSIFYING GROSS NATIONAL INCOME

The income generated in the production of GNP (the items on the left side of the production statement), which we call gross national income, must accrue to either consumers, firms, or government. This knowledge enables us to make a simple but useful classification of GNY. Let us first look at consumer income. What income do consumers have at their *disposal* for spending? We have already mentioned *personal income*, a measure of income earned by or given to consumers. To get it we subtract some items from the left side which do not represent income earned by persons, or consumers. These are (1) capital consumption allowances, undistributed corporate profits, and inventory valuation adjustment, which accrue to business firms; and (2) government income—indirect business taxes, corporate profits taxes, social security contributions, and the surplus of government enterprises less government subsidies. On the other hand, some income received and used for spending by consumers does not show up anywhere on the left side and thus must be added—*government transfer payments, net government interest*, and net interest paid by consumers (PINT). These items do not show up on either side of the GNP accounts because, as we noted earlier, they do not represent payments for *production* or for services rendered. But to consumers, they *are* income and must so be counted. The adjustments give us personal income—income *earned* by persons. But we want to measure their *disposable personal income* (DPY)—income available for spending or saving. Therefore, we must subtract from personal income all personal income taxes (and some other nontaxes, such as tuition for state schools) which come out of income and thus cannot be spent. Making all the above adjustments, we obtain *disposable personal income.*

Table 2-5 ADJUSTMENTS MADE IN OBTAINING GNY FROM THE PRODUCTION STATEMENT

	Items taken out (A)	Items put in (B)
DPY − PINT = GNP − A + B	Capital consumption allowance Indirect business taxes Undistributed corporate profits Corporate profits tax accruals Inventory valuation adjustment Personal tax and nontax payments Employer's social security contributions Employee's social security contributions Surplus of government enterprises less subsidies Net interest paid by consumers	Net government interest Net interest paid by consumers Government transfer payments
DBY = Σ of items B		Capital consumption allowances Undistributed corporate profits Inventory valuation adjustment
DGY = Σ of items B − Σ of items A	Net government interest Government transfer payments	Indirect business taxes Surplus of government enterprises less subsidies Corporate profits tax accruals Personal tax and nontax payments Employer's social security contributions Employee's social security contributions

Now what about *disposable business income* (DBY)? Three items on the left side of the production statement constitute business income—capital consumption allowances, undistributed corporate profits, and inventory valuation adjustment. So we put in two of the items eliminated in reaching a figure for disposable personal income.

Finally, we come to *disposable government income* (DGY). This consists of all the various types of taxes (plus the surplus of government enterprises less government subsidies) *less* transfer payments and net interest paid by government. In short, what the government has to use as income to purchase goods and services consists of its tax revenue, net revenue from its enterprises (less subsidies), *less* that part used for spending on transfer payments and net interest, or *net taxes* (T_n). Thus we put back in all the taxes taken out in reaching a figure for disposable personal income, and at the same time we take *out* the transfer payments and government interest that were put in in reaching that figure.

Table 2-5 shows all these adjustments made in obtaining DPY, DBY, and DGY and how they cancel out so that the left side, which we may call gross national income, is seen to be

$$\text{GNY} = \text{DPY} - \text{PINT} + \text{DBY} + \text{DGY}$$

DEFICITS AND SURPLUSES IN THE NATIONAL INCOME ACCOUNTS

Consider DPY − PINT for a moment. Consumers have two choices in disposing of their income after paying interest—they can make consumption expenditures or they can *save* (not spend); that is, $\text{DPY} - \text{PINT} = C + S_P$, where S_P is *personal saving.* Disposable business income is also called *business saving*, S_b, and DGY can be replaced by net taxes, T_n. Thus we can rewrite the equation for GNY above as

$$\text{GNY} = C + S_P + S_b + T_n$$
or
$$\text{GNY} = C + S + T_n$$

In brief, the income generated in producing GNP may be classified as consumption, savings, and net taxes.

We know that the right side of the production statement for the economy must equal the left side, since these are just two measures of the same thing. That is,

$$\text{GNY} = \text{GNP}$$
or
$$C + S + T_n = C + I + G$$

C can be dropped from both sides. Thus when we measure GNP in any period,

$$S + T_n = I + G$$
or
$$S - I = G - T_n$$

The left side is the surplus (if positive) or deficit (if negative) of spending over income by the private sector,[6] and the right side is the deficit (if positive) or surplus (if negative) of the government. In any period, then, the private sector's surplus must have a matching *deficit* by government; i.e., if the private sector is running a surplus, the government must be running a deficit. Likewise, when the government is running a surplus, the private sector must be running a deficit. These are accounting identities, and they say nothing about economic *behavior*.

We now have a basic grasp of the measures of output and income. It should be remembered that all we have discussed is how *actual* output is measured. We have said nothing about what makes that output what it is.

MEASURING PRICE CHANGES

We noted that in addition to output we are concerned with *prices*. When we speak of "price levels" and "prices" and their movements, our general meaning is clear. *Inflation* we clearly recognize as a condition of rising prices, and *deflation* refers to a situation where prices are falling.

When it comes to *measuring* price movements, however, things become less clear. Do we say "prices" are rising when some are rising and others are falling? How can we say "prices rose 5 percent" when others may have fallen?

Economists of course gauge price level movements with *price indexes*, which generally express "average" prices in one period as a percentage of "average" prices in another period. The price indexes currently published are generally *Laspeyres indexes*. The basic idea followed in this type of index is to obtain the total value at prevailing prices of a representative "basket" of goods for some period, called the "base period," we wish to compare other periods with. Then, for another period, the value of the *same* basket of goods is computed and expressed as a percentage of the value of the basket of goods computed at "base period" prices.

There is a huge literature, both theoretical and empirical, on the proper definition and construction of price indexes. We do not propose to review it here.[7] For many practical reasons, the main United States price indexes used are of the Laspeyres type. These are the *Consumer Price Index* (CPI), which measures the changes in prices of goods bought by families of urban wage earners and clerical workers, the *Wholesale Price Index* (WPI), which represents changes in the general level of prices of some 2,000 commodities at the wholesale level; and the *Implicit GNP Deflator*, a measure of changes in the prices of goods and services contained in gross national product.

---

[6] It may not be clear why the expression $S - I$ is the private sector's surplus (or deficit). Recall that private spending is $C + I$. Private *income* is DPY + DBY, or $C + S$. If we subtract spending from income, we get $(C + S) - (C + I) = S - I$.

[7] A good treatment of the theory of index numbers is to be found in Stigler (1966). For a good discussion of the deficiencies of existing United States price indexes and proposed revisions, see *Government Price Statistics, Hearings* (1961a).

"Deflating" GNP—Real versus Money GNP

A very crucial distinction in economic analysis is between *money* quantities and *real* quantities. In the case of GNP, we distinguish between *real GNP* and *money GNP*. *Real GNP* is GNP with the effect of price changes taken out; *money GNP* is GNP with no adjustment for price changes.

Take two years and compare the GNP figures as stated at market (current) prices. GNP may *rise* because the quantity of goods produced rises *or* because prices increase. Or a fall in GNP may represent either a fall in prices or a fall in output. When we "deflate" GNP, we take out the effect of price-level changes, leaving only changes due to underlying movements of real output.

The technique of deflation is straightforward. Suppose, for example, we have the following data on GNP in current prices (money GNP) and the implicit price deflator for GNP for the years 1958 and 1965:

	GNP in current prices (billions of dollars)	Implicit price deflator (1958 = 100)
1958	$500	100
1965	600	110

It is clear that in this example both output *and* prices rose over the period. Prices rose 10 percent; thus GNP in current prices would have risen by 10 percent, or from $500 billion to $550 billion, if output had stayed the same as in 1958. But how much would 1965 GNP have been if *prices* had remained at their 1958 levels?

To answer this, let us denote output in real terms as q, the average price of GNP as p, and GNP in money terms as R. Then 1965 GNP expressed in 1965 prices would be

$$R_{65} = p_{65}q_{65}$$

Expressed in 1958 prices, 1965 GNP would be

$$p_{58}q_{65}$$

and 1958 GNP in 1958 prices is

$$R_{58} = p_{58}q_{58}$$

The index of prices (1958 = 100) for 1965 is $p_{65}100/p_{58}$. Dividing 1965 output in 1965 prices by the price index for 1965, we get

$$\frac{p_{65}q_{65}}{100p_{65}/p_{58}}$$

When we invert the denominator and multiply, we obtain

$$\frac{p_{58}q_{65}}{100}$$

Thus we can express 1965 GNP in 1958 prices by the formula

$$\frac{\text{GNP}_{65}}{I_{65}} \times 100$$

where GNP_{65} is GNP in 1965 prices and I_{65} is the price index (1958 = 100) for GNP in 1965.

In our example, we find 1965 GNP would have been

$$\tfrac{600}{110} \times 100 = \$546 \text{ billion}$$

if prices had remained at their 1958 level. The \$46 billion change thus measures the change in *real* GNP, or, as it is sometimes called, "GNP in constant dollars."

When we want to discuss changes in output or the forces determining the level of output, we always shall mean "real GNP," or "GNP in constant dollars."

In actual practice the GNP deflator is not used to obtain real GNP from current GNP. The deflator *is itself* obtained by a comparison of real GNP and current GNP; it is the price index that *would be required* if one were to use a general price index to deflate current GNP to real GNP. Real GNP is in fact obtained by a component-by-component deflation of GNP; separate price indexes (obtained mainly from the WPI and CPI series) are used to deflate different types of consumption expenditures, investment outlays, and government purchases into real terms, and the real series for the various components of GNP are then added together to obtain an estimate of GNP in constant dollars. Reversing the deflating procedure above, the implicit GNP deflator is then

$$\frac{p_{65}q_{65}}{p_{58}q_{65}} \times 100 = \frac{100 p_{65}}{p_{58}}$$

THE LABOR FORCE, EMPLOYMENT, AND UNEMPLOYMENT

Our third concern was the level of employment and unemployment. Let us briefly review the definitions used for unemployment and employment.

At any time, a society has a certain number of persons who are willing and able to work. This is the "labor force." In 1972, for example, the United State's labor force (including the armed services) was about 89 million. The *civilian labor force* was about 86.5 million. When not all of the labor force is employed, we have *unemployment*. In 1972, some 4.8 million persons, or 5.6 percent of the civilian labor force, were classified as unemployed.

The estimates of the labor force, employment, and unemployment are prepared monthly by the Census Bureau for the Bureau of Labor Statistics. These estimates are based on a survey of a scientifically chosen sample of some 50,000 households spread throughout the United States. The *unemployed* are defined as those over 16 years of age (not in an institution or the armed forces) who are not classified as "employed," and who either have actively sought work in the past four weeks or did not seek it because they (1) have a job but are laid off or (2) are waiting to start a new job. The *employed* are considered to be those who during the week surveyed are at work for an employer, are self-employed, or are unpaid family workers for 15 hours or more. Included are those not at work because of vacation, labor dispute, or bad weather, as well as those taking time off for various reasons.

Not all unemployment is of a kind to give us concern. There is always an irreducible minimum of unemployment reflecting the fact that the economy is not perfect. This is what we call *frictional unemployment*. It represents the "normal" unemployment due to people switching jobs. Thus when we refer to "unemployment," we shall *always* mean unemployment in *excess* of the normal, frictional unemployment.

How much unemployment is frictional? There are differences of opinion on this question; some say frictional unemployment is no more than 2 percent of the labor force; others are willing to accept figures as high as 4 percent.

A basic problem is that frictional unemployment is likely to vary over time and to some extent with business conditions. Whatever frictional unemployment is, the problem of unemployment that concerns us is the amount over and above that considered frictional.

FULL-EMPLOYMENT GNP (FEGNP)

We have seen that GNP is a measure of aggregate output and spending. At the same time, however, GNP also generates employment. The demand for goods and services reflected in GNP is also an indirect demand for labor and other resources used in production.

At any given time there is a maximum *potential* GNP that is consistent with full employment of the nation's labor force. That is, given the size of the labor force, the average workweek and workyear, and the average productivity of labor per man-hour, there is some GNP that *could* be produced if the labor force were all employed, *allowing for frictional unemployment*. If we denote the available labor supply after subtracting frictional unemployment in man-hours by N and the average productivity of an hour of labor by O, then FEGNP is given by NO. Suppose, for example, that the available labor supply is 180 billion man-hours (90 million workers working 40 hours a week 50 weeks a year). If average productivity per man-hour were $6.40, FEGNP would be $1,152 billion.

However, the concept of FEGNP is inherently fuzzy since the concept of full employment is fuzzy. Given the uncertainty about the unemployment rate that represents only frictional unemployment, full employment is essentially an arbitrary concept. Since the 1960s, it has been conventional, even if arbitrary, to define full employment as a 96 percent *employment rate*, or a 4 percent unemployment rate. FEGNP would thus be the GNP consistent with a 4 percent rate of unemployment.

Actual GNP may be less than FEGNP (the unemployment rate exceeds that chosen to represent full employment) or even bump against and exceed FEGNP (when the actual unemployment rate falls below the arbitrary "full-employment benchmark" amount). When actual GNP falls below FEGNP, we have unemployment. When it tends to bump against and exceed FEGNP, the total demand for goods and services is stronger relative to available supply, with the likelihood of pressures for prices to rise. Full employment exists only when actual GNP = FEGNP.

FEGNP obviously does not remain unchanged with the passage of time. We can expect growth in the labor force, so long as it more than offsets reductions in the workweek and workyear, to increase the available labor supply N. Likewise, research and development and the addition of new capital equipment will make the average productivity of labor O rise. Thus to maintain full employment, *actual* GNP must grow with FEGNP.

The relation between actual GNP and FEGNP is obviously crucial to an understanding of the problems of inflation, unemployment, and growth and what can be done about them through federal budget policy. FEGNP is to some extent beyond the scope of public policy. The rate of growth of the labor force is not something that public policy can do much about, and the average workweek and workyear are not easy to affect either. There are a number of ways to affect the growth in labor productivity, e.g., through stimulating research and its application and through education.

But the *immediate* answers to the problems posed usually lie in influencing actual GNP rather than potential GNP. Therefore we must obtain some understanding of the primary forces at work determining actual GNP, and thus its relation to FEGNP. In Part 3, we shall come back to the forces determining the rate of growth in FEGNP or, as it is often called, "potential GNP."

READINGS FOR CHAPTER 2

ACKLEY, G.: *Macroeconomic Theory* (New York: St. Martin's, 1967), chaps. 2–3, and pp. 78–90 and 90–92.

BAILEY, M. J.: *National Income and Price Level: A Study in Macroeconomic Theory*, 2d ed. (New York: McGraw-Hill, 1971), chap. 12, "The Concept of Income."

Economic Report of the President, President's Council of Economic Advisers, 1962, pp. 49–52, 1966, pp. 39–44.

Government Price Statistics, Hearings before the Joint Economic Committee, Jan. 24 and May 1–5, 1961*a*, parts I and II, especially "Report of NBER Price Statistics Review Committee," pp. 659–665, also pp. 573–611 and 739–776.

Government Price Statistics, Report of the Joint Economic Committee, July 21, 1961*b*.

KEYNES, J. M.: *The General Theory of Employment, Interest and Money* (London: Macmillan, 1936), chap. IV.

National Income: A Supplement to the Survey of Current Business, U.S. Department of Commerce, 1954, pp. 27–50.

Report on Employment and Unemployment, Joint Economic Committee, 1962.

SHAPIRO, EDWARD: *Macroeconomic Analysis*, rev. ed. (New York: Harcourt, Brace & World, 1970), chap. 2–5.

STIGLER, G.: *The Theory of Price*, 3d ed. (New York: Macmillan, 1966), pp. 74–78.

Subcommittee on Economic Statistics: *Unemployment: Terminology Measurement, and Analysis*, Joint Economic Committee, 1961.

Survey of Current Business, U.S. Department of Commerce, August 1965, pp. 6–65.

3

BASIC MACROECONOMIC MODELS: A REVIEW AND CRITIQUE

We begin our analysis of the determinants of output, prices, employment, and the balance of payments by reviewing basic static equilibrium models of economic activity. This provides the essential framework for refinements and extensions in the chapters that follow and allows us to point out the major controversies over the structure of macroeconomic models.

THE FRAMEWORK: AGGREGATE DEMAND AND SUPPLY

The essential properties of different macroeconomic models may be conveniently summarized with the tools of supply and demand analysis. Aggregate *demand* for real national output comes, as we saw in the previous chapter, from government (government purchases) and the private sector (consumption, investment, and net exports). It seems intuitively plausible (and we prove it later) that the lower the price of output (the GNP deflator), the greater the quantity of output demanded by the private sector and, given government demand for output, the greater the total demand for real output. Thus, in Figure 3-1, we draw the familiar downward-sloping demand schedule D, relating prices p and real output demanded Y. On the other

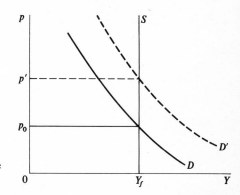

FIGURE 3-1
Aggregate supply and demand in the
neoclassical model.

hand, the shape of the aggregate *supply* curve S is a matter of dispute. Three possibilities are most often cited: (1) a vertical supply curve (the "neoclassical" model); (2) a horizontal supply curve (the "Keynesian" model); and (3) a positively sloped supply curve which, at some level of real output, turns vertical, or nearly so (the "intermediate" case).

The shape of the aggregate supply curves reflects fundamental assumptions made about the short-run behavior of the economy. For the neoclassical curve, shown as S in Figure 3-1, the assumption is that both wages and prices are flexible enough so that no matter what happens to the price level, output will always be at the level where full employment of labor (and capital) occurs, i.e., at Y_f. Shifts in total demand in this model only affect prices, not real output. For example, if total demand for real output at each price level increases (the D curve shifts rightward to D'), prices rise from p_0 to p', while output remains at full employment. The neoclassical model, then, makes output "supply-dominated" and prices "demand-dominated."

At the other extreme are the simple Keynesian models which most intermediate textbooks begin with. In this case (Figure 3-2), the price level is assumed constant at some level p_0; the aggregate supply curve is thus in effect assumed to be horizontal at this price level, as with S' in Figure 3-2. In this setting, output becomes demand-dominated and prices supply-dominated. With the aggregate demand curve D and the horizontal supply curve S', real output will be Y_0, which may or may not correspond to full-employment output Y_f. Increases in aggregate demand (to D') raise real output (to Y') but do not affect prices: decreases in aggregate demand (to D'') lower real output (to Y'') but also do not affect prices.

The third possibility for the aggregate supply curve—that over some range it has a positive slope—is consistent with the assumption that money wage rates are constant.[1] If money wage rates w are constant, then a higher price level means that

---

[1] It is consistent with other assumptions about the money wage rate that are discussed later, but at this point the exposition is simplified by assuming constancy of money wage rates.

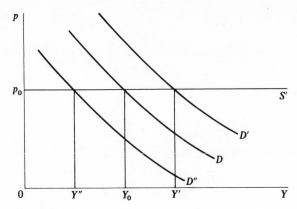

FIGURE 3-2
Aggregate supply and demand in the simple Keynesian model.

producers will hire more workers and produce more output because the additional revenue produced by the additional output from a unit of labor is raised. Or to explain it another way, elementary price theory shows that, given the price of labor (and other inputs), higher prices produce increases in output by competitive firms until price equals marginal cost. This intermediate supply curve is shown as S'' in Figure 3-3. Note that, at full-employment output Y_f, the curve turns vertical—increases in prices beyond this point cannot result in more output.

In this setting, as long as the aggregate demand curve cuts the supply curve on the positively sloped portion, policies affecting aggregate demand can affect both prices and real output. For example, if aggregate demand can be raised to D', so that the demand curve cuts the supply curve at point A, full-employment output can be reached, at the expense of some rise in the price level.

Thus the first major difference in alternative macromodels is in the shape of the aggregate supply curve. The assumptions made about the nature of this curve are crucial to the potential of using aggregate demand policies to affect output, prices, or both.

The second issue can be stated very simply: *How much effect do fiscal policy and monetary policy have on the aggregate demand curve?* Some economists take the view that fiscal actions (changes in government expenditures or net taxes) have little impact on demand while monetary policy actions (e.g., changing the supply of money) have a major impact. Others believe fiscal policy is a potent influence on aggregate demand and monetary policy is not. Still other writers believe both are powerful in their effects, although their impacts on demand occur through different channels and affect different sectors differently.

In the following sections, we shall construct more rigorous versions of alternative models and explore these issues more carefully. To begin, we take up the simple Keynesian model.

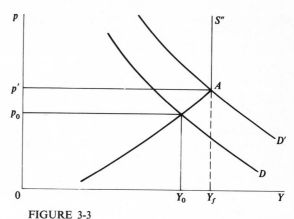

FIGURE 3-3
Aggregate supply and demand in the intermediate case.

THE SIMPLE KEYNESIAN MODEL

In the simple Keynesian model, we assume:

1 There is no foreign trade.
2 Prices and wages are constant—all changes in money income represent changes in output and not prices.
3 All corporate income is received by stockholders (or, alternatively, there are no corporations; all business firms are partnerships or proprietorships).
4 The only tax is a personal income tax levied at a flat rate on some proportion of GNP.
5 The values of all variables are expected to remain the same in future periods; e.g., income and interest rates are always expected to remain at their current values.

Total real demand E is the sum of planned real spending by consumers, business firms, and government (at all levels), and so we may write

$$E = C + I + G \qquad (3\text{-}1)$$

where C, I, and G represent planned real consumption, investment, and government goods and services purchases, respectively. Real consumption expenditures C are assumed to depend on real disposable personal income Y_d:

$$C = C(Y_d) \qquad \frac{\partial C}{\partial Y_d} = C_{Y_d} > 0 \qquad (3\text{-}2)$$

(The subscript notation for a partial derivative is used throughout the book.) Real gross private domestic investment I is assumed to depend negatively on the rate of interest i:

$$I = I(i) \qquad \frac{\partial I}{\partial i} = I_i < 0 \qquad (3\text{-}3)$$

In Chapter 5 we will explore investment theory thoroughly. For the moment, it is sufficient to note that the assumed dependence of I on the rate of interest is generally rationalized by a marginal-efficiency-of-investment approach to the investment decision of the firm. The firm is assumed to carry investment to a level where the marginal rate of return on investment [the marginal efficiency of investment (MEI)] equals the rate of interest (the marginal cost of funds to the firm). If the marginal rate of return on investment declines as investment increases, a decrease in i will then *increase* I as the firm seeks to drive the MEI down to the (lower) i; thus we can assume that $I_i < 0$. Real government purchases of goods and services G are assumed to be an exogenous variable—determined by forces not included in the model which we take as given. These would include, for G, all the forces shaping legislative budget decisions at the federal, state, and local level. Thus we can express planned aggregate spending as

$$Y = C(Y_d) + I(i) + \bar{G} \qquad (3\text{-}3a)$$

where the bar over G denotes an exogenous variable.

In Chapter 2, we found that real disposable personal income was equal to real gross national income or product Y, *minus* real corporate saving S_b, *minus* net real taxes T:

$$Y_d = Y - S_b - T \qquad (3\text{-}4)$$

Since we have assumed that all corporate income is received by stockholders, there is no corporate saving—all saving is on personal account—and so $S_b = 0$. Thus Y_d is

$$Y_d = Y - T \qquad (3\text{-}5)$$

We assume that all taxes are in the form of income taxes. *Net taxes* are gross income tax receipts less net government interest and transfer payments. We assume that taxes depend on *money income*; i.e., the net tax function is of the form

$$pT = \bar{T} + \tau(pY) \qquad (3\text{-}6)$$

where $\bar{T} < 0$ and τ, the marginal tax rate, is between zero and unity. In short, we apply the single tax rate τ to the difference between money GNP (pY) and a negative term $\bar{T}$. Net *real taxes* then are

$$T = \frac{\bar{T}}{p} + \tau Y \qquad (3\text{-}7)$$

Net taxes at any level of GNP may thus be *cut* by lowering the tax rate τ or by making $\bar{T}$ more negative—by an increase in personal exemptions, government interest paid, or transfer payments.

Now we add the money market. The money stock is assumed to consist of demand deposits at banks and currency in the hands of the public. The *supply* of nominal money M_s is assumed controlled by the monetary authority through its control over the monetary base H; i.e., the money supply equation is of the form

$$M_s = m\bar{H} \qquad (3\text{-}8)$$

where m is the money multiplier. In fact, the monetary authority does not control H without some "slippage." Furthermore, the money multiplier is affected by the behavior of the economy (particularly interest rates). These problems are discussed later in Chapter 10, but we assume here that m is constant and H is an exogenous variable controlled by the central bank.

We further assume that the demand functions for currency and demand deposits are identical, and so we may aggregate and speak of the demand for *money* (deposits plus currency) by households and firms. In simple income models commonly used, the demand for *real money* M/p is assumed to be negatively related to the rate of interest i and positively related to the level of real income Y. The rationale for these assumptions will be developed more fully in a later chapter, but they can be justified here briefly. Since money bears no objective return (assuming demand deposits carry no interest), the cost of holding money is the interest foregone from not holding interest-earning securities.[2] The higher i, the greater the cost of holding money and the less, *ceterus paribus*, will be held. The demand for real money is assumed to vary positively with Y on grounds that a higher Y increases the demand for money for transactions purposes, since a higher Y involves a greater total real value of transactions.

The demand for real money $(M/p)_d$ is thus given by the following equation:

$$\left(\frac{M}{p}\right)_d = L(Y,i) \qquad L_Y > 0 \qquad L_i < 0 \qquad (3\text{-}9)$$

Putting together our supply and demand equations for money, we have the equilibrium condition for the money market:

$$m\bar{H} = pL(Y,i) \qquad (3\text{-}10)$$

Substitute Eq. (3-7) into (3-5), (3-5) into (3-2), and (3-2) and (3-3) into (3-1). Together with the money market equilibrium condition (3-10) and the assumption that prices are constant

$$p = p_0 \qquad (3\text{-}11)$$

the model can be reduced to three equations and the three unknowns Y, i, and p:

$$Y = C\left[Y(1-\tau) - \frac{T}{p}\right] + I(i) + \bar{G} \qquad (3\text{-}12)$$

$$m\bar{H} = pL(Y,i) \qquad (3\text{-}13)$$

$$p = p_0 \qquad (3\text{-}14)$$

Equations (3-12) and (3-13) together describe the aggregate demand curve in Figure 3-2. From the money market, we can solve for the interest rate that equates the supply of and demand for money:

$$i = \phi(\bar{H},Y,p) \qquad \phi_H < 0 \qquad \phi_Y > 0 \qquad \phi_p > 0 \qquad (3\text{-}15)$$

---

[2] Note that implicit in the addition of i, the rate of interest on securities, is the existence of a market for securities. However, we need not analyze it explicitly.

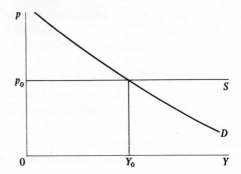

FIGURE 3-4
Equilibrium in the Keynesian model.

so that the total demand for output becomes

$$Y = C\left[Y(1 - \tau) - \frac{\overline{T}}{p}\right] + I[\phi(\overline{H}, Y, p)] + \overline{G} \qquad (3\text{-}16)$$

Differentiating (3-16) totally, setting the increments in the exogenous variables equal to zero, we obtain

$$dY = C_{Y_d}\left[dY(1 - \tau) + \frac{\overline{T}\,dp}{p^2}\right] + I_i\phi_Y\,dY + I_i\phi_p\,dp \qquad (3\text{-}17)$$

The slope of the demand curve is then

$$dY[1 - C_{Y_d}(1 - \tau) - I_i\phi_Y] = dp\left[\frac{C_{Y_d}\overline{T}}{p^2} + I_i\phi_p\right]$$

$$\frac{dp}{dY} = \frac{1 - C_{Y_d}(1 - \tau) - I_i\phi_Y}{C_{Y_d}\overline{T}/p^2 + I_i\phi_p} \qquad (3\text{-}18)$$

As long as the marginal propensity to consume (C_{Y_d}) is between zero and unity, dp/dY is negative (the aggregate demand curve is downward-sloping). With $0 < C_{Y_d} < 1$, the numerator of (3-18) is positive. The denominator is definitely negative since, by assumption, $\overline{T}$ and I_i are negative and ϕ_p is positive.

Equations (3-16) and (3-14)—the aggregate demand and supply curves—provide a solution for p and Y. The price level is, of course, fixed at p_0 by assumption. When p_0 is substituted for p in (3-16), the equilibrium value of $Y(Y_0)$ is obtained, as shown in Figure 3-4.

Alternatively, we can solve for equilibrium output Y and the *interest rate i*, from Eq. (3-12) and (3-13), using the assumption in (3-14) that p is constant. The equilibrium solution may be shown graphically through the use of the familiar *IS* and *LM* curves in Figure 3-5. In Eq. (3-12), given values for the exogenous variables τ, $\overline{T}$, and $\overline{G}$, different pairs of output and the rate of interest will produce equilibrium —an equality of output Y [the left side of (3-12)] and planned expenditures [the right side of (3-12)]. The *IS* curve in Figure 3-5 is drawn with a negative slope—a fall in

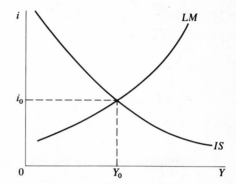

FIGURE 3-5
The Keynesian model: *IS* and *LM*
curves.

i requires a rise in Y to keep planned spending (E) equal to output (Y). As the rate of interest falls, planned investment and thus total planned spending will rise. An *increase* in Y also increases planned spending (E) by increasing consumption (C). The negative slope of the *IS* curve implies that an increase in Y increases Y more than E; the additional C induced by the rise in Y is less than the rise in Y. Thus, when i falls and E rises, a higher level of Y is required to make $Y = E$ again; the rise in Y increases E and Y but Y more than E. On the other hand, if a rise in Y increases E *more* than the rise in Y, then when i falls, a *fall* in Y is required to again make $E = Y$, and the *IS* curve has a positive slope. In short, the *IS* curve has a negative slope if $dE = \partial E/\partial Y\, dY < dY$, or if $\partial E/\partial Y < 1$. If we totally differentiate Eq. (3-12) and solve for di/dY, we obtain directly the slope of the *IS* curve

$$dY = C_{Y_d}\left(dY - \tau dY - Y d\tau - \frac{d\bar{T}}{p} + \frac{\bar{T} dp}{p^2}\right) + I_i\, di + d\bar{G} \qquad (3\text{-}19)$$

Since only i and Y are assumed to change, set $dT = d\tau = dG = 0$. Then we get

$$dY - C_{Y_d}[dY(1 - \tau)] = I_i\, di$$

or

$$\left.\frac{di}{dY}\right|_{IS} = \frac{1 - [C_{Y_d}(1 - \tau)]}{I_i} \qquad (3\text{-}20)$$

The bracketed expression in the numerator of (3-20) is $\partial E/\partial Y$. Since the relationship between planned investment and the rate of interest is a negative one—$I_i < 0$—then $di/dY|_{IS}$ is negative as long as $0 < E_Y < 1$. We assume this to hold here.

The *LM* curve shows paths of values for i and Y which, *given* the monetary base $\bar{H}$ and thus the stock of money $m\bar{H}$, satisfy the money market equilibrium condition, Eq. (3-13). Totally differentiating (3-13) we obtain an expression for the slope of the *LM* curve:

$$0 = p(L_Y\, dY + L_i\, di) + L(Y, i)\, dp$$

Since $dp = 0$ (that is, $p = p_0$),

$$-pL_i\, di = pL_Y\, dY$$

$$\left.\frac{di}{dY}\right|_{LM} = -\frac{L_Y}{L_i} \qquad (3\text{-}21)$$

Since $L_Y > 0$ and $L_i < 0$,

$$\left.\frac{di}{dY}\right|_{LM} > 0$$

The equilibrium values for the interest rate and the level of output (given p_0) are those that produce equilibrium in both markets, that is, i_0 and Y_0 in Figure 3-5.

We now consider the comparative-statics multipliers for changes in policy variables—the fiscal policy variables $\bar{G}$, $\bar{T}$, and τ and the monetary policy variable $\bar{H}$. Totally differentiating Eq. (3-16), we get

$$dY = C_{Y_d}\left[dY - \tau\, dY - Y\, d\tau - \frac{(p\, d\bar{T} - \bar{T}\, dp)}{p^2}\right]$$

$$+ I_i(\phi_H\, d\bar{H} + \phi_Y\, dY + \phi_p\, dp) + d\bar{G}$$

or collecting terms and setting $dp = 0$ (since $p = p_0$), we obtain

$$dY = -\frac{C_{Y_d}(Y\, d\tau + d\bar{T}/p) + I_i\phi_H\, d\bar{H} + d\bar{G}}{1 - C_{Y_d}(1 - \tau) - I_i\phi_Y} \qquad (3\text{-}22)$$

Consider the terms ϕ_H and ϕ_Y—measures of the response of the interest rate to changes in the monetary base and real output (from the money market equation). From total differentiation of (3-13), we see that

$$m\, d\bar{H} = p[L_Y\, dY + L_i\, di] + L(Y, i)\, dp$$
$$m\, d\bar{H} = pL_Y\, dY + pL_i\, di \qquad (\text{since } dp = 0)$$

and thus

$$\phi_H = \frac{\partial i}{\partial \bar{H}} = \frac{m}{pL_i} \qquad (3\text{-}23)$$

$$\phi_Y = \frac{\partial i}{\partial Y} = -\frac{L_Y}{L_i} \qquad (3\text{-}24)$$

Substituting (3-23) and (3-24) into (3-22) and taking changes in each of the exogenous policy variables one at a time (setting increments in the others equal to zero), we have the familiar "multipliers" (for convenience we set $p = p_0 = 1$)

$$\frac{dY}{d\bar{G}} = \frac{1}{1 - C_{Y_d}(1 - \tau) + I_i L_Y/L_i} \qquad (3\text{-}25)$$

$$\frac{dY}{d\bar{T}} = -\frac{C_{Y_d}}{1 - C_{Y_d}(1 - \tau) + I_i L_Y/L_i} \qquad (3\text{-}26)$$

$$\frac{dY}{Yd\tau} = -\frac{C_{Y_d}}{1 - C_{Y_d}(1 - \tau) + I_i L_Y/L_i} \qquad (3\text{-}27)$$

$$\frac{dY}{d\overline{H}} = \frac{m(I_i/L_i)}{1 - C_{Y_d}(1 - \tau) + I_i L_Y/L_i} \qquad (3\text{-}28)$$

The multipliers may also be derived from the *IS-LM* curve framework. Taking $\overline{G}$ first, we totally differentiate (3-12) and (3-13), as we did in finding the slopes of the *IS* and *LM* curves, and set all increments or decrements in exogenous variables *except dG* equal to zero (again we assume $p_0 = 1$):

$$dY = C_{Y_d}(dY - \tau dY) + I_i\, di + d\overline{G}$$
$$0 = L_Y\, dY + L_i\, di$$

Rearranging terms and dividing both equations by dG, we get

$$\frac{dY}{d\overline{G}}[1 - C_{Y_d}(1 - \tau)] - I_i \frac{di}{d\overline{G}} = 1$$

$$\frac{dY}{d\overline{G}} L_Y + L_i \frac{di}{d\overline{G}} = 0$$

Using Cramer's rule, we may solve the two equations for the two unknowns $dY/d\overline{G}$ and $di/d\overline{G}$:

$$\frac{dY}{d\overline{G}} = \frac{\begin{vmatrix} 1 & -I_i \\ 0 & L_i \end{vmatrix}}{\begin{vmatrix} L_Y & L_i \\ [1 - C_{Y_d}(1 - \tau)] & -I_i \end{vmatrix}} = \frac{L_i}{L_i[1 - C_{Y_d}(1 - \tau)] + I_i L_Y}$$

and obtain Eq. (3-25). Applying the same technique to the other three multipliers, we get the same expressions shown in Eqs. (3-26) to (3-28).

Looking first at the fiscal multipliers, (3-25) to (3-27), we see that each of these is absolutely larger the absolutely larger the responsiveness of the demand for money with respect to the interest rate (L_i) is, and absolutely smaller the absolutely larger the responsiveness of investment to the rate of interest (I_i) and the larger the responsiveness of the demand for money with respect to real income (L_Y). These relationships can be explained as follows. An increase in government purchases or a cut in taxes causes the demand for real money balances to rise as it causes Y to rise. This in turn puts upward pressure on the interest rate as firms and households seek to sell securities to obtain cash. Because of the dependence of I on i, this reduces I, partially offsetting the stimulatory effects of the fiscal action, and it also *reduces* the demand for money, bringing M_d and M back toward equality. Thus the money market pressures causing i to rise reduce the impact on Y of any fiscal action. The more the induced rise in Y causes M_d to rise (the absolutely *larger* L_Y is), the more this causes i to rise in order to again make $M_d = M$ (the absolutely *smaller* L_i is);

the more the rise in i reduces I (the absolutely *larger* I_i is), the less the impact of any fiscal action on Y (the absolutely *smaller* the fiscal multipliers). In summary,

The absolutely larger	The effect on the fiscal multiplier
I_i	$-$
L_Y	$-$
L_i	$+$

Now consider the effect on Y of a change in the monetary base shown by Eq. (3-28), which is facilitated by multiplying the numerator and denominator by L_i:

$$\frac{dY}{d\bar{H}} = \frac{mI_i}{L_i[1 - C_{Y_d}(1 - \tau) - I_Y] + I_i L_Y} \qquad (3\text{-}29)$$

$dY/d\bar{H}$ will be *larger* the *larger* (absolutely) I_i is. An increase in $\bar{H}$ and thus M spills over into the market for securities causing the interest rate to *fall* until $M_d = M$ again. The more this increases I (the larger I_i), the more the effect on Y. $dY/d\bar{H}$ is larger the (absolutely) smaller L_i is—with an increase in $\bar{H}$ and thus M, the smaller L_i is, the greater the decrease in i required to make $M_d = M$ and thus the larger the effect on Y. $dY/d\bar{H}$ is larger the *smaller* L_Y is; increases in Y also serve to increase M_d (along with the fall in i), and the larger the increase in Y required to raise M_d back to M, the more i has to fall to accomplish this. The value of $dY/d\bar{H}$ is larger the larger m is: the larger m, the greater the change in the money supply for a given change in $\bar{H}$.

Putting all our conclusions together, we get the following comparison of the fiscal and monetary multipliers:

The absolutely larger	The effect on the money multiplier	The effect on the fiscal multiplier
I_i	$+$	$-$
L_Y	$-$	$-$
L_i	$-$	$+$

Two versions of this model which are often noted in the literature occur where I_i and L_i take on extreme values. Comparing (3-25) and (3-28) we see that monetary policy is completely ineffective ($dY/d\bar{H} = 0$) and fiscal policy is extremely effective when $I_i = 0$ or when $L_i \rightarrow -\infty$.

In terms of Figure 3-4, this case is where fiscal policy has great impact on the position of the aggregate demand curve and monetary policy has little. In terms of the IS and LM curves, over ranges of the IS curve where $I_i \rightarrow 0$, the slope of the IS curve approaches $-\infty$ (becomes vertical), and over ranges of the LM curve where $L_i \rightarrow -\infty$, the slope of the LM curve approaches zero (becomes horizontal). Thus, in Figure 3-6, an increase in $\bar{G}$ which shifts the IS curve rightward has a maximum effect on Y as the shift occurs over the horizontal range of the LM curve [panel (a)]. However, an increase in $\bar{H}$ and thus M merely "stretches out" the flat part of the LM curve, and

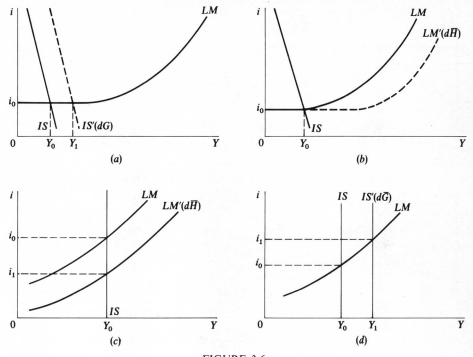

FIGURE 3-6
Effects of fiscal and monetary policy as $I_i \to 0$, $L_i \to -\infty$.

does not affect Y at all [panel (b)]. This special case is the well-known "liquidity trap" emphasized by Keynesians. In (c) and (d), where the IS curve becomes vertical—investment becomes perfectly interest-inelastic—$d\bar{H}$ also has no effect on Y and $d\bar{G}$ has a large effect.

The liquidity-trap case and the interest-inelastic investment case will be given special attention in Part 4 (Chapter 20) in connection with *disequilibrium* analysis. In either of the two cases, the aggregate demand curve tends to have a special form so that there is no way to restore full employment. This unemployment *dis*equilibrium produces severe intermarket pressures which may drive the whole system into an unstable situation, depending upon the degree of rigidity of prices and money wages.

In contrast, (3-25) and (3-28) also show that when I_i is very large or $L_i = 0$, fiscal policy is very ineffective ($dY/d\bar{G} \to 0$ as I_i becomes large or $L_i = 0$). The larger I_i, the more horizontal the IS curve; the smaller L_i, the more vertical the LM curve. Figure 3-7 shows how these effects on the IS and LM curves affect the behavior of Y when $d\bar{H}$ or $d\bar{G}$ changes. Increases in $\bar{G}$, shown in panels (b) and (c), have little or no effect on Y. Increases in $\bar{M}$ [panels (a) and (d)] have large effects on Y.

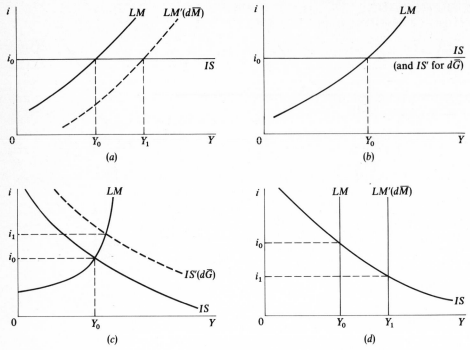

FIGURE 3-7
Effects of fiscal and monetary policy as $I_i \to -\infty$, $L_i \to 0$.

It is apparent that whether changes in real income will largely reflect monetary influences or fiscal influences will depend crucially on the values of I_i and L_i. This may also be stated in terms of the *interest elasticity* of investment and the demand for real money balances. Let us define $e_{I,\,i}$ and $e_{M/p,\,i}$—the interest elasticity of investment and the demand for money, respectively:

$$e_{I,i} = I_i \frac{i}{I} \qquad (3\text{-}30)$$

$$e_{M/p,i} = L_i \frac{i}{M/p} \qquad (3\text{-}31)$$

If I_i and $L_i \to -\infty$, so will $e_{I,\,i}$ and $e_{M/p,\,i}$; if I_i and $L_i \to 0$, then so will $e_{I,\,i}$ and $e_{M/p,\,i}$. The larger $e_{M/p,i}$ and the smaller $e_{I,i}$, the more important fiscal policy is in affecting aggregate demand; and the smaller $e_{M/p,i}$ and the larger $e_{I,\,i}$, the more changes in output reflect monetary policy.

In our more extensive discussions of the investment function and the demand for money, in Chapters 5 and 9, respectively, we shall explore our knowledge of the size of $e_{I,i}$ and $e_{M/p,i}$.

A DIGRESSION: STABILITY CONDITIONS AND THE CORRESPONDENCE PRINCIPLE

At this point, it is useful to consider the dynamic properties of the Keynesian model above for two reasons. First, the dynamic properties of a model can render the results of comparative-statics analysis (e.g., the multipliers discussed above) erroneous. Second, where the results of comparative-statics analysis are ambiguous, investigation of the dynamic properties of the system may enable us to remove such ambiguity.

To illustrate this, consider the $\bar{H}$ multiplier given in Eq. (3-28). We *assumed* the marginal propensity to consume out of an extra dollar of GNP—$[1 - C_{Y_d}(1 - \tau)]$ —was between zero and unity. An increase in $\bar{H}$ will *increase* Y (as we assumed in our discussion) only if the denominator of (3-28) is positive. But we cannot *prove* this is the case. If $[1 - C_{Y_d}(1 - \tau)] < 0$, the positive term $I_i L_Y/L_i$ may be swamped by this negative marginal propensity to consume out of real output. That is, if $|1 - C_{Y_d}(1 - \tau)| > |I_i L_Y/L_i|$, and $[1 - C_{Y_d}(1 - \tau)] < 0$, then the *IS* curve is positively sloped [Eq. (3-20)] *and* has a greater slope than the *LM* curve [Eq. (3-21)];

$$\left. \frac{di}{dY} \right|_{IS} = \frac{1 - C_{Y_d}(1 - \tau)}{I_i} > 0 \qquad (3\text{-}32)$$

$$\left. \frac{di}{dY} \right|_{LM} = -\frac{L_Y}{L_i} > 0 \qquad (3\text{-}33)$$

and therefore

$$\frac{\left. \dfrac{di}{dY} \right|_{IS}}{\left. \dfrac{di}{dY} \right|_{LM}} = \frac{1 - C_{Y_d}(1 - \tau)}{-\dfrac{L_Y I_i}{L_i}} > 1 \qquad (3\text{-}34)$$

As Figure 3-8 shows, under these conditions an increase in the monetary base and thus the money supply *lowers* equilibrium Y, from Y_0 to Y_1, and equilibrium i falls from i_0 to i_1. *Yet this comparative-statics result is erroneous.* Rather than falling from Y_0 to Y_1, income would rise without limit—the equilibrium point Y_0, i_0 is unstable. The downward shift in the *LM* curve caused by an increase in H and thus M lowers the interest rate to i_2 at output level Y_0. But this *increases* desired investment (I_i is still assumed to be negative) and causes income to rise. And while a rise in Y causes i to rise as the demand for money rises—along *LM*—the rise in i is not fast enough to choke off the rise in income. In short, comparative-statics analysis of equilibrium points may lead to erroneous conclusions if the dynamic properties of the model are not explicitly explored.[3]

---

[3] Another example is given by the case where $1 - C_{Y_d}(1 - \tau)$ is not so large in value as to make the denominator negative but makes the slope of the *IS* curve positive but less than the slope of the *LM* curve. In this case, a rise in the money supply *raises* the interest rate (and Y), a result not suggested by the usual assumption of a negative sloped *IS* curve.

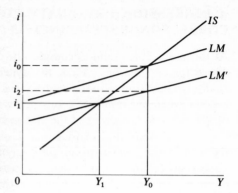

FIGURE 3-8
Unstable case with positively sloped *IS* curve.

The second use of analysis of the dynamic stability properties of the model is to ascertain the signs and relative values of coefficients such as L_Y, L_i, and I_Y. That is, we may not *know* the signs of some of these parameters, or even if we know the signs, we may want to ascertain their relative magnitudes. We can often (though not always) determine signs and relative values of parameters of such a qualitative model by *assuming* stability of the system.

Let us illustrate how to consider the dynamic properties of a model by using the Keynesian model developed in the previous section. The first step is to write out our assumptions concerning the dynamic properties of the model. In this case, we may assume (with $p_0 = 1$):

$$\frac{dY}{dt} = K_1[C(Y_d) + I(i) + G - Y] \qquad (3\text{-}35)$$

$$\frac{di}{dt} = K_2[L(Y, i) - \overline{M}] \qquad (3\text{-}36)$$

That is, the time derivatives of Y and i are linear functions of excess demands in the output and money markets, respectively. The K's are positive constants, and the sign of each term reflects an assumption about the direction of effect on the time derivative of each excess demand.

Using Taylor's theorem, we can obtain a linear approximation to the solution of the system in the neighborhood of equilibrium (Y_0, i_0) by writing it as[4]

$$\frac{dY}{dt} = [K_1(C_{Y_d}(1 - \tau) - 1)] \, d\overline{Y} + [K_1 I_i] \, di \qquad (3\text{-}37)$$

$$\frac{di}{dt} = [K_2 L_Y] \, d\overline{Y} + [K_2 L_i] \, di \qquad (3\text{-}38)$$

---

[4] For good discussions of the techniques used here as well as proofs of some of the theorems used, see Baumol (1970) and Dernburg and Dernburg (1969).

where $d\bar{Y}$ and $d\bar{\imath}$ represent small displacements of Y and i in the neighborhood of Y_0 and i_0. If we denote the bracketed expressions as a_{11}, a_{12}, a_{21}, and a_{22}, respectively, the system of simultaneous differential equations is

$$\frac{dY}{dt} = a_{11}\, d\bar{Y} + a_{22}\, d\bar{\imath} \qquad (3\text{-}39)$$

$$\frac{di}{dt} = a_{21}\, d\bar{Y} + a_{22}\, d\bar{\imath} \qquad (3\text{-}40)$$

For such systems of first-order differential equations, the determinant of the characteristic equation is

$$|A(x)| = \begin{vmatrix} a_{11} - x & a_{12} \\ a_{21} & a_{22} - x \end{vmatrix} = 0$$

which expands to a polynomial in x of the same degree as the number of equations in the system:

$$x^2 - (a_{11} + a_{22})x + (a_{11}a_{22} - a_{21}a_{12}) = 0 \qquad (3\text{-}41)$$

For the system to be stable, the real parts of the roots of the characteristic equation must be negative. In general form, the characteristic equation is

$$x^n + R_1 x^{n-1} + \cdots + R_{n-1}x + R_n = 0 \qquad (3\text{-}42)$$

It can be shown that:

1 R_1, the coefficient of x^{n-1}, is equal to the *sum* of the roots multiplied by -1.

2 R_n, the constant term in the characteristic equation, is equal to the *product* of the roots, multiplied by $(-1)^n$.

3 R_1 is simply equal to *minus* the sum of the principal diagonal elements in the determinant with x set equal to zero.

4 R_n is equal to the value of the determinant with x set equal to zero, times $(-1)^n$.

Since the criterion for stability is that the real parts of the roots be negative for roots that are not complex, the roots must sum to less than zero and their product must be positive if the number of roots is even and negative if the number of roots is odd. That is, a *necessary* condition for stability is that

$$R_1 > 0$$
$$R_n > 0 \qquad \text{if } n \text{ is even}$$
$$R_n < 0 \qquad \text{if } n \text{ is odd}$$

But since

$$R_1 = -tr|A(0)|$$
$$R_n = (-1)^n |A(0)|$$

it is necessary, but not sufficient for stability, that

$$tr|A(0)| < 0 \tag{3-43}$$

$$|A(0)| > 0 \qquad \text{for even number of equations} \tag{3-44}$$

$$|A(0)| < 0 \qquad \text{for odd number of equations} \tag{3-45}$$

For the model studied here, in order for the system to be stable

$$a_{11} + a_{22} < 0 \tag{3-46}$$

and

$$a_{11}a_{22} - a_{21}a_{12} > 0 \tag{3-47}$$

That is, the system will be stable only if

$$K_1[C_{Y_d}(1 - \tau) - 1] + K_2 L_i < 0 \tag{3-48}$$

Since $K_2 L_i < 0$ and $K_1 > 0$, then, for stability,

$$K_1[1 - C_{Y_d}(1 - \tau)] - K_2 L_i > 0$$

or

$$K_1[1 - C_{Y_d}(1 - \tau)] > K_2 L_i \tag{3-49}$$

That is, while the bracketed term can be negative (the *IS* curve can have a positive slope), it cannot be too negative for a stable system. Just how negative it can be is determined from the other necessary condition for stability (3-47):

$$\{K_1[C_{Y_d}(1 - \tau) - 1]\}(K_2 L_i) > (K_1 I_i)(K_2 L_Y)$$

or rearranging terms

$$[C_{Y_d}(1 - \tau) - 1] > \frac{I_i L_Y}{L_i}$$

$$[1 - C_{Y_d}(1 - \tau)] < - \frac{I_i L_Y}{L_i}$$

$$\frac{[1 - C_{Y_d}(1 - \tau)]}{- L_Y I_i / L_i} < 1 \tag{3-50}$$

which is the stability condition discussed earlier (3-34) where the slope of the *IS* curve, if positive [i.e., if the numerator in (3-50) is negative], must not exceed the (positive) slope of the *LM* curve.

THE NEOCLASSICAL MODEL

We now consider the neoclassical model. The assumptions remain the same as for the Keynesian model, except that assumption (2)—constant prices—is replaced with the assumptions that (1) pure competition exists in both the product market and the factor (labor) market and prices and wages move in response to excess demand or supply in these markets and (2) workers supply labor in response to *real wages*. In short, the *total demand* for output is the same as before [Eq. (3-16)]:

$$Y = C\left[Y(1 - \tau) - \frac{\bar{T}}{p} \right] + I[\phi(\bar{H}, Y, p)] + \bar{G} \quad (3\text{-}16)$$

On the other hand, *aggregate supply* is no longer infinitely elastic at a given price level; it is determined by the addition of an aggregate production function relating output supplied to variations in labor input (given the capital stock).

$$Y = F(N, K_0) \quad (3\text{-}51)$$

where N = labor, input (in man-hours)
K_0 = capital stock

The production function is assumed to be twice differentiable, and to exhibit diminishing returns to inputs of labor (that is, $F_N > 0$; $F_{NN} < 0$).

Given the production function (3-51), the supply of output is known (for a given capital stock) with the determination of the amount of labor (N) employed. This is found by considering the market for labor. The *demand* for labor (N_d) is obtained from the familiar profit-maximizing condition for the competitive firm:

$$\text{VMP}_N = w \quad (3\text{-}52)$$

The value of the marginal product of labor (VMP_N) must equal the price of labor—the money wage rate w. Recall $\text{VMP}_N = F_N \times p$, and by assumption the marginal product of labor F_N is a decreasing function of N. Let $F_N = f(N)$, then (3-52) can be written

$$\frac{w}{p} = f(N) \quad (3\text{-}52a)$$

$$w_d = pf(N) \quad (3\text{-}53)$$

where w_d denotes the demand price of labor.

The aggregate supply of labor is assumed to be a positive function of the real wage rate and the potential labor force L:

$$N_s = N\left(\frac{w}{p}, L \right)$$

where $N_{w/p} > 0$. Given L, this can also be written in inverse form as

$$\frac{w}{p} = \phi(N) \quad (3\text{-}54)$$

or
$$w_s = p\phi(N) \quad (3\text{-}55)$$

where w_s denotes the supply price of labor.

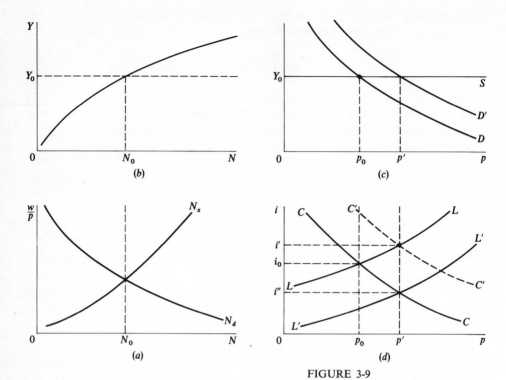

FIGURE 3-9
Equilibrium in the neoclassical model.

The whole model can now be written out, using (3-51), (3-53), and (3-55) from above and (3-12) and (3-13) from the Keynesian model:

$$Y = C\left[Y(1 - \tau) - \frac{\overline{T}}{p}\right] + I(i) + \overline{G} \quad (3\text{-}12)$$

$$m\overline{H} = pL(Y, i) \quad (3\text{-}13)$$

$$Y = F(N, K_0) \quad (3\text{-}51)$$

$$f(N) = \phi(N) \quad (3\text{-}56)$$

It is clear that Eqs. (3-51) and (3-56) determine real output Y (given the capital stock). The labor market equilibrium condition is solved for the amount of N that clears this market, and substitution of N into (3-51) determines Y. Given N and Y from the supply side, Eqs. (3-12) and (3-13) are solved (given $\overline{G}$, $\overline{H}$, and $\overline{T}$) for the equilibrium values of the price level p and the interest rate i.

The neoclassical model is thus dichotomized into a "real" and a "demand" sector. The former determines real output and employment; prices and the rate of interest are determined by the demand sector. In Figure 3-9, we find N_0, equilibrium labor input, from panel (*a*). Substituting this into the production function [panel (*b*)] yields equilibrium, full-employment output Y_0. In panel (*c*), this translates into the supply curve vertical at Y_0, and, given the demand curve *D*, the equilibrium price level is p_0.

Panel (*d*) shows market equilibrium curves for the commodity and money markets, given a real output of Y_0. The *CC* curve shows pairs of *i* and *p* that satisfy (3-12), given Y_0, $\bar{G}$, $\bar{T}$, and τ. Since a rise in *p* makes $\bar{T}/p$ less negative, real taxes *rise*. Given Y_0, then *i* must *fall* in order to increase investment demand enough to equate the demand for output and input. The *LL* curve is the locus of points where the stock of money $m\bar{H}$ equals the demand for it [Eq. (3-13)], given $\bar{H}$ and Y_0. A rise in *p* increases the demand for nominal money, and since the stock of nominal money is fixed $(=m\bar{H})$, then *i* must rise to bring the demand for nominal balances back down to the equilibrium level. Thus the *LL* curve has a positive slope.

Now consider the effect of an increase in government purchases $\bar{G}$ or the monetary base $\bar{H}$. Since *Y* and *N* are determined by (3-51) and (3-56) and must remain at Y_0 and N_0, we can solve (3-12) and (3-13) for the effects on *p* and *i*. Taking the change in $\bar{G}$ first, we obtain

$$0 = -C_{Y_d}\frac{(-\bar{T}dp)}{p^2} + I_i\, di + d\bar{G}$$

$$0 = pL_i\, di + \frac{m\bar{H}}{p}\, dp$$

Rearranging, we get

$$-d\bar{G} = C_{Y_d}\frac{\bar{T}}{p^2}\, dp + (I_i)\, di$$

$$0 = \frac{m\bar{H}}{p}\, dp + (pL_i)\, di$$

and by Cramer's rule,

$$dp = \frac{\begin{vmatrix} -d\bar{G} & I_i \\ 0 & pL_i \end{vmatrix}}{\begin{vmatrix} C_{Y_d}\dfrac{\bar{T}}{p^2} & I_i \\ \dfrac{m\bar{H}}{p} & pL_i \end{vmatrix}} \qquad di = \frac{\begin{vmatrix} C_{Y_d}\dfrac{\bar{T}}{p^2} & -d\bar{G} \\ \dfrac{m\bar{H}}{p} & 0 \end{vmatrix}}{\begin{vmatrix} C_{Y_d}\dfrac{\bar{T}}{p^2} & I_i \\ \dfrac{m\bar{H}}{p} & pL_i \end{vmatrix}}$$

$$dp = \frac{-pL_i\, d\bar{G}}{\dfrac{C_{Y_d}\bar{T}pL_i}{p^2} - \dfrac{m\bar{H}I_i}{p}} \qquad di = \frac{d\bar{G}\left(\dfrac{m\bar{H}}{p}\right)}{\dfrac{C_{Y_d}\bar{T}pL_i}{p^2} - \dfrac{m\bar{H}I_i}{p}}$$

Solving for dp first, we get

$$dp = \frac{d\bar{G}}{\frac{1}{p^2}\left[\frac{m\bar{H}I_i}{L_i} - \bar{T}C_{Y_d}\right]} \qquad (3\text{-}57a)$$

which, by assumption about the signs of I_i, L_i, and $\bar{T}$, is positive. Solving for di, we get

$$di = \frac{d\bar{G}}{\frac{C_{Y_d}\bar{T}I_i}{m\bar{H}} - I_i} \qquad (3\text{-}57b)$$

which is also positive. In this case, the higher level of G is made possible by a fall in both categories of private spending—C and I. The rise in prices reduces consumption by increasing real taxes; the rise in interest rates means I must be lower.

An increase in the monetary base also causes prices to rise, but in this case interest rates fall. In Figure 3-9 this is equivalent to a rightward shift in the LL curve with the CC curve remaining in the same position. Solving for dp, we get

$$dp = \frac{\begin{vmatrix} 0 & I_i \\[4pt] m\,d\bar{H} & pL_i \end{vmatrix}}{\begin{vmatrix} \dfrac{C_{Y_d}\bar{T}}{p^2} & I_i \\[8pt] \dfrac{m\bar{H}}{p} & pL_i \end{vmatrix}} \qquad dp = \frac{-mI_i\,d\bar{H}}{\dfrac{C_{Y_d}\bar{T}L_i}{p} - \dfrac{m\bar{H}I_i}{p}}$$

$$dp = \frac{-d\bar{H}}{\dfrac{C_{Y_d}\bar{T}L_i}{pmI_i} - \dfrac{\bar{H}}{p}} > 0 \qquad (3\text{-}57c)$$

Solving for di, we obtain

$$di = \frac{\begin{vmatrix} \dfrac{C_{Y_d}\bar{T}}{p^2} & 0 \\[8pt] \dfrac{m\bar{H}}{p} & m\,d\bar{H} \end{vmatrix}}{\begin{vmatrix} \dfrac{C_{Y_d}\bar{T}}{p^2} & I_i \\[8pt] \dfrac{m\bar{H}}{p} & pL_i \end{vmatrix}} \qquad di = \frac{\dfrac{C_{Y_d}\bar{T}m\,d\bar{H}}{p^2}}{\dfrac{C_{Y_d}\bar{T}L_i}{p} - \dfrac{m\bar{H}I_i}{p}} = \frac{\dfrac{C_{Y_d}\bar{T}m\,d\bar{H}}{p}}{C_{Y_d}\bar{T}L_i - m\bar{H}I_i} < 0 \qquad (3\text{-}57d)$$

In the case of an expansion of $\bar{H}$, private investment rises (since i falls) at the expense of private consumption (since p rises). Government purchases remain the same.

THE INTERMEDIATE CASE: A POSITIVELY SLOPED AGGREGATE SUPPLY CURVE

Thus far we have considered cases where the aggregate supply curve is horizontal (prices are constant) and where demand dominates movements in Y, and the neoclassical case where Y is completely determined by the labor market and the production function and shifts in aggregate demand affect only the price level and the rate of interest. The intermediate case—where, at least over certain ranges, the aggregate supply curve has a positive slope—is the object of discussion in this section.

To explain the intermediate case, let us reconsider the labor market discussed in the previous section. Where the aggregate supply of and demand for labor depend on the real wage rate (given L, the potential labor force), we have the labor demand, supply, and equilibrium conditions (3-53), (3-55), and (3-56):

$$\text{Labor demand}: w_d = pf(N) \qquad \text{(3-53)}$$

$$\text{Labor supply}: \quad w_s = p\phi(N) \qquad \text{(3-55)}$$

$$\text{Equilibrium}: f(N) = \phi(N) \qquad \text{(3-56)}$$

At this point, it is useful to look at a graph of this model of the labor market, Figure 3-10. Given the price level p_0, the market is cleared at the money wage w_0 and labor input N_0. Suppose the price level *rises* to p_1. Since the demand-for-labor curve is the VMP_N curve, the demand shifts to the right proportionate to the relative increase in prices, i.e., to $p_1 f(N)$. More labor will be demanded at each money wage rate. On the other hand, the supply of labor shifts to the *left* at each money wage rate; the higher price level lowers *real* wages for every money wage and reduces the supply of labor. In the neoclassical model, the shifts in the two curves offset each other; when prices rise, the labor market again returns to equilibrium at N_0 and at a money wage w_1 such that real wages are unchanged.

Thus, as we saw, price-level changes do not affect the amount of labor employed or output produced in this model. A change in employment can only occur if, for some reason, price-level changes do not bring about offsetting shifts in the labor supply and demand curves as in Figure 3-10. The most plausible explanation is that workers, in the short run, do not fully perceive the change in prices, or if it is perceived, they are prevented, by the nature of their contracts or by something else, from completely adjusting their labor supplied. That is, instead of (3-55), we have the labor supply function

$$w_s = h(N, p) \qquad \text{(3-58)}$$

where $h_N > 0$ and $h_p > 0$; i.e., either an increase in N or an increase in prices raises the supply price—w_s—of labor. Now, however, we may assume workers do not respond to prices at all in supplying labor, that they respond, but not as much as in the

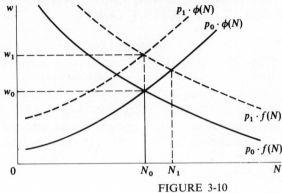

FIGURE 3-10
Labor market equilibrium.

neoclassical case, or that they respond fully, as in the neoclassical case. Differentiating (3-58) and (3-53) with respect to p, we get these cases:

Neoclassical case: $\qquad\qquad\qquad\qquad f(N) = h_p$ $\qquad\qquad$ (3-59)

Intermediate case: $\qquad\qquad\qquad\qquad f(N) > h_p$

Or at the extreme: $\qquad\qquad\qquad\qquad f(N) > h_p, \qquad h_p = 0$ $\qquad$ (3-60)

The complete model for the intermediate case is, then,

$$Y = C\left[Y(1 - \tau) - \frac{\overline{T}}{p}\right] + I(i) + \overline{G} \quad \text{(3-12)}$$

$$m\overline{H} = pL(Y, i) \quad \text{(3-13)}$$

$$Y = F(N, K_0) \quad \text{(3-51)}$$

$$pf(N) = h(N, p) \quad \text{(3-61)}$$

with the unknowns Y, i, p, and N. Alternatively, the model may be put in terms of the aggregate demand and supply functions. From (3-16) earlier, aggregate demand is

$$Y = C\left[Y(1 - \tau) - \frac{\overline{T}}{p}\right] + I[\phi(\overline{H}, Y, p)] + \overline{G} \quad \text{(3-16)}$$

Aggregate supply is given by solving (3-61) for N (given a value of p) and substituting this value into the aggregate production function (3-51). If we write (3-61) as

$$N = q(p) \qquad q_p > 0 \quad \text{(3-62)}$$

we get, for the aggregate supply function,

$$Y = F[q(p), K_0] \quad \text{(3-63)}$$

The slope of the aggregate supply function is obtained by differentiating (3-61), the labor market equilibrium condition:

$$pf_N \, dN + f(N) \, dp = h_N \, dN + h_p \, dp$$

and solving for dN:

$$dN(pf_N - h_N) = [h_p - f(N)] \, dp$$

$$dN = \left[\frac{h_p - f(N)}{pf_N - h_N}\right] dp$$

Since, by (3-60), $f(N) > h_p$, the numerator is negative. Given diminishing marginal product of labor, $f_N < 0$, and h_N is by assumption positive. Thus, the denominator is also negative so that the whole bracketed expression is positive—an increase in prices ($dp > 0$) *increases* labor input.

From the production function we have

$$dY = F_N \, dN = f(N) \, dN$$

Substitution of dN as derived from the labor market yields

$$dY = f(N)\left[\frac{h_p - f(N)}{pf_N - h_N}\right] dp$$

The slope of the aggregate supply curve is then

$$\left.\frac{dp}{dY}\right|_s = \frac{pf_N - h_N}{f(N)[h_p - f(N)]} \qquad (3\text{-}64)$$

which is clearly positive. Note that as $h_p \to f(N)$, the slope of the supply function approaches infinity—the neoclassical vertical supply curve. At another extreme, if workers take no account of prices in supplying labor—$h_p = 0$—the value of dp/dY gets smaller (the slope becomes more horizontal).

Differentiating (3-16) totally, we get

$$dY = C_{Y_d}\left(dY - \tau \, dY - Y \, d\tau - \frac{p \, d\overline{T} - \overline{T} \, dp}{p^2}\right)$$

$$+ \, I_i(\phi_H \, d\overline{H} + \phi_Y \, dY + \phi_p \, dp) + d\overline{G}$$

To get the multipliers for $\overline{G}$ and $\overline{H}$, we set increments in all the other exogenous variables ($\overline{T}$ and τ) equal to zero and rearrange and collect terms:

$$dY[1 - C_{Y_d}(1 - \tau) - I_i\phi_Y] = \left(\frac{C_{Y_d}\overline{T}}{p^2} + I_i\phi_p\right) dp + I_i\phi_H \, d\overline{H} + d\overline{G} \qquad (3\text{-}65)$$

From (3-64), the change in the price level, dp, is

$$dp = dY\left\{\frac{pf_N - h_N}{f(N)[h_p - f(N)]}\right\}$$

Substituting this in (3-65) yields the multipliers for $\bar{G}$ and $\bar{H}$:

$$dY\left[1 - C_{Y_d}(1 - \tau) - I_i\phi_Y - \left(\frac{C_{Y_d}\bar{T}}{p^2} + I_i\phi_p\right)\left(\frac{pf_N - h_N}{f(N)[h_p - f(N)]}\right)\right] = I_i\phi_H \, d\bar{H} + d\bar{G}$$

so that the change in Y is

$$dY = \frac{I_i\phi_H \, d\bar{H} + d\bar{G}}{1 - C_{Y_d}(1 - \tau) - I_i\phi_Y - \left(\dfrac{C_{Y_d}\bar{T}}{p^2} + I_i\phi_p\right)\left(\dfrac{pf_N - h_N}{f(N)[h_p - f(N)]}\right)}$$

Since from (3-23), (3-24), and (3-8)

$$\phi_Y = -\frac{L_Y}{L_i} \qquad \phi_H = \frac{m}{pL_i} \qquad \phi_p = -\frac{M_s}{p^2 L_i}$$

then

$$\frac{dY}{d\bar{G}} = \frac{1}{\left(1 - C_{Y_d}(1 - \tau) + \dfrac{I_i L_Y}{L_i}\right) - \dfrac{1}{p^2}\left(C_{Y_d}\bar{T} - \dfrac{I_i M_s}{L_i}\right)\left(\dfrac{pf_N - h_N}{f(N)[h_p - f(N)]}\right)} \qquad (3\text{-}66)$$

and

$$\frac{dY}{d\bar{H}} = \frac{\dfrac{mI_i}{pL_i}}{1 - C_{Y_d}(1 - \tau) + \dfrac{I_i L_Y}{L_i} - \dfrac{1}{p^2}\left(C_{Y_d}\bar{T} - \dfrac{I_i M_s}{L_i}\right)\left(\dfrac{pf_N - h_N}{f(N)[h_p - f(N)]}\right)} \qquad (3\text{-}67)$$

From our earlier analysis of simple Keynesian multipliers, we know that the horizontal shift in the aggregate demand curve (call it dX) is

$$dX_G = \frac{1}{1 - C_{Y_d}(1 - \tau) + \dfrac{I_i L_Y}{L_i}} \, d\bar{G}$$

The slope of the aggregate demand curve [Eq. (3-18)] is

$$\left.\frac{dp}{dY}\right|_D = \frac{1 - C_{Y_d}(1 - \tau) + \dfrac{I_i L_Y}{L_i}}{\dfrac{1}{p^2}\left[C_{Y_d}\bar{T} - \dfrac{M_s I_i}{L_i}\right]}$$

Therefore, Eq. (3-66) can be written

$$dY = \left[\frac{1 \left/ \left(\frac{1}{p^2} C_{Y_d} \overline{T} - \frac{M_s I_i}{L_i} \right) \right.}{\left. \frac{dp}{dY} \right|_D - \left. \frac{dp}{dY} \right|_S} \right] d\overline{G}$$

or
$$dY = \frac{\left. \frac{dp}{dY} \right|_D}{\left. \frac{dp}{dY} \right|_D - \left. \frac{dp}{dY} \right|_S} dX_{\overline{G}} \qquad (3\text{-}68)$$

The size of the change in Y brought on by a change in government purchases thus depends on the slopes of the aggregate supply and demand curves and on the shift (dX) in the aggregate demand curve. The less the slope of the supply curve—the "flatter" it is—the greater the change in Y for a given change in $\overline{G}$. The greater the (absolute value of) slope of the aggregate demand curve, the larger the government purchases multiplier will be. The larger the horizontal shift in the demand curve (dX), the larger the change in Y (all other things being equal); and a smaller dX reduces dY.

Similarly, the horizontal shift in the aggregate demand curve, when the quantity of high-powered money changes, is given by

$$dX_{\overline{H}} = \frac{\dfrac{m I_i}{p L_i}}{1 - C_{Y_d}(1 - \tau) + \dfrac{I_i L_Y}{L_i}} d\overline{H}$$

Therefore, the multiplier for high-powered money—Eq. (3-67)—may be written

$$dY = \left[\frac{\dfrac{m I_i}{p L_i} \left/ \left\{ \dfrac{1}{p^2} \left(C_{Y_d} \overline{T} - \dfrac{I_i m}{L_i} \right) \right\} \right.}{\left. \dfrac{dp}{dY} \right|_D - \left. \dfrac{dp}{dY} \right|_S} \right] d\overline{H}$$

$$= \left[\frac{\left. \dfrac{dp}{dY} \right|_D}{\left. \dfrac{dp}{dY} \right|_D - \left. \dfrac{dp}{dY} \right|_S} \right] dX_{\overline{H}} \qquad (3\text{-}69)$$

Looking at the equations for $(dp/dY)|_D$ and $(dp/dY)|_S$, we can summarize the influence of each of the parameters on $(dp/dY)|_D$, $(dp/dY)|_S$, $dX_{\overline{G}}$, and $dX_{\overline{H}}$ and thus on dY:

The (absolutely) larger (+) or smaller (−)	$\left.\dfrac{dp}{dY}\right\|_D$	$\left.\dfrac{dp}{dY}\right\|_S$	$dX_{\bar{G}}$	$dX_{\bar{H}}$
L_Y	+	0	−	−
I_i/L_i	+	0	−	+
m	−	0	0	+
f_N	0	+	0	0
h_N	0	+	0	0
$f(N)$	0	−	0	0
h_p	0	+	0	0
$d\bar{H}$	0	0	0	+
$d\bar{G}$	0	0	+	0

Consider first the familiar "demand-shift" effects summarized in the last two columns above. The amount of change in Y reflects, *ceteribus paribus*, the horizontal shift in the demand curve. As we saw earlier (pp. 34–35), the *smaller* the ratio I_i/L_i, the larger the shift for a given change in $\bar{G}$. The larger the ratio I_i/L_i, the greater the effect a change in high-powered money has on demand $dX_{\bar{H}}$. $dX_{\bar{H}}$ is, of course, also larger (given $d\bar{H}$) the larger the "money supply multiplier" m; and given m, $dX_{\bar{H}}$ is larger the larger $d\bar{H}$ is. $dX_{\bar{G}}$ is smaller or larger the smaller or larger $d\bar{G}$ is. Finally, the larger L_Y (again, from the earlier discussion of the Keynesian case), the smaller the demand shift effect of *both* $d\bar{G}$ and $d\bar{H}$.

Given the size of the demand shift, the change in Y will reflect all the parameters influencing the slopes of the supply and demand curves in the neighborhood of the equilibrium point. L_Y tends to increase the (absolute) value of the slope of the demand curve and thus the resulting change in Y. On the other hand, an increase in I_i/L_i[5] or m increases the (absolute) value of the slope and thus dY.

Parameters which *increase* the slope of the supply function reduce the effect on Y of any given dX. These include increases in (the absolute values of) the rate at which the marginal productivity of labor diminishes f_N, the response of the supply price of labor to a change in prices (h_p), and the response of the supply price of labor to a change in $N(h_N)$. The only parameter which decreases the slope of the supply of output is a rise in the marginal product of labor $f(N)$.

Shifts in the Supply Schedule

Over time, both the aggregate demand and supply curves shift. If it is assumed that markets are continuously cleared, then the time path of output and prices is traced by the relative shifts in the supply and demand curves.[6] The persistent forces operating to increase supply are (1) those causing upward (or rightward) shifts in the *demand* for labor—increases in the capital stock K or shifts in the production function

[5] Note that an increase in I_i/L_i increases $dY/dX_{\bar{G}}$ through the "slope effect" but decreases it through the "shift effect."

[6] Part 4 analyzes the more realistic case where markets are not continuously cleared.

(technical change)—and (2) those producing a downward (or rightward) shift in the *supply* of labor. More specifically, the rightward shift of the aggregate supply curve, measured at a given p (call it dR) is given by the production function (3-51) and the labor market equilibrium condition (3-61):

$$Y = F(N, K_0) \qquad (3\text{-}51)$$

$$pf(N) = h(N, p, L) \qquad (3\text{-}61)$$

where the potential labor force L is included in (3-61), for it is assumed here to vary.

To incorporate a technical change in terms of an increase in labor productivity, we define *effective labor input* as

$$E_t = N_t e^{\lambda t} \qquad (3\text{-}70)$$

Thus, effective input of man-hours E_t grows at the rate λ, given N. λ is the rate of growth of output per man-hour. Solving (3-61) for N_t where the potential labor force L is explicitly in the labor supply function, we get

$$N_t = q(p_t, L_t) \qquad q_p > 0 \qquad q_L > 0 \qquad (3\text{-}71)$$

and the aggregate supply function is

$$Y_t = F[e^{\lambda t} q(p_t, L_t), K] \qquad (3\text{-}72)$$

Then, given p, the shift in the supply curve per unit of time is

$$dR = \frac{dY}{dt} = F_N\left(\lambda e^{\lambda t} N_t + e^{\lambda t} \frac{dN}{dt}\right) + F_K \frac{dK}{dt} \qquad (3\text{-}73)$$

Denote the rate of growth of the labor force as $g_L(= dN/dt \cdot 1/N)$, and for simplicity assume $Y =$ net national product so that I is *net investment*. Then dR is

$$dR = \frac{dY}{dt} = F_N[e^{\lambda t} N_t(\lambda + g_L)] + F_K I \qquad (3\text{-}74)$$

The shift in the supply will thus reflect F_N (the marginal product of *effective* man-hours of labor), the rate of growth of output per man-hour λ, the rate of growth of the labor force g_L, and net investment I. The larger any of these, the greater the rightward shift of the supply curve at any given (initial) p.

Thus, the net effect of the forces affecting aggregate supply and demand is the combined effect of dX and dR. In the neighborhood of the initial equilibrium, the change in Y is

$$dY = \frac{\left|\dfrac{dp}{dY}\right|_D |dX| + \left|\dfrac{dp}{dY}\right|_S |dR|}{\left|\dfrac{dp}{dY}\right|_D + \left|\dfrac{dp}{dY}\right|_S} \qquad (3\text{-}75)$$

Without pursuing the matter further at this point (it is discussed further in Parts 3 and 4), we note from (3-74) that in certain instances aggregate demand policies can be seen to affect *both* supply and demand. Policies which affect I affect supply as well as demand. A reduction in $\bar{H}$ will thus reduce aggregate demand by causing interest rates to rise and investment to fall; this effect is accentuated by the *leftward* shift in the supply curve. At the same time, while the leftward shift in the aggregate demand curve causes prices to fall, this is damped to some extent by the concurrent leftward shift in the supply curve. Furthermore, if $\bar{G}$ has an investment component, then there is an additional direct link between demand policies and aggregate supply.

CONCLUSION

In this chapter, we have reviewed the structure of basic macromodels—the Keynesian model, the neoclassical model, and intermediate case. While the behavioral assumptions have been greatly oversimplified, the basic framework for analyzing government macropolicy actions has been provided—fiscal and monetary actions exert their impact on aggregate demand, and to a lesser extent on aggregate supply. Over time, prices and output, the key targets of macropolicy, will trace paths reflecting the relative shifting of the economy's aggregate demand and supply curves, and the basic effect of any action can be analyzed by using this framework and by understanding how it "fits in."

The next part of the book amplifies the discussion by incorporating refinements that economists have made in attempting to explain aggregate demand and supply. Chapters 4 to 11 deal with refinements in the underlying models for consumption and investment (residential construction and inventories as well as business fixed investment), the existence of a foreign sector, refinements in the monetary equations (the supply and demand for money), and the implications of the constraint that the government faces in financing its deficit or surplus. In Chapter 12, the supply-side forces are explored in more detail. Part 3 deals with the dynamics touched upon lightly above—forces determining the time path of output, unemployment, and prices. And perhaps most important, Part 4 deals with the problem of explaining macrobehavior in a world where markets are liable to be continuously in disequilibrium.

READINGS FOR CHAPTER 3

BAUMOL, W.: *Economic Dynamics*, 3d ed. (London: Macmillan, 1970), pp. 365–378.

BRANSON, WILLIAM H.: *Macroeconomic Theory and Policy* (New York: Harper & Row, 1972), chaps. 4–9.

DERNBURG, T., and J. DERNBURG: *Macroeconomic Analysis* (Reading, Mass.: Addison-Wesley, 1969), chaps. 12–14.

DERNBURG, T. F., and D. M. MCDOUGALL: *Macroeconomics*, 2d ed. (New York: McGraw-Hill, 1963), Mathematic app. to chaps. 10 and 15, also chap. 15.

HOLBROOK, ROBERT S.: "The Interest Rate, the Price Level, and Aggregate Output," in W. Smith and R. Teigen (eds.), *Readings in Money, National Income, and Stabilization Policy*, rev. ed. (Homewood, Ill.: Irwin, 1970), pp. 43–65.

SMITH, W., and R. TEIGEN: "Monetary and Fiscal Policies and Aggregate Demand Theory," in Ibid., pp. 1–43.

PART TWO

Refinements and Extensions of the Basic Equilibrium Model

4

CONSUMPTION

In the previous chapter we have defined total planned spending as the sum of planned spending by consumers, business, and government. In this chapter we will explore further the present state of our knowledge of the determinants of planned spending by consumers (consumption).

DEFINITION OF CONSUMPTION AND THE SCOPE OF THE SURVEY

Consumption has been defined earlier to mean total current expenditures by households on goods and services, whether or not these were actually consumed during the period, and consumption thus defined was assumed to depend solely on disposable personal income.

A more meaningful definition of consumption, from the point of view of economic theory, is that of total expenditures by households on nondurable goods and services (adjusted for inventory changes) plus the flow of current services from consumer durables (Suits, 1963, chap. 4). Expenditures on durables, such as automobiles, will not be included in consumption. However, consumption expenditures can be explained once an explanation of consumption is developed.

The precise relationship between income and consumption, whether consumption depends on current disposable income or on past or future income, is subject to a great deal of controversy. In the last 13 years an enormous body of literature has evolved around this issue, and empirical investigation has yielded not one consumption function, but many, each purporting to explain the changes in consumption. It would be fruitless to attempt to survey the whole body of consumption-function literature in this study since this would leave no time for evaluation and comparison. We will, therefore, outline rather briefly major competing hypotheses about the determinants of consumption in order to select the most useful one for our purpose.

The consumption function is a hypothesis about the relation between consumption and income, wealth, and/or other variables. The hypothesis is usually stated in the form of an equation which makes consumption a function of one or more of these variables. Four of these hypotheses will be discussed in this chapter. We begin with the absolute-income hypothesis.

THE ABSOLUTE-INCOME HYPOTHESIS

In *The General Theory* Keynes stated an a priori relationship between consumption and income. His specific formulation of this relationship contains several propositions. The most important of these are:

1 Real consumption is a stable function of real income.
2 The marginal propensity to consume (MPC) is positive but less than unity.

$$0 < \text{MPC}\left(= \frac{\partial C}{\partial Y}\right) < 1$$

Keynes also supposed, but less positively, that the marginal propensity to consume is less than the average propensity to consume [which implies that the average propensity to consume (APC) declines as Y rises] and that the marginal propensity to consume falls as income rises.

Empirical Studies of the Absolute-Income Consumption Function

Short-run consumption-function estimates The absolute-income hypothesis implies more than merely a correlation between income and consumption. More carefully stated, it implies that an increase (or decrease) in income is associated with a simultaneous increase (or decrease) in consumption *and* saving. The Keynesian consumption function has been subjected to a number of empirical investigations. These have taken the form of family-budget studies and time-series analyses.

Cross-section In the family-budget studies, data on the size and disposition of income have been collected for a "cross section" of families for a given period of time (Allen and Bowley, 1935; Brady and Friedman, 1947; Gilboy, 1938; *Study of Consumer Expenditures*, 1957; and Houthakker, 1957). In one of these studies—the Wharton School of Finance and Commerce Study—the data were collected from a sample of 12,500 urban United States families for the year 1950. These data show for the given period how much of each family's income was devoted to consumption expenditures. The Wharton study, as well as other budget studies, revealed a relationship between family income and family consumption similar to that postulated by Keynes for the whole economy—the average propensity to consume falls as income rises, and the marginal propensity to consume is less than 1 (between 0.6 and 0.8) and falls as income rises.

The fact that family-budget studies generally showed close "fits" of money consumption to money disposable income led economists in the early postwar period to be confident in the Keynesian consumption function. However, some questions remained concerning the applicability of estimates taken from cross-section data to the aggregate consumption function. The problem of aggregation—from the individual family level to the aggregate level—can be illustrated in the following example. Suppose we want to estimate the effect of a 50 percent rise in disposable income on consumption expenditures. Suppose as income rises, assuming no change in the number of families or the distribution of income, each and every family enjoys a 50 percent increase of its disposable income. At the higher level of aggregate income, the Keynesian hypothesis suggests that there will be a lower average propensity to consume, for it assumes the ratio of aggregate consumption to aggregate disposable income falls as aggregate income rises. Would this result be supported by examining a family's behavior as its income rises? In other words, assuming that as income rises, 9,000 families each initially with $1,000 incomes move up to the $1,500 bracket. Can we expect their behavior to be identical to those previous $1,500-income families? We would expect such a behavior only if the *absolute* level of family income influenced the family consumption decision. For each family now feels that it is absolutely better off than before. However, since the distribution of income remains the same, the relative position of every family also remains the same; that is, each family is no better or worse off than before relative to the position of other families. In view of this it seems unlikely that the consumption behavior of the new families in the $1,500 bracket will be similar to that of the previous $1,500-income families.

Another source of empirical evidence is found in time-series data; unlike family-budget studies, *time-series data show specifically how aggregate* consumption expenditures have varied through time with aggregate income.

Early empirical studies of the consumption function using time-series annual data tended to confirm the Keynesian postulate.[1] Calculations made by Mosak of

---

[1] Mosak (1945) formulated an estimating equation using annual data for the period 1929–1940 (in billions of dollars):

$$C = 8.621 + 0.803\,Y_d \qquad R = 0.995$$

L. Paridiso also developed a regression equation to measure the relationship between consumption and income. It was used by the National Planning Association in computing the national budget for full employment. The estimating equation for the period 1923–1940 (in billions of dollars) is

$$C = 5.50 + 0.828\,Y_d + 0.04(T - 1935)$$

where T = the current year (see *National Budget for Full Employment*, 1945). A similar relationship has also been estimated by Bennion (1946) and Woytinsky (1946).

the consumption function using 1924–1940 annual data (in billions of dollars) suggested that a linear consumption function was applicable, of the form

$$C = C_0 + C_1 Y_d \qquad (4\text{-}1)$$

where

$$\frac{\partial C}{\partial Y_d} = C_1 = \text{MPC}$$

and

$$\frac{C}{Y_d} = \frac{C_0}{Y_d} + C_1 = \text{APC}$$

Clearly this implies APC > MPC and a falling APC as disposable income rises:

$$C_1 < \frac{C_0}{Y_d} + C_1$$

As Y_d rises, $C_0/Y_d + C_1$ falls; $C_0/Y_d + C_1 \rightarrow C_1$ as $Y_d \rightarrow \infty$.

Estimates made by Smithies (1945) for the period 1923–1940 also supported the Keynesian hypothesis.[2] Smithies's estimates, however, relate per capita consumption to per capita disposable income in billions of constant dollars. His estimating equation differs slightly from Mosak in that he expresses consumption as a linear function of disposable income and a time trend, of the form

$$\frac{C}{N} = C_0 + C_1 \frac{Y_d}{N} + C_2(T) \qquad (4\text{-}2)$$

Where C/N is per capita consumption, Y_d/N is per capita disposable income, and T is a time trend.

Some Statistical Problems

Some of the statistical problems encountered in empirically testing the Keynesian consumption function need now to be briefly illustrated.

1 Real or money income The fundamental relationship between consumption and income as postulated by Keynes is one in real terms.[3] Thus data expressed in money terms may fail to reveal such a relationship, since the money value of consumption is a function not only of money income but also of the price level. We can write money consumption as a function of money income only if the consumption function is linearly homogeneous in Y so that

$$C = C_1 Y_d \qquad \text{is equivalent to} \qquad PC = C_1 P Y_d$$

---

[2] Smithies' estimating equation is
$$C/N = 76.58 + 0.76(Y_d/N) + 1.15(T - 1922)$$
where $T =$ the current year; e.g. in 1923, $T = 1923$.

[3] What Keynes asserts was that consumers were not subject to money illusion. This may or may not be an assertion of fact.

where C and Y_d are real consumption and real disposable income, respectively, and P is an index of the general price level.

For the prewar period 1929–1940, it made little difference for "the goodness of fit" of the consumption function whether money terms or real terms were used because prices moved with real income in the United States during that period. In other periods, however, where this relationship does not hold true, real income and real consumption are the relevant data to be used in testing the consumption function.

2 Net national product or disposable income Keynes was not explicit regarding the appropriate concept of income which should be used in testing the consumption function. Keynes's proposition refers to net national product (NNP) rather than disposable income as the independent variable in the consumption function. Both NNP and Y_d were used in testing the Keynesian function. The results did not, however, favor one over the other for the goodness of fit of the consumption function. Yet, clearly, if personal consumption, rather than consumption out of net national product, is to be estimated, disposable personal income rather than net national product is the relevant concept to be used for such purposes.

3 Aggregate or per capita income For long periods, the consumption function should be corrected for population changes, so that we may isolate the effect of a rise in consumption which is due to population changes from that which results from a rise in consumers' disposable income. Thus per capita consumption and per capita income rather than the aggregate magnitudes are the relevant data to be used in testing the consumption-function hypothesis.

4 Bias in the estimating procedure In most of the empirical tests of the consumption function we have surveyed, the investigators have regressed consumption on disposable income. Yet a large component of disposable income is consumption, which means that we are in effect correlating consumption with something largely composed of consumption.

Ferber (1953) and Ackley (1961, pp. 234–235) as well as others have suggested an alternative method for estimating the consumption function which would reflect the dependence of consumption on disposable income yet eliminate some of the bias inherent in regressing consumption on disposable income.

Ackley suggested a consumption function of the following form:

$$C = C(S_p) \qquad (4\text{-}3)$$

relating consumption to personal saving.

Let us consider this relation more carefully. From Eq. (4-1) we have

$$C = C_0 + C_1 Y_d \qquad (4\text{-}1)$$

and we know that

$$Y_d = C + S_p \qquad (4\text{-}4)$$

Substituting for Y_d in (4-1) we get

$$C = C_0 + C_1(C + S_p)$$

or

$$C = \frac{C_0}{1 - C_1} + \frac{C_1}{1 - C_1} S_p \quad (4\text{-}1a)$$

Equation (4-1a) yields information on $C_0/(1 - C_1)$ and $C_1/(1 - C_1)$ which can then be used to indirectly estimate the consumption function as expressed in Eq. (4-1).[4]

However, this method does not completely eliminate the bias in the consumption function. Ando and Modigliani have shown that biases still remain in regressing consumption on saving and that no definite implication about the correlation between consumption and saving can therefore be made.[5]

Long-Run Estimates of the Consumption Function

In 1946 Kuznets published data on net national product and consumption expenditures for overlapping decades for the 1869–1938 period which showed consumption to have been a stable proportion of total (and also of per capita) income.[6] Kuznets's data were consistent with the hypothesis that consumption is a stable function of income but did not support the hypothesis that MPC < APC found in the earlier studies of the 1923–1940 or 1929–1940 periods. Instead, his data, supported by new evidence from Goldsmith's study (1955), showed the marginal propensity to consume to be equal to the average propensity to consume and within the range 0.89 to 0.87.

This inconsistency between the consumption function estimated using data covering short periods and that suggested by long-run data led to discarding the absolute-income hypothesis, and to various attempts to reconcile long- and short-run consumption functions. Out of these attempts the relative-income, permanent-income, and the life-cycle hypotheses have emerged as bases for the consumption function.

THE RELATIVE-INCOME HYPOTHESIS

Duesenberry (1949) proposed the relative-income hypothesis to reconcile the long-run and short-run consumption function.[7] According to Duesenberry, relative rather than absolute income is the basis for the consumer spending-saving decision. Briefly

---

[4] For the period 1929–1941 Ackley's estimation of the consumption function based on Eq. (4-1a) yielded results close to those directly estimated for Eq. (4-1). The value of C_0 is, however, slightly higher and the new slope (C_1) is slightly lower.

[5] For detailed explanation on this point see Ando and Modigliani (1965, especially pp. 694–706).

[6] Also see his study (1942) covering the period 1879–1928.

[7] One of the first attempts at reconciliation was that of Smithies (1945). Smithies explained the discrepancy between long-run and short-run estimates of the consumption function by the effect of the time-trend variable in his consumption function. He reasoned that the consumption function drifts up over time and such an upward drift just offsets the tendency of the APC to fall as income grows.

stated, he expressed the ratio of saving to disposable income (S/Y_d) to be a function of current disposable income *relative* to the highest (peak) disposable income Y_d^* previously reached. If in some period t, for instance, disposable income at time $t(Y_{dt})$ were to fall below previous peak level, consumers would defend their consumption by reducing savings and (S_t/Y_{dt}) would fall. On the other hand, if Y_{dt} were to rise at a relatively steady rate (if Y_{dt} grows at 4 percent per year, Y_{dt}/Y_d^* is always 1.04), consumption would progressively adjust itself to the new high level of disposable income, and S_t/Y_d^* would be constant. The resulting consumption function may be written in the following form:[8]

$$\frac{S_t}{Y_{dt}} = a \frac{Y_{dt}}{Y_d^*} + b \qquad \text{(saving function)} \qquad (4\text{-}5)$$

or

$$\frac{C_t}{Y_{dt}} = 1 - \frac{S_t}{Y_{dt}} \qquad \text{(consumption function)} \qquad (4\text{-}6)$$

$$= 1 - \left(a \frac{Y_{dt}}{Y_d^*} + b \right)$$

where S_t = personal saving in period t

Y_{dt} = disposable personal income in period t

Y_d^* = previous (to period t) peak disposable income

a = constant > 0

b = some constant ≤ 0

Income growth is, however, not steady; it fluctuates up and down with the phases of the business cycle. Since consumption responds to short-run fluctuations in income with a certain lag, then in observing the consumption-income relation over the short-run we lose sight of the long-run relationship. On the other hand if we view the whole history—the long-run relation—it is clear that consumption fluctuates in proportion to income. To illustrate the short-run relation of consumption to income, Duesenberry fitted his formulation to data for the period 1923–1940, and obtained the values $a = 0.165$ and $b = 0.066$.[9] The results were then evaluated for goodness of fit and for ability to predict the early prewar years. Two basic conclusions emerged from his study:

1 Consumption behavior is explained better in terms of a dynamic-type formulation, such as that given by Eq. (4-5), than by the absolute-income hypothesis.

---

[8] An alternative formulation of the relative-income hypothesis has also been suggested by Ferber (1953). In Ferber's formulation the Saving-income ratio depends on the difference between present and previous peak disposable income expressed as a fraction of present disposable income,

$$\frac{S_t}{Y_{dt}} = a \frac{Y_{dt} - Y_d^*}{Y_{dt}} + b$$

[9] Y_d and S_t are both corrected for price and population change. For more detail see his article published in 1948.

2 The observable difference between short-run and long-run results found in earlier empirical studies can be explained by the relative-income hypothesis.

To demonstrate the ability of his formulation to predict Kuznets's stable long-run relationship between consumption and income, Duesenberry showed that in a period when income is slightly rising with only minor cyclical fluctuations, Y_{dt}/Y_d^* should be about 1.02 in each year. Substituting $Y_{dt}/Y_d^* = 1.02$ in Eq. (4-5), we get

$$\frac{S_t}{Y_{dt}} = 0.165 \frac{Y_{dt}}{Y_d^*} - 0.066 = 0.102$$

or $C_t/Y_{dt} = 0.898$, which is close to Kuznets's estimate for the period 1869–1938. The relative-income hypothesis, however, failed to explain the observable difference between consumer behavior in the prewar and postwar periods found in the empirical studies of the consumption functions for these two periods.

THE PERMANENT INCOME HYPOTHESIS

The Hypothesis

The second reconciliatory effort was by Friedman (1957), who sought to explain the long-run–short-run consumption-function discrepancy by developing the permanent-income hypothesis. His exposition of the relationship of consumption to income led the way toward recent studies which seek to root the consumption function in the microeconomic behavior of the household.

The essence of Friedman's hypothesis is that the consumption of a spending unit, which he denotes as "permanent consumption," is a function of its permanent income. During any particular time period, the *observed* consumption expenditure of a spending unit is assumed to differ in random fashion from its "true," *permanent* consumption due to such transitory factors as the timing of outlays for durables, vacations, emergencies, and similar causes. Similarly, during any time period the *observed* level of income will differ from its *permanent* level due to the timing of receipts, fluctuations in economic conditions, and the like. Over longer periods, however, these short-run factors smooth out and reveal underlying relationships of a more permanent nature.

Let us begin with the consumption of the household. In Figure 4-1, we picture a spending unit (household) with a two-period horizon where there is complete certainty. The spending unit has y_1 receipts in period 1 and expects y_2 receipts in period 2. Let i be the interest rate the spending unit would earn or pay when it lends or borrows. The maximum amount the spending unit can spend in year 1 (if nothing is spent in year 2) is $OZ[= y_1 + y_2/(1 + i)]$. In year 2 the maximum amount it

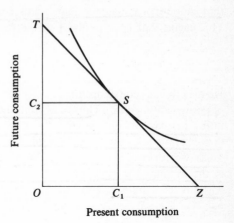

FIGURE 4-1
Household consumption in a two-period
setting.

can spend (if nothing is spent in year 1) is $OT[= y_1(1 + i) + y_2]$. The budget line is
then TZ, and its slope is given by

$$\frac{OT}{OZ} = \frac{y_2 + y_1(1 + i)}{y_1 + y_2/(1+i)}$$

$$= 1 + i$$

Given the budget line TZ and the spending unit's indifference map, the optimum combination of c_1 and c_2 is where the budget line is tangent to an indifference
curve, point S in Figure 4-1. From Figure 4-1 it is clear that the budget line is determined by the values of y_1, y_2, and i. However, consumption OC_1 depends not on these
three variables but only on two, the slope of the budget line TZ and its position.[10]
In other words, OC_1 depends on i and $[y_1 + y_2/(1 + i)]$. A change in current receipts
y_1 does not directly affect OC_1; it affects OC_1 only through its effects on $[y_1 + y_2/(1+i)]$.
What we need then to determine OC_1 is only two variables rather than three: i and
$[y_1 + y_2/(1 + i)]$ or wealth v_1. v_1 and i can thus be taken as the two independent
variables in the consumption function of the spending unit:

$$c_1 = f(v_1, i) \qquad (4\text{-}7)$$

where c_1 is consumption—the value of services (not stocks) the spending unit is
planning to consume during period 1. In Eq. (4-7), v_1 is the spending unit's wealth
in year 1.

Friedman, however, defines a concept of income, permanent income y_p—which
he uses as the independent variable in lieu of v in the consumption function—to be

---

[10] Note that a change in the interest rate does not shift the budget line but changes its
slope around point S in Figure 4-1.

that amount a consumer unit could consume while maintaining its wealth intact. This means that y_p in period 1 would be equal to

$$y_{p1} = \left[iy_1 + \frac{iy_2}{1+i} \right] \qquad (4\text{-}8)$$

He also defines consumption as permanent consumption (c_p) and makes it a function of permanent income. Thus, if current receipts in period 1 were to exceed the spending unit's permanent income, that is, $y_1 > iv$, part of y_1 must be "saved" to provide depreciation allowances to be added to receipts in period 2, so that the spending unit's wealth remains intact at $v_2 = v_1$. On the other hand, if $y_1 < iv$, the difference is the amount the spending unit can borrow to spend in addition to its receipts without reducing v_2. The spending unit's consumption function can now be written as

$$c_{p_1} = h(y_{p_1}, i) \qquad (4\text{-}9)$$

or $$c_{p_1} = g(iv_1, i) \qquad (4\text{-}9a)$$

Equation (4-7) can be considered as a special case of Eq. (4-9). According to Eq. (4-7) the initial wealth of the spending unit is spent on consumption during the two-year period (time horizon) rather than being maintained. Equation (4-9) is regarded as a generalization to a longer horizon where consumers do not plan to spend their entire wealth during their time horizon.

The only assumptions underlying this model thus far have been certainty, convexity, and the negative slope of the indifference curves. With a few other assumptions[11] concerning the shape of the indifference curves, Eq. (4-9) can be written as

$$c_p = k(i, U)y_p \qquad (4\text{-}9b)$$

U represents a number of factors such as spending units' tastes, age, and family composition—the factors that determine the shape of the indifference curve. k is the fraction of y_p consumed and depends on i and U and not the level of y_p.

The Effects of Uncertainty on the Permanent-Income Hypothesis

If the certainty assumption is removed, the above analysis must be modified in two ways: (1) the indifference curve and the budget line in the previous analysis must be altered to account for the direct effects of uncertainty on consumers' utility functions and future receipts and prices and for the indirect effects of this uncertainty on the possibility of lending and borrowing; (2) because uncertainty introduces an additional motive for saving, i.e., the availability of a reserve for emergencies, it becomes necessary to distinguish between different kinds of wealth, for all forms of

---

[11] *1* Indifference curves are symetrical around the 45° line.
2 Indifference curves have common slopes where they intersect any other line through the origin. (i.e., the U function is not only symmetrical but also homogeneous in c_1 and c_2).
3 The U function is homogeneous to degree 1.

wealth are not equally satisfactory for this motive. Friedman dismisses for lack of evidence the effect of uncertainty on the shape assigned to the consumption function [Eq. (4-9)], but modifies his analysis to account for the second factor. To account for the effect of uncertainty on the motives for holding wealth, Friedman includes in Eq. (4-9b) the ratio of nonhuman wealth to permanent income (ω) as a variable determining k, the ratio of consumption to permanent income. The higher ω is, the less the need is for additional reserves and the higher consumption may be expected to be. Thus Eq. (4-9b) can be written as

$$c_p = k(i, \omega, U)y_p = k(i, \omega, U)iv \qquad (4\text{-}9c)$$

where all variables refer to the same period of time. Assuming Eq. (4-9c) to apply to every common unit in a group, the aggregate consumption function may be written as[12]

$$C_p = K(i, \omega, U)iV \qquad (4\text{-}9d)$$

where K may be interpreted as a function of the mean values of i, ω, U, and their variances, and the covariance among them or other similar parameters may be interpreted as describing the distribution of individuals by i, ω, and U.

Income and Consumption Data and the Permanent-Income Hypothesis

Suppose y is a spending unit's measured income for a certain period, for example, a year. y is then the sum of two components: a permanent component y_p and a transitory component y_t, or

$$y = y_p + y_t \qquad (4\text{-}10)$$

where the permanent component is to be interpreted as reflecting the effects of such factors that determine the spending unit's wealth. The permanent component is analogous to the "expected" value of a probability distribution. The transitory component reflects all "other factors" which are treated by the spending units as windfalls or accidental income.

Similarly let c represent the spending unit's expenditures during the year. c is then the sum of a permanent component c_p and a transitory component c_t, or

$$c = c_p + c_t \qquad (4\text{-}11)$$

where $c_p = k(i, \omega, U)iv$ [Eq. (4-9c)].

In its general form, Friedman's permanent-income hypothesis is specified by the above three equations. Equation (4-9c) defines the relationship between permanent consumption and permanent income. Equations (4-10) and (4-11) define the relationship between the permanent components and the measured magnitudes.

---

[12] For a detailed discussion on the aggregation procedure, see Friedman (1957, pp. 18–19).

For the application of his hypothesis Friedman makes the following three assumptions[13]:

1 Permanent income and transitory income are uncorrelated.
2 Permanent consumption and transitory consumption are uncorrelated.
3 And most importantly, transitory consumption and transitory income are uncorrelated, or $\rho_{y_p y_t} = \rho_{c_t c_p} = \rho_{y_t c_t} = 0$, where ρ is the correlation coefficient between the variables designated by the subscripts.

A special and rather simple case of the hypothesis arises if in addition to the previous conditions it is assumed that the mean transitory components of consumption and income are zero; that is, $\mu_{y_t} = \mu_{c_t} = 0$.

Suppose now that we have consumption and income data for a number of families for whom k can be supposed to be the same. From these, we estimate a consumption function of the form

$$C = \alpha + \beta Y \qquad (4\text{-}12)$$

where C is the mean consumption for a given value of Y. It is assumed here that the spending unit's consumption deviates from this value by chance. The relationship between the mean value of C and Y is assumed here to be linear.[14] Regressing C on Y using the least-squares method of estimation, β and α can be computed. The estimates of β and α are

$$\beta = \frac{\sum(C - \bar{C})(Y - \bar{Y})}{\sum(Y - \bar{Y})^2} \qquad (4\text{-}13)$$

$$\alpha = \bar{C} - \beta\,\bar{Y} \qquad (4\text{-}14)$$

where $\bar{C}$ and $\bar{Y}$ stand for mean C and mean Y of the group and the summation is over the group.

In the expression for β we can make the following substitutions:

1 Replace, in the numerator, Y and C by their equivalents from Eqs. (4-10) and (4-11).
2 From Eq. (4-9*d*), substitute for C_p

$$C_p = KY$$

The expression for the numerator thus becomes

$$\sum(C - \bar{C})(Y - \bar{Y}) = K\sum(Y_p - \bar{Y}_p)^2 + K\sum(Y_p - \bar{Y}_p)(Y_t - \bar{Y}_t)$$

$$+ \frac{1}{K}\sum(C_p - \bar{C}_p)(C_t - \bar{C}_t) + \sum(C_t - \bar{C}_t)(Y_t - \bar{Y}_t)$$

---

[13] For a detailed discussion on these points see Friedman (1957, pp. 26–30).
[14] According to Friedman's hypothesis, this relation is linear only under special conditions (1957, p. 31, footnote 8).

Given the condition specified earlier, that is, $\rho_{y_p y_t} = \rho_{c_t c_p} = \rho_{y_t c_t} = 0$, the above equation reduces to (ignoring sampling error)[15]

$$\sum (C - \bar{C})(Y - \bar{Y}) = K \sum (Y_p - \bar{Y}_p)^2$$

Thus β can be written as equal to

$$\beta = \frac{K \sum (Y_p - \bar{Y}_p)^2}{\sum (Y - \bar{Y})^2}$$

or

$$\beta = KP_y \qquad (4\text{-}15)$$

where P_y is the fraction of total variance of income in the group contributed by Y_p. It can also be interpreted as the fraction of any change in Y that, on the average, is contributed by a change in Y_p.

In short, β, the ratio of the change in consumption to the change in income (dC/dY) depends on K and the fraction of dY composed of dY_p. If $P_y = 0$, all the change in income is transitory. Since $\rho_{y_t c_t} = 0$, the change in measured income due to these transitory elements will not be associated with any systematic change in consumption. β is therefore zero.

On the other hand, if $P_y = 1$, all the change in income is due to permanent component, and the effect on consumption will be equal to $K\, dY_p$. β is in this case equal to K.

Substituting Eq. (4-15)—the expression for β—in Eq. (4-14) we get

$$\alpha = \bar{C} - KP_y \bar{Y} \qquad (4\text{-}16)$$

We know that

$$\bar{C} = \bar{C}_t + \bar{C}_p$$
$$\bar{Y} = \bar{Y}_t + \bar{Y}_p$$

and also

$$\bar{C}_p = K\bar{Y}_n$$

Equation (4-14) can be written as[16]

$$\alpha = \bar{C}_t + K\bar{Y}_p - KP_y(\bar{Y}_t + \bar{Y}_p)$$

or

$$\alpha = \bar{C}_t + K\bar{Y}_p(1 - P_y) - KP_y \bar{Y}_t \qquad (4\text{-}16a)$$

The Income Elasticity of Consumption

At any point, say (C_0, Y_0), on the estimated consumption function, the elasticity of consumption with respect to income is equal to

$$\varepsilon_{cy} = \frac{\partial C}{\partial Y} \frac{Y}{C} = \beta \frac{Y}{C} = KP_y \frac{Y}{C} \qquad (4\text{-}17)$$

---

[15] The second, third, and fourth terms $\neq 0$ only because of sampling fluctuations. They $\rightarrow 0$ as the sample size is increased. For the purpose of this analysis Friedman (1957, p. 32) assumed the sample to be sufficiently large.

[16] In the case where $\bar{Y}_t = \bar{C}_t = 0$, Eq. (4-16a) can be further reduced to $\alpha = K\bar{Y}_p(1 - P_y)$.

If the mean transitory components of Y and C are zero, then $\bar{Y} = \bar{Y}_p$ and $\bar{C} = \bar{C}_p$. In this case $\bar{C}_p = K\bar{Y}_p$ becomes $\bar{C} = K\bar{Y}$, and

$$\frac{\bar{Y}}{\bar{C}} = \frac{1}{K} \qquad (4\text{-}18)$$

Suppose that (C_0, Y_0), the point on the consumption function where ε_{cy} is computed, is the sample mean. In this case the elasticity of consumption with respect to income becomes equal to P_y:

$$\varepsilon_{cy} = KP_y \frac{1}{K} = P_y \qquad (4\text{-}17a)$$

Graphical Presentation of the Relations between Measured Consumption and Measured Income

The relationship between measured consumption and measured income when the mean transitory components of income and consumption are equal to zero ($\bar{Y}_t = \bar{C}_t = 0$) is illustrated graphically in Figure 4-2. In this figure, we plot on the line IF measured consumption against measured income. On the line OE we plot permanent consumption against permanent income.

Let us consider consumer units with a certain measured income (say, Y_0) which is above the mean measured income $\bar{Y}$ for the group as a whole. Since transitory income Y_t is correlated with measured income Y (but not with Y_p), these consumer units will have an average permanent income below Y_0—because $Y_0 > \bar{Y}$ and $\bar{Y} = \bar{Y}_p + \bar{Y}_t$. But since $\bar{Y}_t = 0$, it follows that $Y_0 > \bar{Y}_p$. Such a relatively high measured income Y_0 of this group is more likely to be the result of favorable transitory effects; that is, Y_t for this group is greater than zero. Given the assumption that $\bar{C}_t$ and $\bar{Y}_t$ are uncorrelated, the average transitory component of consumption of these consumer units $\bar{C}_t$ tends to average out to the average for the group of consumers as a whole, which is assumed to be zero. Thus we may say that the average consumption of the consumer units with Y_0 measured income is equal to their average permanent consumption. This is by hypothesis equal to

$$C_p = KY_p$$

Since average permanent income $Y_p < Y_0$, average measured consumption $Y_0 F$ in Figure 4-2 will be less than $Y_0 E$, average permanent consumption. If, however, Y_0 was also the permanent income of these consumer units, their average permanent consumption would be $KY_0 = Y_0 E$.

By the same hypothesis, for those consumer units with an income equal to the mean income $\bar{Y}$ of the group as a whole, the average transitory component of consumption is zero ($\bar{C}_t = 0$), and thus measured consumption for this group is equal to permanent consumption, as at point Q in the graph.

$$C = C_p = KY_p = K\bar{Y}$$

Similarly, for consumer units with an income below the mean of the group as a whole, the average transitory component of income is negative ($\bar{Y}_t < 0$); thus their average measured consumption is greater than that of their average permanent consumption.

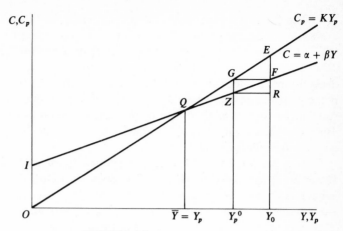

FIGURE 4-2
Measured consumption and income when $\bar{Y}_t = \bar{C}_t = 0$.

In Friedman's terms then, the usually plotted consumption function IF (in Figure 4-2) depends both on the relation of Y_p/Y_t at each level of measured income and on the value of K.

Consider again, in Figure 4-2, the income group with Y_0 measured income. At Y_0, measured consumption $C = Y_0 F$ is the equivalent of a permanent consumption out of a permanent income equal to $GY_p{}^0$. $Y_p{}^0$ is therefore the average permanent-income component of members of the consumer units having Y_0 as measured income, and $Y_0 - Y_p{}^0$ is the average transitory-income component of this group. The slope of IF at $Y_0(FR/ZR)$ is equal to β (the marginal propensity to consume) $= KP_y$, where $K = EF/ZR$ (since $ZR = GF$) and $P_y = (Y_p{}^0 - \bar{Y})/(Y_0 - \bar{Y})$.[17]

---

[17] The equation for IF is

$C = \alpha + \beta Y$ or from Eq. (4-16a) $C = K(1 - P_y)\bar{Y} + KP_y Y$
$C = K[\bar{Y} - P_y \bar{Y}] + KP_y Y$
$dC = KP_y dY$

From Figure 4-2, $K = EF/FG = EF/ZR$. But $FR = dC = KP_y dY$; if we substitute EF/ZR for K, we get

$$FR = \frac{EF}{ZR} P_y dY$$

$$dY = ZR$$

Substituting for dY, we get

$$FR = \frac{EF}{ZR} P_y ZR$$

Dividing both sides by ZR, we get

$$\frac{FR}{ZR} = \frac{EF}{ZR} P_y$$

$$P_y = \frac{Y_p{}^0 - \bar{Y}}{Y_0 - \bar{Y}}$$

The fraction of the deviation of the spending unit's average income from the average for the group contributed by transitory component of income is $(Y_0 - Y_p^0)/(Y_0 - \overline{Y}) = 1 - P_y$. Given K, the *shape* of IF depends on the values of P_y. IF may coincide with OE if $P_y = 1$ or may become horizontal if $P_y = 0$. The *position* of IF depends on $\overline{Y}_t$, the mean transitory income. If $\overline{Y}_t = 0$, then IF passes through point Q in Figure 4-2, where $\overline{Y} = \overline{Y}_p$. But if $\overline{Y}_t > 0$, then IF shifts down and intersects OE to the left of Q; if $\overline{Y}_t < 0$, IF shifts up and intersects OE to the right of Q. The parameters K, P_y, and $\overline{Y}_t$ thus determine the shape and position of the measured consumption function (IF).

It is clear that if $K < 1$, permanent consumption is less than permanent income. However, as illustrated in Figure 4-2, it does not follow that measured consumption is necessarily less than measured income. A rise in K shifts both OE and IF upward —they still intersect where $\overline{Y} = \overline{Y}_p$, since $\overline{Y}_t = 0$ and vice versa. If, however, $\overline{Y}_t = 0$, the curve IF is shifted vertically by a corresponding amount. The measured consumption function will shift upward when $\overline{Y}_t > 0$ and downward if $\overline{Y}_t < 0$. Clearly such a shift in IF cannot be identified from a shift due to a change in K.

In summary, Friedman's hypothesis led to the following specified relationships concerning the consumption function: *First*, the *expected* level of consumption is some proportion of the level of permanent income regardless of the level of that income, and *second*, this proportion varies with the ratio of nonhuman wealth to permanent income, interest rates, the composition and age of the spending units, etc.

Empirical Tests of the Permanent-Income Hypothesis

Friedman sought to interpret a wide range of empirical findings of budget studies and time series in terms of the permanent-income hypothesis. Three broad empirical findings to be explained that contradict the impression that consumption is a stable function of absolute real income are given below:

1 The similarity of the average propensity to consume computed from budget studies at different dates
2 The rough constancy of the average propensity to consume over the last 50 years as measured by time-series data
3 A sharply higher average propensity to consume in the United States after World War II

Consistency of the Permanent-Income Hypothesis with Time-Series Studies

If i, ω, and U remain constant over time, C_p/Y_p will remain constant over time. Thus, averaging short-run fluctuations in C and Y (e.g., over business cycles) so that $C_t \cong Y_t \cong 0$, the long-run C/Y ratio will remain constant and not exhibit any trend. This is consistent with empirical evidence on the average propensity to consume.

To *test* the permanent-income hypothesis with time-series data, empirical approximations for Y_p and C_p are necessary. It is assumed that $C = C_p$, and Y_p is approximated by the weighted average of past and present *measured Y*, with exponentially declining weights:

$$(Y_p)_T = \beta \int_{-\infty}^{T} e^{(\beta - \alpha)(t - T)} Y_t \, dt$$

where β = adjustment coefficient between Y and Y_p
   α = average annual growth rate of disposable income
   T = present time period
   t = index of time periods; $t = T$ back to $-\infty$

For discrete income and time, Friedman uses

$$(Y_p)_t = \beta(Y_t + e^{-(\beta - \alpha)} Y_{t-1} + e^{-2(\beta - \alpha)} Y_{t-2} + \cdots + e^{-17(\beta - \alpha)} Y_{t-17})$$

$$(e^{-(\beta - \alpha)} = \lambda \text{ in Koyck transformation})$$

He estimates

$$C_t = \gamma + K[Y_{p_t}]$$

and gets $\gamma = 0$ and $K = 0.88$, close to 0.877, the observed APC over the sample period. To make the function more wieldy for econometric work where Y_p cannot be directly observed, we can write

$$C_t = K\beta(Y_t + \lambda Y_{t-1} + \lambda^2 Y_{t-2} + \cdots + \lambda^N Y_{t-N})$$

We know that

$$C_{t-1} = K\beta(Y_{t-1} + \lambda Y_{t-2} + \cdots + \lambda^{N-1} Y_{t-N})$$
$$\lambda C_{t-1} = K\beta(\lambda Y_{t-1} + \lambda^2 Y_{t-2} + \cdots + \lambda^N Y_{t-N})$$

and
$$C_t - \lambda C_{t-1} = K\beta Y_t$$

so that $C_t = K\beta Y_t + \lambda C_{t-1}$. In this form, only the *current value of income* and lagged consumption are *required*.[18]

To find the long-run MPC (or APC), *we must allow for growth*. It should be noted that the long-run MPC is *not* where

$$C = C_{t-1}$$

or
$$C_t(1 - \lambda) = K\beta Y_t$$

$$C_t = \frac{K\beta}{(1 - \lambda)} Y_t$$

---

[18] However, it turns out that econometric problems reduce the gain from being able to use this form of the hypothesis. For details see Evans (1969, chap. 2).

It should be where

$$C = (1 + \alpha)C_{t-1}$$

where $\alpha =$ the long-run rate of growth of C and Y.

Consistency of the Permanent-Income Hypothesis with Budget Studies

Examination of several cross-section studies for the United States for different dates from 1888–1890 to 1951–1952 revealed the following evidence:

1 The APC in these studies is almost the same (evaluated at the mean), ranging between 0.89 and 0.92. The only deviation from this range is for 1944.
2 The MPC and the income elasticity of consumption ε_{cy} vary more widely from the average propensity to consume. The value of the MPC ranged between 0.67 and 0.79 (farm families excluded), and ε_{cy} was between 0.74 and 0.87. Again estimates for 1944 deviate from these estimates.
3 The marginal propensity to consume was always less than the average propensity to consume—MPC < APC—so that ε_{cy} is uniformly less than unity. Because MPC < APC as shown in these studies implied $\varepsilon_{cy} < 1$, it is quite evident from these regressions that a stable relation between consumption and income, as postulated by Keynes, does not exist. $\varepsilon_{cy} < 1$ implies that an increase in income results in a reduction in the average propensity to consume; but the observed APC computed from budget studies of 1880–1950 are virtually the same, despite a substantial rise in average income during this period. Thus Friedman (1957) concludes that "this stability in average propensity is therefore inconsistent with stability in the relation itself" (p. 44).

Friedman explains the stability of the APC over the period examined in the following way:

1 After correcting the data for price changes (the original computations used current dollars) Friedman estimates the APC from two regressions, one for 1888–1890 and the other for 1950. If the regression of 1888–1890 is assumed to be valid throughout the period and for the different groups, consumption at the arithmetic mean income falls from 94 percent in 1901 to 77 percent in 1950. Similarly, if the 1950 regression is taken as valid, consumption falls from 109 in 1901 to 94 percent in 1950. What actually happened is that the consumption functions shifted over time (such as C_1 or C_2) in such a way that consumption remained roughly the same percentage of the mean income. This is illustrated in Figure 4-3.
2 Using the permanent-income hypothesis Friedman explains the shift in the computed regression to be the direct result of the change in average real income during this period. The interpretation of the results by the permanent-income hypothesis is shown in Figure 4-3. The solid line is an assumed relation between the permanent components; i.e.,

$$C_p = 0.9Y_p$$

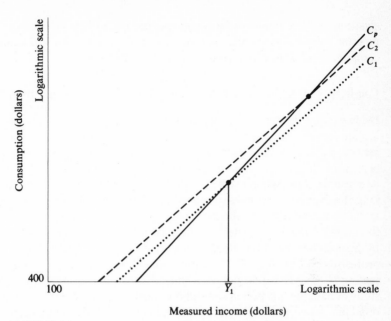

FIGURE 4-3
Regression of consumption on income, 1888–1890 and 1950. (Mean consumption and mean income in eight studies.) (1935–1939 prices.) *Source: Friedman (1957, p. 59).*

If Y_t and C_t were equal to zero for each of the studies separately, and assuming that K has stayed the same over time, the points defining $\bar{Y}$ and $\bar{C}$ would fall on the C_p line. The data show $\bar{C}$ and $\bar{Y}$ for each study to cluster around such a line. For any given study, however, the consumption function is as $C_1, C_2, \ldots$ in Figure 4-3 because of the transitory component of income (Y_t); C_1 is above C_p, to the left of $\bar{Y}_1$, because of the large negative Y_t component, and C_1 is below it to the right because of the positive Y_t component.

The constancy of the average propensity to consume over the period examined —while consistent with the permanent-income hypothesis—is not required by it. The APC, for a group and dates where $\bar{Y}_t = 0$, depends on i, ω, U, etc. A change in the value of these variables will affect APC through its effect on K. There is no reason whatsoever to assume that changes in these variables would tend to cancel one another.[19]

Friedman's interpretation of ε_{cy} From our earlier discussion we know that $\bar{Y}/\bar{C} = 1/K$ if $\bar{Y} = \bar{Y}_p$ and $\bar{C} = \bar{C}_p$. Then $\varepsilon_{cy} = dC/dY \cdot \bar{Y}/C = \beta\bar{Y}/C = P_y$. That is, the income elasticity of consumption measures P_y—the fraction of total variance of income contributed by Y_p—if $Y_t = 0$. Generally ε_{cy} rises with time—the income

[19] Evidence for different countries and for different groups—farm versus nonfarm white versus black—has also been presented and discussed by Friedman (1957, pp. 54–84).

elasticity of C is found to be higher (at the mean) for later studies. This suggests that the permanent component of income is more important than the transitory component in producing income differences over time.

Consistency of the Permanent-Income Hypothesis with Evidence from Time Series

Evidence from long-run time series points to the constancy of the average propensity to consume over the period 1897–1949 (Goldsmith, 1955, vol. I, pp. 393–400). The general pattern of data and regression lines reported by Goldsmith seems to fit the permanent hypothesis remarkably well. The constancy of the average propensity to consume, although consistent with the permanent-income hypothesis (since, in the long run, Y_t variations tend to cancel out so that $Y = Y_p$ and C/P is a constant equal to K), is not required by the permanent-income hypothesis. The average propensity to consume, and thus K, depends on factors (i, ω, U) other than the level of income. If these factors have remained the same during the period 1897–1949, the average propensity to consume (C/Y) would remain constant, which means that data representing C_p and Y_p would fall on a single straight line through the origin. A detailed study of data for this period showed the consumption-income points to cluster around this line. Some points, however, did lie below the line and others above it. Some points of major interest are those of 1942, 1943, 1944, and 1945. These are all years of wartime inflation in which we might expect both a positive mean transitory component of income and a negative mean transitory component of consumption. A positive $\bar{Y}_t$ can be explained by the fact that war time incomes were regarded by spending units as abnormally high and temporary. The negative $\bar{C}_t$ can be explained by the inavailability of goods during war years. Both of these factors account for the observed low ratio of measured consumption to income during that period.

Friedman then turns to examine the factors underlying the secular constancy of K. No conclusive evidence can be found to explain its constancy, however. Interest rates varied considerably over the period; so did the ratio of nonhuman wealth to total wealth and the factors underlying U. The only interpretation he offers is that the changes in the variables that determine K must have been offsetting during this period. The two major offsetting forces he speculates upon are (1) the declining relative importance of farming, which would tend to raise K, and (2) the declining average size of families, which would tend to reduce K. An additional offsetting effect on K (measured from the available statistics) was the changing role of the government in the provision of security, which tends to raise K.

The Permanent-Income Hypothesis—Further Empirical Evidence

One of the basic assumptions underlying the Friedman hypothesis has been subjected to extensive empirical investigation to determine its validity—the stipulation that transitory income and transitory consumption are uncorrelated $(\rho_{c_t y_t} = 0)$. This implies that transitory income does not give rise to consumption on a systematic basis. The empirical evidence presented in testing this proposition is, however, inconclusive.

The first evidence was reported by Bodkin (1959). Bodkin employed data from the 1950 Bureau of Labor Statistics (BLS) Survey of Consumer Expenditures. The National Service Life Insurance (NSLI) dividends paid out early in 1950 were regarded as windfall income, and two regressions were computed using a subsample of 1,414 dividend recipients.[20] In both regressions, disposable income and windfall income were used as independent variables. In the first equation total consumption (including expenditures on durables) was the dependent variable, while in the second equation expenditures on durables were excluded from the definition of consumption. The regressions showed the marginal propensity to consume out of windfall income to be equal to 0.966 when durables were included in consumption, and 0.723 when durables were excluded from consumption. Thus, using Friedman's definition of consumption, the marginal propensity to consume out of transitory income would be between 0.966 and 0.723, which contradicts the Friedman assumption of $\rho_{c_t y_t} = 0$. Friedman (1957, p. 215) argues that the marginal propensity to consume out of transitory income in fact could be expected to be in the neighborhood of 0.3, on the assumption of an average 3-year horizon. Since Bodkin's results are much higher than this, he is led to question the validity of the permanent-income hypothesis, at least insofar as it depends on the assumption that consumption and windfall income are uncorrelated.

Kreinin (1961) offered additional evidence which contradicts Bodkin's result and gives support to Friedman's stipulation. In this case the data used were from the Israeli Survey of Family Savings of 1957–1958 on the behavior of recipients of lump-sum personal restitution payments from Germany. To determine the effect of such windfall gains on consumption Kreinin examined the behavior of consumer units receiving such payments as compared to that of nonrecipients belonging to the same socioeconomic groups. Two regressions were fitted to the data. In one regression, consumption was defined to include expenditures on durables, the other exclusive of durables. In both regressions, disposable income (exclusive of restitution) and the restitution payments were used as the independent variables. Kreinin's estimating equations give a value for the marginal propensity to consume nondurables out of windfall income of 0.156 and a marginal propensity to consume of 0.167 when expenditures on durables were included. The smallness of these estimates clearly gives support to Friedman's prediction and thus is consistent with the permanent-income hypothesis.

Reid (1962) supplied additional evidence on the Friedman proposition, using the 1950 BLS data. Reid's findings are consistent with the Friedman hypothesis.

[20] Friedman (1957) discusses the likely impact of this dividend on consumption. He states that "on our hypothesis, the windfall should affect consumption only insofar as it raises permanent income; for the rest it should be treated as transitory components" (p. 215). The estimating equations are

(1) $C = 964 + 0.747\,Y + 0.966d$ $R^2 = 0.601$
       (76)   (0.017)   (0.145)

(2) $C' = 959 + 0.560\,Y + 0.723d$ $R^2 = 0.601$
       (57)   (0.012)   (0.104)

Her results indicate (p. 734) that "virtually none of the windfall gains goes to the consumption of items not commonly classed as consumer capital and much of it goes to savings in the form of an increase in net assets apart from personal insurance."

Bird and Bodkin (1965) reexamined the Friedman proposition by further examination of the NSLI data. Their estimates suggest a value for MPC out of windfall income equal to 0.65 (when consumption is defined to include durables) and 0.38 exclusive of durables (regarding the dividend as windfall income). However, Bodkin and Bird argued that no conclusive evidence can be found either to support or to refute the Friedman proposition (p. 508): "When formal statistical tests are made, the outcome is inconclusive. Our results are clearly consistent with an absolute income hypothesis, while they do not decisively refute a strict PIH (*Permanent Income Hypothesis*)." Shapiro (1974) conducted further tests using the 1961–1962 BLS survey and found some support for Friedman's position.

From the contradictory evidence presented above it is clear that further study needs to be undertaken to provide conclusive evidence to support or reject the proposition that transitory consumption and transitory income are uncorrelated.

THE LIFE-CYCLE HYPOTHESIS

The Hypothesis

A similar hypothesis to that of Friedman has been developed by Modigliani and Brumberg (1954), by Watts (1958), and by Ando and Modigliani (1963). The so-called life-cycle hypothesis of Modigliani and Brumberg and Ando and Modigliani will be explored briefly in this section as well as some of the empirical tests of the hypothesis.

Let us begin with Brumberg-Modigliani model. Assuming the price level of consumables is not expected to change over the spending unit's life-span, and the interest rate is expected to remain constant, they start, as did Friedman [Eq. (4-7)], with the basic proposition that the consumption of an individual of a given age may be written in the following form:

$$c_t = f(v) \qquad f(v) > 0 \qquad (4\text{-}19)$$

This says that (given the interest rate) an individual's consumption at time t is an increasing function of his wealth (the present value of his current and future income as of time t).

However, unlike Friedman, Modigliani and Ando do not revert to defining a proxy for v— permanent income—but proceed directly to attempt to put the consumption-wealth relationship in a form amenable to empirical testing. First, they posit that *age* is a crucial variable in determining the relation of consumption to

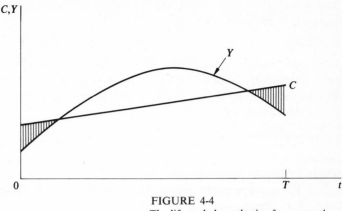

FIGURE 4-4
The life-cycle hypothesis of consumption.

measured income, and perhaps the relation between consumption and wealth. The typical life cycle for consumption and income is shown in Figure 4-4. Over their lifetimes individuals experience an income path shown by the Y line; income is low in the initial earning years, rises to a peak in middle or late working years, and falls off sharply with old age and retirement. On the other hand, the typical consumption pattern is much "flatter"—the typical individual would choose a gently rising or stable path of C over his lifetime. As a consequence, in his youth and old age he dissaves (the shaded areas in Figure 4-4), and saves in his middle years to repay debt incurred earlier and to provide for retirement.

This hypothesis explains the cross-section studies showing the C/Y ratio falling as Y rises with MPC < APC. The higher the level of Y in a typical cross section, the greater the proportion of middle-aged individuals whose incomes are high *because* they are of that age group and the lower the C/Y ratio. The persons observed at low-income levels contain both the groups at either end of the life cycle—the aged and the young—with a consequently high ratio of C to Y. Thus, the life-cycle hypothesis, if true, explains why a cross-section study would show a falling C/Y ratio as Y rises.

If it is assumed that the individual consumer of a given age "spreads" any increase in wealth more or less proportionate to consumption in present and future periods, we have[21]

$$c_t = \lambda v_t{}^i \qquad (4\text{-}20)$$

---

[21] Note the similarity to Friedman's permanent-income hypothesis:

$$C_p = kiv$$

given i, we may interpret ki as Ando and Modigliani's λ_t. Friedman's k, like Ando and Modigliani's λ_t, depends on tastes, i, and age. Here also consumption is defined as expenditure on nondurable goods and services (adjusted for inventory changes) plus current depreciation of income-yielding durables.

And if the distribution of the population by age groups is fairly stable over time, the aggregate consumption function can be written

$$C_t = \alpha V_t \qquad (4\text{-}21)$$

Ando and Modigliani made this more useful empirically by defining V—the present value of resources—(for time $t = 0$) as the sum of net worth (conventionally measured) A_0 and the present value of nonproperty income individuals expect to earn over the rest of their earning lives; i.e.,

$$V_t = A_0 + Y_0{}^L + \sum_1^T \frac{Y_t{}^L}{(1 + i)^t} \qquad (4\text{-}22)$$

where $Y_0{}^L$ = current nonproperty income
  $Y_t{}^L$ = nonproperty income the individual expects at time zero to earn t years
    from now
  T = remaining years of life
  i = the rate of discount, assumed to be the same for all periods
If we define the *average* expected labor income in time zero, $Y_0{}^e$, we obtain

$$Y_0{}^e = \frac{1}{T - 1} \sum_1^T \frac{Y_t{}^L}{(1 + i)^t} \qquad (4\text{-}23)$$

Then the wealth at time $t = 0$ can be written

$$V_0 = A_0 + Y_0{}^L + (T - 1)Y_0{}^e \qquad (4\text{-}24)$$

and the form of the aggregate consumption function (Ando and Modigliani, 1963, p. 58) is

$$C_0 = \alpha Y_0{}^L + \alpha(T - 1)Y_0{}^e + \alpha A_0 \qquad (4\text{-}25)$$

i.e., consumption in any year t is assumed to be a linear function of aggregate current nonproperty income ($Y_0{}^L$), average expected annual nonproperty income ($Y_0{}^e$), and assets at the beginning of the period (A_0).

The main empirical difficulty with the life-cycle hypothesis is the measurement of average expected labor income $Y_0{}^e$. Ando and Modigliani tried two alternatives for measurement of $Y_0{}^e$: (1) that average expected nonproperty income is the same as current income except for a scale factor[22]:

$$Y_0{}^e = \beta Y_0{}^L \qquad 1 > \beta > 0 \qquad (4\text{-}26)$$

and (2) that, for those *employed*, expected nonproperty income is equal to current nonproperty income $Y_0{}^L$ adjusted for a scale factor:

$$Y_0{}^e = \beta_1 \frac{Y_0{}^L}{E_0} \qquad (4\text{-}27)$$

---

[22] We may note that Ando and Modigliani have discarded Friedman's assumption that Y_t^e can be measured as an exponentially weighted average of past incomes. See Friedman (1957, pp. 142–145).

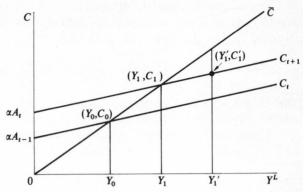

FIGURE 4-5
Short- and long-run consumption functions.

where $Y_0{}^e$ is average expected nonproperty income of the employed and E_0 equals the number of persons employed.[23] The first hypothesis seems to work better, with the estimate of the C function[24]:

$$C_t = 0.7Y_t{}^L + 0.06A_{t-1} \qquad (4\text{-}28)$$

In terms of (4-25) and (4-26), the coefficient of $Y_t{}^L$ is $\alpha[1 + \beta(T - 1)]$, and that of A_{t-1} is α.[25] If T is assumed to be 38 (the average worker is 35 years old), then Eq. (4-28) indicates that β would be given by $0.06(1 + 38\beta) = 0.7$, or $\beta = 0.3$. Thus, a \$1 rise in current labor income causes *expected labor income* to use some 30 cents.

Now consider the implications of the Ando–Modigliani consumption function for reconciliation of the long- and short-run consumption functions. In the short run, with assets fairly stable, the consumption function would appear as shown in Figure 4-5. The intercept of the function would be αA_{t-1}, and C would vary along the C_t line, with the APC showing a tendency to fall as labor income rises {the slope

----

[23] For an *unemployed* person $Y_0{}^e$ is assumed to be proportional to the $Y_0{}^e$ of the employed:

$$Y_0{}^{eu} = \beta_2 \frac{Y_0}{E_0} \qquad \beta_2 < \beta_1$$

[24] The data are from later estimates by Ando and Modigliani using net worth figures not available when the original article was published. See their note in the March 1964 issue of *American Economic Review*. In the same issue, J. J. Arena reports results of independent tests of his own which (though containing some definitional differences) also support the life-cycle hypothesis.

[25] Ando and Modigliani tested for a shift in parameters by computing a number of regressions involving a dummy variable with value zero for the years 1929–1940, and a value of 1 for 1947–1959. The results suggest only a moderate downward shift in the parameter α of the measured consumption function from the prewar to postwar period.

of C_t is, of course, equal to $\alpha[1 + \beta(T - 1)]\}$. Over the long run, however, the growth in assets would shift the C function up—the intercept αA_{t-1} would increase. Dividing Eq. (4-28) by *total income Y*, we get

$$\frac{C_t}{Y_t} = 0.7 \frac{Y_t^L}{Y_t} + 0.06 \frac{A_{t-1}}{Y_t} \qquad (4\text{-}29)$$

The constant C/Y ratio observed by Kuznets will follow as long as the ratios Y_t^L/Y_t and A_{t-1}/Y_t exhibit secular stability—and they have. Labor income has been around 0.75 of total income, and the asset-income ratio for households is in the neighborhood of 5. The implied long-run APC is then

$$\frac{C}{Y} = 0.7(0.75) + 0.06(5) \qquad \frac{C}{Y} = 0.525 + (0.30) = 0.825 \qquad (4\text{-}30)$$

which is close to the values obtained by Kuznets (cited earlier). In Figure 4-5, the line $\bar{C}$ represents the long-run C function.

Thus, the Ando–Modigliani hypothesis provides an explanation of the inconsistencies between the long-run constancy of the APC as estimated from secular data and the declining APC exhibited in estimates of the consumption function using cross-section and short-run time-series data. However, the formulation has one major flaw: it assumes that changes in *current* (after-tax) labor income always generate changes, in the same direction, of expected *future* labor income. This makes the function difficult to use in cases where the change in current Y^L is clearly temporary, as, for example, when the temporary income tax surcharge was imposed in 1968–1969.

THE LONG-RUN PROPERTIES OF CONSUMPTION FUNCTION CONTAINING WEALTH AS AN ARGUMENT

It is instructive to explore the results of hypotheses which make consumption a function of wealth. The long-run implications of the form in which such functions are specified yield considerable information about their consistency with observed data, and enable us to immediately discard some "wealth versions" of the consumption function.

Consider first a consumption function of the form

$$\frac{C}{Y} = a + b \frac{A_{-1}}{Y} \qquad (4\text{-}31)$$

This resembles the life-cycle consumption function, but Y here is *total income* rather than nonproperty income. By definition,

$$S = Y - C \qquad \text{and} \qquad S = \Delta A \qquad (4\text{-}32)$$

Then
$$\frac{C}{Y} = \frac{Y - S}{Y} = a + b \frac{A_{-1}}{Y}$$

or

$$\frac{Y - \Delta A}{Y} = a + b \frac{A_{-1}}{Y}$$

Therefore, since $\Delta A = A - A_{-1}$,

$$\frac{Y - A + A_{-1}}{Y} = a + b \frac{A_{-1}}{Y}$$

$$1 - \frac{A}{Y} + \frac{A_{-1}}{Y} = a + b \frac{A_{-1}}{Y}$$

$$1 - \frac{A}{Y} = a - (1 - b) \frac{A_{-1}}{Y}$$

and

$$(1 - b) \frac{A_{-1}}{Y} = a - 1 + \frac{A}{Y}$$

If A grows at the constant long-run rate, then

$$A = (1 + \gamma) A_{-1}$$

$$\frac{(1 - b)}{(1 + \gamma)} \frac{A}{Y} = a - 1 + \frac{A}{Y}$$

$$\frac{A}{Y} \left[1 - \frac{(1 - b)}{(1 + \gamma)} \right] = 1 - a$$

$$\frac{A}{Y} = \frac{1 - a}{1 - \frac{(1 - b)}{(1 + \gamma)}} = \frac{1 - a}{\frac{(1 + \gamma) - (1 - b)}{(1 + \gamma)}}$$

$$\frac{A}{Y} = \frac{1 - a}{\left[\frac{(\gamma + b)}{(1 + \gamma)} \right]} = \frac{(1 + \gamma)(1 - a)}{(\gamma + b)}$$

If $\gamma = 0$, i.e., if there is *no growth in A*, then

$$\frac{A}{Y} = \frac{1 - a}{b}$$

Substituting this in the original C function, we get

$$\frac{C}{Y} = a + b \frac{A_{-1}}{Y} \qquad (A = A_{-1})$$

$$\frac{C}{Y} = a + \frac{b(1 - a)}{b} = 1$$

(4-33)

With no growth, the long-run MPC = 1. With growth, the *actual long-run MPC* (=APC) *depends on the rate of growth of Y.*

Suppose the hypothesis is that consumption is *proportional* to wealth:

$$C = kA \qquad (4\text{-}34)$$

This form of the wealth hypothesis has been advanced by Ball and Drake (1964) and by Spiro (1962). As shown by Evans (1969, pp. 36–40), this form of consumption function implies a long-run *and* short-run MPC that is inconsistent with observed data and most other empirical studies of the consumption function. Again, we have

$$S = Y - C = \Delta A$$

and

$$C = Y - S$$

$$= Y - A + A_{-1}$$

$$= Y - \frac{C}{k} + \frac{C_{-1}}{k}$$

Factoring out C, we get

$$C + \frac{C}{k} = Y + \frac{C_{-1}}{k}$$

$$C\left(1 + \frac{1}{k}\right) = Y + \frac{1}{k}C_{-1}$$

or

$$C = Y\left(\frac{1}{1 + \frac{1}{k}}\right) + \left(\frac{1}{k}\right)\left(\frac{1}{1 + \frac{1}{k}}\right)C_{-1}$$

$$= Y\left(\frac{k}{k+1}\right) + \left(\frac{1}{k}\right)\left(\frac{1}{\frac{k+1}{k}}\right)C_{-1}$$

$$= Y\left(\frac{k}{1+k}\right) + \left(\frac{1}{1+k}\right)C_{-1}$$

With no growth in income, wealth, or consumption ($C = C_{-1}$),

$$C\left(1 - \frac{1}{1+k}\right) = Y\left(\frac{k}{1+k}\right)$$

$$C\left(\frac{1+k-1}{1+k}\right) = Y\left(\frac{k}{1+k}\right)$$

$$C = Y\left(\frac{\frac{k}{1+k}}{\frac{k}{1+k}}\right) = Y$$

Thus the long-run MPC ($=APC$) is also unity where no growth occurs for this version of the consumption function.

With income and wealth growing at a constant growth rate, the proportionality consumption function yields a long-run MPC of less than unity. Again, we have

$$A = (1 + \gamma)A_{-1}$$

$$C = kA$$

$$C = Y - S$$

$$= Y - \Delta A$$

$$C = Y - (A - A_{-1})$$

$$C = Y - \frac{C}{k} + \frac{C}{k(1 + \gamma)}$$

$$C\left(1 + \frac{1}{k}\right) = Y + \frac{C}{k(1 + \gamma)}$$

$$C\left(\frac{k + 1}{k}\right) = Y + \frac{C}{k(1 + \gamma)}$$

$$C = Y\left(\frac{k}{k + 1}\right) + \frac{k}{(k + 1)k} \frac{C}{(1 + \gamma)}$$

$$C\left[1 - \frac{1}{(k + 1)(1 + \gamma)}\right] = Y\left(\frac{k}{k + 1}\right)$$

$$\frac{C}{Y} = \frac{\dfrac{k}{(k + 1)}}{1 - \dfrac{1}{(k + 1)(1 + \gamma)}} = \frac{k}{(k + 1) - \dfrac{1}{1 + \gamma}}$$

$$\frac{C}{Y} = \frac{k}{\dfrac{(k + 1)(1 + \gamma) - 1}{1 + \gamma}} = \frac{k}{1 + \gamma k + \gamma + k - 1} = \frac{k}{\gamma(1 + k) + k}$$

The data show that $C/A = k \approx 0.2$. This implies a *yearly* MPC out of disposable personal income $[=k/(k + 1)]$ of only about 0.16. This is too low when the yearly MPC is observed from other studies. Furthermore, the long-run MPC $\{=k/[\gamma(1 + k) + k]\}$ would be only 0.80 for the 3 percent average growth rate since World War II, whereas with this growth rate it has actually been about 0.93 over the postwar period.

On the other hand, as noted above, the Ando–Modigliani consumption function does not yield long-run results that are a priori inconsistent with the data.

In summary, the long-run MPC depends crucially on γ, the rate of growth. The Ball–Drake, Spiro, and Ando–Modigliani consumption functions all yield a long-run MPC = 1 for no growth. However, they yield different results where growth is assumed. In this case, the Ando–Modigliani function is not inconsistent with other estimates (where $\gamma > 0$); the functions assuming $C = kA$ are inconsistent.

COMPARISON AND EVALUATION OF
CONSUMPTION-FUNCTION HYPOTHESES

It is quite obvious from the survey in this chapter that a simple relation between consumption and income such as the one illustrated by Keynes does not exist. We have selected to review three alternative hypotheses in this chapter to illustrate the complexity in defining a stable consumption function. The three hypotheses discussed agree that current income alone is not a sufficient explanatory variable in a stable consumption function. While the list of other influences upon consumption spending can be made vary large, e.g., including lagged income, relative income, the amount of permanent income, assets, the rate of interest and/or terms of installment credit, the size and composition of the consumer unit, the occupation of the head of the house-hold, and prices, the resulting information about the consumption function would be unmanageable if it included all such influences as explanatory variables. A more useful approach is to limit the number of variables to those which dominate consumption behavior over time and yield a stable function.

What of the alternative hypotheses discussed in this chapter? Which should one choose as the basis for constructing a macromodel useful for analyzing critical policy decisions? It seems clear that the failure of the relative-income hypothesis to predict post-World War II consumption should lead us to reject it.

This leaves us to choose between the permanent-income and life-cycle hypotheses. Although the permanent-income hypothesis is generally considered an improvement over previous hypotheses of the consumption function, it does leave something to be desired. On the one hand there is the unresolved controversy over Friedman's assumption that transitory income and consumption are uncorrelated. This issue is so crucial to the permanent-income hypothesis that additional investigation is needed to support or refute this basic proposition. Even more, however, Friedman seems to have avoided completely the distinction between *personal* and *disposable permanent income*. How can one define *permanent taxes*? In using permanent disposable income, *some* concept of permanent taxes is implied. One might use weighted-average personal taxes of the last 3 to 5 years as a proxy of permanent taxes; yet the tax rate is an exogenous variable which presumably could vary with the level of economic activity, wars, or domestic government fiscal programs. Previous tax rates are by no means an indication of what future tax rates are likely to be.

The life-cycle hypothesis of Ando and Modigliani avoids some but not all of the difficulties associated with the permanent-income hypothesis. Their consumption function includes current income, expected income, and consumer units' net worth as explanatory variables. However, the problems of estimating expected income are present in this case also. As we have seen earlier, Ando and Modigliani discarded Friedman's proposition that expected income can be measured as an exponentially weighted average of past income. Instead they have assumed expected income to be the same as current income except for a scale factor. However, the life-cycle hypothesis is more easily estimated with existing data, and the results of the tests by Ando and Modigliani indicate it gives at least as good a "fit" as the permanent-income hypothesis, at least for annual data. It also successfully explains the long-run stability and the cyclical variability of the consumption-income ratio.

For these reasons the Ando–Modigliani hypothesis may be considered as an improvement over both the absolute-income hypothesis and the permanent-income hypothesis.

CONSUMER DURABLES AND TOTAL CONSUMER EXPENDITURES

With a theory of *consumption* in hand, the analysis can be extended to explain *consumer expenditures*, the consumption concept used in the GNP accounts. Consumer expenditures (C_E) are equal to

$$C_E = C_N + E_D \qquad (4\text{-}35)$$

where C_N = consumption of nondurable goods
E_D = current expenditure on durable goods

But *consumption* of the services of durable goods reflects the rental value (depreciation plus interest) of the average *stock* of durables during the period:

$$C_D = (r + \delta_D)\bar{K}_D \qquad (4\text{-}36)$$

The average stock of durables during the period can be written

$$\bar{K}_D = K_{D-1} + \gamma E_D$$

where K_{D-1} is the stock at the beginning of the current period and γ represents a proportion of E_D to be added to the stock of durables. Thus, consumption of durables is given by

$$C_D = (r + \delta_D)\gamma E_D + (r + \delta_D)K_{D-1} \qquad (4\text{-}37)$$

Given total consumption from the Ando–Modigliani consumption function above

$$C = 0.7Y^L + 0.06A_{t-1} \quad (4\text{-}28a)$$

we can proceed to estimate the *durable and nondurable components* of C, i.e., C_N and C_D, where specific variables reflecting credit conditions and other factors causing consumption of the components of consumption are represented by $X_i(i = 1, \ldots, N)$:

$$C_N = \alpha_N C + \sum_i^N \beta_{N_i} X_i \qquad (4\text{-}38)$$

$$C_D = \alpha_D C + \sum_i^N \beta_{D_i} X_i \qquad (4\text{-}39)$$

The constraints are that $\alpha_N + \alpha_D = 1$ and $\sum_i^N (\beta_{N_i} + \beta_{D_i}) = 0$. This is the procedure followed, for example, in the 1968 version of the Federal Reserve-MIT model.

Given estimates of C_N and C_D, Eq. (4-40) can be used to explain total consumer expenditures:

$$C_E = C_N + \frac{C_D - (r + \delta_D)K_{D-1}}{(r + \delta_D)\gamma} \quad (4\text{-}40)$$

Consider the β_{N_i} and β_{D_i}—the variables explaining the "mix" of total consumption as between durables and nondurables. What variables will be important here? There are three which are commonly used: (1) the *relative prices* of durables and nondurables (P_N/P_D); (2) some variable reflecting *credit conditions* (cost and availability, Cr); and (3) a *consumer attitudes index* (A).[26] Thus,

$$C_N = \alpha_N C + \beta_{N_0}\left(\frac{P_N}{P_D}\right) + \beta_{N_1}(\text{Cr}) + \beta_{N_2}(A)$$

$$C_D = \alpha_D C + \beta_{D_0}\left(\frac{P_N}{P_D}\right) + \beta_{D_1}(\text{Cr}) + \beta_{D_2}(A)$$

And the consumer expenditures sector is closed with the definitions

$$C_E = C_N + E_D \quad (4\text{-}35)$$
$$C_D = (r + \delta_D)\gamma E_D + (r + \delta_D)K_{D-1} \quad (4\text{-}37)$$

and with the Ando–Modigliani equation for C,

$$C = 0.7Y^L + 0.06A_{t-1} \quad (4\text{-}28a)$$

READINGS FOR CHAPTER 4

ACKLEY, G.: *Macroeconomic Theory* (New York: Macmillan, 1961), chaps. 10–12.

ALLEN, R. G., and A. L. BOWLEY: *Family Expenditures* (London: 1935).

ANDO A., and F. MODIGLIANI: "The Life-Cycle Hypothesis of Saving: Aggregate Implications and Tests," *American Economic Review*, pp. 55–84, March 1963; also see their "Correction" in the March 1964 issue of *American Economic Review*, pp. 111–113.

———: "Velocity and the Investment Multiplier," *American Economic Review*, September 1965.

ARENA, J. J.: "The Wealth Effect and Consumption: A Statistical Inquiry," *Yale Economic Essays*, vol. 111, pp. 251–303, 1963.

———: "Capital Gains and the 'Life Cycle' Hypothesis of Saving, "*American Economic Review*, pp. 107–110, March 1964.

BALL, R. J., and P. S. DRAKE: "The Relationship between Aggregate Consumption and Wealth," *International Economic Review*, vol. V, pp. 63–81, January 1964.

BENNION, E. G.: "The Consumption Function Cyclically Variable," *Review of Economics and Statistics*, November 1946.

[26] Evans (1969, chap. 6) provides a detailed discussion of how these variables may be specified.

BIRD, R. C., and R. G. BODKIN: "The National Service Life Insurance Dividend of 1950 and Consumption: A Further Test of the 'Strict' Permanent Income Hypothesis," *Journal of Political Economy*, pp. 499–515, October 1965.

BODKIN, R: "Windfall Income and Consumption," *American Economic Review*, pp. 602–614, September 1959.

———: "Windfall Income and Consumption: Comment," *American Economic Review*, pp. 445–447, June 1963.

BRADY, D., and R. FRIEDMAN: "Saving and the Income Distribution," *Studies in Economic Wealth*, National Bureau of Economic Research, 1947, vol. 10.

DUESENBERRY, J.: "Income-Consumption Relations and Their Implications," in *Income, Employment and Public Policy: Essays in Honor of Alvin Hansen* (New York: Norton, 1948), pp. 54–81.

———: *Income, Saving, and the Theory of Consumer Behavior* (Cambridge, Mass.: Harvard, 1949).

EVANS, MICHAEL, K: "The Importance of Wealth in the Consumption Function," *Journal of Political Economy*, vol. 75, pp. 335–351, part 1, April 1967.

———: *Macroeconomic Activity: Theory, Forecasting, and Control* (New York: Harper & Row, 1969).

FERBER, R.: *A Study of Aggregate Consumption Functions*, National Bureau of Economic Research, Technical Paper 8, 1953.

FRIEDMAN, M.: *A Theory of the Consumption Function* (Princeton N.J.: Princeton, 1957), especially chaps. 1, 2, 6, and 9.

———: "The Concept of Horizon in the Permanent Income Hypothesis," in C. F. Christ et al. (eds.) *Measurement in Economics: Studies in Mathematical Economics and Econometrics in Memory of Yehuda Grunfeld* (Stanford, Calif.: Stanford, 1963).

GILBOY, E.: "The Propensity to Consume," *Quarterly Journal of Economics*, pp. 120–140, November 1938.

GOLDSMITH, R.: *A Study of Saving in the United States* (Princeton, N.J.: Princeton, 1955).

HANSEN, A. H.: *A Guide to Keynes* (New York: McGraw-Hill, 1953), chap. 3.

HOUTHAKKER, H.: "An International Comparison of Household Expenditure Patterns," *Econometrica*, pp. 532–551, October 1957.

———: "The Permanent Income Hypothesis," *American Economic Review* (review of Friedman), June 1958; also comments by Eisner, Friedman, and Houthakker, *American Economic Review*, December 1958.

KEYNES, J. M.: *The General Theory of Employment, Interest, and Money* (New York: Harcourt, Brace, 1936), chaps. 7–9.

KREININ, M. E.: "Windfall Income and Consumption: Additional Evidence," *American Economic Review*, pp. 388–390, June 1961.

KUZNETS, SIMON: "Uses of National Income in Peace and War," Occasional Paper 6, National Bureau of Economic Research, New York, 1942.

———: *National Product Since 1869*, New York, 1946.

LANSBERGER, M.: "Windfall Income and Consumption: Comment," *American Economic Review*, pp. 534–540, June 1966, and Bodkins "Reply" in same issue, pp. 540–545.

MODIGLIANI, F., and R. BRUMBERG: "Utility Analysis and the Consumption Function: An Interpretation of Cross Section Data," in *Post-Keynesian Economics* (New Brunswick, N. J. Rutgers, 1954).

————: "Utility Analysis and the Consumption Function," in K. Kurihara (ed.), *Post-Keynesian Economics* (London: G. Allen, 1955), pp. 388–436.

MOSAK, J.: "Forecasting Postwar Demand III," *Econometrica*, pp. 25–53, January 1945.

National Budget for Full Employment, National Planning Association, Washington, 1945.

REID, M.: "Consumption, Savings and Windfall Gains," *American Economic Review*, pp. 728–737, September 1962.

SHAPIRO, IRWIN A.: *A Test of the Effect of Windfall Receipts on Consumption* (unpublished doctoral dissertation, Clark University, 1974), chap. 4.

SMITHIES, A.: "Forecasting Postwar Demand I," *Econometrica*, pp. 1–14, January 1945.

SPIRO, A.: "Wealth and the Consumption Function," *Journal of Political Economy*, vol. 70, pp. 339–354, August 1962.

Study of Consumer Expenditures, Income and Savings, Wharton School of Finance and Commerce, 1957.

SUITS, D. B.: "The Determinants of Consumer Expenditure: A Review of Present Knowledge," in *Impacts of Monetary Policy*, Commission on Money and Credit (Englewood Cliffs, N.J.: Prentice-Hall, 1963), pp. 1–53.

TOBIN, J.: "Relative Income, Absolute Income, and Savings," in *Money, Trade and Economic Growth: Essays in Honor of John H. Williams* (New York: Macmillan, 1951), pp. 135–156.

WATTS, H.: "Long Run Income Expectations and Consumer Saving, " in *Studies in Household Economic Behavior*, Yale Studies in Economics (New Haven, Conn.: Yale, 1958), vol. 9.

WOYTINSKY, W.: "Relationship between Consumer's Expenditures, Saving and Disposable Income," *Review of Economics and Statistics*, February 1946.

ZELLNER, A.: "Short-Run Consumption Functions," *Econometrica*, 1958.

5

BUSINESS FIXED INVESTMENT

In the previous chapter we discussed the major hypotheses put forth to explain consumption expenditures. In this chapter we turn to another component of planned spending: business investment expenditures. Investment expenditures will be broken down into three components: business investment in plant and equipment (business fixed investment), housing investment, and inventory investment, with the latter two covered separately in Chapters 6 and 7.

In Chapter 3, investment was rather eclectically assumed to be a function of the rate of interest—the investment function was $I = I(i)$. In this chapter we attempt to broaden our understanding of the investment process, the decision to invest, and the factors that determine the rate of investment. It is not our purpose, however, to give a comprehensive survey of the literature on the theory of investment but rather to focus attention on the major theoretical developments of recent years. Specifically, most of this chapter deals with the *neoclassical investment model*, as it has come to be called.

Let us begin by defining the term investment.[1] The term investment has been

---

[1] Investment is defined here as investment in physical assets; investment in other forms of assets are thus excluded.

used, in the literature, in a manner which could easily confuse the modern student of economics (Haavelmo, 1960). It has been used by classical economists to denote the transfer of certain amounts of wealth from one ownership or employment to another; to denote the replacement, per unit of time, required to maintain the total stock of capital; or to denote the nonconsumption of a given amount of capital. In the macroeconomic models that grow out of the experience of the 1930s, investment was looked upon as the active element determining the total amount of saving that the economy was capable of offsetting. With the recent development of the theory of investment, especially since Lerner's famous work on the marginal efficiency of investment, net investment is defined as the time rate of change of the stock of capital, or $I_N = dK/dt$.

If net investment is the rate of change in the capital stock, the decision to invest (to change the capital stock) depends on changes in the desired stock of that asset. Such a decision will thus be made when the actual stock of the asset (K) differs from the desired stock (K^*).

Two obvious questions must now be raised. First, what determines the desired (optimum) stock of capital—K^*? Second, what causes K^* to change?

To be able to explain the underlying factors that determine the desired stock of capital we must begin at the microlevel, i.e., with the firm's demand for capital services.

MICROFOUNDATIONS OF THE INVESTMENT FUNCTION: THE NEOCLASSICAL INVESTMENT MODEL

In recent years, the literature on investment theory has centered around models developed on the ground work laid by Irving Fisher (1930) and later expanded by Herschliefer (1958, 1970), Bailey (1959), and Witte (1963). Although these models differ in many respects, they have in common a basic element—a specific relation between microeconomic variables and aggregate investment. They incorporate a theory of the demand for a flow of capital goods based on the profit-maximizing theory of the firm, and, in addition, a distributed lag stock-adjustment hypothesis.[2]

In deriving an aggregate investment function we begin with a model that describes the firm's demand for a flow of capital services. Unlike its demand for other inputs, such as labor, the firm is unable to purchase capital services independently of the sources of these services. Thus, in order to acquire capital services, the firm must purchase and maintain a stock of capital goods. To overcome this problem (flow-stock demand) we make the standard assumption in production theory that the flow of capital services resulting from a given stock is proportional to the size of that stock. With this assumption, varying the rate of capital services can be accomplished by varying the size of the capital stock.

---

[2] The main models we refer to are those of Jorgenson (along with several different collaborators) and Bischoff (1968). The pioneering study by Jorgenson is Jorgenson (1963).

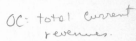

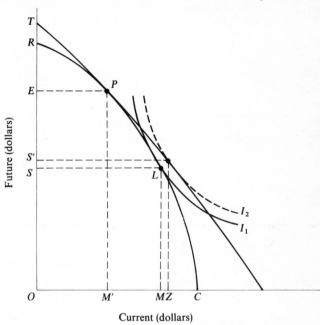

Current (dollars)

FIGURE 5-1
Intertemporal choice by a firm.

Based on the neoclassical theory of the firm, the demand for capital, or the optimum capital stock, is determined in the process of *maximizing the present value of the firm*, defined as the present value of a stream of net proceeds—total revenue less labor costs, taxes, and gross investment—and subject to two constraints: (1) a production function; and (2) the time rate of change of the stock of capital, at time t, is equal to gross investment less depreciation at time t.

This may be made clearer by considering a firm with a two-period horizon, which is also assumed to use only capital as an input. In Figure 5-1, the horizontal axis represents current dollars and the vertical axis represents "future" dollars. The firm's *production function* is shown by the line RC—which indicates all combinations of present and future income the firm can produce by use of its current gross revenues OC. The utility function of the firm's owners is shown by indifference curves I_1 and I_2; they indicate all combinations of present and future income received by them from the firm which produce equal satisfaction.

If the firm does not have access to credit markets, the utility of the owners would clearly be best served by investing CM of its current revenues, leaving the owners on the highest indifference curve tangent to the production possibilities line

RC (that is, I_1). In this case, at point L, the owners would be receiving OM of current income and OS of future income.

However, with access to credit markets, the firm maximizes the utility of the owners by investing CM' of its current revenues, borrowing MM' in the market, and paying the owners OZ of current income and OS' of future income—which places them on the higher indifference curve I_2. *In short, by choosing the most efficient production point (P), and then borrowing or lending to achieve the desired time distribution of income to the owners, the firm maximizes its utility.* But this is equivalent to maximizing the *present value of the flow of net proceeds* (PVR) to the firm, i.e., current revenues less gross investment. In our example (Figure 5-1) this is

$$\text{PVR} = OM' + \frac{OE}{1 + i}$$

where i is the market rate of interest. Given access to the capital markets, then, maximizing PVR is equivalent to maximizing utility. This is the cornerstone of neoclassical investment models.

More formally, let us assume that the firm produces one homogeneous output, Y, and uses only two inputs—one homogeneous factor input on current account (labor) and one homogeneous factor input on capital account (capital). Let N_t be period t labor input and Y_t be period t output. Let K_t be the stock of capital at the beginning of period t. The firm's production function is then given by

$$Y_t = F(N_t, K_t) \qquad (5\text{-}1)$$

Let p_t, w_t, and q_t be, respectively, the price of a unit of output, the wage rate, and the price of a unit of capital at the beginning of period t. (Hereafter, when price, stock, or flow variables appear unsubscripted, they are understood to carry the subscript t). Let I be gross investment in capital, in real terms, and T be taxes. Then net proceeds R is defined as

$$R = pY - qI - wN - T \qquad (5\text{-}2)$$

or total revenues less total expenditures on factor inputs and taxes.

The value of the firm V is defined as the present value of the anticipated stream of net proceeds, at some time $t = 0$, or

$$V = \int_0^\infty e^{-it}(pY - qI - wN - T)\, dt \qquad (5\text{-}3)$$

where i is the "relevant" rate of discount and is presumed to be independent of t.

Derivation of Optimum Capital Stock

The problem then is to maximize (5-3) subject to the constraints of the production function

$$F(Y, K, N) = 0 \qquad (5\text{-}1a)$$

and the definition of gross investment

$$I_t = \delta K_t + \frac{dK}{dt} \qquad (5\text{-}4)$$

and

$$I_N = \frac{dK}{dt} = \dot{K}(t) = I(t) - \delta K(t) \qquad (5\text{-}4a)$$

where δK_t is economic depreciation. Economic depreciation is assumed to be proportional to the capital stock, with the rate of economic depreciation equal to δ.[3]

It is convenient to approach the maximization problem first in a setting where firms are not subject to direct taxation, i.e., where $T = 0$. We want to maximize

$$V = \int_0^\infty e^{-it}(pY - qI - wN)\, dt \qquad (5\text{-}3)$$

$$V = \int_0^\infty e^{-it} R(t)\, dt$$

subject to

$$F(Y, K, N) = 0 \qquad (5\text{-}1a)$$

$$\dot{K}(t) = I(t) - \delta K(t) \qquad (5\text{-}4a)$$

To do so, we form the Lagrangian expression

$$L = \int_0^\infty [e^{-it} R(t) + \lambda_0(t)F(Y, N, K) + \lambda_1(t)(\dot{K} - I - \delta K)]\, dt \qquad (5\text{-}5)$$

$$L = \int_0^\infty f(Y, N, I, K, \dot{K}, \lambda_0, \lambda_1, t)\, dt \qquad (5\text{-}6)$$

The Euler conditions necessary for a maximum of the present value of the firm then are[4]

$$\frac{\partial f}{\partial Y} = e^{-it}p + \lambda_0(t)\frac{\partial F}{\partial Y} = 0 \qquad (5\text{-}6a)$$

$$\frac{\partial f}{\partial N} = -e^{-it}w + \lambda_0(t)\frac{\partial F}{\partial N} = 0 \qquad (5\text{-}6b)$$

---

[3] The implications of the depreciation assumption on the survival time path of capital are given in the Appendix to this chapter.
[4] If $f = f(t, K, \dot{K})$, and we want to maximize $\int f\, dt$, then according to the Euler equation, $\partial f / \partial K - d/dt\, \partial f / \partial \dot{K} = 0$, and (5-6d) is obtained. For further explanation, see Allen (1956, p. 530).

$$\frac{\partial f}{\partial I} = -e^{-it}q - \lambda_1(t) = 0 \tag{5-6c}$$

$$\frac{\partial f}{\partial K} - \frac{d}{dt}\frac{\partial f}{\partial \dot{K}} = \lambda_0(t)\frac{\partial F}{\partial K} + \delta\lambda_1(t) - \frac{d}{dt}\lambda_1(t) = 0 \tag{5-6d}$$

$$\frac{\partial f}{\partial \lambda_0} = F(Y, N, K) \tag{5-6e}$$

$$\frac{\partial f}{\partial \lambda_1} = \dot{K} - I + \delta K = 0 \tag{5-6f}$$

Equation (5-6d) is the condition for the optimal growth path of K. Combining (5-6a) and (5-6b), we obtain the marginal productivity condition for labor services:

$$\lambda_0(t)\frac{\partial F}{\partial N} = e^{-it}w$$

$$\lambda_0(t)\frac{\partial F}{\partial Y} = -e^{-it}p$$

$$\frac{\partial F/\partial N}{\partial F/\partial Y} = -\frac{\partial Y}{\partial N} = -\frac{w}{p}$$

$$\frac{\partial Y}{\partial N} = \frac{w}{p} \tag{5-7}$$

The marginal product of labor is equal to the real wage. It should be noted that since output, labor, wages, and prices are all functions of time, condition (5-7) is one which holds for every point in time over the indefinite future. In static analysis of the firm, (5-7) holds only for a given point in time.

The marginal productivity condition for the services of capital are obtained from (5-6a), (5-6c), and (5-6d). First, from (5-6c) we obtain an expression for $\lambda_1(t)$:

$$\lambda_1(t) = -e^{-it}q \tag{5-8}$$

Substituting this in (5-6d), we obtain

$$\lambda_0(t)\frac{\partial F}{\partial K} - \delta e^{-it}q + \frac{d}{dt}(e^{-it}q) = 0$$

$$= \lambda_0(t)\frac{\partial F}{\partial K} - \delta e^{-it}q + (-ie^{-it}q + e^{-it}\dot{q}) = 0$$

$$= \lambda_0(t)\frac{\partial F}{\partial K} - e^{-it}q\left(\delta + i - \frac{\dot{q}}{q}\right) = 0 \tag{5-9}$$

Combining (5-9) and (5-6a), we get the marginal productivity condition for capital services:

$$\lambda_0(t)\frac{\partial F}{\partial K} = e^{-it}q\left(\delta + i - \frac{\dot{q}}{q}\right)$$

$$\lambda_0(t)\frac{\partial F}{\partial Y} = -e^{-it}p$$

$$\frac{\partial F/\partial K}{\partial F/\partial Y} = -\frac{\partial Y}{\partial K} = -\frac{q(\delta + i - \dot{q}/q)}{p} = -\frac{c}{p}$$

$$\frac{\partial Y}{\partial K} = \frac{q(\delta + i - \dot{q}/q)}{p} = \frac{c}{p} \qquad (5\text{-}10)$$

The marginal product of capital equals the real user cost of capital. The user cost, or implicit rental value per unit of capital (c) in Eq. (5-10), is given by

$$c = \left(\delta + i - \frac{\dot{q}}{q}\right)q \qquad (5\text{-}11)$$

Equation (5-10) simply says that the firm will reach an equilibrium level of capital stock when the value of marginal product of capital p ($\partial Y/\partial K$) is always equal to its implicit rental value (c)[5]:

$$p\frac{\partial Y}{\partial K} = q\left(\delta + i - \frac{\dot{q}}{q}\right) \qquad (5\text{-}12)$$

The logic behind user cost c is simple: the rent on a unit of capital must be such that it just covers the opportunity cost of lending the funds used to buy it (i) *plus* the economic depreciation or decay per unit (δ) *less* the expected rate of capital gains per period due to a rise in the unit price of capital goods ($\dot{q}/q$).

The marginal condition (5-12) determines the equilibrium capital stock of the firm. Using, for example, the CES (constant elasticity of substitution) production function,[6] we obtain

$$Y = \gamma[\delta K^{-\phi} + (1 - \delta)N^{-\phi}]^{-1/\phi} \qquad (5\text{-}13)$$

where γ = the scale parameter in the CES production function
  Y = output
  ϕ = the substitution parameter = $1/\sigma - 1$ where σ is the elasticity of substitution ($\sigma > 0$)
  δ = the distribution parameter in the CES production function

[5] For further detail on the implicit rental value of capital services see the Appendix to this chapter.
[6] The nature of the CES production function and the derivation of the marginal product of capital from it are discussed in Chapter 12.

The marginal product of capital is given by

$$\frac{\partial Y}{\partial K} = \left(\frac{Y}{K}\right)^{(1+\phi)} \gamma^{-\phi}\delta \qquad (5\text{-}14)$$

Substituting Eq. (5-14) into (5-12), we find the optimum stock of capital (K^*) of the firm with the CES production function[7]:

$$p\left[\left(\frac{Y}{K}\right)^{(1+\phi)} \gamma^{-\phi}\delta\right] = c \qquad (5\text{-}15)$$

or

$$K^* = A(p/c)^\sigma Y \qquad (5\text{-}15a)$$

where $A = (\gamma^\phi \delta^{-1})^{-\sigma}$, a constant.

The optimum capital stock rises with an increase in output Y, or a reduction in the "user cost" of capital c relative to prices p. A rise in the real user cost of capital or a fall in output reduces the optimum capital stock. Equation (5-15) gives the expression for K^* for the CES production function and where the user cost is defined in the absence of taxation.

Now we introduce direct taxation. Since most investment (about 80 percent) is undertaken by the corporate sector, the tax variable is the corporate tax rate u. Total tax payments by corporations are determined by applying the corporate tax rate to business income with deductions allowed for interest payments and for depreciation on capital assets. However, capital gains income is subject to a differential rate g. A tax credit (investment tax credit) which reduces a firm's tax liability is also allowed on the purchase of capital assets.

Introducing taxation to the model requires two modifications: (1) the rate of return before tax (which we now denote by ρ, to distinguish it from i) is one which allows for the deductibility of interest payments; (2) the discount rate is the *after-tax rate* $[(1 - u)\rho]$, and the stream of values of rentals of capital services is the *after-tax stream* $[(1 - u)c(t)]$. Because the corporate tax allows the firm a depreciation deduction for tax purposes, the firm's taxes are reduced by that amount of taxes *not* paid in each period due to the depreciation deduction claimed. In addition, the investment tax credit leads to the reduction in the acquisition cost of the asset.

Now let us define z to be the present value of depreciation deductions over the life of an asset.[8] The user cost or the implicit rental value of capital services can be

---

[7] Equation (5-15a) is derived as follows: Equation (5-15) is rewritten as:

$$p Y^{(1+\phi)} K^{-(1+\phi)} \gamma^{-\phi}\delta = c \qquad \text{and} \qquad K^{-(1+\phi)} = \frac{c}{p} Y^{-(1+\phi)}(\gamma^\phi \delta^{-1})$$

Substituting for $\phi = 1/\sigma - 1$ we get

$$[K^{(-1/\sigma)}]^\sigma = \left(\frac{c}{p}\right)^\sigma Y^{-1}(\gamma^\phi \delta^{-1})^\sigma$$

[8] Where z is given by

$$z = \int_s^\infty e^{-(1-u)\rho(t-s)} q(s) D(t-s)\, dt$$

For more detail see the Appendix to this chapter.

written as

$$c = \frac{[(1 - u)\rho + \delta - (\dot{q}/q)(1 - gu)](1 - k - uz)q}{1 - u}$$

$$= \frac{q[(1 - u)\rho + \delta - (\dot{q}/q)(1 - gu)](1 - k - uz)}{1 - u} \qquad (5\text{-}16)$$

where ρ = before-tax rate of return

u = corporate tax rate

g = differential tax rate applicable to capital gains income

k = rate of tax credit per dollar of asset

z = present value of depreciation deductions

q = price per unit of capital

If asset prices are expected to remain constant, capital gains or losses resulting from changes in the value of the asset are zero. The rental price per unit of capital then is[9]

$$c = \frac{[(1 - u)\rho + \delta](1 - k - uz)q}{1 - u} \qquad (5\text{-}17)$$

From Eq. (5-17) it is clear that the acquisition cost per unit is now $q(1 - k - uz)$. This is equal to the price per unit of capital (q) less the sum of (1) the tax savings via the investment tax credit (kq) and (2) the tax savings via depreciation deductions which, over time, sum to the price of the asset (uzq). Since (5-17) is derived from the same conditions as the "no-tax" version (5-11), we proceed to find the optimum capital stock from condition (5-12) for the CES production function. This is given by (5-15a):

$$K^* = A(p/c)^\sigma Y \qquad (5\text{-}15a)$$

where c now reflects the tax treatment of corporate income.

Equations (5-16) and (5-17) enable us to describe how taxes affect investment through their effect on the implicit rental value of capital. If there were no corporate tax or capital gains tax (u and $g = 0$), or investment credit ($k = 0$), then, as noted in (5-11), the user cost of capital would be

$$c = q(\delta + i - \dot{q}/q) \qquad (5\text{-}11)$$

Comparison of (5-11) and (5-17) shows that the corporate tax affects the cost of capital because of the tax treatment of depreciation, the deductibility of interest ($\rho \neq i$), the investment tax credit, and the preferential treatment of capital gains ($g \neq 1$). To put it another way, the corporate tax would be neutral in its effect on investment if g were unity—capital gains taxed at some rate at other income—if interest payments were not deductible, and if the present value of tax savings through

---

[9] The economic rationale for the rental price of capital with direct taxation is shown in the Appendix to this chapter.

depreciation deductions and the investment tax credit under the tax laws were the same as the present value of the tax savings from deducting economic depreciation.[10] In this case the user cost of capital is reduced to

$$c = q(i + \delta) \qquad (5\text{-}18)$$

Thus, the user cost of capital is sensitive to the tax treatment of income from capital.

If the tax laws provide depreciation and tax credits that have a present value *greater* than the present value of economic depreciation, the cost of capital is lowered. The cost of capital is increased if tax laws have the opposite effect.

Now consider how the corporate tax rate itself affects c. If the *before-tax rate of return* (ρ) *is constant*, a fall in the corporate tax rate *raises* the cost of capital if tax depreciation and credits are greater than economic depreciation; a fall in corporate taxes *reduces* the cost of capital if the present value of economic depreciation exceeds the present value of tax depreciation plus the investment tax credit. At the other extreme, if the *after-tax rate-of-return* $[(1 - u)\rho]$ is constant, a fall in the corporate tax rate will *reduce* c as long as the present value of tax depreciation plus the investment tax credit is less than the cost of the capital asset.[11]

In empirical work using the concept of the optimum stock of capital K^* two main issues must be resolved: (1) the appropriate assumption about the elasticity of substitution σ and (2) the appropriate rate of discount or return (ρ) to employ. In short, which production function is "best" in terms of yielding the appropriate elasticity of capital with respect to relative prices (p/c) and which rate of return is most consistent with available time-series data?

Jorgenson and his various collaborators, as well as Bischoff, have argued that the assumption that $\sigma \cong 1$ is consistent with observed data. While Eisner and Nadiri (1968) have questioned the appropriateness of Jorgenson's original assumption, and produced empirical results seemingly inconsistent with it, replies by Jorgenson and

---

[10] The present value of economic depreciation (z^*) is approximately

$$z^* = \frac{\delta}{i(1 - u) + \delta}$$

Thus, if $uz^* = uz + k$, and $g = 1$ and $\rho = i$, c reduces to

$$c = \frac{q[\delta + (1 - u)i]\left[\dfrac{1 - u\delta}{i(1 - u) + \delta}\right]}{1 - u}$$

$$= q(i + \delta)$$

The corporate tax in this case has no effect on investment.

[11] Different results concerning the effect of a change in the corporate tax rate on the cost of capital are obtained depending on whether "depreciation for tax purposes ($uz + k$) is greater than, less than, or equal to economic depreciation." For more detail see the Appendix to this chapter. This paragraph and a further extension, Appendix C, were taken with minor changes from *Reforming the Federal Tax Structure, Commission to Revise the Tax Structure*, published by Fund for Public Policy Research, 1973.

Stephenson (1968) and by Bischoff (1969)[12] questioned the empirical techniques used by Eisner and Nadiri, and produced further evidence to the effect that the assumption $\sigma = 1$ is not inconsistent with the data.

As for the rate of return, the principal difference is between Jorgenson and Bischoff. The former uses a constant rate of return, letting the empirical results tell him which rate to use. Bischoff, on the other hand, approximates the rate of return as a weighted average of various market rates using the statistical properties of the regression equations to choose the weights, with the constraint that the weights sum to unity; i.e., the Bischoff formulation is

$$\rho = w_1(\text{div}) + w_2(r_b)$$

where $w_1 + w_2 = 1$, and div is the dividend-price ratio, and r_b is the corporate bond rate.

From Stock Equilibrium to Investment Flow

However one resolves the problem of how to define ρ and the proper value of σ, the optimization process described above yields an optimum stock of capital K^* summarized in Eq. (5-15a), and this in turn produces an equation for business fixed investment. Net investment results when there is a change in the optimum stock— $K_t^* - K_{t-1}^* > 0$. If the adjustment process is instantaneous, then in the discrete case $I_{Nt} = K_t^* - K_{t-1}^*$. However, the usual assumption is that net investment in any period t is some proportion of the projects initiated in previous periods when there is a change in the optimum capital stock

$$I_{Nt} = I_t - \delta K_{t-1}^* = M_0(K_t^* - K_{t-1}^*) + M_1(K_{t-1}^* - K_{t-2}^*) + \cdots \qquad (5\text{-}19)$$

where the M's represent the proportion of investment orders in each previous period which come to fruition in period t as net investment and where δK_{t-1} represents replacement investment. Clearly, a critical question is the pattern of the M's, or lags, in the adjustment process. This is a much-disputed issue which will not be explored in detail here.[13]

For the moment, let us assume away the problem of lags, so that *net investment* is equal to the change in K^*:

$$I_N = dK^* \qquad (5\text{-}20)$$

From (5-15a), assuming a unitary elasticity of factor substitution ($\sigma = 1$), the optimum capital stock is

$$K^* = A \frac{p}{c} Y$$

[12] The bibliographies attached to these two articles provide excellent compendiums of writings on the neoclassical theory of investment by both proponents and critics.

[13] In general, most recent studies use estimating techniques involving rational distributed lag functions, which allow great flexibility in the pattern that the sequences of M's may take on.

Net investment is thus

$$dK^* = d\left(\frac{ApY}{c}\right)$$

or

$$dK^* = I_N = Yd\left(\frac{Ap}{c}\right) + \left(\frac{Ap}{c}\right) dY \qquad (5\text{-}21)$$

As seen from Eq. (5-21), net investment reflects changes in the *real* user cost of capital (c/p) and output (Y). Since gross investment is equal to net investment plus depreciation [from (5-4)], we have

$$I = Yd(Ap/c) + (Ap/c)\, dY + \delta K \qquad (5\text{-}22)$$

Equation (5-22) is the neoclassical investment function. As the equation shows, gross business fixed investment reflects *changes* in the real user cost of capital and output and the existing *stock* of capital.

Numerous empirical studies have been conducted using variants of the neoclassical investment function. In general, the long-run elasticity of gross investment with respect to relative prices (p/c) was found to be in the range of -0.3 to -0.9. The elasticity with respect to Y is generally found to be close to unity.[14] In addition to showing a greater *total* response to changes in output, the studies showed investment responding more *quickly* to output changes than to relative prices (Bischoff, 1971, p. 28).

This pattern of response can be explained in terms of the "putty-clay" nature of the firm's production function.[15] That is, production possibilities are "putty" ex ante—firms can choose the mix of capital and labor from numerous possibilities in making an investment in a plant. However, once the investment plant is built and in operation, the K/N ratio is fixed—capital and labor are used in fixed proportions. Thus, when the demand for output increases past the capacity of the firm, if the firm wants to respond to it, an *immediate* addition to the plant is necessary. The fixed proportion of capital and labor thus causes net investment to respond quickly to a change in output demanded.

On the other hand, a change (say, p/c rises) in Ap/c causes the firm to want to increase the K/N ratio, *given* the level of output. Since the existing production technique is "clay," firms will only be able to change the K/N ratio—build a new *kind* of plant—as existing capital wears out and is replaced (or becomes obsolete considering costs). Thus, the effect of a relative price change is much slower in having an impact on investment than is the impact of a change in output.

---

[14] These studies are summarized in Bischoff (1971).
[15] For a discussion of the "putty-clay" nature of the production function, see Chapter 15.

ALTERNATIVE THEORIES OF INVESTMENT

The neoclassical investment function may now be contrasted with others presented in the literature on investment.

Keynes's Marginal Efficiency of Capital

Perhaps the most familiar investment function is the marginal efficiency of investment.[16] According to this approach, the decision to invest in a given asset depends on two rates: the internal rate of return from investing in that asset called the marginal efficiency of investment and the current rate of interest. It is an internal rate in that it is determined "subjectively" by the firm. If the internal rate of return exceeds the current rate of interest, investment in that asset should be undertaken, and vice versa. The optimum or equilibrium amount of investment will thus be determined when the internal rate equals the current rate of interest. Keynes (1936) defines the marginal efficiency of investment (the internal rate) as "being equal to the rate of discount which would make the present value of the series of annuities given by the returns expected from the capital asset during its life just equal its supply price" (p. 135). We can represent this definition symbolically as follows.

Let a_1, a_2, a_3,... represent an expected stream of future returns associated with a given investment project. If $a_n(n = 1,\ldots,\infty)$ are discounted at some appropriate interest rate i, the present value of the investment project, V, is

$$V = \sum_{n=1}^{\infty} \frac{a_n}{(1 + i)^n} \qquad (5\text{-}23)$$

To undertake the investment project, a certain cost (C) must be incurred. A comparison between the project cost and its present value gives a clue to its profitability. The rate of discount—call it i_m—which equates the discounted value of the stream of returns $(a_1,\ldots,a_n)$ to the cost of the project, C:

$$C = \sum_{n=1}^{\infty} \frac{a_n}{(1 + i_m)^n} \qquad (5\text{-}24)$$

is the marginal efficiency of investment.

[16] The term marginal efficiency of investment, MEI, should be distinguished from Keynes's marginal efficiency of capital, MEC. The MEC schedule discussed by Keynes is a demand curve for capital which shows the optimum stock of capital at each rate of interest. Each point on this curve is defined not only in terms of a given expectation of yields, but also in terms of a cost of capital goods which would prevail if net investment were zero. It is a downward-sloping curve reflecting an inverse relation between the optimum capital stock and the rate of interest. The MEI schedule is a curve defining expected yields from new capital goods as the actual capital stock moves toward its optimum level. The MEI curve declines as the rate of investment (addition to existing stock) rises, reflecting the fact that higher investment raises the cost of producing capital goods. For further discussion, see Lerner (1944, chap. 25).

If all possible investment projects are ranked according to their "marginal efficiency," a schedule showing the internal rate of return i_m as a function of the level of investment may be derived. If the external rate, the interest rate i, is specified and if investors desire to undertake all profitable investment programs, the level of desired net investment may be found. This marginal efficiency of investment schedule is also an investment demand schedule where the interest rate is taken as the independent variable. Thus, the investment function can be written as

$$I = \phi(i) \qquad (5\text{-}25)$$

However, the marginal-efficiency-of-investment approach raises a number of questions. As noted above in the neoclassical theory, optimal investment behavior should involve maximizing the present value of the firm. The MEI approach can be inconsistent with maximization of the present value of the firm.[17] This is because Keynes's internal rate of return (i_m), which equates present values of all investment projects to the cost of each, involves only one and not several optimal investment projects. *Ranking of investment options on the basis of internal rates of return will be correlated with present-value ranking if the only investment options compared are a particular investment and an option to invest at the market rate of interest.* But if there are two investment projects alternative to market lending, the internal rate of return of the two investment options will not rank them consistently with their present value (Alchian, 1955, pp. 68–69).

To illustrate this point let us suppose that each of two investment alternatives, A and B, requires the same amount of outlay, C. Suppose that A yields an income stream of \$$X$ per year for 10 years and B yields \$$Y$ in the first year, \$$2Y$ in the second year, and \$$3Y$ in the third year, etc., up to 10 years. Figure 5-2 shows the present value of net income streams of A and B for different discount rates. Line CC represents the cost C. The discount rate (internal rate of return) at which line CC intersects AA (where the present value of $A = \text{cost}$) is r_A. Line BB cuts CC at r_B, and BB intersects AA at r_m. If the rate of interest i is lower than r_m, that is, $i < r_m$, option B is preferable to option A because it has the larger present value; at $i > r_m$, A is preferable, according to the maximum present value criterion. Thus, ranking investments once and for all according to their internal rates of return is not feasible since the ranking changes as the rate of interest changes (Alchian, 1955, p. 69).

Eisner and Strotz (1963) have also criticized the marginal-efficiency-of-investment approach on several grounds. Their main criticisms center around the expectation hypothesis and the internal rate of return used for discounting. Let us consider these in order.

In assessing the profitability of an investment project the investor must form some sort of an expectation hypothesis concerning the future stream of returns associated with that project. Keynes's marginal-efficiency approach, however, lacks an explicit account of such an expectation hypothesis which would reflect the investor's

---

[17] See Alchian (1955) and Hirschliefer (1958).

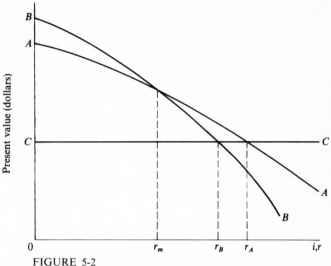

FIGURE 5-2
Internal rates of return and present value of investment options.

feeling about the probability distribution of the possible return streams. To overcome this problem Eisner and Strotz suggested that investors are interested only in the mathematical expected return of each given date, or that the stream $a_1, a_2, \ldots, a_n$ represents "certainty equivalents" to the probability distribution. This would require, however, that $a_1, a_2, \ldots, a_n$ be statistically independent, an assumption which might be unrealistic (Eisner and Strotz, 1963, pp. 88–89).

A further difficulty with the Keynesian approach arises in computing the present value of an investment project due to the ambiguity of the proper rate of interest which would be used for discounting. In the case of a perfect capital market, the market rate of interest is the rate which is used. But the market rate must be regarded as one which prevails for loans of comparable risk. The lending rate and the borrowing rate for a firm may not be the same, and thus one has to be careful in selecting the rate of interest the investor compares to the marginal efficiency of investment.

The Accelerator Theory of Investment

The fundamental idea of the acceleration principle for the explanation of the investment behavior of the firm goes back to Aftalion (1911), although its modern form was given by Clark (1917) and Frisch (1933). The simple, or naïve, form of the acceleration principle postulates a certain fixed relationship between the desired capital stock K^* and output Y. Stated symbolically, the relationship is

$$K^* = \beta Y \quad (\beta > 0) \quad (5\text{-}26)$$

From (5-15a), we know that (5-26) is a special case of the neoclassical theory—where the real user cost of capital is assumed constant. That is, the β in (5-26) is the same as Ap/c in (5-18). The acceleration principle, then, makes net investment proportional to the *change* in output. Differentiating Eq. (5-26) with respect to time, we get

$$\frac{dK}{dt} = \beta \frac{dY}{dt} \qquad (5\text{-}27)$$

or net investment at time t is equal to

$$I_{Nt} = \beta \frac{dY}{dt} \qquad (5\text{-}28)$$

and the rate of change in investment at time t is given by

$$\frac{dI_{Nt}}{dt} = \beta \frac{d\left(\dfrac{dY}{dt}\right)}{dt} \qquad (5\text{-}29)$$

i.e., the rate of change in net investment is determined by the *acceleration* (the rate of change of the rate of change) of output.

If we assume, as before, that depreciation in time t is proportional to the capital stock, gross investment I_t will be

$$I_t = \beta \frac{dY}{dt} + \delta K_t \qquad (5\text{-}30)$$

Substituting for K, from Eq. (5-26) we get

$$I_t = \beta \frac{dY_t}{dt} + \delta(\beta Y_t) \qquad (5\text{-}31)$$

The relationship between investment and output given in Eq. (5-31) breaks down if $\beta \, dY_t/dt$ is negative and absolutely larger than $\delta(\beta Y)$. This occurs when output is falling and the required rate of disinvestment exceeds the actual rate of depreciation. Gross investment, however, will not be negative (unless capital is destroyed). To prevent disinvestment from being larger (numerically) than depreciation, we have to add to Eq. (5-31) the boundary condition

$$I_t \geq 0 \qquad (5\text{-}32)$$

Another limitation to the acceleration principle is the possible existence of idle capacity. When output is falling or fails to rise, the capital goods industry may experience idle capacity. In this case, gross investment will not take place until existing capacity is fully utilized—until output rises sufficiently or the excess capital stock is depreciated away. In short, the existence of idle capacity also breaks down the acceleration principle.

Because of these limitations, as well as others, various attempts have been made to modify in a number of ways the simple acceleration theory described above. One modification is to assume that the firm bases its capital requirements on the previous period's output rather than current output, and thus K_t is proportional to Y_{t-1} rather than Y_t. Equations (5-26) and (5-27) are thus modified to read

$$K_t = \beta Y_{t-1}$$

and

$$I_{Nt} = \beta \frac{dY_{t-1}}{dt} \qquad (5\text{-}33)$$

Treating (5-33) in the discrete case, it may be written

$$I_{Nt} = \beta(Y_{t-1} - Y_{t-2}) \qquad (5\text{-}34)$$

While this version of the accelerator hypothesis may be considered in some way an improvement over the simple one, the limitations mentioned previously still apply.

Goodwin and Chenery have suggested still another variant of the accelerator hypothesis.[18] Their model is a stock-adjustment model of the following form:

$$I_{Nt} = \alpha(K_t^* - K_{t-1}) \qquad (5\text{-}35)$$

where α is the adjustment coefficient. The desired capital stock at time t is defined

$$K_t^* = \beta Y_t \qquad (5\text{-}36)$$

where β is the proportionality relation. Substituting Eq. (5-36) into Eq. (5-35), we get

$$I_{Nt} = \alpha(\beta Y_t - K_{t-1}) \qquad (5\text{-}37)$$

$$I_{Nt} = \alpha(\beta Y_t) - \alpha K_{t-1} \qquad (5\text{-}37a)$$

Equation (5-37) defines net investment to be proportionate to the level of output. It can be modified slightly by dividing both sides by K_{t-1}

$$\frac{I_{Nt}}{K_{t-1}} = \alpha\left(\frac{\beta Y_t}{K_{t-1}} - 1\right) \qquad (5\text{-}37b)$$

where the ratio Y_t/K_{t-1} may be taken as a measure of capacity utilization by the firm.

The relationships between these three variants of the acceleration approach to investment theory were examined by Koyck (1954). Koyck points out that the three versions of the accelerator principle described also unrealistically assume a lagless world or a world with only a one-period lag. To remedy this deficiency he suggested a distributed lag investment function where the capital stock requirements are dependent on the output of a number of periods in the past. Thus Eqs. (5-26) and (5-27) are replaced by

$$K_t = \beta(\lambda^0 Y_t + \lambda^1 Y_{t-1} + \lambda^2 Y_{t-2} + \cdots) \qquad (5\text{-}38)$$

and

$$K_{t-1} = \beta(\lambda^0 Y_{t-1} + \lambda^1 Y_{t-2} + \lambda^2 Y_{t-3} + \cdots) \qquad (5\text{-}38a)$$

[18] For detail, see Chenery (1952) and Goodwin (1951).

Using Koyck transformation and Eqs. (5-38) and (5-38a) we can write

$$K_t = \beta Y_t + \lambda K_{t-1} \qquad (5\text{-}39)$$

Since net investment is equal to

$$I_{Nt} = K_t - K_{t-1} \qquad (5\text{-}40)$$

by substituting Eq. (5-39) into (5-40), the following equation defines net investment:

$$I_{Nt} = \beta Y_t - (1 - \lambda)K_{t-1} \qquad (5\text{-}41)$$

Gross investment is

$$I_{Nt} = \beta Y_t - (1 - \lambda - \delta)K_{t-1} \qquad (5\text{-}42)$$

where δ is the depreciation rate.

From Eq. (5-42), it is clear that gross investment is positively related to the level of output, Y, and negatively related with existing capital stock, K_{t-1}, provided that $(1 - \lambda - \delta)$ is positive. For $(1 - \lambda - \delta)$ to be positive, $(1 - \lambda)$ must be greater than δ. This is, of course, an empirical issue since λ is in the interval 0,1.

Regardless of its form—naïve or sophisticated—the accelerator approach to investment fails to account for the impact of other factors affecting the real cost of capital—changes in the price of capital, depreciation rules, corporation income tax rates, investment tax credit provisions, and the price of output. The neoclassical model is a more generalized and useful approach to investment which captures not only the accelerator effect but the actions which affect the cost of capital.

APPENDIX TO CHAPTER 5

A IMPLICATION OF THE DEPRECIATION ASSUMPTIONS TO THE SURVIVAL TIME PATH OF CAPITAL

The assumption that economic depreciation is proportional to the capital stock implies that capital of a given vintage has a time path that is geometrically declining. Equation (5-4) written in discrete form implies that

$$K_t = K_{t-1}(1 - \delta) + I_{t-1}$$

where I_{t-1} is gross investment in period $t-1$. The expression of K_{t-1} in terms of K_{t-2} and I_{t-2} can be substituted into the above expression to get

$$K_t = K_{t-2}(1 - \delta)^2 + I_{t-2}(1 - \delta) + I_{t-1}$$

Iteration of this process permits K_t to be expressed in terms of K_{t-m} and the gross investment increments for all intervening periods.

$$K_t = I_{t-1} + I_{t-2}(1 - \delta) + \cdots + I_{t-n}(1 - \delta)^{n-1} + \cdots$$
$$+ I_{t-m}(1 - \delta)^{m-1} + K_{t-m}(1 - \delta)^m$$

Because $(1 - \delta)$ is a positive number less than 1, $(1 - \delta)^m$ tends toward zero as m tends toward infinity. Therefore, if m is chosen sufficiently large, then n can be chosen large enough that all terms with subscripts greater than n can be considered to be negligibly small. Thus K_t can be expressed exclusively in terms of past-period gross investments to any desired degree of accuracy.

$$K_t = I_{t-1} + I_{t-2}(1 - \delta) + \cdots + I_{t-n}(1 - \delta)^{n-1}$$

This expression illustrates the geometric survival pattern of each period's gross investment.

A survival time shape of this type is consistent with the hypothesis that capital is utilized more intensively and therefore consumed more rapidly during the early part of its life than during the latter part. This hypothesis is consistent with a wide variety of experience, but may not apply in many specific industries.

B   THE ECONOMIC RATIONALE FOR THE RENTAL PRICE OF CAPITAL WITH AND WITHOUT DIRECT TAXATION

Equation (5-11) defines $c = (\delta + i - \dot{q}/q)q$ as the implicit rental value of capital services supplied by the firm to itself. This may be justified more formally by considering the relationship between the price of capital goods and capital services. The flow of a unit of capital services over an interval of length dt beginning at time t from a unit of investment goods acquired at time s is

$$e^{-\delta(t-s)} dt \qquad \text{(B-1)}$$

If $c(t)$ is the *price* of capital services at time t, the discounted price of capital services is

$$e^{-it}c(t)e^{-\delta(t-s)} dt \qquad \text{(B-2)}$$

If $q(s)$ is the price of capital goods at time s, the discounted price of capital goods is $e^{-is}q(s)$, so that the *value* of a unit of investment goods acquired *at time s* must also be $e^{-is}q(s)$. However, the value of investment goods acquired at time s is equal to the integral of the discounted value of all future capital services derived from these investment goods:

$$e^{-is}q(s) = \int_s^\infty e^{-it}c(t)e^{-\delta(t-s)} dt \qquad \text{(B-3)}$$

$$= e^{\delta s} \int_s^\infty e^{-(i+\delta)t}c(t) dt$$

and the price of capital goods at time s is

$$q(s) = e^{(i+\delta)s} \int_s^\infty e^{-(i+\delta)t}c(t) dt \qquad \text{(B-4)}$$

$$= \int_s^\infty e^{-(i+\delta)(t-s)}c(t) dt$$

Differentiating this expression with respect to time t, we obtain the price of capital services implicit in this expression:

$$\dot{q}(s) = [i(s) + \delta]q(s) - c(s)$$

or
$$c = q(i + \delta - \dot{q}/q)$$

as given in Eq. (5-11).

In the tax case—where corporate taxes are introduced—the following modifications are introduced. First, if the rate of return before tax ρ is one which allows for the deductibility of interest payments, Eq. (B-4) becomes

$$q(s) = \int_s^\infty e^{-[(1-u)\rho + \delta](t-s)}[(1-u)\overset{\bullet}{c}(t)]\, dt$$

$$+ \int_s^\infty e^{-(1-u)\rho(t-s)}[uq(s)D(t-s)]\, dt + kq(s) \qquad \text{(B-5)}$$

The first part is the same as before, except that the discount rate is the after-tax rate $[(1-u)\rho]$ and the stream of values of rentals of capital services is also the after-tax stream $[(1-u)c(t)]$. The second term reflects the fact that allowing depreciation for tax purposes reduces taxes; the term $uq(s)D(t-s)$ is the taxes *not* paid in each period due to the depreciation deduction claimed, with the latter expressed as a fraction $D(t-s)$ of the cost of the asset at time $s[q(s)]$. Over the life of the asset, $D(t-s)$ sums to unity—$D(t-s)$ is then the depreciation allowance per dollar of initial investment for tax purposes at time s on an asset of age $(t-s)$. The final term in (B-5) represents the reduction in the acquisition cost of the asset due to the investment tax credit, where k is the rate of credit per dollar of asset cost and $q(s)$ is the price per unit of capital assets.

Now let us define

$$z = \int_s^\infty e^{-(1-u)\rho(t-s)}q(s)D(t-s)\, dt \qquad \text{(B-6)}$$

which is the present value of depreciation deductions totaling \$1 over the life of an asset. Then (B-5) may be written

$$q(s) = \int_s^\infty e^{-[(1-u)\rho + \delta](t-s)}[(1-u)c(t)]\, dt + uz + kq(s)$$

As before, differentiating $q(s)$ with respect to time, we obtain an expression for the implicit rental value of capital services:

$$\frac{c(1-u)}{q(1-uz-k)} = \rho(1-u) + \delta - \frac{\dot{q}}{q}(1-gu)$$

where g reflects the differential tax rate applicable to capital gains income. The user cost or implicit rental value of capital services is then

$$c = \frac{[(1-u)\rho + \delta - \dfrac{\dot{q}}{q}(1-gu)](1-k-uz)q}{1-u}$$

$$= \frac{q[(1-u)\rho + \delta - \dfrac{\dot{q}}{q}(1-gu)](1-k-uz)}{1-u} \qquad \text{(B-7)}$$

If asset prices are expected to remain constant, the rental price per unit of capital is

$$c = \frac{[(1 - u)\rho + \delta](1 - k - uz)q}{1 - u} \qquad \text{(B-7}a\text{)}$$

Again, the economic rationale for the rental price of capital is straightforward. Rearranging (B-7):

$$\frac{c(1 - u)}{q(1 - k - uz)} = q\left[(1 - u)\rho + \delta - (1 - gu)\frac{\dot{q}}{q}\right]$$

we see that the marginal after-tax rate of return per dollar *paid* for capital rental per unit of capital—$c(1 - u)/q(1 - k - uz)$—must just cover the after-tax rate of return $(1 - u)\rho$ *plus* the rate of economic depreciation plus the rate of capital gains. The acquisition cost per unit is $q(1 - k - uz)$, i.e., the price per unit (q) less the sum of (1) the tax savings via the investment tax credit (kq) and (2) the tax savings via depreciation deductions which, over time, sum to the price of the asset (uzq).

C   ECONOMIC DEPRECIATION, TAX DEPRECIATION, AND THE EFFECT OF CORPORATE TAXES ON THE COST OF CAPITAL

The effect of a change in the corporate tax rate on the cost of capital may be different from that given in the text depending on whether "depreciation for tax purposes" ($uz + k$) is greater than, less than, or equal to "economic depreciation" $u\delta/(\delta + i(1 - u))$. Depending on which relation is fulfilled, the results obtained are

$$\frac{\Delta c}{\Delta u} < 0 \qquad \frac{\Delta c}{\Delta u} > 0 \qquad \frac{\Delta c}{\Delta u} = 0 \qquad \text{respectively}$$

Let c_w define implicit rental value of capital with corporate tax and c_{wo} define implicit rental value of capital without corporate tax. The following cases can be distinguished:

Case I

ρ constant (*before-tax rate of return constant*). Equations (C-1) and (C-2) define the implicit rental value of capital with and without corporate tax, respectively.

$$c_w = \frac{[\delta + \rho(1 - u)](1 - uz - k)}{1 - u} \qquad \text{(C-1)}$$

$$c_{wo} = \delta + \rho \qquad \text{(C-2)}$$

$$c_{wo} \lesseqgtr c_w \text{ as } \delta + \rho \lesseqgtr \frac{[\delta + \rho(1 - u)](1 - uz - k)}{1 - u}$$

Manipulating the two sides yields

1 $(\delta + \rho)(1 - u) \lesseqgtr [\delta + \rho(1 - u)](1 - uz - k)$

2 $\delta + \rho - u\rho - u\delta \lesseqgtr (\delta + \rho - u\rho)(1 - uz - k)$

3 $\dfrac{\delta + \rho - u\rho}{\delta + \rho - u\rho} - \dfrac{u\delta}{\delta + \rho(1 - u)} \lesseqgtr 1 - uz - k$

4 $-\dfrac{u\delta}{\delta + \rho(1 - u)} \lesseqgtr - uz - k$

5 $\dfrac{u\delta}{\delta + \rho(1 - u)} \gtreqless uz + k$

Therefore, from step 5, if

$$c_{wo} < c_w \rightarrow \frac{u\delta}{\delta + \rho(1 - u)} > uz + k$$

$$c_{wo} = c_w \rightarrow \frac{u\delta}{\delta + \rho(1 - u)} = uz + k$$

$$c_{wo} > c_w \rightarrow \frac{u\delta}{\delta + \rho(1 - u)} < uz + k$$

Case II

$\rho(1 - u)$ constant (*after-tax rate of return constant*). Again the implicit rental value of capital with and without corporate taxes is

$$c_w = \frac{[\delta + \rho(1 - u)](1 - uz - k)}{1 - u}$$

$$c_{wo} = \delta + \rho(1 - u)$$

In this case, $c_{wo} \lesseqgtr c_w$ as $\delta + \rho(1 - u) \lesseqgtr [\delta + \rho(1 - u)](1 - uz - k)/(1 - u)$. Manipulating the two sides yields

1 $\delta + \rho(1 - u) \lesseqgtr \dfrac{[\delta + \rho(1 - u)](1 - uz - k)}{1 - u}$

2 $1 \lesseqgtr \dfrac{1 - uz - k}{1 - u}$

3 $1 - u \lesseqgtr 1 - uz - k$

4 $u \gtreqless uz + k$

Therefore, from step 4, if

$c_{wo} < c_w \rightarrow u > uz + k$

$c_{wo} = c_w \rightarrow u = uz + k$

$c_{wo} > c_w \rightarrow u > uz + k$

READINGS FOR CHAPTER 5

ACKLEY, G.: *Macroeconomic Theory* (New York: Macmillan, 1961), chap. 17, pp. 460–504.

AFTALION, A.: "Les Trois Notions de la Producitité et les Revenus," *Revue d'Economie Politique*, 1911.

ALCHIAN, A. A.: "The Rate of Interest, Fisher's Rate of Return Over Cost, and Keynes' Internal Rate of Return," *American Economic Review*, vol. 45, pp. 938–943, December 1955. See also the comment by Robinson in *American Economic Review*, vol. 46, pp. 972–973, December 1956.

ALLEN, R. G. D.: *Mathematical Analysis for Economists* (New York: Macmillan, 1956).

BAILEY, M.: "Formal Criteria for Investment Decisions," *Journal of Political Economy*, vol. LXVII, pp. 476–488, October 1959.

BAUMOL, W. J.: *Economic Dynamics*, 2d ed (New York: Macmillan, 1959), pp. 169–224.

BISCHOFF, C. W.: "Lags in Fiscal and Monetary Impacts on Producer's Durable Equipment," *Cowles Foundation Discussion Paper*, no. 250. New Haven, June 11, 1968.

———: "Hypothesis Testing and the Demand for Capital Goods," *Review of Economic Studies*, pp. 354–368, August 1969.

———: "Business Investment in the 1970's: A Comparison of Models," *Brookings Papers on Economic Activity* (Washington: The Brookings Institution, 1971).

BRANSON, WILLIAM H.: *Macroeconomic Theory and Policy* (New York: Harper & Row, 1972), chap. 11.

CHENERY, H. B.: "Overcapacity and Acceleration Principle," *Econometrica*, vol. 20, pp. 1–28, 1952.

CLARK, J. M.: "Business Acceleration and the Law of Demand," *Journal of Political Economy*, vol. 25, pp. 217–235, March 1917.

COMMISSION TO REVISE THE TAX STRUCTURE: *Reforming the Federal Tax Structure* (Washington, D.C.: Fund for Public Policy Research, 1973).

DUESENBERRY, J. S.: *Business Cycles and Economic Growth*, (New York: McGraw-Hill, 1958), chaps. 3–5.

ECKHAUS, R. C.: "The Acceleration Principle Reconsidered," *Quarterly Journal of Economics*, vol. 67, pp. 209–230, May 1953.

EISNER, R.: "The Demand for Investment Goods: An Experiment with Distributed Lags," *Econometrica*, vol. 58, January 1960.

——— and M. I. NADIRI: "Investment Behavior and Neoclassical Theory," *Review of Economic Studies*, vol. 50, pp. 369–382, August 1968.

——— and R. H. STROTZ: "Determinants of Business Investment," *Impact of Monetary Policy*, Commission on Money and Credit 1963, pp. 60–233.

FISHER, I.: *The Theory of Interest* (New York: Macmillan, 1930).

FRISCH, R.: "Propagation Problems and Impulse Problems in Dynamic Economics," in *Essay in Honor of Gustav Cassel* (London: G. Allen, 1933).

GOODWIN, R. M.: "The Nonlinear Accelerator and the Persistence of Business Cycles," *Econometrica*, vol. 19, pp. 1–17, January 1951.

GRILICHES, Z., and N. WALLACE: "The Determinants of Investment Revisited," *International Economic Review*, vol. VI, pp. 311–329, September 1965.

HAAVELMO, T.: *A Study in the Theory of Investment* (Chicago: The University of Chicago Press, 1960).

HALL, R. E., and D. W. JORGENSON: "Tax Policy and Investment Behavior," *American Economic Review*, vol. LVII, pp. 391–414, June 1967.

HAMBERG, D.: *A Study in the Theory of Investment* (Chicago: The University of Chicago Press, 1960), app. to chap. 8.

HANSEN, A. H.: *A Guide to Keynes* (New York: McGraw-Hill, 1953), chaps. 6–8.

———: *Business Cycles and National Income* (New York: Norton, 1951), chap. 11.

HICKS, J. R.: *A Contribution to the Theory of the Trade Cycle* (Oxford: Oxford, 1950), chaps. I–VI and math. app.

HIRSCHLIEFER, J.: "On the Theory of the Optimal Investment Decision," *Journal of Political Economy*, vol. LXVI, pp. 329–352, August 1958).

———: *Investment, Interest and Capital* (Englewood Cliffs, N.J.: Prentice-Hall, 1970), chaps. 2–4.

JORGENSON, D. W.: "Capital Theory and Investment Behavior," *American Economic Review*, pp. 247–257, May 1963.

———: "The Theory of Investment Behavior," in R. Ferber (ed.), *Determinants of Investment Behavior* (New York: Columbia, 1967).

——— and J. A. STEPHENSON: "Issues in the Neoclassical Theory of Investment Behavior," *Review of Economic Studies*, pp. 346–353, August 1969; also references to their other articles cited therein.

——— and C. D. SIEVER: "A Comparison of Alternative Theories of Corporate Investment Behavior," *American Economic Review*, vol. 58, pp. 681–712, September 1968.

KEYNES, J. M.: *The General Theory of Employment, Interest and Money* (London: Macmillan, 1936), chap. 11–12.

KOYCK, L. M.: *Distributed Lags and Investment Analysis* (Amsterdam: North-Holland Publishing Company, 1954).

LERNER, A. P.: *The Economic of Control* (New York: Macmillan, 1944).

———: "On the Marginal Efficiency of Capital and the Marginal Efficiency of Investment," *Journal of Political Economy*, vol. 61, pp. 1–14, February 1953.

MEYER J. R. and E. KUH: "Acceleration and Related Theories of Investment: An Empirical Inquiry," *Review of Economics and Statistics*, vol. 37, pp. 217–300, August 1955. See "Comment" by Morrissett in February 1957 issue and "Reply" by Meyer and Kuh in same issue.

NEISSER, H.: "Critical Notes on the Acceleration Principle," *Quarterly Journal of Economics*, vol. 68, pp. 253–274, May 1954.

SAMUELSON, P. A.: "Interaction between the Multiplier Analysis and the Principle of Acceleration," *Review of Economics and Statistics*, vol. 21, May 1939; reprinted in *Readings in Business Cycle Theory*, American Economics Association (Homewood, Ill.: Irwin, 1951).

SMITH, V. L.: *Investment and Production* (Cambridge, Mass.: Harvard, 1966).

STOCKFISCH, J.: "The Relationships between Money Cost, Investment, and the Rate of Return," *Quarterly Journal of Economics*, vol. 70, pp. 295–302, May 1956.

THUROW, L.: "A Disequilibrium Neoclassical Investment Function," *Review of Economics and Statistics*, pp. 431–435, November 1969.

WITTE, J.: "The Micro-Foundations of the Social Investment Function," *Journal of Political Economy*, October 1963.

6

INVESTMENT IN RESIDENTIAL CONSTRUCTION

The second component of gross private domestic investment is residential construction expenditures I_h. This component of aggregate demand is particularly important for business-cycle analysis because it exhibits sharp swings over the cycle and because housing expenditures are particularly susceptible to policy actions, especially monetary policy. The postwar behavior of housing outlays (in real terms) is shown in Figure 6-1.

Housing expenditures represent investment by consumers in a durable good which yields a stream of consumption services (housing) over a long period of time. Thus the obvious starting point for examining expenditures on new housing is the demand for the services provided by housing, and, in turn, for a stock of housing.

THE DEMAND FOR HOUSING

To keep the analysis simple, at least at the outset, suppose all housing is homogeneous and income from housing is taxed at the same rate as other income, at the margin, for each taxpayer. Units of housing are then demanded by households for the stream

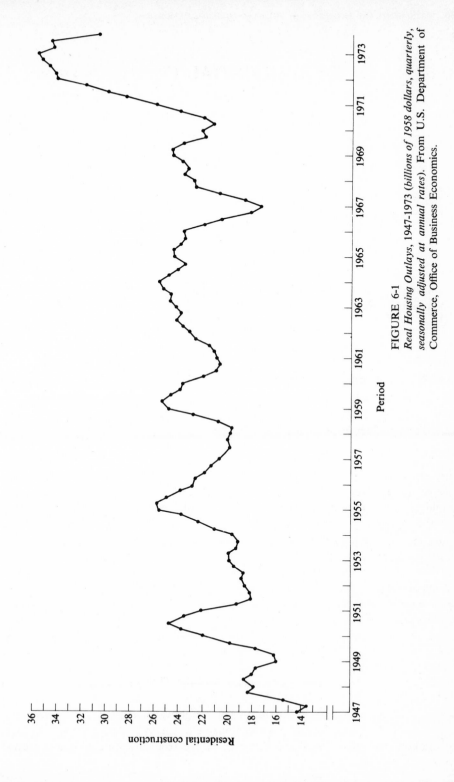

FIGURE 6-1

Real Housing Outlays, 1947-1973 (billions of 1958 dollars, quarterly, seasonally adjusted at annual rates). From U.S. Department of Commerce, Office of Business Economics.

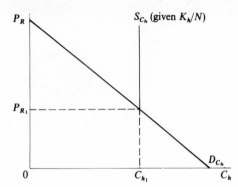

FIGURE 6-2
The demand for housing services.

of housing services C_h they yield. The demand for housing services per capita at some point in time may then be written as

$$\frac{C_h}{N} = \gamma\left(\frac{P_R}{P_c}, \frac{C}{N}\right) \qquad (6\text{-}1)$$

where C_h = flow of housing services
N = population
P_R = rent per unit of housing
P_C = implicit deflator or price index for all consumption goods
C = total consumption

The equation says that per capita demand for housing services depends on the relative price of housing versus all consumption goods and total consumption per capita. Graphically, this is illustrated in Figure 6-2. Total consumption C is determined from the aggregate consumption function discussed in Chapter 4. If we assume that N and P_C are given, then the demand curve D_{C_h} relates desired housing services to the price of such services—P_R. The supply of housing services S_{C_h} may be taken as proportional to the stock of housing K_h. Given the stock of housing K_h, the flow of housing services is determined at (say) C_{h_1}, and the rental price will then be P_{R_1}. An increase in the stock of housing per capita, which increases the supply of housing services per capita, will shift the S_{C_h} curve so as to lower the rental price. An increase in total consumption per capita shifts the demand curve to the right—the rental price then increases for any given per capita stock of housing. An increase in the consumer goods deflator P_C also shifts the demand curve to the right; the *relative* price of housing services P_R/P_C is decreased, and the demand increases for any given P_R. Finally, an increase in population increases the total demand for housing services. The demand curve in Figure 6-2 shifts rightward, and the rental price rises.

The demand curve for the *stock* of housing can now be derived from Eq. (6-1) and the condition that the after-tax rate of return from investing in housing must

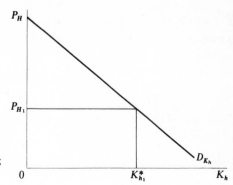

FIGURE 6-3
The demand for the stock of housing K_h^*.

be equal, at the margin, to the net (after-tax) rate of return on alternative investment:

$$\frac{P_R}{P_H} = (1 - t)i \qquad \text{or} \qquad P_R = P_H(1 - t)i \qquad (6\text{-}2)$$

where P_H = demand price per unit of housing
$\quad\quad\ t$ = average personal income and property tax rates per dollar of housing
$\quad\quad\ i$ = the appropriate long-term interest rate

Substituting P_R in (6-2) for P_R in (6-1), we get, as the demand function for housing services, or alternatively, for the stock of housing K_h^*,

$$C_h = N\gamma\left(\frac{P_H(1 - t)i}{P_c}, \frac{C}{N}\right) \qquad (6\text{-}3)$$

Given C, N, t, P_c, and i, the desired stock of housing capital then varies inversely with P_H. This is shown in Figure 6-3. The demand curve D_{K_h} relates the desired housing stock to P_H—given values for C, N, P_c, i, and t. If $P_H = P_{H_1}$, then $K_h^* = K_{h_1}^*$. A change in C, N, i, t, or P_c will cause K_h^* to change for any P_H. A rise in C, N, or P_c will shift D_{K_h} to the right for each value of P_H; a rise in the interest rate will shift D_{K_h} to the left. A rise in the personal tax rate has ambiguous effects: on the one hand it lowers the rental cost of housing and shifts D_{K_h} to the right for any C level; but total C would also tend to fall, thus reducing K_h^*.

It is convenient to write Eq. (6-3), in terms of K_h^*, on the assumption that the function γ is log-linear (de Leeuw and Gramlich, 1969, p. 270):

$$K_h^* = N\left[\frac{P_H(1 - t)i}{P_c}\right]^{\gamma_1}\left(\frac{C}{N}\right)^{\gamma_2} \quad (\gamma_1 < 0; \gamma_2 > 0)$$

Then

$$\log K_h^* = (1 - \gamma_2) \log N + \gamma_1 \log P_H + \gamma_1 \log (1 - t) + \gamma_1 \log i$$
$$- \gamma_1 \log P_c + \gamma_2 \log C \qquad (6\text{-}4)$$

Equation (6-4) makes it clear that the desired housing stock increases when t, P_c, or C rises, and falls when the rate of interest or P_c rises (since γ_1 is negative). A change in the population N *alone* has two effects on the desired stock of housing. It reduces per capita consumption C/N and thus tends to reduce the desired stock of housing. At the same time, for any value of C/N, there is an *increase* in the demand for housing, stemming from the premultiplicative N in (6-3). Thus an *equal* percentage change in C and N, keeping per capita consumption unchanged, increases the demand for the stock of housing due to the "pure" population effect by the percentage amount

$$d \log K_h^* = (1 - \gamma_2) \, d \log N + \gamma_2 \, d \log C$$

and since $d \log N = d \log C$ if per capita consumption is constant,

$$d \log K_h^* = d \log N \qquad (6\text{-}5)$$

The elasticity of K_h with respect to N, with per capita consumption unchanged, is thus unity.

At this point, it should be clear that, at least as a first step, the demand for *net investment* in housing and housing construction expenditures can be approached in the same manner as business fixed investment. That is, current additions to the housing stock (net housing investment) are some proportion of the value of projects initiated in previous periods when the optimum stock of housing changes:

$$I_{h_t} - \delta_h K_{h_{t-1}} = H_0(K_{h_t}^* - K_{h_{t-1}}^*) + H_1(K_{h_{t-1}}^* - K_{h_{t-2}}^*) + \cdots \qquad (6\text{-}6)$$

or

$$I_{h_t} = \left(\sum_{i=0}^{n} H_i \, \Delta K_{h_{t-i}}^* \right) + \delta_h K_{h_{t-1}}$$

where the H's represent the proportion of the value of housing starts initiated in each previous period which come to fruition in period t as net investment and where $\delta_h K_{h_{t-1}}$ represents replacement investment.

In short, a theory of housing construction outlays can be constructed by combining the consumption function—which explains the demand for housing services —with the neoclassical investment approach—which translates the demand for the services of housing capital into a theory of net investment.

At the same time, the housing sector has certain peculiarities all its own, particularly on the supply side, to necessitate refinement and extension of this approach.

SPECIAL FEATURES OF THE HOUSING SECTOR

The important characteristics about housing and the housing industry which make explanation of I_h more complicated than simply extending the consumption function and neoclassical investment theory to cover this case are:

1 It is generally recognized that *the housing sector receives residual supplies of factors of production and credit from the economy*. In particular, business fixed investment and consumer durables preempt inputs and credit. Since expenditures on these goods are generally *procyclical*, this in large part accounts for the *countercyclical* behavior of housing (Figure 6-1).

2 Expenditures on housing construction are on an accrual basis. That is, the outlays are counted as construction progresses, not as purchases are made and deliveries of finished houses occur. In comparison, say, with business purchases of equipment, I_h includes *purchases* of new houses plus the net change in housing inventories. Thus, the *supply* of housing must be given careful consideration —along with demand—in explaining the behavior of I_h.

3 Housing purchases are heavily dependent upon credit. Taken together with (1), this accentuates the countercyclical nature of I_h, both because credit is generally "tighter" in periods of prosperity and easier in recessions and because the housing sector receives a larger share of total credit available in recessions than in periods of prosperity.

4 The housing market is really two markets—one for single-family (largely owner-occupied) homes and another for multifamily homes. Since real construction costs per unit of single-family homes is much higher than for multifamily housing units, shifts in the "mix" of housing construction will change the amounts of real outlays for housing construction.

CREDIT AVAILABILITY AND HOUSING EXPENDITURES

The importance of credit in home purchases is that, in effect, buyers of homes (or builders of apartments) may *want* to purchase housing, but mortgages are either not available on acceptable terms or simply not available. In general, this will reflect general credit conditions, but it may also reflect special conditions which make tight (or easy) money more or less severe in its impact on housing. As noted above, the housing sector is generally considered to be a residual claimant on the total supply of credit. This largely reflects the practices of financial institutions supplying mortgage funds, but it also reflects government constraints. The largest suppliers of mortgage funds are savings and loan associations and mutual savings banks. They have evolved as institutions which accept savings deposits of thousands of small savers. Until recent years, interest rates paid on these accounts have typically been the same for all accounts. When market interest rates rise (including mortgage rates), the savings and loan institutions and mutual savings banks were thus unable to raise the rates paid to their deposits in step with other rates. Since they paid the same rate to all depositors, to raise their deposit rates *at the margin* required raising rates on *all* outstanding deposits. Yet the rise in the yields they earned on mortgages generally applied only to *new* loans made. Thus, during expansions, when interest rates rise generally, savings and loan institutions and mutual savings banks found themselves (as long as they followed these practices) unable to compete for funds. The inflow of deposits into these mortgage-lending institutions slackens or even declines absolutely as yields on alternative assets (Treasury bills, commercial paper, etc.) rise. Thus the flow of funds into mortgages slackens or ceases.

To account for the impact of tight money on the terms and availability of mortgage funds, we can add a term to (6-6) which represents the tightness of monetary policy—the differential between long-term and short-term interest rates:

$$I_h = \sum_{i=0}^{N} h_i(\Delta K^*_{h_{t-i}}) + \sum_{i=0}^{N} h'_i(i_L - i_S)_{t-i} + \delta_H K_{h_{t-1}} \qquad (6\text{-}6a)$$

In short, the demand for new housing reflects (lagged) changes in the optimum stock of housing (ΔK^*_h), but its *realization* also reflects general credit conditions.

It should be noted that since the mid-sixties savings and loan institutions have developed techniques to vary interest rates paid to marginal investors, via so-called certificates of deposit. While the rates they may pay on these issues are regulated by the Federal Home Loan Bank Board, it is now possible for mortgage-lending institutions to vary marginal rates. In addition, many savings and loan institutions are moving toward variable interest rate mortgages, whereby they may protect themselves on the lending side also during periods of credit restraint. Thus the housing sector is less affected by credit conditions than in earlier years.

At times, the supply of mortgage funds to demanders of new housing has also reflected other factors. First, when market rates rise above the ceilings imposed on yields on government-guaranteed mortgages—FHA and VA—the supply of funds for these types of mortgages has been severely reduced or even eliminated. Since borrowers seeking these mortgages typically do so because of lower down-payment requirements, they are cut off from purchasing homes when FHA and VA loans are not available. The nonavailability of mortgages is thus exacerbated when ceilings on FHA and VA mortgages are not allowed to rise in periods of high interest rates. Given the total supply of funds for new mortgages and the total demand for new housing at any time of "tight credit" conditions, some demanders of housing who still might have obtained FHA or VA loans are squeezed out. This may mean more of the total supply of funds are then available for conventional mortgages. To the extent that marginal borrowers of conventional mortgage funds who would have been denied loans will now get them (instead of marginal borrowers seeking FHA or VA loans), the squeeze on government-guaranteed loans will not have any *net* impact on total housing. The funds that would have gone into FHA or VA financing will flow into conventional loans, and total construction will not suffer. However, since the two markets may not function perfectly, periods where long-term market yields are higher than FHA-VA ceilings *may* have an additional impact on residential construction. To account for this possibility, we modify Eq. (6-6a):

$$I_h = \sum_{i=0}^{N} h_i(\Delta K^*_{h_{t-i}}) + \sum_{i=0}^{N} h'_i(i_L - i_S)_{t-i} + h_1 i_{F_{t-1}} + \delta_H K_{h_{t-1}} \qquad (6\text{-}6b)$$

where
$$i_F = i_L - (0.5 i_{FHA} + 0.5 i_{VA})$$

The i_F term is lagged one quarter to account for the delay between new mortgage lending and resultant construction. The definition of i_F follows that employed in recent work on the Federal Reserve–MIT model (de Leeuw and Gramlich).

The other credit effect on housing demand realizations is Federal Reserve policy in setting the ceiling rates that commercial banks pay on time and savings deposits. Around 1962, commercial banks developed a new time deposit liability called certificates of deposit (CDs). These are negotiable instruments with fixed maturity dates which banks sell to business firms and others seeking liquidity but also interested in returns comparable to short-term interest rates. With this instrument, commercial banks have developed a technique for competing for funds in the money market without raising interest rates on all their time and savings accounts; like savings and loan institutions, they can vary *marginal* rates of return without a comparable adjustment of the *average* rate of interest paid to depositors.

The Federal Reserve System prescribes ceilings to the rates that banks can pay on CDs, as they do for passbook savings accounts. These ceilings vary with the denominations in which the CDs are issued. From the point of view of the housing industry, the importance of Regulation Q (which defines these ceilings) is that if banks are allowed—during periods of tight money—to keep CD rates competitive with short-term market rates of interest generally, while savings and loan institutions and mutual savings banks are unable to match these increases, then added incentives are given to depositors of mortgage-lending institutions to shift to CDs and away from savings and loan and mutual savings bank deposits. This was particularly evident in 1966, when CD ceilings were raised as interest rates rose and savings and loan institutions and mutual savings banks suffered staggering withdrawals of deposits. However, as noted above, savings and loan institutions now also use the CD to ease their deposit losses, subject to Federal Home Loan Bank Board rate ceilings.

To take account of this added credit effect on the effective demand for residential construction is difficult, since CDs have only been important since 1962. One approach is to define a dummy variable DCD, which is set equal to 1 when short-term rates exceed the CD rate and zero at all other times. The resulting form of the housing investment equation thus is

$$I_h = \sum_{i=0}^{N} h_i(\Delta K^*_{h_{t-i}}) + \sum_{i=0}^{N} h_i'(i_L - i_S)_{t-i} + h_1 i_{F_{t-1}} + h_2 \text{DCD} + \delta_H K_{h_{t-1}} \quad (6\text{-}6c)$$

The housing sector is closed with the identity defining the stock of housing (in 1958 dollars):

$$K_h = 0.994 K_{h_{t-1}} + I_h \quad (6\text{-}7)$$

This implies an *annual* depreciation rate of 2.4 percent (0.6 percent per quarter) for the existing stock of housing.

Supply Conditions and Housing Investment

As we noted at the beginning of this chapter, the actual amount of I_h during any period depends on supply conditions as well as demand.

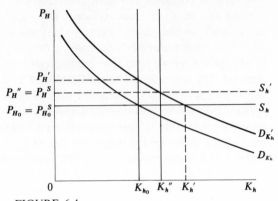

FIGURE 6-4
The supply price of housing and housing expenditures.

Costs in the housing construction industry are largely variable costs, and variable costs are dominated by labor costs. Business investment in structures uses the same pool of construction workers employed in housing. However, workers prefer working in the business construction area, where fluctuations in employment are somewhat less than in housing, and where wages and working conditions tend to be better. When an economic expansion occurs, business investment rises, and workers are bid away from housing to commercial construction. Since the total supply of construction workers is very inelastic in the short run, wages of housing construction workers tend to rise, and this exerts a powerful force on the price of housing. As a result, the supply price of new housing P_H^S *tends to fluctuate over the cycle, lending further impetus to the countercyclical performance of housing construction.*

Consider Figure 6-4. Suppose the housing market is in equilibrium at P_{H_0} and K_{h_0}, and the supply curve of housing is horizontal at $P_{H_0} = P_{H_0}^S$ the housing industry is a constant-cost industry (in real terms). Now in economic expansion, with rising consumption, shifts the demand for housing capital to D_{K_h}'. In the short run, the demand price for housing would rise to P_H', and *with no changes in the real supply price,* the wedge between the demand and supply price would increase the housing stock to K_h'. But if P_H^S rises as the expansion occurs, the supply curve will shift to S_h', thus cutting back the increase in the housing stock so that, in this case, it rises to K_h'' rather than K_h'.

In short, supply conditions make the response to a change in housing demand K_h^* depend on the business cycle, most importantly on the share of business fixed investment in total output I_B/Y.

One further point needs to be made which comes out of the behavior of I_h of the early 1960s. Two peculiarities about I_h manifested themselves in the 1961–1963 period:

1 I_h rose in 1962–1963 as the expansion began, rather than falling as it had done in coming out of other post-World War II recessions.

2 I_h turned down in 1964 (far later than during other recovery periods).

As Evans (1969) points out, the recovery in 1962–1963 did *not* coincide with a rapid rise in business fixed investment and its ratio to GNP. Since the "residual-claimant" approach to housing construction behavior stresses that I_h suffers at the expense of I_B, the failure of I_B to rise much relative to Y is why I_h continued strong in 1962–1963. When I_B rose in 1964, I_h turned down. In addition, the rise that did occur in I_B in 1962–1963 occurred when there were still considerable resources in the economy that were not being utilized.

To account for these inferences, we modify our I_h function by including the ratio of business investment to GNP as a variable and also adding a variable representing the GNP "gap" as a ratio to GNP. Equation (6-6c) thus becomes

$$I_h = \sum_{i=0}^{N} h_i(\Delta K^*_{h_{t-i}}) + \sum_{i=0}^{N} h'_i(i_L - i_S)_{t-i} + h_1 i_{F_{t-1}} + h_2 \text{DCD}$$

$$+ h_3\left(\frac{I_B}{Y}\right) + h_4\left(\frac{Y - Y_F}{Y}\right) + \delta_H K_{h_{t-1}} \qquad (6\text{-}4d)$$

Single-family versus Multifamily Housing

A further complication in explaining total outlays for residential construction is that there are essentially two housing markets: (1) that for single-family dwellings (mostly owner-occupied) and (2) that for apartments, or multifamily dwellings. The distinction between these two is important because differences exist in the tax treatment of income generated by the two types of housing and because the *real* cost of an average unit of multifamily housing is much less than that for single-family housing.

First, consider the tax treatment of the two types of housing. A person who lives in single-family housing and also owns it has an implicit rental income per dollar of housing P_{RS} under present law of

$$\frac{P_{RS}}{P_{HS}} = i(1 - t) + tp(1 - t) - \frac{\dot{P}_{HS}}{P_{HS}}$$

$$P_{RS} = P_{HS}\left[i(1 - t) + tp(1 - t) - \frac{\dot{P}_{HS}}{P_{HS}}\right] \qquad (6\text{-}7)$$

where i = before-tax rate of return on alternative investments
    t = marginal personal income tax rate of the investor
    tp = property tax rate per dollar of house value
    $\dot{P}_{HS}$ = expected change in P_{HS}
    P_{HS} = price per house

That is, the owner, in effect, "rents" the house to himself. No tax is applied to this imputed income, P_{RS}, and so he equates the *before-tax rate of return* from such housing, P_{RS}/P_{HS}, to the sum of (1) the *after-tax return* per dollar on alternative investments $i(1 - t)$; (2) the *after-tax property tax rate* per unit of implied rental income tp —this cost being deductible against the federal income tax—*less* (3) the gross expected capital gain income accruing per dollar invested in the house $(\dot{P}_{HS}/P_{HS})$, this also being free of even capital gains taxes, in most circumstances.

On the other hand, the rental price of a unit of multifamily housing (P_{RM}) will be

$$(1 - t_M)P_{RM} = P_{HM}(1 - t_M z_{HM})\left[i(1 - t_M) + tp(1 - t_M) - (1 - gt_M)\frac{\dot{P}_{HM}}{P_{HM}}\right]$$

$$P_{RM} = P_{HM}(1 - t_M z_{HM})\left[i + tp - \frac{(1 - gt_M)}{(1 - t_M)}\frac{\dot{P}_{HS}}{P_{HS}}\right] \tag{6-8}$$

where P_{HM} = price per unit of multifamily housing

t_M = marginal tax rate of investees in multifamily housing

z_{HM} = present value of depreciation under tax laws totaling \$1 over the life of the multifamily housing unit

g = the ratio of the effective tax rate on capital gains in housing to the tax rate on ordinary income

The tax laws specify that the present value of depreciation deductions of \$1 of the life of a unit of multifamily housing, z_{HM}, is greater than economic depreciation totaling \$1(z_{HM}^*). In addition, some tax is applicable (allowing for deferral of realization and exclusion of a portion of the gain) to accrued capital gains on rental housing. Furthermore, the owner of rental housing is allowed to deduct depreciation in computing taxes, and so the "cost"—for rate-of-return purpose—of rental housing is $P_{HM}(1 - t_M z_{HM})$ rather than P_{HM}. Finally, since a large fraction of multifamily housing is owned by corporations, t_M is likely to be close to the corporate income tax rate and be affected by it.

It can thus be seen that the rental price of single-family (mostly owner-occupied) housing and multifamily housing can vary *relative* to each other especially as changes occur in tax provisions—the corporate tax rate, the treatment of capital gains on the two types of housing, the exclusion of gross rental income from owner-occupied housing in income for computing tax, etc. Therefore, the model for residential construction expenditures should be modified by changing (6-3) to

$$K_{HS}^* = h_S\left(\frac{P_{RS}}{P_c}, \frac{P_{RM}}{P_c}, \frac{C}{N}\right)$$

$$K_{HM}^* = h_M\left(\frac{P_{RS}}{P_c}, \frac{P_{RM}}{P_c}, \frac{C}{N}\right)$$

$$I_{hs} = \delta_s K_{hs_{t-1}} + \phi_1(K_{HS_t}^* - K_{HS_{t-1}}^*) + \phi_2(K_{HS_{t-1}}^* - K_{HS_{t-2}}^*) + \cdots$$

$$I_{hm} = \delta_m K_{hm_{t-1}} + \phi_1(K_{HM_t}^* - K_{HM_{t-1}}^*) + \phi_2(K_{HM_{t-1}}^* - K_{HM_{t-2}}^*) + \cdots$$

$$I_h = I_{hs} + I_{hm}$$

where P_{RS} and P_{RM} are defined as indicated in the discussion above.

READINGS FOR CHAPTER 6

ABRAMOVITZ, M.: *Evidences of Long Swings in Aggregate Construction Since the Civil War*, National Bureau of Economic Research (Princeton, N.J.: Princeton, 1964).

ALBERTS, W. W.: "Business Cycles, Residential Construction Cycles, and the Mortgage Market," *Journal of Political Economy*, vol. 70, pp. 263–281, June 1962.

DELEEUW, F., and E. GRAMLICH," The Channels of Monetary Policy: A Further Report on the Federal Reserve—MIT Model," *Journal of Finance*, vol. XXIV, pp. 265–290, May 1969.

———: "The Federal Reserve–MIT Econometric Model," *Federal Reserve Bulletin*, pp. 11–40, January 1968.

EVANS, M.: *Macroeconomic Activity: Theory, Forecasting and Control* (New York: Harper & Row, 1969), pp. 198–200.

GRAMLICH, E.: "A Housing Sector for June," unpublished working paper for the Fed–MIT model (mimeo.).

GREBLER, L. and S. J. MAISEL: "Determinants of Residential Construction: A Review of Present Knowledge," *Impacts of Monetary Policy*, Commission on Money and Credit (Englewood Cliffs, N.J.: Prentice-Hall, 1963).

GUTTENTAG, J.: "The Short Cycle in Residential Construction," *American Economic Review*, vol. 51, pp. 275–298, June 1961.

MAISEL, S. J.: "A Theory of Fluctuations in Residential Construction Starts," *American Economic Review*, vol. 53, pp. 359–383, June 1963.

———: "The Effects of Monetary Policy on Expenditures in Specific Sectors of the Economy," *Journal of Political Economy*, vol. 76, no. 4, part II, pp. 796–814, July–August 1968.

MUTH, RICHARD: "The Demand for Non-Farm Housing," in A. Harberger (ed.), *The Demand for Durable Goods* (Chicago: The University of Chicago Press, 1960), pp. 29–96.

SPARKS, G. R.: "An Econometric Analysis of the Role of Financial Intermediaries in Postwar Residential Building Cycles," in R. Ferber (ed.), *Determinants of Investment Behavior* (New York: National Bureau of Economic Research, 1967), pp. 301–302.

7
INVENTORY INVESTMENT

The crucial role inventories play in generating fluctuations in economic activity stands in marked contrast to the limited attention given to the study of inventory behavior. Although works by Klein and Popkin (1961), Darling (1959), Metzler (1941), Mills (1957), Abramovitz (1950), Stanback (1961), and Lovell (1964) have shed some light on inventory behavior, nevertheless, relative to the voluminous literature on consumption or business fixed investment, studies of the determinants of inventory investment have been relatively scant.

Since World War II, inventory investment has fluctuated more than any other component of demand during recessions; for the five postwar recessions the average decline in GNP (in 1958 dollars) has been about $9.4 billion while the average decline in real inventory investment amounted to $7 billion. On the average, inventory investment has thus accounted for three-fourths of the decline in real GNP during postwar recessions. This pattern of fluctuation in GNP and inventory investment can be seen in Table 7-1. To understand business fluctuations and the appropriate policy instruments to deal with them, an understanding of the determinants of inventory investment and its relation to GNP is clearly required.

MOTIVES FOR HOLDING INVENTORIES

Inventory models are based on several assumed motives for holding inventory stocks. The most frequently discussed motives for business firms holding inventory stocks are (1) transactions, (2) speculation, (3) buffer stocks, and (4) backlog of demand.

Transactions Demand

As with the transaction demand for money (see Chapter 9), firms are assumed to desire to hold a certain amount of inventories for daily business activities. Since there are costs to holding inventories (interest cost and reordering cost), each firm considers the costs of holding or not holding inventories and thus seeks some optimal inventory-sales ratio that minimizes the cost of holding inventories. Following Whitin (1957), inventory transactions costs, under certain restrictive assumptions, will be minimized according to the formula

$$K_I^* = \sqrt{\frac{2bS^e}{i}}$$

as follows.

Let K_I^* = desired stock of inventories
K_I = actual stock of inventories
b = broker cost per order
S^e = expected sales
i = interest rate at which working capital is borrowed or could be lent
O = size of each order in money terms
n = number of times orders are placed
π_I = total transaction costs

The transactions costs of holding inventories (π_I) fall into two categories—interest costs of tying up working capital in inventories and broker costs associated with the number of orders placed. Thus

$$\pi_I = i\frac{K_I}{2} + bn \qquad (7\text{-}1)$$

Table 7-1 FLUCTUATIONS IN INVENTORY INVESTMENT
AND GNP DURING POSTWAR RECESSIONS
(1958 dollars; billions of dollars)

Recession periods	Total change in inventory investment	Total change in GNP
1948:4–1949:4	−9.5	−5.4
1953:3–1954:2	−4.7	−11.6
1957:3–1958:1	−8.9	−15.7
1960:3–1961:1	−7.2	−7.1
1969:3–1970:4	−4.7	−7.1

SOURCE: U.S. Department of Commerce.

where $i(K_I/2)$ is the interest cost on the average inventory stock during a period and bn is broker costs per period. Assuming that orders O are placed in equal-sized amounts during the period, $K_I/2 = O/2$. In addition, $bn = b(S^e/O)$ (since S^e/O expected sales divided by the number of orders is number of orders n). Equation (7-1) can be written as

$$\pi_I = i\frac{O}{2} + b\frac{S^e}{O} \qquad (7\text{-}2)$$

Differentiating Eq. (7-2) with respect to the size of each order O and setting the result equal to zero, we obtain

$$\frac{d\pi_I}{dO} = \frac{i}{2} - \frac{bS^e}{O^2} = 0 \qquad (7\text{-}3)$$

or

$$\frac{i}{2} = \frac{bS^e}{O^2}$$

and

$$O^2 = \frac{2bS^e}{i} \qquad (7\text{-}4)$$

Thus the desired stock of inventories—that order size that minimizes transactions cost—is given by

$$K_I = O = \sqrt{\frac{2bS^e}{i}} \qquad (7\text{-}4a)$$

Speculative Motive

As with the case for speculative demand for money (Chapter 9), firms may desire to hold more inventories than needed for transaction purposes for speculation. If prices are expected to rise, firms would then receive capital gains on their inventory holdings. Another reason for holding inventories under this heading is to hedge against future shortages in supply which would either increase the cost of new orders or deplete the firm's stock of inventories.

Buffer Stocks

Because of errors in forecasting expected sales, firms will also attempt to hold inventory stock to smooth out order filling and to avoid accumulation or depletion of their inventory stocks. This is the essence of the "buffer motive."

Backlog of Demand

Firms may desire to hold inventories, in addition to the above motives, to smooth out the time flow of goods. Like a pipeline, orders are going in one end and goods are shipped from the other. If shipping proceeds at a certain rate, but orders accumulate much faster, then backlog of orders occurs. In this case the firm will attempt to stock more inventories in response to the established demand than in periods when the backlog of orders is low.

A SIMPLE-ACCELERATOR MODEL

As we will see in this and the following sections, the determinants of inventory behavior hinge on the motives assumed for holding inventories. The specific forms in which these motives enter into the models will be spelled out in each case.

A simple explanation of aggregate inventory behavior is provided by the acceleration theory of investment. In its elementary form the acceleration theory states that businessmen aim at maintaining their stocks of inventory at an equilibrium level which is linearly related to sales.

Let $K_{I_t}^*$ denote equilibrium stock of inventories at time t
S_t denote sales at time t
I_I denote inventory investment

We have

$$K_{I_t}^* = a + bS_t \qquad (7\text{-}5)$$

Equation (7-5) implies that actual inventory investment $(dK_{I_t} = I_I)$ is proportional to changes in sales, or

$$I_I = b(dS_t) \qquad (7\text{-}6)$$

An empirical estimate of this type of model is given in Smyth (1960) for the period 1948–1958. The change in the stock of inventories was explained by changes in GNP, and the coefficient of dGNP was significant and equal to 0.3.

Several modifications of this simple-accelerator model can be introduced. Abramovitz, in a monumental study for the National Bureau of Economic Research, pointed out that, in contrast to the simple-accelerator model, inventory investment is *not* proportional to changes in sales or GNP. Metzler (1941) and Lundberg (1957) indicated that errors made by firms in forecasting sales in future time periods could cause sales and inventory investment to move in opposite directions. If sales estimates are too high—actual sales exceed expected sales—the buffer of finished goods inventories carried to prevent runouts is depleted. Conversely, if actual sales are below expected sales, unplanned inventory accumulation occurs.

Other factors in addition to sales may influence entrepreneurs' desire for a given inventory stock. Several attempts were made to explore, within the framework of the accelerator model, the possible effects of monetary policy or credit conditions, the role of speculation, and price hedging, as well as other influences on inventory investment. In the next section we will examine four variants of the accelerator model. These are referred to as (1) the Metzler transactions-and-expectational-errors model, (2) Klein's flexible-accelerator model, (3) Darling's variable-accelerator model, and (4) the expectational-error model of Lovell. In the section after these models are discussed, other determinants of inventory investment will be explored.

OTHER ACCELERATOR MODELS

The Metzler Inventory Model

Metzler developed a model of inventory behavior based on two hypotheses: (1) that the basic reason for holding inventories is *transactions* (expected sales) and (2) that *errors* in forecasting future sales occur. To account for the transaction motive, firms are assumed to seek some optimal inventory-sales ratio α; thus the desired stock of inventory K_I^* can be written as being proportional to sales, viz., $K_I^* = \alpha S$.

Combining this simple transactions demand model with a stock-adjustment model, Metzler's inventory model explains inventory investment as follows. First, inventory investment in any period is the difference between desired and actual stocks:

$$I_{I_t} = K_{I_t}^* - K_{I_{t-1}} \qquad (7\text{-}7)$$

Second, this period's expected sales are assumed to be the same as actual sales in the last period:

$$S_t^e = S_{t-1} \qquad (7\text{-}8)$$

The desired stock of inventory is proportional to the expected sales:

$$K_{I_t}^* = \alpha S_t^e \qquad (7\text{-}9)$$

where (7-9) is the same as the simple-accelerator models.

Since inventory stocks at time $t-1$ are equal to inventory stocks at time $t-2$ less depletions in time $t-1$, and depletions in time $t-1$ equal the change in sales

$$K_{I_{t-1}} = K_{I_{t-2}} - d(S_{t-1}) \qquad (7\text{-}10)$$

Then
$$K_{I_{t-1}} = K_{I_{t-2}} - d(S_{t-1}) \qquad (7\text{-}11)$$

Substituting Eqs. (7-9) and (7-11) into (7-7) we get

$$I_{I_t} = \alpha S_{t-1} - K_{I_{t-2}} + d(S_{t-1}) \qquad (7\text{-}12)$$

Equation (7-12) is the basic Metzler equation.[1]

To allow for expectational errors, Metzler introduces into the model an "expectations elasticity" η, where η is defined as the ratio of the expected change in sales between period t and $t-1$ and the observed change in sales between $t-1$ and $t-2$.

$$\eta = d(S_t^e)/d(S_{t-1})$$

where $0 < \eta < 1$.

---

[1] Assuming inventory investment, in any period, to be equal to the difference between desired and actual inventory stocks, the proportionality of α has been questioned by Abramovitz. He pointed out that actual inventory is not proportional to changes in output or sales and thus α should be treated as a variable quantity. This is incorporated in the variable-accelerator model discussed below.

Rewriting S_t^e in terms of the expectations elasticity we have

$$S_t^e = S_{t-1} + \eta \, d(S_{t-1}) \qquad (7\text{-}13)$$

and $K_{I_{t-1}}$ is now expressed as

$$K_{I_{t-1}} = K_{I_{t-2}} - (S_{t-1} - S_{t-1}^e)$$
$$= K_{I_{t-2}} - d(S_{t-1}) + \eta \, d(S_{t-2}) \qquad (7\text{-}14)$$

since $S_{t-1} - S_{t-2} = d(S_{t-1})$. From Eqs. (7-9) and (7-14), Eq. (7-7) can be written as

$$I_{I_t} = \alpha S_t^e - K_{I_{t-2}} + d(S_{t-1}) - \eta \, d(S_{t-2})$$
$$= \alpha S_{t-1} + \alpha\eta \, d(S_{t-1}) - K_{I_{t-2}} + d(S_{t-1}) - \eta \, dS_{t-2} \qquad (7\text{-}15)$$

Combining terms in (7-15) gives

$$I_{I_t} = \alpha S_{t-1} + (1 + \alpha\eta) \, d(S_{t-1}) - \eta \, d(S_{t-2}) - K_{I_{t-2}} \qquad (7\text{-}15a)$$

Equation (7-15a) shows inventory investment being determined by last period's sales, the change in last period's sales, the change in sales two periods ago, and inventory stocks two periods past. Thus, introducing expectational errors leads to a desire to hold inventory, in addition to inventory held for transaction purposes to smooth out fluctuations in inventory stocks.

Klein's Flexible-Accelerator Model

A basic flaw in the Metzler model is the assumption that firms adjust their inventory stock toward equilibrium or desired stock within a single period. An alternative procedure, frequently employed in econometric studies, is to assume that the firm attempts only a *partial* adjustment of its inventories during one period. Thus actual inventory investment is assumed to be a fraction λ of the discrepency between last period's stock and the current desired level;

$$I_{I_t} = \lambda(K_t^* - K_{t-1}) \qquad 0 < \lambda < 1 \qquad (7\text{-}16)$$

Only when the adjustment coefficient λ is exactly equal to unity will inventories be fully adjusted to the equilibrium level. When $\lambda < 1$, only through passage of time will the discrepancy between the equilibrium level of inventories and the actual stock be removed.

Introducing Eq. (7-16) into the Metzler model we get

$$I_{I_t} = \lambda\alpha S_{t-1} + \lambda(1 + \alpha\eta) \, d(S_{t-1}) \qquad (7\text{-}17)$$
$$- \lambda\eta \, d(S_{t-2}) - \lambda K_{I_{t-2}}$$

Using annual inventory data for the period 1921–1940, Klein (1950) found the adjustment coefficient λ to be approximately equal to 0.52 rather than 1.0, the value implied in the simple-accelerator model of Smyth [Eq. (7-5)] described above.

Darling's Variable-Accelerator Model

Darling explains inventory behavior using an accelerator model similar to Metzler's but modified in two respects: (1) that α, the inventory-sales ratio, varies over the cycle and (2) that actual inventory stock is adjusted toward the equilibrium stock over time—$\lambda < 1$. Darling suggests that α will be higher, the higher the ratio of unfilled orders U to sales, and lower the lower this ratio is. Thus α can be written as

$$\alpha = a_0 + a_1 \left(\frac{dU}{S}\right)_{t-1} \qquad a_1 > 0 \qquad (7\text{-}18)$$

Substituting this relation (7-18) into (7-12) as modified for the flexible accelerator (the coefficient λ) and dropping the $d(S_{t-1})$ term, we get

$$I_{I_t} = \lambda\left(a_0 + a_1 \frac{dU_{t-1}}{S_{t-1}}\right) S_{t-1} - \lambda K_{I_{t-2}}$$

or
$$I_{I_t} = \lambda a_0 S_{t-1} + \lambda a_1 d(U_{t-1}) - \lambda K_{I_{t-2}} \qquad (7\text{-}19)$$

According to Darling's model, net investment in inventories I_I is explained by lagged sales S_{t-1}, the previous period's change in unfilled orders $d(U_{t-1})$, and inventory stocks lagged two periods $K_{I_{t-2}}$. Quarterly data from 1947:3 to 1958:3 were used to find the reaction coefficient λ. λ was found to be equal to 0.212 per quarter, implying that the adjustment by firms is equal to one-fifth of the discrepancy between desired and actual stock of inventory in each quarter.

Lovell's Errors-in-Anticipating-Sales Model

Except for those cases where a firm produces goods to specific order, a firm's sales may exceed or fall short of the anticipated level. Since production of finished goods requires time, a "buffer-stock" motive then partly explains firms' desires to hold inventories. Using the buffer-stock motive, which stems from forecasting errors, Lovell introduces two modifications to the basic accelerator model. These are (1) replacing what he calls *anticipated* sales $\hat{S}$ for actual sales in the equation determining inventory behavior and (2) allowing for the impact of errors in anticipating sales on the level of inventory.

These two modifications suggest that finished goods inventory behavior is explained by the following equation:

$$I_{I_t} = \lambda(K_{I_t}^* - K_{I_{t-1}}) + u(\hat{S}_t - S_t) \qquad (7\text{-}20)$$

where λ again is the adjustment coefficient and u is the production adaptation coefficient—the degree to which the firm succeeds in compensating for errors made in anticipating sales during the period. If $u = 0$, production plans are assumed to be completely flexible, while if $u = 1$, production plans are assumed to be completely inflexible and finished goods inventory would fall below the planned level by the full amount. A value $0 < u < 1$ means that the firm is able to partially offset errors made in anticipating sales.

If K_I^* is rewritten in terms of anticipated sales—$K_I^* = \beta \hat{S}_t$—(7-20) can be written

$$I_{I_t} = \lambda \beta \hat{S}_t - \lambda K_{I_{t-1}} + u(\hat{S}_t - S_t) \qquad (7\text{-}20a)$$

when $\lambda \beta S_t$ is added and subtracted, (7-20a) becomes

$$I_{I_t} = \lambda \beta S_t + (\lambda \beta + u)(\hat{S}_t - S_t) - \lambda K_{I_{t-1}} \qquad (7\text{-}20b)$$

Since $\hat{S}$ is not observed, Lovell hypothesized that the expectations error $(\hat{S} - S)$ is proportional to the change in sales. Quarterly and annual data were used to perform calculations for the cement industry. The regressions run by Lovell suggest that the forecast error is best explained by the change in sales from the preceding period. The expectation-error equation is of the form

$$\hat{S}_t - S_t = -\rho(S_t - S_{t-1}) \qquad (7\text{-}21)$$

and thus

$$\hat{S}_t = \rho S_{t-1} + (1 - \rho)S_t \qquad (7\text{-}21a)$$

where ρ is the "coefficient of anticipations." The coefficient ρ is a measure of the bias of forecasts of current sales toward last period's sales. If $\rho = 1$, firms base their forecasts entirely on last period's sales. A value of $\rho = 0$ means that firms' forecasts are based on this period's sales. A value of ρ between these two extremes, $0 < \rho < 1$, implies that, on the average, firms' anticipations are some fraction of *changes* in sales.

Substituting Eq. (7-21) into Lovell's inventory-behavior equation (7-20b), we get

$$I_{I_t} = \lambda \beta S_t + (\lambda \beta + u)[-\rho(S_t - S_{t-1})] - \lambda K_{I_{t-1}} \qquad (7\text{-}22)$$
$$= \lambda \beta S_t - \rho(\lambda \beta + u) \, d(S_t) - \lambda K_{I_{t-1}}$$

Estimating an inventory-behavior equation for finished goods of all manufacturers using quarterly deflated seasonally adjusted data for 1948 to 1955, Lovell found a value of the coefficient $\lambda \beta = 0.042$, and $-\rho(\lambda \beta + u) = -0.13$. However, the regression estimates do not give a value for ρ, but can only be solved for $u\rho$; it is not possible to segregate the effect of production flexibility from the expectation errors. Thus if u is assumed to be equal to 1, then $\rho = 0.1247$. If $u = 0.5$, then $\rho = 0.24$. A value of ρ equal to or greater than 1 requires a value of production adaptation coefficient less than 9 percent.

OTHER DETERMINANTS OF INVENTORY INVESTMENT

Other variables, such as credit conditions, the role of speculation, and price hedging, have been discussed, in addition to sales, as influences on the desired or equilibrium level of inventories. The possible effects of monetary policy upon inventory investment were studied by Ando et al. (1961), Lovell (1961), and McGouldrick (1961).

The study by Ando et al. contains estimates of the effect of interest rates on short-term loans on manufacturers' inventory holdings. One estimate reported by the authors suggests that a 1 percentage point rise in the interest rate lowers inventory investment by $1.5 billion in the following quarter, with the total effect on inventories being put at $4.8 billion. However, the study is generally somewhat inconclusive as to the influence of credit conditions on inventory. When a complicated lag structure was used in the estimating equation, the study produced an interest coefficient roughly equal to its standard error.

Two other studies also failed to yield a concrete relation between credit conditions and inventory behavior. Lovell and McGouldrick both found the credit-condition variable not significant or with its coefficient having an incorrect sign.

The role of speculation in inventory holdings was examined by Klein (1964), Brown (1964), Lovell (1961), and Darling (1959). The evidence with regard to this variable is not entirely satisfactory. Klein's study shows a significant relation between total inventory investment and the change in the GNP deflator. However, the other two studies found the price variable to be not significant and sometimes having the wrong sign.

SUMMARY

Literature on inventory investment is scant compared to studies on the determinants of fixed business investment or the consumption function. The neglect can perhaps be attributed to the difficulty of the subject and/or lack of data for empirical estimation. In any case, the studies reported here, which are the best known, are but variants of the simple-accelerator model of investment, with allowances made for lags and the impact of errors in anticipating sales.

The simple-accelerator inventory model, as derived by Smyth, explains the change in inventory by changes in GNP. This makes for a proportional and constant relation (α) between changes in inventories and changes in sales or GNP, and the adjustment process of actual inventory toward the equilibrium level takes place within a single period. The constancy of α and the unitary value of the adjustment coefficient are dropped in the modified accelerator models of inventory. The Darling model allows for α to vary over the cycle and also incorporates a lag structure in the model. The speed of adjustment of actual inventory toward equilibrium inventory was found to be around 0.2 per quarter.

Both the Metzler and Lovell models deal with the expectational variable. In the Metzler model an "expectational error elasticity" is introduced to allow for errors in forecasting sales on inventory. Lovell's model is more sophisticated, providing a method for constructing an anticipated-sales variable and for estimating the impact of expectation errors on inventory behavior. It also incorporates a "production-adaptation" variable to allow for possible inflexibility of the production plan of the firm.

Unfortunately, Lovell's model requires an a priori assumption concerning the production-adaptation coefficient u, to infer the value of the anticipation error ρ.

When u is assumed to be equal to unity, ρ is found to be equal to 0.1247, which means that business firms do not rely entirely on past-period sales in determining the desired level of inventory.

Other variables such as prices and interest rate were examined in several econometric studies, but evidence of their influence on I_t has not yet been found to be conclusive.

READINGS FOR CHAPTER 7

ABRAMOVITZ, M.: *Inventories and Business Cycles with Special Reference to Manufacturer's Inventories* (New York: National Bureau of Economic Research, 1950).

ANDO, H., E. C. BROWN, R. SOLOW, and J. KAREKAN: "Lags in Fiscal and Monetary Policy," in *Stabilization Policies*, Commission on Money and Credit (Englewood Cliffs, N.J.: Prentice-Hall 1961), pp. 11–163.

BROWN, T. M.: "A Forecast Determination of National Product, Employment, and Price Level in Canada, from an Econometric Model," in E. Denison and R. Klein (eds.), *Models of Income Determination*, National Bureau of Economic Research (Princeton, N.J.: Princeton, 1964), pp. 59–86.

DARLING, P.: "Manufacturer's Inventory Investment, 1947–1958," *American Economic Review*, vol. 49, pp. 950–963, December 1959.

EVANS, M.: *Macroeconomic Activity, Theory, Forecasting, and Control* (New York: Harper & Row, 1969), chap. 8.

KLEIN, R.: *Economic Fluctuations in the United States, 1921–4*, Cowles Commission Monograph 11 (New York: Wiley, 1950).

———: "A Postwar Quarterly Model: Description and Applications," in Denison and Klein, op. cit., pp. 11–36.

KLEIN, R., and J. POPKIN: "An Econometric Analysis of the Post-War Relationship between Inventory Fluctuations and Changes in Aggregate Economic Activity," *Inventory Fluctuation and Change in Aggregate Economic Activity*, Joint Economic Committee, 1961, Part III, pp. 71–81.

LOVELL, M.: "Manufacturers Inventories, Sales Expectations, and the Acceleration Principle," *Econometrica*, vol. 29, pp. 293–314, July 1961.

———: "Determinants of Inventory Investment," in Denison, and Klein op. cit., pp. 177–220.

LUNDBERG, E.: *Studies in the Theory of Economic Expansion* (London: King, 1957).

MCGOULDRICK, P.: "The Impact of Credit Cost and Availability on Inventory Investment," in *Inventory Fluctuation*, op. cit., part II.

METZLER, L.: "The Nature and Stability of Inventory Cycles," *Review of Economics and Statistics*, vol. 23, pp. 113–129, August 1941.

MILLS, E.: "The Theory of Inventory Decisions," *Econometrica*, pp. 222–239, April 1957.

SMYTH, D.: "The Inventory and Fixed Capital Accelerators," *Economic Record*, August 1960.

STANBACK, T.: *Postwar Cycles in Manufacturers' Inventories*, National Bureau of Economic Research (Princeton, N.J.: Princeton, 1961).

WHITIN, T.: *The Theory of Inventory Management* (Princeton, N.J.: Princeton, 1957).

8

THE FOREIGN SECTOR

The analysis of income-determination models presented in the previous chapters has assumed a "closed economy"—an economy considered in isolation from all others. In this chapter we add a foreign sector to the model so that interrelationships between the domestic economy and the rest of the world can be examined. Introducing a foreign sector to the income model involves the addition of the following variables and equations: (1) a *current account balance equation* where exports, imports, foreign prices (as a ratio of domestic prices, treated as a numeraire), and foreign income appear as variables; (2) a *capital account equation*, reflecting net capital flows resulting from the purchase and sales of assets, as a function of interest rate differentials between the domestic economy and the rest of the world; and (3) a *balance of payments equation*, which is the sum of the current account equation and the capital account equation.

THE FOREIGN TRADE BALANCE EQUATION

The current account balance equation describes the balance between income from sales of United States goods and services abroad and purchases of foreign goods and services by United States residents. The current account records, on one side of the account, income from the sale of currently produced goods and services of one country to the rest of the world. These transactions appear as exports of goods and services (X) in the national income accounts. On the other side of the current account, payments for goods and services purchased from foreigners are entered and appear as imports (IM) in the national income accounts. The current account balance is given by exports minus imports

$$BC = X - IM \qquad (8\text{-}1)$$

and enters the GNP accounts in the aggregate demand equation as follows:

$$Y = C + I + G + (X - IM) \qquad (8\text{-}2)$$

where all variables are in real terms.

The Demand for Exports and Imports

Exports, like the consumption component of aggregate demand, depend on the level of income and prices, except that the relevant variables are *foreign income* and the ratio of foreign to domestic prices. To make the analysis simple, let us assume that the foreign price level p_f is constant, and given the level of aggregate foreign demand Y_f and the exchange rate e,[1] exports will depend only on relative prices expressed in terms of the foreign currency, pe/p_f, which varies here only with the domestic price level p. Thus

$$X = X(pe/\bar{p}_f, \bar{Y}_f) \qquad (8\text{-}3)$$

where $\dfrac{\partial X}{\partial(pe/\bar{p}_f)} < 0$.

The demand for imports IM, on the other hand, depends on the domestic level of income Y and relative prices, or

$$IM = IM(Y, pe/\bar{p}_f) \qquad (8\text{-}4)$$

where $\dfrac{\partial IM}{\partial Y} > 0, \dfrac{\partial IM}{\partial pe/\bar{p}_f} > 0$.

The real current account balance equation is then given by

$$BC = X - IM \qquad (8\text{-}5)$$

$$BC = X(pe/\bar{p}_f, \bar{Y}_f) - IM(Y, pe/\bar{p}_f) \qquad (8\text{-}6)$$

The equilibrium condition in the market for commodities

$$C + I + G + X - IM = Y \qquad (8\text{-}7)$$

can now be written

$$Y = C(Y - \bar{T}/p - \tau(Y), A/p) + I(i) + G$$
$$+ X(\bar{Y}_f, pe/\bar{p}_f) - IM(Y, pe/\bar{p}_f) \qquad (8\text{-}7a)$$

---

[1] The exchange rate is expressed in terms of units of foreign currency (e.g., German marks) per dollar.

(the consumption equation, for simplicity, is written with the assumption that labor income is proportional to personal income). As expressed in Eq. (8-7), foreign purchases of domestic goods X add to the income stream while imports IM have a "leakage effect" on income by diverting demand to foreign-produced goods. In relation (8-7a), equality of savings and taxes to investment and government expenditures, on the one hand, and exports and imports on the other hand, is not required for equilibrium. Equilibrium in the commodity market only requires that the difference between exports and imports be equal to the difference between savings plus taxes and investment plus government spending. (Again imports, exports, savings, taxes, and G are in real terms.)

Higher domestic prices relative to foreign prices will tend to increase imports and reduce exports, and, given real income, reduce the surplus or increase the deficit in the real current account balance:

$$\frac{\partial BC}{\partial(pe/\bar{p}_f)} < 0 \qquad (8\text{-}8)$$

where a deficit in the current account balance is an excess of domestic expenditures (absorption) over domestic income or an excess of investment plus government spending over savings and taxes.[2]

Effect of Exports and Imports on the *IS* Curve

Including the foreign sector affects the *IS* curve. An exogenous increase in exports, with a given $pe/\bar{p}_f$, will shift the *IS* curve out and to the right. On the other hand, an increase in imports will increase the leakage effect $(S + T + IM)$ and thus shift the *IS* curve to the left. The *slope* of the *IS* curve with the foreign sector included is now obtained by differentiating Eq. (8-7a), holding $pe/\bar{p}_f$, τ, $\bar{T}$, A/p, and G constant:

$$dY = C_{Y_d}(dY - \tau\,dY) + I_i\,di - \text{IM}_Y\,dY$$

or

$$\left.\frac{di}{dY}\right|_{IS} = \frac{1 - C_{Y_d}(1 - \tau) + \text{IM}_Y}{I_i} \qquad (8\text{-}9)$$

The slope of the import function IM_Y has been added to the numerator, thus making the *IS* curve "steeper" (more negative) than was the case in a closed economy. The effect of opening the economy to foreign trade is that the size of the simple G multiplier is now reduced—the leverage effect of any fiscal policy change designed to stimulate aggregate demand will be less potent than in a closed economy. A rise

---

[2] This observation is based on the assumption that the sum of the elasticities of demand for exports and imports is greater than 1. If these elasticities sum to less than 1, the opposite result may be obtained. See pp. 145–146.

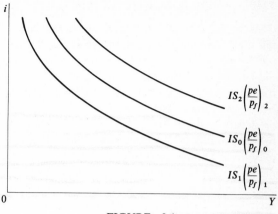

FIGURE 8-1
Shift of *IS* as terms of trade change.

in *G* or a cut in taxes will stimulate aggregate demand and raise *Y* through the multiplier effect, but the increase in *Y* per dollar change in the policy parameter *G* (or *T* or τ in Chapter 3) will be smaller, since some of the stimulated demand will leak abroad in the form of increased imports. The effect on *Y* of a change in *G* per dollar change in *G*, with foreign trade, with a constant interest-rate—the simple multiplier —is now given by

$$\frac{dY}{dG} = \frac{1}{1 - C_{Y_d}(1 - \tau) + IM_Y} \qquad (8\text{-}10)$$

Since the term IM_Y is positive, dY/dG will be smaller than is the case where $IM_Y = 0$ in the closed economy case.

Changes in relative price $pe/\bar{p}_f$ affect the *IS* curve by affecting savings and the demand for imports and exports. A rise in domestic prices relative to foreign prices (*e* constant) increases savings due to the real balance effect and also imports by making foreign goods cheaper than domestically produced goods. The increase in savings and imports increases the leakage effect in the system and tends to shift the *IS* curve to the left. This effect is further reinforced by the decline in exports due to the increased relative prices of domestic goods. The initial *IS* curve, IS_0 in Figure 8-1, would now shift to the IS_1 position. The opposite effect, a shift of the IS_0 curve to the right to IS_2, occurs with a deterioration in the terms of trade. In the graph (the bar over p_f is removed hereafter for simplicity) we have:

$$\left(\frac{pe}{p_f}\right)_2 < \left(\frac{pe}{p_f}\right)_0 < \left(\frac{pe}{p_f}\right)_1$$

THE CAPITAL ACCOUNT AND THE BALANCE OF PAYMENTS

Consider the case of a deficit in the current account of the United States. As exports fall short of imports, the rest of the world (ROW) has an increase in its claims against the deficit country, in this case, the United States. The rise in ROW claims against the United States (or the reduction of their liabilities to the United States) increases their net assets. The *capital account* is a record of such capital transaction with the rest of the world. The type of capital movement described, resulting from a surplus or deficit in the trade account, is representative of "induced" capital movements between countries. "Autonomous" capital movements are also undertaken for several reasons: (1) higher rate of return on foreign securities compared to similar invest- ments at home; (2) anticipated changes in foreign exchange rates; and (3) fear of war, political instability, or inflation which leads residents of a country to transfer their assets abroad.

The capital account records long-term as well as short-term capital movements. Long-term capital movements occur when a country exchanges currently or previously acquired foreign balances (or short-term capital) for stocks, bonds, or physical capital of long-term maturity. Both long-term and short-term capital movements take place when yields on comparable foreign investments change relative to those at home. Thus, the allocation of investment portfolios between home and abroad will depend on domestic and foreign interest rate levels. The higher the level of foreign interest rates relative to home rates, the larger the fraction of foreign invest- ments to total investment portfolios, and vice versa. Given the level of foreign interest rates and exchange rates, the *net inflow* of capital KA, both short and long term, will be an increasing function of the domestic interest rate,

$$KA = KA(i) \qquad KA_i > 0 \qquad (8\text{-}11)$$

where KA = the nominal net capital inflow, in dollars

i = the domestic interest rate

The balance of payments equation can now be written as the sum of the nominal balance, in dollars, in the current account and the capital account.

$$B = [pX - (p_f/e)IM] + KA \qquad (8\text{-}12)$$

or $\qquad B = pX(pe/p_f, \overline{Y}_f) - (p_f/e)IM(Y, pe/p_f) + KA(i) \qquad (8\text{-}13)$

Balance of payments equilibrium ($B = 0$) can be represented by a curve—the BB curve—similar to the IS or LM curve. The BB curve is a locus of points in the i, Y plane where the balance of payments is in equilibrium. B will be equal to zero (no surplus or deficits) when net exports, $pX - (p_f/e)IM$, are just equal to net capital outflows ($-KA$). When B is not equal to zero, balance of payments equili- brium can be achieved with varying combinations of i and Y. This is shown by the BB curve in Figure 8-2. For example, an increase in Y causes imports to rise [$pX - (p_f/e)IM$ is reduced], thus making $B < 0$ and necessitating a higher i to induce a capital inflow to offset the trade deficit and again make $B = 0$. The slope of the

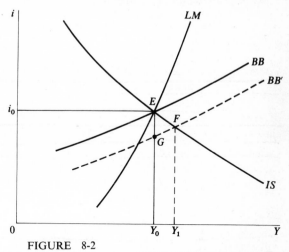

FIGURE 8-2
Balance of payments equilibrium. See Mundell (1963).

BB curve can be seen by totally differentiating Eq. (8-13) and setting $dB = 0$. Assuming prices p and p_f and the exchange rate e to remain constant, we get

$$0 = -\text{IM}_Y \, dY + \text{KA}_i \, di \qquad (8\text{-}14)$$

where the subscripted terms denote partials with respect to the subscripts. Equation (8-14) reduces to

$$\left.\frac{di}{dY}\right|_{B=0} = \frac{\text{IM}_Y}{\text{KA}_i} > 0 \qquad (8\text{-}15)$$

Since IM_Y is positive and KA_i is also positive, the slope of the BB curve in the $i - Y$ space is positive. In Figure 8-2, the BB curve is drawn so that B is very interest-elastic, as may be the case in practice.[3]

Effect of Price Changes on the BB Curve

As seen in Eq. (8-13), the current account balance in current dollars is given by

$$pX(pe/p_f, \, \overline{Y}_f) - (p_f/e)\text{IM}(Y, \, pe/p_f)$$

where both exports and imports are valued in terms of domestic currency (dollars); imports are converted to dollars by using foreign prices p_f divided by the exchange rate e. Since exports depend only on domestic prices (given p_f, e, and $\overline{Y}_f$), a change in domestic prices affects nominal exports as follows:

$$\frac{d(pX)}{dp} = \frac{p \, \partial X}{\partial p} + X = X\left(1 + \frac{p}{X}\frac{\partial X}{\partial p}\right) \qquad (8\text{-}16)$$

[3] See Mundell (1963).

$\text{IM}_Y \doteq$ The income response effect
of imports.
$\text{KA}_i \doteq$ The interest response of capital

Equation (8-16) can be written

$$\frac{d(pX)}{dp} = X(1 + E_{X,p}) \qquad (8\text{-}17)$$

where $E_{X,p}$ is the price elasticity of demand for *real* exports, and is negative; i.e., a rise in domestic prices relative to foreign prices reduces real exports and vice versa.

When domestic prices fall, real exports rise, but the effect on the *money value* of exports is not clearly determined. Whether it rises or falls will depend on the elasticity of exports, in the same manner as total revenue, in the theory of the firm, depends upon the elasticity of demand for the product. If the absolute value of $|E_{X,p}| > 1$, then Eq. (8-17) shows that the money value of exports *falls* when prices rise. It will rise if $|E_{X,p}| < 1$ and remains the same when $|E_{X,p}| = 1$.

With respect to imports, we know that $\partial(\text{IM})/\partial p$ is positive—a rise in domestic prices increases *real* imports. In addition, a rise in p increases *nominal* imports as well. Thus, the effect on the balance in the current account due to a rise in domestic prices will depend on the effect of the price change on exports relative to imports. In general, the change in the nominal current account balance BCN is given by

$$\frac{d(BCN)}{dp} = X(1 + E_{X,p}) - \frac{p_f}{e}\frac{\partial \text{IM}}{\partial p} \qquad (8\text{-}18)$$

or

$$\frac{d(BCN)}{dp} = X(1 + E_{X,p}) - \frac{\text{IM}}{p}\frac{p_f}{e}(E_{\text{IM},p}) \qquad (8\text{-}19)$$

where $E_{\text{IM},p}$ is the elasticity of real imports with respect to domestic prices. If (8-19) is multiplied by p

$$p\frac{d(BCN)}{dp} = pX(1 + E_{X,p}) - \text{IM}\frac{p_f}{e}(E_{\text{IM},p}) \qquad (8\text{-}20)$$

then for $p(d(BCN)/dp) < 0$ (which is also the condition for $d(BCN)/dp < 0$, since $p > 0$), *starting from a position of balance in the current account* $(pX = (p_f/e)\text{IM})$, the condition is

$$pX(1 + E_{X,p} - E_{\text{IM},p}) < 0$$

or

$$1 + E_{X,p} - E_{\text{IM},p} < 0 \qquad (8\text{-}20a)$$

Since $E_{X,p} < 0$ and $E_{\text{IM},p} > 0$, the condition reduces to

$$|E_{X,p}| + |E_{\text{IM},p}| > 1 \qquad (8\text{-}21)$$

That is, starting with balance in the current account, a rise in domestic prices causes the current account to go into deficit as long as the sum of the absolute value of the price elasticities of demand for real exports and imports exceeds unity.

Statistical evidence on the magnitude of the elasticities of real exports and imports with respect to relative prices suggests that their absolute values are near unity,[4] so that the sum of the absolute values is certainly larger than unity.

The reader should be able to establish that the same condition that applied to a change in domestic prices also applies to a change in exchange notes e.

INTERNAL AND EXTERNAL EQUILIBRIUM

In Figure 8-2, the *IS* curve and *LM* curve intersection portrays equilibrium for the commodity and money market at a level of income Y_0 and interest rate i_0. At a given exchange rate and domestic price level, the *BB* curve represents an equilibrium in the balance of payments $(B = 0)$—*external balance*—which, to begin with, is assumed consistent with internal equilibrium at Y_0 and i_0 (where Y_0 refers to full-employment output). Now let us suppose that the capital account improves so that a surplus in the balance of payments develops. A balance of payments surplus shifts the *BB* curve to the right and downward to *BB'*. As shown in Figure 8-2, the twin goals of full employment and external balance cannot be achieved with the existing interest rate i_0 and income level Y_0. The *BB'* curve shows that external balance is not consistent with the internal balance depicted by the intersection of the *IS − LM* curves at point *E*. For a new balance of payments equilibrium to be achieved at full employment, the *IS* and *LM* curves must intersect the new *BB* curve at point *G*, or at some other point if *BB* shifts further. Some combination of a shift in the *LM* curve to the right, the *IS* curve to the left, and the *BB* curve up (to the left), so that the three curves again intersect at Y_0, will achieve equilibrium with full employment at home. Let us explain the possible adjustments involved.

H = Monetary Base : D.D + C.

Effect of Surplus or Deficit on the *LM* and *IS* curves

The first point to note is that a balance of payments surplus may produce an increase in the money supply. Because a surplus results in increased receipts from foreigners over payments to them, commercial banks (when they deposit their receipts with the Federal Reserve) experience an increase in reserves, and thus high-powered money H rises by the amount of the surplus. Given the money multiplier, the money supply will also rise (unless there are offsetting actions by the Federal Reserve). The change in the money supply can be expressed as

$$dM = m \, d\overline{H} = m \, dB \qquad (8\text{-}22)$$

where m is the money multiplier discussed in Chapter 3. Because the surplus increases the money supply, the initial equilibrium point *E* shown in Figure 8-2 is no longer an equilibrium point for the money market, with the balance of payments surplus

---

[4] Houthakker and Magee (1969) found $E_{X,p}$ to be about -1.46 and $E_{\text{IM},p}$ to be around -0.88.

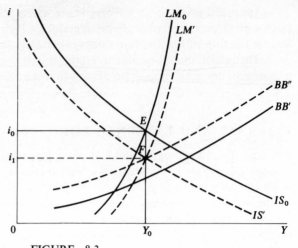

FIGURE 8-3
Effect of surpluses on internal and external equilibrium.

represented by the shift in the *BB* curve to *BB'*. As the money supply increases, the *LM* curve shifts to the right toward the *IS–BB'* intersection, i.e., toward point *F*. However, as the money supply is increased, the interest rate falls, thus generating increased demand for output (moving down the *IS* curve). Since output is already at full employment, prices rise, moderating the shift of the *LM* curve. In addition, the

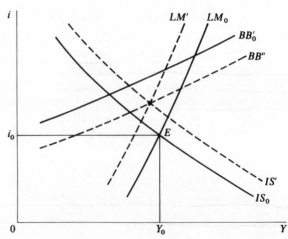

FIGURE 8-4
Effect of balance of payments deficits on internal and external equilibrium.

price increase tends to shift the *IS* curve to the left, via its effect on the wealth variable in the consumption function and on the demand for real exports. As shown in Figure 8-3, the increase in the money supply, and thus in aggregate demand and prices, leads to an increase in output and employment, moving the original internal equilibrium point *E* to the right. Also the rise in prices affects the *BB* curve by reducing real exports, and the *BB* curve shifts upward to *BB"* (Figure 8-3). Full equilibrium—internal and external balance—is achieved when the three curves, *IS*, *LM*, and *BB*, intersect at a new point such as point *F*.

The reverse process takes place with a balance of payments deficit. A balance of payments deficit leads to a reduction in the money supply and prices, and an increase in the interest rate. The *LM* curve in this case shifts to the left, the *IS* curve to the right, and the *BB* curve downward, with full equilibrium again achieved at the common intersection of all three curves. This is shown in Figure 8-4. As long as balance of payments surpluses or deficits exist, the "induced effects" of these surpluses or deficits on the supply of money, aggregate demand, prices, and the interest rate will go on. Only when monetary action is taken to "sterilize" the surplus or "counteroffset" the deficit can we ignore the repercussion of the balance of payments position on internal equilibrium.[5]

INTERNAL AND EXTERNAL BALANCE UNDER FIXED AND FLEXIBLE EXCHANGE RATE SYSTEMS

As we have indicated earlier, an exchange rate is the rate at which a unit of one country's currency can be exchanged for other country's currencies. As a price, similar to prices of other commodities, the exchange rate is determined by the supply of and demand for foreign exchange. The market for the exchange rate, as well as the adjustment mechanism, is usually governed by one of two exchange rate systems. The first, and perhaps the best-known system, is the gold standard, or the fixed exchange system. The second is a system of freely fluctuating exchange rates. We now consider the problem of achieving internal and external equilibrium under each of these systems.

The Fixed Exchange System

Under this system, countries maintain the value of their currencies in "fixed" relation to the value of gold or some other reserve currency by standing ready to sell or buy gold or a reserve currency at constant prices. Thus, if all the currencies of the world each have a fixed relationship to gold, they have a fixed relation to one another. However, because the buying and selling prices of gold are not identical, due to

---

[5] The Federal Reserve System can act to sterilize the balance of payments surpluses by offsetting the increase in bank reserves by open market sales. In the case of a balance of payments deficit, the Federal Reserve System can engage in open market purchases of securities to replace commercial bank reserve losses. See Chapter 10.

transportation, commissions, and insurance costs of moving gold between markets, these costs establish the gold import and export points (mint points). Between the gold points, the price of exchange is set by the demand for and supply of foreign exchange. When a wide change occurs in the demand for or supply of foreign exchange, in the short run gold or reserve currency movements will take place to balance the demand and supply. If such imbalance persists for longer periods, domestic adjustments take place—some combination of constriction of aggregate demand and higher interest rates. In short, under a fixed exchange system, when the balance of payments is not in equilibrium, policies other than exchange rate adjustments are needed to bring about a shift in the BB curve to achieve external balance.[6]

Suppose the macroeconomic goals of society are full employment, price stability, and balance of payments equilibrium. Let us assume that internal balance is achieved at point E with the combination i_0 and Y_0 while the economy is running a deficit in the balance of payments depicted by the curve BB' in Figure 8-4. If the exchange rate is fixed, some combination of a discretionary fiscal policy action (shifting the IS curve) and monetary policy action (shifting the LM curve) can be used to achieve internal-external equilibrium.

From the analysis in Chapter 3, we know that various combinations of fiscal and monetary actions will keep total demand such that the economy will remain at full employment Y_0 (that is, various combinations of the LM and IS curves can be used to keep the economy at Y_0). For expository ease, assume government purchases are used as the fiscal policy tool. The level of the monetary base $\bar{H}$ would be the monetary policy tool, but let us assume the monetary authority fixes the interest rate and then lets $\bar{H}$ be endogenous. Then the higher the level of $\bar{G}$, the higher the interest rate must be to keep the economy at the internal position Y_0, as shown by the line IE in Figure 8-5.

From the balance of payments equilibrium equation discussed earlier, we can see that various combinations of $\bar{G}$ and $\bar{i}$ can be used to keep $B = 0$. In general, the higher the level of $\bar{G}$, the greater the nominal value of imports since a higher $\bar{G}$ means a larger Y. Therefore, a larger value of i is required to maintain equilibrium in the current and capital accounts taken together. The external equilibrium curve (EE)—showing combinations of $\bar{G}$ and $\bar{H}$ keeping B equal to zero—also has a positive slope, as shown in Figure 8-5.

Which policy tool should be directed at which goal? Should fiscal policy be targeted at internal or external equilibrium? What should be the target for monetary policy? The answers to these questions depend on the *relative slopes* of the EE and IE curves in Figure 8-5. To ascertain the relative slope of the two curves, we begin with the internal equilibrium conditions

$$dY = C_{Y_d}(1 - \tau)\, dY + I_i\, d\bar{i} + d\bar{G} - \text{IM}_Y\, dY \qquad (8\text{-}23)$$

$$m\, dH = L_Y\, dY + L_i\, d\bar{i} \qquad (8\text{-}24)$$

---

[6] Changes in the exchange rate do, however, occur by official actions. In the case of deficits, a country may devalue its currency vis-à-vis gold and thus vis-à-vis all other currencies.

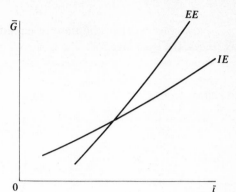

FIGURE 8-5
Internal and external equilibrium curves.

or

$$dY[1 - C_{Y_d}(1 - \tau) + IM_Y] = I_i \, d\bar{\imath} + d\bar{G}$$

$$dY - \frac{m}{L_Y} dH = -\frac{L_i}{L_Y} d\bar{\imath}$$

Solving for dY, we have

$$dY = \frac{\begin{vmatrix} I_i \, d\bar{\imath} + d\bar{G} & 0 \\ -\dfrac{L_i}{L_Y} d\bar{\imath} & -\dfrac{m}{L_Y} \end{vmatrix}}{\begin{vmatrix} 1 - C_{Y_d}(1 - \tau) + IM_Y & 0 \\ 1 & -\dfrac{m}{L_Y} \end{vmatrix}}$$

$$dY = \frac{-(I_i \, d\bar{\imath} + d\bar{G}) \dfrac{m}{L_Y}}{-\dfrac{m}{L_Y} [1 - C_{Y_d}(1 - \tau) + IM_Y]} \qquad (8\text{-}25)$$

$$dY = \frac{I_i \, d\bar{\imath} + d\bar{G}}{[1 - C_{Y_d}(1 - \tau) + IM_Y]} = 0 \qquad \text{(for equilibrium)}$$

Thus for equilibrium

$$d\bar{G} = -I_i \, d\bar{\imath}$$

and

$$\left. \frac{d\bar{G}}{d\bar{\imath}} \right|_{IE} = -I_i \qquad (8\text{-}26)$$

The slope of the *IE* curve is the absolute value of the change in domestic investment per unit change in the interest rate. A rise of 1 percentage point in the interest rate *reduces* aggregate demand by $I_i \, d\bar{\imath}$; it then takes an increase of $-I_i \, d\bar{\imath}$ in real G to offset the change and keep output constant.

Now consider the condition for equilibrium in the balance of payments (ignoring prices, the exchange rate, the other variables held constant):

$$dB = 0 = -IM_Y \, dY + KA_i \, di \qquad (8\text{-}27)$$

Substitute from (8-25) and collect terms:

$$0 = -IM_Y \left[\frac{I_i \, di + d\bar{G}}{1 - C_{Y_d}(1 - \tau) + IM_Y} \right] + KA_i \, di$$

$$IM_Y \left[\frac{d\bar{G}}{1 - C_{Y_d}(1 - \tau) + IM_Y} \right] = IM_Y \left[\frac{-I_i \, di}{1 - C_{Y_d}(1 - \tau) + IM_Y} \right] + KA_i \, di$$

$$\left. \frac{d\bar{G}}{di} \right|_{EE} = -I_i + KA_i[1 - C_{Y_d}(1 - \tau) + IM_Y]/IM_Y \qquad (8\text{-}28)$$

Equation (8-28) shows that the slope of *EE* is *greater* than the slope of *IE*. The reason is that a rise in the interest rate has an additional effect on the balance of payments other than via aggregate demand: *it improves the capital account balance.* This suggests a criterion for pairing the fiscal and monetary instruments and internal and external targets: *monetary policy should be directed at balance of payments equilibrium and fiscal policy at internal equilibrium.* This can be seen in Figure 8-6 where the *EE* and *IE* curves of Figure 8-5 are reproduced.

Suppose the economy is at point *A*—there is domestic equilibrium but the balance of payments shows a deficit (the interest rate would have to be i_1, with $\bar{G}$ at $\bar{G}_1$ to balance the foreign accounts). When the pairing principle above is used, the situation dictates a rise in i. This causes a move to i_1, which restores the balance of payments equilibrium but causes reduced demand and increased unemployment domestically. This in turn suggests the $\bar{G}$ should be increased, and so we move to point *C*. As the graph shows, continuous application of the pairing principle (given stability in the *IE* and *EE* curves) will produce movement toward point *J*, where both targets are achieved. The reader can satisfy himself that opposite pairing will lead to a continuous movement *away* from *J*, and the balance of payments and domestic equilibrium will require larger and larger change in i and $\bar{G}$.

The pairing principle reflects the fact that slope *EE* is greater than slope *IE*, or

$$\left. \frac{d\bar{G}}{di} \right|_{EE} > \left. \frac{d\bar{G}}{di} \right|_{IE}$$

or

$$\left(\frac{dB}{di} \bigg/ \frac{dB}{d\bar{G}} \right) > \left(\frac{dY}{di} \bigg/ \frac{dY}{d\bar{G}} \right)$$

or

$$\left(\frac{dB}{di} \bigg/ \frac{dY}{di} \right) > \left(\frac{dB}{d\bar{G}} \bigg/ \frac{dY}{d\bar{G}} \right) \qquad (8\text{-}29)$$

Equation (8-29) says that the impact of monetary policy is greater on the balance of payments than *Y relative to* the same comparison for $\bar{G}$. Thus the principle in essence is to target the policy instrument where it has its greater *relative* impact.

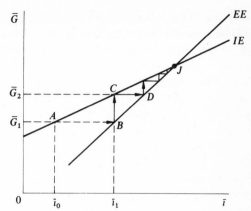

FIGURE 8-6
Internal and external equilibrium.

Since Mundell (1962) originated this argument, others (Ott and Ott, 1968) have shown that the monetary-external and fiscal-internal may not be the appropriate pairing for all cases and countries. In particular, imports may be sensitive not only to changes in the *level* of GNP, but to changes in the *composition* of GNP. Countries which have imports that are largely consumption goods, and which have interest-sensitive domestic investment but interest-insensitive capital accounts, may find that reverse pairing is appropriate for them. And even if the policy instruments are aimed at the correct targets, they may themselves be "bounded" so that large enough fiscal and/or monetary actions are not possible. For example, an interest rate of 12 percent and a tax cut of $30 billion, if that were necessary to close a United States payments deficit, might simply be politically impossible to implement. Thus, in many circumstances, recourse *must* be had to exchange rate changes, and in addition, frequent or even continuous exchange rate adjustments may be desirable for other reasons even if monetary and fiscal policy alone could maintain external-internal equilibrium. The next section discusses internal-external equilibrium under flexible exchange rates.

Flexible Exchange Rates

If the exchange rate is allowed to fluctuate when a balance-of-payments deficit or surplus exists, a depreciation[7] of the home currency (a fall in e) will shift BB down as the improvement in the current-account balance allows a lower interest rate at any level of income to keep the balance of payments in balance. An appreciation in the exchange rate (a rise in e) will have the opposite effects on the BB curve with higher interest rate accompanying the deterioration of the trade balance. With flexible

---

[7] A currency is said to depreciate when its value declines in terms of foreign currencies—when the number of units of foreign currency that can be obtained for a unit of domestic currency is reduced. A currency appreciates when its exchange value in terms of foreign currencies increases. Since we have defined e as, for example, francs per dollar, then depreciation of the dollar means more dollars are required per franc, and so e falls. A rise in e means the home currency has appreciated.

exchange rates, then, domestic or internal balance can be insulated from external adjustment; this is not the case under a fixed exchange system.

Under flexible exchange rates, the exchange rate fluctuates in response to changes in the supply of and demand for foreign exchange. Demand for and supply of foreign exchange are generated by both trade and capital accounts transactions. However, demand for and supply of foreign currencies are somewhat different from the usual concept of demand and supply. For example, the demand for United States currency is in itself a supply of foreign currencies, while the supply of United States currency is also a demand for foreign currencies. This can be illustrated by using our trade and capital accounts balance equation. A demand for foreign currencies arises from United States imports while the supply of foreign exchange results from exports. When United States importers buy foreign goods, they supply United States currency in the foreign exchange market in demanding foreign exchange to pay for imported goods. The demand for foreign currencies also comes from capital transactions. As United States capital flows abroad, dollars are supplied and foreign currencies are demanded. Thus, assuming a net capital inflow, the demand for foreign exchange is given by

$$D_{fe} = \frac{p_f}{e}(\text{IM}) \qquad (8\text{-}30)$$

The supply of foreign currencies arises from the demand by foreign importers for United States dollars, who are thus supplying their own currencies; from the demand by United States exporters exchanging their foreign earnings for United States dollars; and from net capital inflows, or

$$S_{fe} = p(\text{X}) + \text{KA}(i) \qquad (8\text{-}31)$$

The equilibrium rate of exchange (for example, francs per dollar) is established when the demand for foreign exchange equals the supply, at a point such as E in Figure 8-7 given by Eq. (8-32).

$$\frac{p_f}{e}(\text{IM}) = p(X) + \text{KA}(i) \qquad (8\text{-}32)$$

Since the exchange rate equilibrium equation is the equilibrium condition of the balance of payments equation, represented by the BB curve, then under a system of freely fluctuating exchange rates, automatic adjustment of the exchange rate takes place as demand for and supply of foreign exchange occur. A deficit in the balance of payments shifts the D_{fe} curve upward and lowers the exchange rate, while a surplus raises it. As long as e changes to clear the foreign exchange market for each level of i and Y, external equilibrium can be achieved by shifting the BB curve via exchange rate adjustment to intersect the IS–LM curve point of internal equilibrium.

Monetary and Fiscal Rules and Internal and External Balance

Because discretionary monetary and fiscal policy may act with substantial lags, they they may be too little or too late to be effective in achieving internal or external balance, and thus some economists have suggested more reliance on automatic

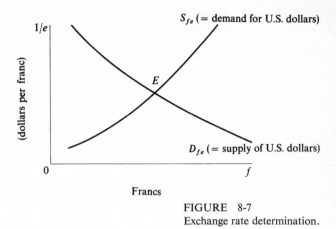

FIGURE 8-7
Exchange rate determination.

stabilization rules.[8] Under a "money rule," the Federal Reserve System would use its open market powers to produce some constant rate of growth in the money stock, to roughly match the secular rate of increase in real output. Under a "fiscal rule," the fiscal authorities would set government expenditures according to "needs" and set taxes to balance the budget at full employment. Surpluses or deficits in the government budget would be reflected in changes in the stock of money (as can be the case with deficits or surpluses in the balance of payments), and the money stock would change only as a sequence of such deficits or surpluses.

How well will these two rules—a balanced budget at full employment and a fixed rate of growth of the money supply—perform to achieve internal and external balance under a fixed or flexible exchange rate?

Start with a full-employment equilibrium position, depicted by point E in Figure 8-8, and assume that (1) government spending G is set at a "needs" level and the tax rate τ is set to produce budget balance at full employment ($G = T$ at Y_F); and (2) the exchange rate e is fixed. Suppose that in the next period there is an autonomous increase in world demand for United States exports and that Y_F is not changing. The BB curve will shift down, say, to BB' in Figure 8-8, since equilibrium in the balance of payments can now be achieved with a lower interest rate at any level of output. At the same time, the IS curve shifts up to IS', for the added export demand increases the interest rate required to preserve commodity equilibrium at any income level. Since under the money rule the money supply only changes as real output changes, the system will tend, in the short run, toward the point at which the IS and LM curves intersect, at least as long as international reserves permit. In Figure 8-8, this would be around point Z, with resulting inflationary pressure and a balance of payments surplus (the higher interest rate—i_2—tends to further increase the balance of payments surplus by causing an improvement in the capital account).

[8] See, for example, Friedman (1959, 1948), Bronfenbrenner (1961), Modigliani (1964), and Ott and Ott (1970).

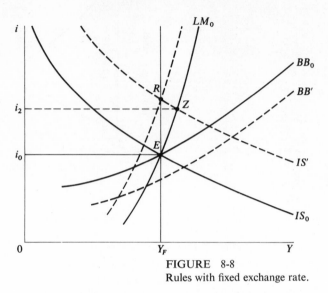

FIGURE 8-8
Rules with fixed exchange rate.

Under the budget rule, the results would be similar. Again assume that budget deficits or surpluses produce changes in the quantity of money (shifts in LM), but balance of payments surpluses or deficits are sterilized. If at the initial position the tax rate was set so that $G = T$ at Y_F, the shift in the IS curve due to the increased demand for exports will produce a budget surplus as aggregate spending rises above Y_F toward Z. This will cause the money stock to fall and the LM curve to shift leftward until it intersects IS' at R in Figure 8-8. Under the fiscal rule, there will be full employment and the rise in prices will cease, but again the balance of payments will shows a surplus. Thus, with *fixed exchange rates, neither* rule will operate to achieve internal and external balance simultaneously. The only solution in this case is to use discretionary policy.

If the exchange rate is allowed to *fluctuate* when a balance of payments deficit or surplus exists, both the BB and IS curves will shift. Suppose, under the money rule, that the four curves, Y_F, IS, LM, and BB, shift over time in a way such that a relationship such as shown in Figure 8-9 is produced in some period. The LM, BB, and Y_F curves all intersect at W, but some fiscal policy action or autonomous change in I has kept the IS curve from also intersecting at W. We assume that the position of the LM curve is set by the money rule. The system would tend toward equilibrium at point A under a fixed exchange rate, but now the balance of payments *deficit* at A (evidenced by the fact that at Y_0 the rate of interest i_0 is below that rate i_1 required for balance of payments equilibrium) will cause the exchange rate to depreciate. This will cause the BB curve to shift *down* and the IS curve to shift up. The new equilibrium output and interest must therefore be somewhere along AW, where the down-

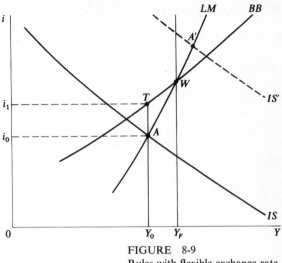

FIGURE 8-9
Rules with flexible exchange rate.

ward-shifting *BB* curve and the upward-shifting *IS* curve intersect one another. Alternatively, a strong increase in aggregate demand could shift the *IS* curve to *IS'*, and the exchange rate *appreciation* would shift *BB* up and *IS'* down to intersect somewhere along *A'W*—a situation where inflationary pressure would exist. Clearly, then, *the money rule will not even tend always to produce all three—full employment, price stability, and balance of payments equilibrium—under flexible exchange rates.*

Now consider the same situation where the fiscal rule is applied—where *budget* deficits or surpluses affect *M*. If the initial situation were as before with *IS*, *LM*, *BB*, and Y_F, but where the budget is set to balance only at Y_F, then as the exchange rate depreciated (beginning at point *A*), a budget deficit ($Y_0 < Y_F$) would exist and the *LM* curve would be shifting down. Not until the *IS*, *LM*, *BB*, and Y_F curves all intersect at the same point would the exchange rate cease to depreciate or the money stock cease to increase. In short, the link between the budget balance and the money stock would work in the proper direction *with* the change in the exchange rate to restore internal and external equilibrium. The adjustment of the exchange rate would shift *BB* and *IS* to intersect at a point on Y_F; the change in *M* brought by budget deficits or surpluses would shift the *LM* curve there too. In contrast, the money rule might not provide the *M* required to make the *LM* curve intersect *IS*, Y_F, and *BB* simultaneously anywhere, and inflationary pressures would develop when aggregate demand (foreign and domestic) grew rapidly and unemployment would persist when aggregate demand grew slowly.

In short, where a society's goals are full employment, price stability, and balance of payments equilibrium and it is desired to rely on fiscal or monetary rules, *flexible rates* are essential!

READINGS FOR CHAPTER 8

BRANSON, WILLIAM H.: *Macroeconomic Theory and Policy* (New York: Harper & Row, 1972), chap. 15.

BRONFENBRENNER, M.: "Statistical Tests of Rival Monetary Rules," *Journal of Political Economy*, pp. 1–14, February 1961.

FRIEDMAN, M.: *A Program for Monetary Stability* (New York: Fordham University Press, 1959), chap. IV.

FRIEDMAN, M.: "A Monetary and Fiscal Framework for Economic Stability," *American Economic Review*, June 1948.

HOUTHAKKER, H. S., and STEPHEN P. MAGEE, "Income and Price Elasticities in World Trade," *Review of Economics and Statistics*, May 1969.

MODIGLIANI, F.: "Some Empirical Tests of Monetary Management and Rules vs. Discretion," *Journal of Political Economy*, pp. 211–245, June 1964.

MUNDELL, ROBERT A.: "The Appropriate Use of Monetary and Fiscal Policy for Internal and External Stability," *IMF Staff Papers*, vol. IX, pp. 70–79, March 1962.

———: "Capital Mobility and Stabilization Policy Levels Fixed and Flexible Exchange Rates," *Canadian Journal of Economics and Political Science*, vol. XXIX, pp. 475–485, November 1963.

OTT, DAVID J., and ATTIAT F. OTT: "Monetary and Fiscal Policy: Goals and the Choice of Instruments," *Quarterly Journal of Economics*, vol. LXXXII, pp. 313–325, May 1968.

———: "The Workings of the Fiscal Rule in a Closed and an Open Economy," *Economic Internazionale*, February 1970.

WHITMAN, MARINA V. N.: *Policies for Internal and External Balance* (Princeton, N.J.: Princeton, 1970).

9

THE DEMAND FOR MONEY AND
OTHER FINANCIAL ASSETS

The only financial asset explicit in the simple income-determination models of Chapter 3 was money—demand deposits plus currency outside banks—and securities issued by business firms. Yet even a cursory look at the financial items in the balance sheets of households and firms in the United States, in Table 9-1, shows how much of an oversimplification this is.

Clearly we could not hope to treat separately with *each* of the assets held by the private sector and still keep our models to manageable size; *some* abstraction from reality is essential. However, it also seems obvious that grouping assets into only two categories—securities and money—limits severely the relevance of any conclusions that might be drawn. To avoid both these difficulties, we will combine the assets held by the private sector into a few categories and treat all the assets in a category as a single asset. The asset categories and the specific assets included in each category are shown in Table 9-2.

The remainder of the chapter discusses demand functions for money, time deposits, savings shares, and securities. Since by far the bulk of the work on asset demand has dealt specifically with money, the bulk of the chapter is devoted to this subject.

Table 9-1 FINANCIAL ITEMS IN THE BALANCE SHEETS OF UNITED STATES HOUSEHOLDS AND FIRMS, DECEMBER 31, 1972
(Billions of dollars)

Households

Financial assets		Financial liabilities	
Demand deposits and currency	156.5	Mortgages	357.9
Time deposits at commercial banks	248.6	Consumer credit	157.5
Savings accounts at savings		Bank loans, n.e.c.	21.0
institutions	319.9	Other loans	23.6
Life insurance reserves	143.7	Security credit	17.7
Pension fund reserves	309.2	Trade credit	6.2
U.S. government securities	92.2	Deferred and unpaid life	
State and local government		Insurance premiums	6.0
securities	46.0		
Corporate and foreign bonds	54.8		
Corporate stock	967.3		
Mortgage	37.3		
Commercial paper	1.1		
Security credit	5.0		
Miscellaneous	31.3		
Total assets	2413.1		590.0

Nonfinancial Business Firms*

Financial assets		Financial liabilities	
Demand deposits and currency	55.3	Corporate bonds	198.3
Time deposits at commercial banks	20.2	Mortgages	202.1
Securities	65.9†	Bank loans, n.e.c.	147.4
Trade credit	215.2	Other loans	55.0
Other	114.4	Trade debt, net	183.1
		Other	28.5
Total assets	470.9	Total liabilities	814.4

* Includes nonfinancial corporations, noncorporate nonfinancial firms, and farm businesses.
† Separate figures by type of security not available for all nonfinancial business.

SOURCE: Board of Governors, Federal Reserve System, *Federal Reserve Bulletin* (September 1973), A 71.20–A 71.21

Table 9-2 ASSET CATEGORIES AND ASSETS INCLUDED IN EACH CATEGORY

Category	Assets included
1 Money	Demand deposits Currency outside banks
2 Commercial bank time deposits	Commercial bank time deposits
3 Savings shares	Savings and loan deposits Mutual savings bank deposits Credit union deposits Life insurance company reserves Assets of pension funds (private)
4 Securities	Federal government securities State and local government securities Corporate bonds Corporate stock Mortgages Trade credit

THE DEMAND FOR MONEY

A great deal of the literature and effort in the field of monetary economics has always been centered on the demand for money. This has been perhaps even more the case in the last fifteen or so years. In large part this reflects the explicit or implicit use of the simple income-determination model of Chapter 3, in which the interest and income responsiveness of the demand for money is so important to the size of the fiscal and monetary policy multipliers. It also is another manifestation of the growing tendency to follow up economic theory with econometric analysis.

Here we shall first discuss the theoretical approaches to the demand for money, which lead to somewhat different testable hypotheses. Then we will attempt a brief summary of the major empirical studies of recent years.

The Theoretical Issues

At least three major theoretical issues surround the demand for money. First, *how is money to be defined*? Some writers (Gurley, 1960) use a broad concept like "liquid assets," embracing currency outside banks, demand deposits, time deposits at commercial banks, and credit unions, as well as short-term government securities. Others (Latané, 1954) use the narrow definition covering only the first two items above. Still others (Friedman, 1959) choose definitions in between, such as currency outside banks and bank deposits (demand *and* time). In the Brookings–SSRC model of the United States economy, de Leeuw (1965) estimated the demand for currency, demand deposits, and time deposits separately. The importance of this question is that the definition of money employed may make considerable difference as to which variables are significant in estimating the demand for money.

We shall use the "narrow" definition; i.e., money will be considered to be currency outside banks plus demand deposits adjusted, or M_1 as it is now commonly called. There are at least two justifications for this. First, this is the most common definition of money employed by researchers in the field of monetary economics. Second, although assets shade almost imperceptibly away from each other in their liquidity, there seems to be a sharper break in liquidity at this point than at any other; all assets other than demand deposits and currency have to be converted into either the deposits or currency in order to be spent, and in this sense, only demand deposits and currency are truly the "medium of exchange."

There is no need to be rigid about this delineation of money. The point to keep in mind is that the demand function derived using different definitions of money may differ in its characteristics, and this we shall watch for as we go along.

This leads to the second major issue: *What variables should be included in the money demand function and how should they be defined*? Bearing directly on this issue is the way of approaching the demand for money. Until recently, and under the particular influence of Keynes's *The General Theory of Employment, Interest and Money*, the demand for money was approached in what may be called a "compartmentalized" fashion; the demand for money was divided up into the "transactions demand," the "precautionary demand," and the "speculative demand," and each was studied separately. The relevant variables in the resulting aggregate demand-for-money function were usually assumed to be income (or the volume of transactions), the rate of interest, and (sometimes) wealth. More recently, monetary theorists have tended to approach the demand for money as a special topic in capital theory, much like the demand for any durable good, and to downgrade the compartmentalized approach. A result of this is that income (or transactions) in the usual sense of the term has been left out as a variable, and the functions have had as their major arguments wealth (as a budget constraint) and rates of interest or return. A very important controversy has been carried on over just how significant interest rates are in the demand function, with some holding them to be insignificant and others finding them very significant. Finally, there are arguments about *which* concepts of "wealth" and interest rates are the proper ones.

The last major issue concerning the demand function for money is the *stability of that function*. The effects of monetary policy actions on the economic system cannot be predicted or explained if the demand for money shifts about often and significantly with (say) changes in expectations or the general institutional setting. So it is of some considerable interest and concern for monetary policy to ascertain the stability of the money demand function.

The Keynesian Approach—Segmenting the Demand for Money

Money is demanded because of the relevance of time, uncertainty, and credit market imperfections to any realistic economic model. The orthodox approach to the demand for money is to split it up into balances held for different reasons—the transactions, precautionary, and speculative demands for cash. Let us first review this approach to the demand for money.

THE TRANSACTIONS DEMAND FOR MONEY

Suppose we could visualize a perfect economy where all transactions occurred in an instantaneous, timeless way. In such an economy, there would be no need for cash; receipts and expenditures would occur simultaneously and people would not need money balances to bridge the gap between receipts and expenditures. It is just because of the fact that receipts and expenditures are *not* synchronized in the real world that we have a transactions demand for cash. Spending units in the real world typically receive income at various points in time, while their expenditures are usually distributed more uniformly in between receipts.[1]

---

[1] Brunner and Meltzer (1971) show that this point can be turned upside down—the presence of a money asset implies that cost-minimizing economic units will be led to adopt a pattern of receipts and expenditures that are not synchronized. However, for expository purposes we shall use the conventional argument.

Even if receipts and expenditures are *not* synchronized, money would still not be demanded to bridge the receipts-spending gap if there were a credit market and it were perfect—if individuals could borrow or loan in infinitely small amounts with certainty of repayment and no costs of investment or disinvestment. A spending unit under such circumstances could loan his receipts until needed to those whose expenditures precede their receipts, receiving repayment as needed for making expenditures. However, we shall assume here, as is the case, that loans *cannot* be made in infinitely small amounts, and that there *are* costs (for trouble and time as well as for the services) involved in making and receiving such loans. These imperfections make necessary a demand for cash balances to bridge receipts-expenditure gaps rather than bridging them with lending and borrowing.

The transactions demand for money balances will arise then when receipts and expenditures are not perfectly synchronized *and* where in such circumstances loans are not perfectly divisible and/or transactions costs are connected with loans. It will be useful for us to pursue these general conclusions in a more rigorous fashion.[2]

Suppose that a certain spending unit, in a particular period, has expenditure transactions of the value T/f, when T is the dollar value of total annual transactions and f is the number of payment periods per year, to be made in a uniform way over the period (where there is no uncertainty as to their timing). Suppose his receipts are certain and come in a lump sum at the end of the period, and suppose during the period he finances his expenditures by borrowing cash. Each time he borrows cash, a "broker's fee" b is charged, which is constant regardless of the size of the borrowing. In addition, he must pay an interest rate i/f on the loans contracted. Suppose he borrows cash in lots of C dollars distributed uniformly throughout the period.

Now it is fairly obvious that any value of C equal to or less than T/f will allow our spending unit to meet his expenditures equally well if he borrows the money often enough. For example, if his planned expenditures are \$100, he can borrow \$100 one time, \$50 twice, or \$25 four times. Thus, whatever the value of each borrowing, C, the *number* of borrowings, will be given by T/fC.[3] If he pays a broker's fee of b at each borrowing, total credit transactions costs will be bT/fC.

Since our spending unit spends each borrowing C in a steady stream and borrows again the moment it is exhausted, his average money balance during the payment period will be given by $C/2$. His interest cost per payment period involved in bridging the expenditure gap by borrowing will be given by $(i/f)\{(T/f + C)/2\}$.[4] The total

---

[2] The following analysis is that presented by Baumol (1952). Virtually the same results were obtained by Tobin (1956).

[3] Thus if the credit market is perfect and credit transactions can be infinitely small $C = 0$ and T/C approaches infinity. Here there would be no transactions demand for cash.

[4] This is derived as follows. The general statement for the total interest cost (R) per payment period is

$$R = C\frac{i}{f} + C\frac{i}{f}\left(1 - \frac{C}{T/f}\right) + C\frac{i}{f}\left(1 - 2\frac{C}{T/f}\right) + \cdots + C\frac{i}{f}\left[1 - (n-1)\frac{C}{T/f}\right]$$

cost involved in obtaining money to bridge the expenditures-receipt gap will then be

$$b\frac{T}{fC} + \frac{i}{f}\left(\frac{T/f + C}{2}\right) \qquad (9\text{-}1)$$

i.e., the sum of the interest costs and broker's fees (credit transactions costs). The rational spending unit would then determine the optimum size of each uniform borrowing (and also the number of borrowings T/Cf and average money balance $C/2$) by selecting a value of C that will minimize total costs, as given in expression (9-1). This is given by setting the derivative of (9-1) with respect to C equal to zero:

$$-\frac{bT}{fC^2} + \frac{i}{2f} = 0$$

That is,[5]

$$C = \sqrt{\frac{2bT}{i}} \qquad (9\text{-}2)$$

---

where $n = T/Cf$. For example, if $T/f = \$100$, $C = \$25$, and $\frac{i}{f} = 0.04$, total interest costs are

$$R = \$25(0.04) + \$25(0.04)(1 - \tfrac{1}{4}) + \$25(0.04)(1 - \tfrac{2}{4})$$
$$+ \$25(0.04)(1 - \tfrac{3}{4})$$
$$= \$1.00 + 0.75 + 0.50 + 0.25$$
$$= \$2.50$$

The above general expression simplifies as follows:

$$R = C\frac{i}{f}\left\{1 + \left(1 - \frac{Cf}{T}\right) + \left(1 - \frac{2Cf}{T}\right) + \cdots + \left[1 - (n-1)\frac{Cf}{T}\right]\right\}$$

There are obviously n number of 1's in the series. Further, the sum of $(n-1)$ Cf/T's multiplied successively by $1, 2, 3, \ldots, n-1$ is $(-1)(n-1)n/2(Cf/T)$. The above then becomes

$$R = C\frac{i}{f}\left[n - \frac{Cf}{T} - 2\frac{Cf}{T} - \cdots - (n-1)\frac{Cf}{T}\right]$$
$$= C\frac{i}{f}n + C\frac{i}{f}\frac{Cf}{T}[-1-2-3-\cdots-(n-1)]$$
$$= C\frac{i}{f}n + \frac{C\frac{i}{f}Cf}{T}\left[\frac{(n-1)n}{2}\right](-1)$$
$$= C\frac{i}{f}\left[n - \frac{Cf}{T}\frac{(n-1)n}{2}\right]$$

Since $Cf/T = 1/n$, we get

$$R = C\frac{i}{f}\left(n - \frac{n-1}{2}\right)$$
$$= C\frac{i}{f}\left(\frac{2n - n + 1}{2}\right)$$
$$= C\frac{i}{f}\left(\frac{n+1}{2}\right) = C\frac{i}{f}\left(\frac{T/Cf + 1}{2}\right) = \frac{i}{f}\left(\frac{T/f + C}{2}\right)$$

[5] Note that even if it is possible for C to equal zero, there still will be a transactions demand for cash if b is positive. If there is a credit transaction cost, or broker's fee as we have termed it, it obviously would not pay an individual to carry on an infinite number of credit transactions and incur a fee of b for each one. He will carry out just that number of borrowings which will minimize the sum of the broker's fees and interest costs. If, on the other hand, interest costs were zero, it would pay our spending unit to carry out just one big borrowing at the first of the period, for then his only concern is to minimize the broker's fee. Tobin (1956) also stresses the point that many units have a "corner solution", i.e., they carry out no bond transaction.

The average cash balance $\bar{C}$ per period ($=C/2$) is thus

$$\bar{C} = \sqrt{\frac{bT}{2i}} \qquad (9\text{-}2a)$$

In our simple example, we find that, *given* the receipts-expenditure pattern, the spending unit's demand for cash balances $\bar{C}$ is positively related to the costs of credit transactions b and the value of *annual* expenditures T and inversely related to the interest rate i. A rise in the costs of credit transactions and/or the value of expenditures will increase the spending unit's transactions demand for money; a fall in b or T will produce a decline in the transactions demand for money. The reverse is of course true for a rise or fall in i, the interest rate.

It is important to note in our simple case that the transactions demand ($9\text{-}2a$) does *not* vary *proportionately* with T, the annual value of expenditures. Instead, it varies in proportion to the *square root* of the value of transactions, or *less* than proportionately. This implies that there are, in effect, economies of scale with respect to the use of money for transactions purposes. At higher and higher expenditure levels, the ratio of cash required for transactions purposes to expenditures could be expected to decline. The nature of the relation of the transactions demand for cash to the value of expenditures suggested by our simple case (assuming i and b given) is indicated in Figure 9-1.[6] If the transactions demand for money of *all* spending units in the economy conform to this general pattern, we may say that, given the receipts-expenditure patterns, the aggregate demand for transactions balances is a function of the value of total transactions, the interest rate, and broker's fees:

$$M_d{}^t = L_1(T, i, b) \qquad (9\text{-}3)$$

where T now refers to the *aggregate* value of transactions.

The form of the transactions demand for cash in logarithms from Eq. ($9\text{-}2a$) would be

$$\log M_d{}^t = 0.5 \log b + 0.5 \log T - 0.5 \log 2 - 0.5 \log i \qquad (9\text{-}2b)$$

Thus the a priori suggestion from this inventory-theoretic model is that the interest and transactions elasticities of the demand for money will be approximately 0.5 (in absolute value).

The simple case used here relates to the transactions demand of spending units in two general situations: that of a spending unit whose receipts come at the end of the period and who borrows during the period (in anticipation of future receipts) to obtain transactions balances, and that of a spending unit who disinvests during the period to obtain cash balances. There is also the possibility that some spending units may have their receipts at the beginning of the period, and thus have the option of

---

[6] However, a doubling of *all* prices, *including b*, *will double* the demand for cash for transactions purposes, as substitution in Eq. ($9\text{-}2a$) will show. This means a doubling of T due to a *doubling* of the *number* of transactions *will not double C* (and $C/2$), while a doubling of T due to a *doubling* of the *average value* of cash transactions *will double C* and $C/2$.

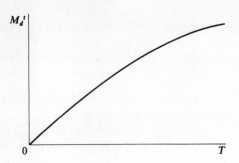

FIGURE   9-1
Transactions and the transactions demand
for cash.

either holding all or part of those receipts in cash until it is needed or investing all or
part of the receipts in a way that the investment will mature over the expenditure
period when needed for expenditures. This case, when followed through, produces
the same results as the simpler case we have already looked at, namely, that C will
vary positively with the square root of the value of expenditures and broker's fees
and negatively with i. Hence it will not be explored here.[7]

The same results also follow if b is allowed to vary with the *value* of borrowing
or disinvesting transactions rather than be assumed constant.[8]

The relation between the value of transactions and the transactions demand for
cash needs to be qualified, however. For when T changes, i.e., when the total amount

[7] In such a situation, bond transactions cost will again be $b\,\dfrac{T}{Cf}$.

Initial bond holdings will be given by

$$\left(\frac{T}{Cf} - 1\right)\left(T\Big/\frac{T}{C}\right) = \left(\frac{T}{Cf} - 1\right)C$$

Average bond holdings will then be given by

$$\left(\frac{T}{Cf} - 1\right)\frac{C}{2}$$

The individuals' interest income will be

$$\left(\frac{T}{Cf} - 1\right)\frac{Ci}{2}$$

where i is the market rate of interest. His total profits will then be

$$P = \frac{\left(\dfrac{T}{Cf} - 1\right)\dfrac{Ci}{f}}{2} - \frac{Tb}{Cf} \tag{1}$$

To find the optimum value of each disinvestment or bond sale, we find dP/dC and
set the results equal to zero.

$$\frac{dP}{dC} = \frac{bT}{C^2 f} - \frac{i}{2f} = 0$$

$$C = \sqrt{\frac{2bT}{i}}$$

[8] If we write the broker's fees as $b + kC$, then in (1) (footnote 7) it becomes

$$\frac{T}{Cf}(b + kC) = \frac{Tb}{fC} + \frac{kT}{f}$$

The additional term kT/f drops out in differentiating, and we have the same result
as before.

of receipts and expenditures rises or falls, there is likely to be an effect on the *timing* or *structure* of receipts or payments. We have assumed that payments are made in a uniform way over the period and that the pattern of receipts is given, that there is a given *structure* of payments and receipts. But when (say) T rises, the structure or timing of payments is unlikely to be unchanged. If an individual's income rises by X percent, it is not likely that all payments will rise in the same proportion. Some will rise more and some less, depending on how the added income is allocated among purchases. This will change the structure or timing of payments, and this will affect the transactions demand apart from the change in the *total* value of transactions (Turvey, 1960). Given the pattern of receipts, if payments coming later in the period are increased more than proportionate to the increase in total payments, then required transactions balances would be increased by a greater proportion than where all payments were still made at a uniform rate. On the other hand, a greater proportionate increase of payments early in the period can cause transactions demand to rise less than it otherwise would for a given increase in total payments.

In short, the effect of a change in T on $M_d{}^t$ will depend on how the change in T affects the timing of receipts and expenditures.

Over the long run, institutional and social changes will also affect the timing or structure of receipts and payments and thus the transactions demand for money. Changes in payment patterns such as installment buying and credit cards will affect the transactions balance. Furthermore, the total transactions demand reflects the *number* of spending units. If they should integrate, the total demand for such balances would fall, and vice versa.

In studying the demand for money over a long period of time, changes in the timing of payments and receipts may be important. Here we shall assume that they are not; we assume given receipts-expenditure patterns and concentrate on the other variables affecting the demand for money.

In much of the theoretical and most of the empirical work on the demand for money in recent years, the assumption is made that aggregate money income is a reliable proxy for the total value of transactions. Let us consider briefly whether the assumption is correct.[9]

Consider the relation between gross national product and the money value of transactions. Starting with GNP, we must make several adjustments to arrive at a figure for total transactions (Turvey, 1960).

1 GNP

2 − all imputed items in GNP and gross business saving (capital consumption allowances and retained earnings)

3 + GNP net of above items

4 + transfer payments and net government and consumer interest payments

5 + intermediate goods and services purchases

6 + payments for existing real and financial assets

[9] The following several paragraphs draw heavily on an unpublished paper by Samuel B. Chase, Jr. (1965).

Item 2 adjusts GNP to exclude nonmonetary transactions. Item 3 is required because the transactions in GNP are two-sided—business has to hold transactions balances to finance factor payments and the recipients of factor payments have to hold money to finance their *purchases* of the goods produced. In item 4 transfer payments and net government and consumer interest are added because they represent transactions excluded from the income and product accounts. The entries in 5 and 6 are for the same reason: transactions in securities and existing physical assets require cash balances but are not in the income and product accounts.

Clearly there is no reason why GNP and T should always move together. In fact GNP is a relatively small proportion of total transactions—GNP was about $676 billion in 1965, while total transactions were on the order of $5 *trillion*, or seven times GNP (Duesenberry, 1967). It would not in fact be at all surprising if the GNP/T ratio varied both over the business cycle and secularly.

Some computations by Chase do in fact suggest considerable divergence in the short-run and long-run movements of T and GNP. Using quarterly, seasonally adjusted data on bank debits, he found very low correlation coefficients between various measures of money income, including GNP, and T for the period 1951–1964.[10]

The significance of this general tendency to employ a poor proxy (income) for total transactions will become clear at a later juncture. For the present, we note simply that an aggregate transactions demand for money may be written as

$$M_d^t = L_1(T, i, b) \qquad (9\text{-}3)$$

$$L_T > 0 \qquad L_i < 0 \qquad L_b > 0$$

or if aggregate money income is an adequate proxy for T, it may be written as

$$M_d^t = L_1(pY, i, b) \qquad (9\text{-}3a)$$

The form of the function suggested by the theory is

$$\log M_d^t = 0.5 \log b + 0.5 \log T - 0.5 \log 2 - 0.5 \log i \qquad (9\text{-}3b)$$

To sum up, we have seen that one element in the demand for money balances is the transactions demand, which arises out of imperfect synchronization of receipts and expenditures and less than perfect credit markets. The demand for money for transactions purposes is a positive function of money income and credit transactions costs, and is negatively related to the interest rate.

THE PRECAUTIONARY DEMAND FOR CASH

The precautionary motive for holding cash is a reflection of uncertainty which exists in the real world. In particular, *uncertainty* regarding the *timing* of receipts and expenditures gives rise to a demand for money over and above the transactions demand,

---

[10] The measures of income used by Chase were GNP, GNP minus government purchases of goods and services, net national product, disposable personal income, and "permanent net national product." The highest correlation coefficient was 0.372, for disposable personal income.

which is caused by lack of synchronization of receipts and payments even though their *timing* is certain (as in the model above).

The optimal balance to hold as a precaution against the uncertain timing of a spending unit's receipts and expenditures can be derived in a manner somewhat analogous to the optimum transactions balance.[11] Consider the variables that must be weighed in deciding on the optimal quantity of precautionary balances. First, there is the expected *cost of illiquidity*—the costs of selling off securities or other assets to cover an unexpected deficit (like the broker's fee b above), the cost of unplanned borrowing, or even possibly the cost of bankruptcy where the unit has no assets that can be sold or used to provide collateral for the borrowing needed to cover the deficit. If we denote the cost of covering an unplanned deficit as c, per occurrence, the expected cost of illiquidity is the probability of a deficit p times its cost, or pc.

In addition to the cost of illiquidity, the spending unit must consider the opportunity cost of tying up resources in the form of cash. If money pays no pecuniary return, the opportunity cost of holding M^p dollars of precautionary balances is the rate of interest i times M^p (if money pays interest, it is the difference between the bond rate of interest and the money rate of interest).

Thus the cost E of guarding oneself against illiquidity by holding precautionary balances is

$$E = M^p i + pc \qquad (9\text{-}4)$$

Now we must find an expression for the probability of a deficit p. Suppose the probability distribution of expected net deficits has a mean zero and a dispersion defined by the standard deviation. Then a given degree of certainty against unexpected deficits can be defined as some multiple K of the standard deviation s of net expected deficits. That is, the probability that the net expected deficit will deviate from its mean by *more* than Ks can be shown to be equal to or less than $1/K^2$.[12] With the expected value of net deficits assumed to be zero, any value of K can be written

$$K = M^p/s \qquad (9\text{-}5)$$

The probability of illiquidity is then

$$p \le \frac{1}{(M^p/s)^2} \qquad (9\text{-}6)$$

and for the most conservative behavior,

$$p = s^2/(M^p)^2 \qquad (9\text{-}6a)$$

Substituting (9-6a) into (9-4), we get, for the costs of managing precautionary cash balances,

$$E = M^p i + [s^2/(M^p)^2]c \qquad (9\text{-}4a)$$

[11] The analysis in this section relies heavily on an article by Edward L. Whalen (1966).
[12] See Whalen (1966, p. 317).

As with transactions balances, we solve for the optimum balance (for precautionary purposes now) by setting the derivative of (9-3a) with respect to M^p equal to zero:

$$0 = i - 2cs^2(M^p)^{-3}$$

$$M^p = \sqrt[3]{\frac{2s^2c}{i}} \qquad (9\text{-}7)$$

This equation is analogous to the transactions demand equation derived earlier. In fact, if a normal distribution of net deficits is assumed and if T changes because of changes in the number of transactions and not their average size, then s^2 varies proportionately with T, so that (9-7) can be written

$$M_d{}^p = \sqrt[3]{\frac{2\gamma Tc}{i}} \qquad (9\text{-}8)$$

where γ is the proportionality factor between s^2 and T.

The precautionary demand for money in (9-8) can be combined with the transactions demand in (9-3b) to get

$$\log M_d{}^t + \log M_d{}^p = 0.5 \log b + 0.83 \log T$$

$$+ 0.33 \log c - 0.83 \log i + Q \qquad (9\text{-}9)$$

where Q represents logs of constant terms not shown separately. In general form, we have thus far

$$M_d{}^{t+p} = L(T, i, b, c) \qquad (9\text{-}10)$$

or where pY is a good proxy for T:

$$M_d{}^{t+p} = L(pY, i, b, c)$$

THE SPECULATIVE DEMAND FOR MONEY: THE DEMAND FOR MONEY AS AN ASSET

Uncertainty is important in giving rise to still a third motive for demanding cash under the Keynesian approach. This uncertainty is that regarding the *future prices of claims to given streams of income*. It is argued that money balances are demanded because spending units speculate on future interest rates; this speculation is related to *uncertain* expectations of the levels of future interest rates.

The reason spending units are concerned with future interest rates is that capital values of claims to streams of income, because of imperfect credit markets, vary inversely with market interest rates. In present-day economies, bonds or other claims to income are issued subject to the rate of interest prevailing at the time of issue. If the market rate at time of issue is 3 percent, a bond representing claim to $30 per year in perpetuity will cost $1,000. If there is imperfect contract renegotiation, the price of this claim will vary as the market rate of interest varies. Should the market rate rise to 4 percent, the claim to $30 per year will cost only $750. In other words, if the coupon rate is fixed at 3 percent, but the market rate of interest varies, the *price* of the claim has to be adjusted to bring the coupon rate and market rate into equality. If there were perfect contract renegotiation, however, the coupon rate could be adjusted to every change in the market rate, and the capital value of the claim would not vary.

Since perfect contract renegotiation is not common, capital values of claims, such as bonds, are subject to considerable fluctuation as market rates of interest vary. It is this fluctuation in capital value that could give rise to the desire of spending units to hold cash as an asset rather than purchase interest-earning assets. Suppose an individual is offered a perpetuity bond bearing a coupon rate of 3 percent at a time when the market rate of interest is also 3 percent. If he decides to purchase it, during the first year he will earn an interest income of $30. However, he will decide against buying the asset if he suspects a change in interest rates will occur that will lower the capital value of the security by more than $30 at the time he expects to sell it—in such a circumstance he would rather hold cash, if this is the alternative. This means that if he expects interest rates to rise between the time of purchase and next year from 3.00 to 3.09 percent, he would hold cash rather than purchase the asset. On the other hand, it would clearly be to his advantage to purchase the asset if he expected interest rates either to rise by *less* than 0.09 percentage points or to fall between this year and next year.

To put the point differently (Tobin, 1958), suppose the individual expects a certain rate of interest i_e at the end of the year when redemption is to occur. For every dollar he invests in perpetuity bonds today he will earn i interest and a capital gain or loss g. It is clear that g is[13]

$$g = \frac{i}{i_e} - 1 \qquad (9\text{-}11)$$

Given his expected i_e, the individual will buy all bonds if

$$i + g > 0$$

and hold all cash if

$$i + g \leq 0$$

[13] In the previous example, if i is 3.0% and i_e is 4.0%, then

$$\$1000g = \frac{\$1000i}{i_e} - \$1000$$

$$= \frac{30}{0.04} - \$1000$$

$$= -\$250$$

$$g = -\$0.25$$

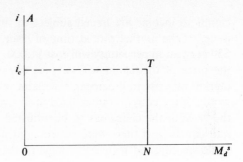

FIGURE 9-2
Individual's speculative demand for money.

But $i + g$ are equal to

$$i + \frac{i}{i_e} - 1$$

and solving for the i that makes this equal to zero we get i_c, the *critical* current rate of interest,

$$i\left(1 + \frac{1}{i_e}\right) = 1$$

$$i = \frac{1}{1 + 1/i_e}$$

$$i_c = \frac{i_e}{1 + i_e} \qquad (9\text{-}12)$$

At current rates of interest *above* i_c, the individual will hold none of his assets in cash. At $i \leq i_c$ he will hold *all* his assets in the form of cash.

In short, when the individual has taken care of his transactions and precautionary requirements, his *speculative demand* for money will appear as in Figure 9-2. At a current rate of interest *above* i_c, the individual will hold no cash in his asset portfolio; at rates below i_c he will hold his total portfolio in the form of cash. His speculative demand for cash is shown by $Ai_c TN$.

So far we have assumed that the individual's i_e does not change as i does. Instead we may assume that as i changes, i_e varies:

$$i_e = \phi(i)$$

and therefore

$$i_c = \frac{\phi(i)}{1 + \phi(i)} = g(i)$$

This is illustrated in Figure 9-3. Line i_e shows the relation of i and i_e; i_c shows the relation of i_c and i. Again, where $i_c = i$, that is, at i_0, the individual is on the margin of holding all cash or all bonds. At $i > i_0$ (and i_c), he will hold all bonds. At $i < i_0$ (and i_c) he will hold all cash. Plotting his speculative demand for cash against i will yield the same "step" function shown in Figure 9-2.

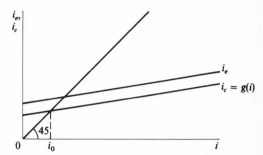

FIGURE 9-3
Relation between the expected rate of
interest, the critical rate of interest, and
the current rate of interest.

However, suppose the $g(i)$ function—the critical rate of interest—has a slope *greater* than unity, as in Figure 9-3a. In this case, as i rises above i_0, where $i_c = i$, the critical rate of interest rises *above* i, and so the individual will hold all cash. As i falls below i_0, the individual will hold all bonds since in this case $i > i_c$. That is, if the $g(i)$ function has the shape shown in Figure 9-3a, the demand for money is *positively* related to the rate of interest. The conditions under which this might arise are given by differentiating $g(i)$ with respect to i:

$$i_c = \frac{\phi(i)}{1 + \phi(i)}$$

$$\frac{di_c}{di} = \frac{\phi_i[1 + \phi(i)] - \phi_i\phi(i)}{[1 + \phi(i)]^2} \tag{9-13}$$

and

$$g_i = \frac{di_c}{di} = \frac{\phi_i}{[1 + \phi(i)]^2} \tag{9-13a}$$

Since $[1 + \phi(i)]^2 > 1$, for g_i to be greater than unity $\phi_i > [1 + \phi(i)]^2$ or $di_e/di > (1 + i_e)^2$.

Another assumption was implicitly made above that must now be clarified. In Figure 9-2, we spoke of the "given" asset portfolio of our individual (ON). We must now consider that as the current rate of interest i varies, the *value* of the financial assets held by our individual will vary, since the market value of bonds varies inversely

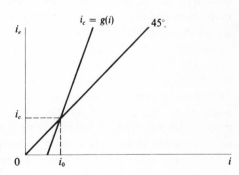

FIGURE 9-3a
Elastic expectations and the critical rate
of interest.

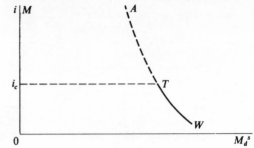

FIGURE 9-4
Individual's speculative demand for
money.

with that rate. Suppose, in Figure 9-4, the curve AW shows, on the horizontal axis,
the value of the individual's financial assets at each i. His speculative demand for
money then is $Mi_c TW$. If we could assume that different individuals have varying
i_c's (their expectations of future rates as related to the current rate are different),
then aggregating their individual demand curves for speculative money balances
would produce a curve such as the heavy one shown in Figure 9-5. If expectations
concerning i_e (and its relations to i) were the *same* for each individual, the speculative
demand for money would be as $Mi_c TW$ in Figure 9-4, where AW represents the
financial assets of the whole community instead of one individual. Note that at some
high i in Figure 9-5 (i_h) the demand for speculative balances is zero; this is that i
which is just above the *highest* i_c of any individual. At a low i, i_L in Figure 9-5, the
aggregate demand for money for speculative purposes becomes equal to the aggregate
value of the community's assets (shown in Figure 9-5 by the curve AW); this is that
i just *below* the *lowest* i_c of any individual in the community.

It is important to stress again that the speculative demand for money rests on
the assumption that expectations of individuals regarding future interest rates *are*
uncertain. If everyone had certain expectations regarding future interest rates, there
would be no speculative demand for money. In this case, it would always pay to
hold an earning asset rather than money. If an individual knew with certainty that
interest rates would rise by 1 percentage point on next May 15, he could buy an earning
asset now, sell it on May 14 at the same interest rate at which it was bought (the
same price), and buy another asset on May 15, holding it until just prior to the next
change in interest rates, and so on, preserving all the while the original value of his
investment and receiving the interest income. It is essential to the speculative motive
for money that individuals' expectations regarding future interest rates be uncertain;
it is in this sense that uncertainty gives rise to a speculative demand for money.

The theory of the speculative demand for money is unsatisfactory. Most
important, it produces the conclusion, not at all in accord with what we actually
observe of individual behavior, that an investor holds *either* all money *or* all earning
assets in his portfolio. If, as the actual facts seem to indicate, investors typically
diversify their portfolios, holding some cash and some earning assets, this approach,
to hold money as an asset, certainly seems to have basic limitations.

An alternative and more general approach to the demand for money as an asset

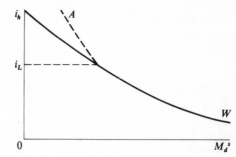

FIGURE 9-5
Aggregate demand for speculative balances.

was developed by Tobin (1958) and Markowitz (1952, 1959). While this "portfolio-choice" model produces basically the same aggregative results as the speculative-demand model, it was designed to rationalize the holding of cash *and* earning assets by the individual investor. Basically, the portfolio-selection model views investors as choosing between risk and return on a portfolio. The higher the proportion of bonds in a portfolio, the greater the return, but the risk is also greater because of the increased probability of capital losses. The normal, "risk-averter" investor will thus choose a mix of bonds and money which gives him the most preferred mix of return and risk, which, it is shown, is one containing *both* assets.

The portfolio-selection model is discussed in the Appendix to this chapter, for the reader interested in its details. However, unfortunately it does not solve the problem it was addressed to. There will be no "asset motive" for holding money in the Tobin sense. As he himself noted in a later unpublished work (1959), consideration of the complete spectrum of assets in practice eliminates the basis for holding money for portfolio diversification. Many assets, such as bank time deposits, savings and loan shares, and Treasury bills, "dominate" money, in the sense that like money they have a virtually certain and unchanging nominal value, but *in addition* they bear a positive nominal return. In short, why would anyone hold money—which pays no interest—in his portfolio when he can have all the security that money provides *and* earn interest?

In Tobin's view, since assets nearly always dominate money, the only distinguishable demand for money is a transactions demand. And in a recent article, S. C. Tsiang (1972) has shown that this analysis cannot justify the asset demand for money even if it is not dominated by another asset. Furthermore, another group of theorists have risen who abjure *any* partitioning of the demand for money into "transactions" or "asset" demands, and build their analysis on the concept of money as an asset yielding a stream of services. Their work has been substantial and impressive, and deserves the attention we give it in the following section.

The "Chicago School" Approach to the Demand for Money

One of the more striking developments in monetary theory since the 1950s has been a trend toward viewing the demand for money as simply a special topic in capital theory, involving, as in the case of other durable goods, a constraint of wealth or income and the terms of substitution—the rates of return on various assets. Milton Friedman of the University of Chicago had more to do with this development than perhaps anyone else, and we thus have titled this approach the "Chicago School approach." The essence of the Chicago School approach to the demand for money was clearly stated by Friedman in his classic article (1956):

To the ultimate wealth-owning units in the economy money is one kind of asset, one way of holding wealth. To the productive enterprise, money is a capital good, a source of productive services that are combined with other productive services to yield the products that the enterprise sells. Thus the theory of the demand for money is a special topic in the theory of capital . . . (p. 4).[14]

That is, the demand for money is viewed as analogous to the demand for a consumer durable good or capital. As in these cases, it reflects (1) the total wealth to be held in various forms (the constraint), (2) the price and return on this form of wealth and on alternative forms, and (3) the tastes and preferences of the wealth-owning units. There are no separate "transactions," "precautionary," or "asset" demands for money; these are viewed as one asset, not three, and the demand for the one asset reflects wealth, relative prices, and tastes. Let us look more closely at the various versions of this approach, beginning with Friedman himself.

First, what is the "wealth" spoken of by Friedman as the constraint on the demand for money? As with his basic theory of the consumption services, in particular it includes the productive capacity of human beings ("human wealth"), and it excludes "transitory" fluctuations in income. From the discussion of the concept of permanent income in Chapter 4, we know that the total wealth of a society (V) may be written (approximately) as

$$V = \frac{Y_p}{i} \qquad (9\text{-}14)$$

which expresses the relation between the stock (wealth) and the flow (permanent income), via the rate of interest i. We may classify this wealth as human (V_h) and nonhuman (V_n). One variable in the demand for money is thus total wealth, Y_p/i, which in turn may be written in terms of permanent income and the rate of interest. Friedman considers five ways in which this wealth may be held: (1) money; (2) bonds, interpreted as claims to perpetual streams of payments that are fixed in nominal units; (3) equities, interpreted as claims to pro rata shares of the returns of enterprises; (4) physical nonhuman goods; and (5) human capital or wealth. The way total wealth will be held will depend on the return to each form in which it may be held.

The return to money may be in nominal money units, when interest is paid on demand deposits. Assuming it is not, the return to money is subjective in the form of convenience, security, etc.. that having money gives a person. The yield on money

---

[14] This is the most rigorous theoretical statement of Friedman's on his approach to the demand for money. Several other articles dealing with his empirical work on the subject will be discussed below.

may be thought of as a fictional deposit rate representing the money value of these services per dollar of money. The real value of these services will also reflect the general price level, and so it will enter as a specific variable in the demand function. So far, then, the demand function for money contains the variables Y_p/i and p, wealth and the price level, respectively.

The return to bonds reflects the nominal interest payments plus any appreciation in the price of bonds over the time period they are held (or less any depreciation in the price of bonds). The *rate* of return on bonds thus may be written

$$i_{b_0} + \left(\frac{dB}{dt}\right)\frac{1}{B_0} \tag{9-15}$$

where i_{b_0} is the yield of the bond at time zero and B_0 is the price at time zero. Assume each bond is a promise to pay \$1 per period in perpetuity. Then $1/i_{b_0}$ is the price of a bond at time zero, and the expression for the nominal rate of return on bonds becomes

$$i_{b_0} + i_{b_0}\frac{d\left(\frac{1}{i_{b_t}}\right)}{dt}$$

or

$$i_{b_0} - \frac{i_{b_0}}{i_{b_t}^2}\frac{di_{b_t}}{dt}$$

which at time zero equals

$$i_{b_0} - \frac{1}{i_{b_0}}\frac{di_{b_0}}{dt} \tag{9-16}$$

If the bond rate of interest is not expected to change, the nominal return to holding bonds at any time t is simply i_{b_t}.

The return to equities takes the form of a nominal return per period which varies as the price level varies (in the form of changing prices of equities) and as the nominal returns to firms vary. At time zero, this may be expressed by

$$i_{e_0} + \frac{dp}{dt}p - \frac{di_{e_0}}{dt}i_{e_0} \tag{9-17}$$

where i_{e_0} is the nominal rate of payment (dividend yield) per equity share at time zero and p is the general price level.

The return to physical capital is in the form of goods. Thus the nominal or money value of the return from a dollar of physical capital depends on the yield of physical capital i_k and the behavior of prices, in a manner analogous to equities:

$$i_k + \frac{dp}{dt}p - \frac{di_k}{dt}i_k \tag{9-18}$$

The return to human capital is not defined by market prices or returns, since there is only a limited market in it except in slave societies. However, we shall include as a variable d the ratio Y_h/V_h, the yield on human wealth.

Combining the variables discussed in connection with the returns to different forms of wealth and the wealth constraint, we have the money demand function, given the tastes of wealth owners,

$$M_d = f\left(p, i_b - \frac{1}{i_b}\frac{di_b}{dt}, i_e + \frac{dp}{dt}\frac{1}{p} - \frac{di_e}{dt}\frac{1}{i_e}, i_k + \frac{dp}{dt}p - \frac{di_k}{dt}i_k, d, \frac{Y_p}{i}\right) \qquad (9\text{-}19)$$

We notice first that the money demand function contains five rates of return—i_b, i_e, i_k, d, and i—with the latter, as a yield on all assets, representing some sort of weighted average of the other rates. It also has as arguments the expected rates of change of i_b, i_k, i_e, and p, as well as total wealth Y_p/i.

Assume all yields and prices are expected to remain the same. Then we have

$$M_d = f^*\left(p, i_b, i_e, i_k, d, \frac{Y_p}{i}\right) \qquad (9\text{-}19a)$$

Now, as in demand theory applying to a commodity, it is assumed that the demand for "real" money balances must be independent of the nominal units of measurement employed; i.e., the demand function for money is assumed to be homogeneous to degree one in prices and the money value of wealth, so that

$$f^*\left(\lambda p, i_b, i_e, i_k, d, \lambda\frac{Y_p}{i}\right) = \lambda f^*\left(p, i_b, i_e, i_k, d, \frac{Y_p}{i}\right) = \lambda M_d$$

Since λ is any arbitrary constant, let it be $1/p$. Then the demand for *real* money balance is

$$\frac{M_d}{p} = f^*\left(i_b, i_e, i_k, d, \frac{Y_p}{ip}\right) \qquad (9\text{-}19b)$$

The demand for real money balances depends upon the rates of return on alternative forms of holding wealth (assumed to be a negative relation; that is, $\dfrac{\partial \frac{M}{p}}{\partial i_b}$, $\dfrac{\partial \frac{M}{p}}{\partial i_e}$, $\dfrac{\partial \frac{M}{p}}{\partial i_k}$, and $\dfrac{\partial \frac{M}{p}}{\partial d}$ are all assumed to be less than zero) and real wealth (a positive relation). Suppose the rates of return i_b, i_e, i_k, and d all move together and can be represented by a single rate i^*. Then the demand function becomes

$$\frac{M}{p} = g\left(i^*, \frac{Y_p}{pi}\right) \qquad g_{i^*} \leq 0, \qquad g_{Y_p/pi} \geq 0 \qquad (9\text{-}19c)$$

The demand for real balances is then a function of some interest rate variable and real wealth. Alternatively, we can assume i also moves with the other rates of return and represent it too with the variable i^*, wherein M/P becomes

$$\frac{M}{p} = \left(i^*, \frac{Y_p}{p}\right) \qquad (9\text{-}19d)$$

This is the general form in which the demand function has been empirically tested by Friedman (1959), Meltzer (June 1963), Bronfenbrenner and Mayer (1960), and others, although the specification of the interest rate and wealth variables has differed from study to study. Note that the major difference from the transactions demand function is that *current income* is not included as a separate variable, and is reflected only insofar as it is manifested in Y_p/pi, the real wealth variable, or Y_p/p, the permanent-income variable.

Summary and Comparison of Demand-for-Money Hypotheses

Our survey of the theoretical literature on the demand for money suggests the following a priori hypothesis about the demand for money:

1 The demand for money is basically a transactions and precautionary demand, since near-moneys dominate it insofar as it might be held for portfolio diversification. The demand function for real money balances is thus of the general form

(a) $$\frac{M_d}{p} = L(Y, b, i, c) \qquad L_Y > 0 \qquad L_b > 0 \qquad L_i < 0 \qquad L_c > 0$$

Y is real GNP, b is the broker's fee, c is the cost of illiquidity, and i is a vector of interest rates on the "near-money" alternatives to money in which cash balances may be invested until needed for transactions. (This assumes pY is a suitable proxy for T).

2 The demand for money is analogous to the demand for any other asset, and thus depends on the constraint and price variables considered in choosing the amounts held of all assets. In general form, this yields the demand function for real money balances:

(a) $$\frac{M_d}{p} = Z\left(i_n, i_b, i_e, i_k, i_h, \frac{Y_p}{ip}\right)$$

where i_b is the bond rate of interest, i_e is the rate of return on equities, i_k is the rate of return on physical assets, i_h is the rate of return on human capital, Y_p is permanent income, and i is the discount rate applicable to permanent income. The partial derivative $Z_{Y_p/i}$ is positive, while the others are negative.

If it is assumed that i varies with the other rates, M_d can be written as a function of permanent income:

(b) $$\frac{M_d}{p} = Z\left(i_n, i_b, i_e, i_k, i_h, \frac{Y_p}{p}\right)$$

If one interest rate is taken as a proxy variable for all the other interest rates (say, i_b), then the Chicago School hypothesis can be reduced to

(c) $$\frac{M_d}{p} = g\left(i_b, \frac{Y_p}{ip}\right)$$

or

$$(d) \quad \frac{M_d}{p} = g* \left(i_b, \frac{Y_p}{p} \right)$$

In short, different a priori hypotheses about the demand for money lead to different specifications of explanatory variables in the money demand function. The basic issues in this connection are (1) Is the relevant constraint or scale variable current income, permanent income, or wealth? (2) Is the relevant price variable some short-term rate of return on "near-moneys"—savings shares in our terminology—or should a long-term rate of return be used? (3) Can a single rate of return be used to represent the movement of all relevant rates of return—the whole spectrum of financial and physical assets or the array of "near-moneys," depending on the hypothesis—or must a number of separate price variables be used?

Virtually all of the *empirical* money demand work has come within the past two decades, and the money demand functions tested reflect the use of different hypotheses and thus different explanatory variables.[15] A major point of contention has been over the constraint variable.

Teigen (1964), Stedry (1959), Tobin (1958), and Chase (1965) have all argued that the demand for money is basically a transactions demand, and have used as their scale variable various measures of current income or transactions. On the other hand, Friedman (1959) conducted empirical work on money demand, and followed his argument in the theoretical article discussed earlier by using a measure of *permanent income* as the scale variable in his money-demand-function estimates.

A large number of investigators have used *nonhuman wealth* as the scale variable. Among these are Meltzer (June 1963), Brunner and Meltzer (1963), and Lydall (1958). Note that to say $M_d/p = g(i_b, Y_p/ip)$—the demand for real balances is a function of the (bond) rate of interest and *total* wealth—is *not* the same as positing that $M_d/p = h(r_b, W_n)$—the demand for real balances depends on the (bond) rate of interest and nonhuman wealth. But it is in the same tradition as the Chicago School; as Meltzer (June 1963) put it, "the [nonhuman] wealth constraint emphasizes the rate of money as a productive asset and focuses attention on the equilibrium of the balance sheet, the allocation of assets, and the services that money provides" (p. 232). It is basically an attempt to reformulate Friedman's hypothesis to substitute a variable that is directly measurable—nonhuman wealth—for one that is not directly measurable—total wealth or, alternatively, permanent income.

Put another way, the wealth variable in the Chicago School approach could be approached in the same fashion as Ando and Modigliani approached it in formulating their consumption function (Chapter 4). This would yield a demand function for *real* balances of the form

$$\frac{M_d}{p} = g' \left(i, Y^L, \frac{A}{P} \right) \qquad (9\text{-}20)$$

[15] For a good, relatively brief discussion of empirical studies of money demand functions, see Laidler (1969, chaps. 7–9).

However, as of this writing, no estimates of this form of a money demand function have been attempted.

The major problem in choosing between the alternative scale variables has been a statistical one. The measures of current income, nonhuman wealth, and permanent income or wealth are all highly correlated with each other. That is, when two (or more) competing scale variables are included in a money demand function, the fact that one is statistically significant while the other (or others) lacks explanatory power is difficult to interpret when the scale variables are highly correlated with each other.

As one might expect with such wide divergences in the specification of the scale variable, the relation obtained between it and the demand for money has varied considerably. Friedman (1959), using a definition of money which includes commercial bank time deposits, found the elasticity of the demand for real money balances with respect to permanent income to be about 1.8. Meltzer found the wealth elasticity of the demand for real money balances to be near unity. Teigen (1965), on the other hand, found an *income* elasticity of the demand for money of 0.5. Clearly this issue is not yet closed.

Somewhat less specific attention has been focused on questions (2) and (3) relating to the proper "price" variables to be included in the money demand equation. Most studies *have* used single interest rates to represent the movement of the whole array of rates. However, Brunner and Meltzer (1963) and de Leeuw (SSRC model, 1965) have sought to include rates of return on physical assets in addition to the bond yield. All but a few studies—Teigen, Stedry, and Bronfenbrenner and Mayer—have taken the relevant interest rate variable to be *some* measure of *long-term* rates. Virtually all investigators have found *some* interest rate variable to be statistically significant in explaining the demand for money. Friedman is sometimes cited as an exception, but careful reading of his original article and a later article by him (1969) makes it clear that while he tends to feel the interest elasticity of the demand for money is quite low, he does believe it to be significantly different from zero. However his findings of a low (but significantly different from zero) interest elasticity of the demand for money has been shown to reflect his broader definition of money and certain of his statistical techniques.[16] Excluding Friedman's results, estimates of the interest elasticity of the demand for money generally range between −0.5 and −0.9.[17]

---

[16] Shifts between money (defined as demand deposits plus currency) and time deposits when all interest rates change may be obscured if money is defined to *include* time deposits. If all market rates of interest rise, individuals and firms may well shift from money to time deposits *and* other assets. If money is defined to include time deposits, then to the extent the shift is to time deposits there is no shift out of money and the interest sensitivity of the demand for money is thereby reduced. See Meltzer (June 1963, pp. 234–236), Brunner and Meltzer (1963, p. 350), and Teigen (1965, p. 56).

[17] See the summary tables presented in Teigen (1965, pp. 52 and 64). The only estimate falling outside this range is that by Bronfenbrenner and Mayer (1963, p. 539), and their results have been shown by Meltzer (June 1963, pp. 221 and 231) to be suspect because of the definition of wealth employed.

Thus the issue of the "best" empirical money demand function remains unsettled, as is likely to continue to be the case.

Our own choice is to write the demand for money in a Ando–Modigliani form of the Chicago approach, with the price variables being rates of return on securities as well as both of the two types of "near-moneys"—time deposits and savings shares. The demand for money in real terms is thus

$$\frac{M_d}{p} = L\left(Y^L, i, i_s, i_t, \frac{A}{p}\right) \qquad (9\text{-}21)$$

where Y^L is real labor income, i is the rate of interest on securities, i_s is the rate of return on savings shares, i_t is the rate of interest on commercial bank time deposits, and A/p is real private nonhuman wealth.

Before leaving the subject, however, we need to deal briefly with one further aspect of the problem: differences between the demand for currency and the demand for demand deposits.

THE DEMAND FOR DEMAND DEPOSITS AND THE DEMAND FOR CURRENCY

If two goods are perfect substitutes, they may be treated as one good from the point of view of demand analysis. We have assumed thus far that currency and demand deposits are perfect substitutes, enabling us to speak of the demand for "money." The same assumption is implicit in most empirical work on the demand for money. Yet the evidence seems clear that currency and demand deposits are *not* perfect substitutes.

For one thing currency by law carries no pecuniary return, but demand deposits have paid interest in the past and probably carry a positive nonpecuniary return today. In addition, the two assets are not perfect substitutes for all transactions; for example, currency is more useful for illegal transactions. And over time the substitutability of the two varies—insurance of bank deposits probably made them closer substitutes for currency, while the growth of vending machines has reduced the substitutability between the two. Discussion of the causes of the imperfect and changing subsitutability between currency and demand deposits is to be found in studies by Cagan (1958), McDonald (1956), and Kaufman (1966).

We shall thus split the demand for money by the public into two demand functions, one for currency (X^p) and one for demand deposits held by the non-bank public (DD^p):

$$\frac{X_d^p}{p} = \mu\left(Y^L, i, i_s, i_t, \frac{A}{p}\right) \qquad (9\text{-}22)$$

$$\frac{DD_d^p}{p} = \lambda\left(Y^L, i, i_s, i_t, \frac{A}{p}\right) \qquad (9\text{-}23)$$

THE DEMAND FOR TIME DEPOSITS AND SAVINGS SHARES

Relatively little work has been done on the demand for financial assets other than money. Those who define money to include time deposits have treated with the demand for this asset (though usually not separately), and the demand functions for time and savings deposits (savings and loan deposits, mutual savings bank deposits, and credit union deposits) form part of some large-scale econometric models.[18] Yet as we shall see in a later chapter, the form of the demand functions for these assets is at least as important to economic policy formulation as the demand for money.

Our discussion of the theoretical literature gives us the basis for specifying a demand function for savings shares—our composite asset for savings and loan deposits, mutual savings bank deposits, and credit union deposits—and time deposits. (The rationale for this grouping will become more apparent at a later juncture). The demand functions for real savings shares S and time deposits DT may be treated, along Friedmanian lines, in the following manner:

$$\frac{S_d}{p} = \pi\left(Y^L, i, i_s, i_t, \frac{A}{p}\right) \qquad (9\text{-}24)$$

$$\frac{DT_d}{p} = \theta\left(Y^L, i, i_s, i_t, \frac{A}{p}\right) \qquad (9\text{-}25)$$

i.e., the demands for savings shares and time deposits are assumed to depend on the array of rates of return (on securities, savings shares, and time deposits) and on total labor income and private nonhuman wealth. We assume the rates of return on physical capital i_k and human capital i_h to be given for our purposes and thus not relevant in the form of the function. The partial derivatives of each function with respect to Y^L, A/p, and the "own" rate of return are assumed to be positive; the partials with respect to the other rates of return are assumed to be negative.

THE DEMAND FOR SECURITIES

Our grouping of assets called "securities" contains assets which differ sharply from each other in risk, rate of return, and term to maturity. We cannot pretend to posit a single demand function for a group of assets which includes long-term federal government securities, Treasury bills, tax-exempt state and local securities, equities, and corporate bonds. On the other hand, to present a separate demand function for each asset would involve us in a model far too complex for qualitative analysis. So we simply abstract from the differences between the different assets included in the securities category and assume a homogeneous type of security. By analogy with the

---

[18] For example, see de Leeuw and Gramlich (1968). Feige (1963) studied the demand for demand deposits, savings and loan deposits, time deposits, and mutual savings bank deposits. Teigen (1969) estimated a demand function for time deposits.

demand functions for savings shares and time deposits, the demand for real securities B_d/p is assumed to be of the form

$$\frac{B_d}{p} = \varepsilon\left(Y^L, i, i_s, i_t, \frac{A}{p}\right) \qquad (9\text{-}26)$$

with the partial derivatives $\dfrac{\partial(B_d/p)}{\partial i}$, $\dfrac{\partial(B_d/p)}{\partial Y^L}$, and $\dfrac{\partial(B_d/p)}{\partial \dfrac{A}{P}}$ positive and the partial

derivatives $\dfrac{\partial(B_d/p)}{\partial i_t}$ and $\dfrac{\partial(B_d/p)}{\partial i_s}$ negative.

SUMMARY

In this chapter we have compared in some detail alternative theoretical approaches to the demand for money, namely the Keynesian approach, where the demand for money is compartmentalized into transactions, precautionary, and asset demands, and the Chicago approach, where the demand for money is viewed as analogous to the demand for any other asset. We saw that the Keynesian approach essentially reduces to the transactions and precautionary demands since other "near-moneys" dominate money in portfolio diversification. The transactions approach suggests a money demand function which includes a measure of current income, or transactions, and various yields on "near-moneys" as arguments. The Chicago approach, on the other hand, leads to a real money demand function containing as arguments rates of return on the spectrum of financial assets and physical assets, together with a measure of real total wealth (real labor income and real nonhuman wealth) or permanent income.

Attention was also given to approaching the demand for money from the point of view of life cycle hypothesis, with current real labor income, rates of return on alternative assets, and real nonhuman wealth as the appropriate variables.

After a brief survey of the empirical literature on the demand for money, we noted that since currency and demand deposits are not perfect substitutes, separate demand functions should be specified for each, and this was done using the same independent variables as in the aggregate demand function.

The demand functions for savings shares, time deposits, and securities were developed using the life cycle approach to the demand for assets, where the independent variables were assumed to be the real labor income, the spectrum of yields on financial and physical assets, and real nonhuman wealth.

APPENDIX TO CHAPTER 9: TOBIN-MARKOWITZ AND THE DIVERSIFICATION OF DEMAND FOR MONEY

When the demand for money as an asset was treated in the text as a speculative demand, the treatment did not *explicitly* deal with *uncertainty*. It is intuitively obvious that uncertainty might be introduced by using a *probability distribution* to describe the range and likelihood of various outcomes of an investment in a portfolio of securities and money. In a classic article published in 1958, Tobin did this and attempted to provide a rationale for mixed portfolios of money and securities in a two-asset world.

The basic idea is to conceive of the individual investor as having a utility function for *expected* returns (expected utility function) which he maximizes in choosing his portfolio. To take a simple example first, suppose an investor has a utility function for rates of return on a portfolio of the form $U = R^2$, where U is an index of utility and R is the rate of return on a portfolio. If he has a choice between portfolio A, with a 50 percent chance of yielding \$10 or \$20, and portfolio B, with a 60 percent chance of a \$15 yield and a 40 percent chance of a \$25 yield, he would choose B by comparing the *expected* utilities of the two portfolios, calculated as follows:

$$E(U)_A = 0.50(10) + 0.50(20) = 15$$
$$E(U)_B = 0.60(15) + 0.40(25) = 19$$

Now we distinguish between utility-of-rates-of-return functions of three types, shown in Figure A9-1. Function I is one with constant marginal utility; utility rises as the rate of return rises but at a constant rate. Functions II and III show decreasing and increasing marginal utility of returns, respectively. The shape of the investor's utility function has an important bearing on his investment behavior.

Let us continue to assume, as before, that there are two assets—perpetuity bonds and money. We further assume now that the yield on bonds, in the mind of the investor, is a random variable with a normal distribution and that the investor is of type II—he has the quadratic utility function

$$U(R) = aR^2 + bR \qquad \text{(A9-1)}$$

where $-1 < a < 0$ and $b > 0$. If $U(R)$ is the utility function of R and $f(R)$ is the probability distribution of R, the expected value of utility of R, $E[U(R)]$, is

$$E[U(R)] = \int_{-\infty}^{\infty} U(R) f(R) \, dR \qquad \text{(A9-2)}$$

Substituting in for the utility function $U(R)$, we get

$$E[U(R)] = \int_{-\infty}^{\infty} (aR^2 + bR) \left(\frac{1}{\sigma_R \sqrt{2\pi}} e^{-1/2(R - \mu_R)^2/\sigma_R^2} \right) dR \qquad \text{(A9-3)}$$

where μ_R is the mean expected rate of return and σ_R^2 is the variance of $f(R)$. Integrating by terms we obtain

$$E[U(R)] = \frac{1}{\sigma_R \sqrt{2\pi}} a \int_{-\infty}^{\infty} R^2 (e^{-1/2(R - \mu_R)^2/\sigma_R^2}) \, dR$$

$$+ \frac{1}{\sigma_R \sqrt{2\pi}} b \int_{-\infty}^{\infty} R(\sigma^{-1/2(R - \mu_R)^2/\sigma_R^2}) \, dR \qquad \text{(A9-4)}$$

From the properties of the normal distribution, this is seen to be

$$E[U(R)] = aE(R^2) + bE(R)$$

or

$$E[U(R)] = aE(R^2) + b\mu_R \qquad \text{(A9-5)}$$

Let us find an expression for the expected value of R^2—$E(R^2)$ in terms of the variance σ_R^2. The variance of a normal distribution of rates of return on the portfolio is

$$\sigma_R^2 = E(R - \mu_R)^2$$
$$= E(R^2 + \mu_R^2 - 2\mu_R R) \qquad \text{(A9-6)}$$

Thus

$$E(R^2) = \sigma_R^2 - \mu_R^2 + 2\mu_R^2$$
$$= \sigma_R^2 + \mu_R^2 \qquad \text{(A9-7)}$$

$E[U(R)]$ therefore can be written

$$E[U(R)] = a(\sigma_R^2 + \mu_R^2) + b\mu_R \qquad \text{(A9-7a)}$$

In short, where the investor has a quadratic utility function and a normal subjective probability distribution, the expected utility of the portfolio depends only on two characteristics of that portfolio, the mean return μ_R and variance σ_R^2. The individual may be pictured as comparing the mean and variance of returns on alternative portfolios in maximizing expected utility.

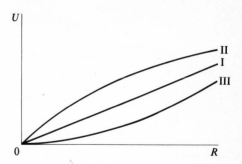

FIGURE   A9-1
Constant, decreasing, and increasing marginal utility of returns.

Let us find the properties of the indifference curves implied in Eq. (A9-7a) for $E[U(R)]$. Differentiating (A9-7a) with respect to the *standard deviation* σ_R of returns on the portfolio and setting the result equal to zero, we get

$$2a\mu_R\left(\frac{d\mu_R}{d\sigma_R}\right) + 2a\sigma_R + b\left(\frac{d\mu_R}{d\sigma_R}\right) = 0$$

or

$$\frac{d\mu_R}{d\sigma_R} = \frac{-2a\sigma_R}{2a\mu_R + b} \qquad \text{(A9-8)}$$

The following properties of the indifference curves between σ_R and μ_R emerge:

1 When $\sigma_R = 0$, the investor's indifference curves have a zero slope.

2 If the coefficient a is negative, as assumed here, the investor's indifference curves have a *positive* slope (with μ_R on the vertical axis) and vice versa. The reason is that the denominator $(2a\mu_R + b)$ is the marginal expected utility at the mean return μ_R, which is positive. Hence the sign of $d\mu_R/d\sigma_R$ depends on the sign of a.

In short, for a *risk averter* with diminishing marginal utility attached to expected returns $(a < 0)$, the indifference curve slopes up and to the right; for a *risk lover* who has *increasing* marginal utility of expected return, the indifference curve slopes down and to the right. These cases are shown in Figure A9-2. It can also be shown that the indifference curves of a risk averter will be *concave upward*, while those of a risk lover will be *concave downward*.[1]

---

[1]

$$\frac{d^2\mu_R}{d\sigma_R{}^2} = \frac{-2a}{2a\mu_R + b} + \sigma_R\left[\frac{(2a)^2\,\dfrac{d\mu_R}{d\sigma_R}}{(2a\mu_R + b)^2}\right]$$

$$= \frac{-2a}{2a\mu_R + b} + \frac{2a\sigma_R}{2a\mu_R + b}\,\frac{\dfrac{d\mu_R}{d\sigma_R}\,(2a)}{2a\mu_R + b}$$

$$= \frac{-2a}{2a\mu_R + b} - \frac{2a\left(\dfrac{d\mu_R}{d\sigma_R}\right)^2}{2a\mu_R + b}$$

$$= \frac{-2a\left[\left(\dfrac{d\mu_R}{dR}\right)^2 + 1\right]}{2a\mu_R + b}$$

If $a < 0$ and $\dfrac{d\mu_R}{d\sigma_R} > 0$, then $\dfrac{d^2\mu_R}{d\sigma_R{}^2} > 0$. If $a > 0$ and $\dfrac{d\mu_R}{d\sigma_R} < 0$, then $\dfrac{d^2\mu_R}{d\sigma_R{}^2} < 0$.
In both cases we assume $2a\mu_R + b > 0$ as before.

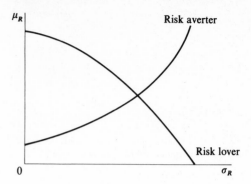

FIGURE A9-2
Indifference curves of risk averters and risk lovers.

We should note that the expression for $E[U(R)]$ contained only two parameters of the probability distribution of R because we assumed a second-degree polynomial utility function for R. In general, if $U(R)$ equals some polynomial expression containing R in each term (except for a constant), then $E[U(R)]$ is some sum of integrals where each term in the sum contains *one* of the powers of R appearing in $U(R)$. Since by definition the kth moment of $f(R)$ is $\int_{-\infty}^{\infty} R^k f(R)\, dR$, $E[U(R)]$ will contain one moment of $f(R)$ for each power of R appearing in $U(R)$. The number of properties of $f(R)$ relevant to the investor's choice will depend on the degree of the polynomial defining the utility function. The specific properties of $f(R)$ that are relevant will depend on the terms in $E[U(R)]$, each of which contains some moment of $f(R)$.

Let us consider now the opportunity locus of the investor. The return on a dollar of bonds is $i + g$, that is, the sum of the interest and capital gains "rates." As a result, the return on a dollar of assets (bonds *and* money) is $R = A_2(i + g)$, where A_2 is the percentage of the portfolio held in bonds. But since R was assumed to be a random variable normally distributed (with mean μ_R and variance σ_R^2), g will be also normally distributed (with mean zero and variance σ_g^2). Therefore the expected return on a portfolio (μ_R) will be $\mu_R = A_2 i$. The *risk* on a portfolio will be the standard deviation of returns, or

$$\sigma_R = A_2(\sigma_g) \qquad \text{(A9-9)}$$

We thus obtain

$$A_2 = \frac{\sigma_R}{\sigma_g} = \frac{\mu_R}{i}$$

or

$$\mu_R = \frac{i}{\sigma_g} \sigma_R \qquad \text{(A9-10)}$$

which gives us the slope of the investor's opportunity loci as i/σ_g. As shown in Figure A9-3, the investor maximizes $E[U(R)]$ by choosing a portfolio of bonds and money which puts him on the highest possible indifference curve. The possible outcomes are shown in the two panels of Figure A9-3, (*a*) and (*b*). The "normal" outcome, shown in panel (*a*), involves a tangency between an indifference curve and the opportunity locus and a mixed portfolio of bonds and money. *This kind of maximum can occur only for a risk averter.*

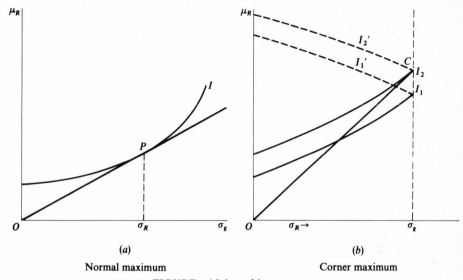

(a)

Normal maximum

(b)

Corner maximum

FIGURE   A9-3a and b
Possible outcomes in maximizing expected utility from a portfolio.

Another possible outcome is a *corner maximum* with a portfolio of all bonds and no money, or where $\mu_R = i$ and $\sigma_R = \sigma_g$, as at C in panel (*b*). This can occur either for a *risk averter* (indifference curve sloping up, concave upward) or for a *risk lover* (indifference curve sloping downward, concave downward). For a risk averter it will occur where his indifference curves have slopes less than that of the opportunity locus everywhere to the left of point C. It is clear that a *risk lover* will *always* have a corner maximum with a portfolio composed entirely of risky assets.

Is an outcome where only money is held possible? Not with the assumptions employed here. It would be conceivable that a risk averter could hold only money if the slope of the opportunity locus OC at the origin O and everywhere else to the right was *exceeded* by that of any indifference curve, as in Figure A9-4. However, as we have seen, the slope of all indifference curves where they intersect the vertical axis is zero, and so this possibility is ruled out.

The Tobin analysis thus suggests that at least in a two-asset world money will be held to diversify asset portfolios to reduce risk. Given investors tastes, the *proportion* of assets held in money for such purposes will reflect (1) the rate of interest and (2) the risk attached to bonds (σ_g). Our interest does not lie in σ_g, so assume it is constant. Then the total asset demand for money depends on the rate of interest *and* the total amount of assets of investors:

$$M_A = L_2(A,i) \qquad \text{(A9-11)}$$

where A is the total assets of individuals and i is the rate of interest.

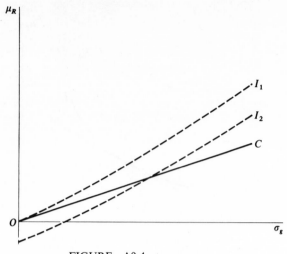

FIGURE A9-4
A corner maximum where only money is held.

What does the Tobin analysis tell us about the effect on M_A of changes in the rate of interest? First, consider investors who are *risk averters*. Clearly, changes in i (illustrated in Figure A9-5) may cause the investor to increase or decrease the proportion of his portfolio in money—the outcome depends on the relative strengths of the familiar income and substitution effects. An increase in the rate of interest tends to increase the incentive to take risk—the substitution effect will thus tend to increase A_2, the proportion of the portfolio in bonds. At the same time, a higher i raises the real income of the investor and allows him to enjoy *more* security along with more income—the income effect will thus likely work against

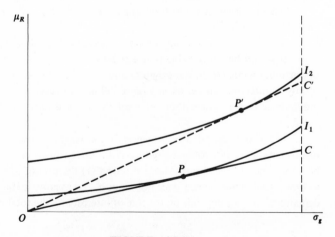

FIGURE A9-5
A case of increase in bond-holdings as i rises.

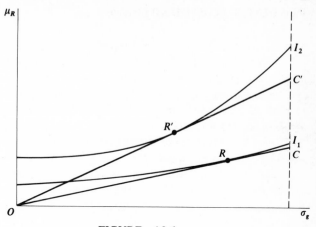

FIGURE   A9-6
A case of decrease in bond-holdings as i rises.

A_2 being increased. In Figure A9-5, the increase in i raises the attainable ratio of μ_R/σ_g (since $\mu_R = i$) and causes the opportunity locus to rotate upward to OC'. In the case shown in Figure A9-5 the investor chooses to increase A_2, the proportion of his portfolio held in bonds, and ends up at P'. It would be possible, however, for him to behave as in Figure A9-6 and reduce the percentage of his portfolio in bonds, moving from point R to R'. So we cannot be certain of a "normal" relation between i and M_A in the case of risk averters.[2]

---

[2] For the quadratic utility function used here, the "normal" relation between i and M_A can be given more support than this. We have already observed that at $\sigma_R = 0$ the indifference curves derived from the maximization of expected utility will have zero slopes, and at this point $A_2 = 0$. Clearly, as i rises from zero, so will bond holdings A_2. It can even be shown that A_2 increases with i for $i < \sigma_g$. We know the maximization condition is where the slope of the opportunity locus is equal to the slope of the indifference curve:

$$\frac{i}{\sigma_g} = \frac{-2a\sigma_R}{2a\mu_R + b}$$

or since $\sigma_R = A_2\,\sigma_g$ and $\mu_R = A_2 i$,

$$\frac{i}{\sigma_g} = -\frac{A_2\,\sigma_g}{b/2a - A_2 i}$$

From this we can write A_2 as a function of r:

$$A_2 = \frac{i}{\sigma_g^2 + i^2}\left(\frac{-b}{2a}\right)$$

Differentiating, we get

$$\frac{dA_2}{di} = \frac{-b}{2a}\left[\frac{\sigma_g^2 - i^2}{(\sigma_g^2 + i^2)^2}\right]$$

The *elasticity* of A_2 with respect to i is therefore

$$\frac{dA_2}{di}\frac{i}{A_2} = -\frac{b}{2a}\left[\frac{\sigma_g^2 - i^2}{(\sigma_g^2 + i^2)^2}\right]\frac{-(\sigma_g^2 + i^2)2a}{b}$$

$$= \frac{\sigma_g^2 - i^2}{\sigma_g^2 + i^2}$$

The elasticity is positive—the share of bonds in the portfolio increases as i increases —for any i less than σ_g. The demand for bonds is less interest-elastic the higher the rate of interest, and A_2 may increase over all ranges of i if $i < \sigma_g$.

READINGS FOR CHAPTER 9

BAUMOL, W. J.: "The Transactions Demand for Case: An Inventory-Theoretic Approach," *Quarterly Journal of Economics*, 545ff, November 1952.

BRONFENBRENNER, M., and T. MAYER: "Liquidity Functions in the American Economy," *Econometrica*, pp. 810–34, October 1960: also see July 1963 issue for "Comments" by Meltzer and Eisner and "Reply" by Bronfenbrenner and Mayer.

BRUNNER, K., and A. H. MELTZER: "Predicting Velocity: Implications for Theory and Policy," *Journal of Finance*, pp. 319–354, May 1963.

———: "The Uses of Money: Money in the Theory of an Exchange Economy," *American Economic Review*, vol. 61, pp. 784–805, December 1971.

CAGAN, P.: "The Demand for Currency Relative to the Total Money Supply," *Journal of Political Economy*, pp. 303–328, 1958.

CHASE, S. B.: "The Scale Variable in the Demand for Money," unpublished (mimeo.), 1965.

CHETTY, V. K.: "On the Long-Run and Short-Run Demand for Money: Some Further Evidence," *Journal of Political Economy*, pp. 921–930, November–December 1969.

CHOW, GREGORY, C.: "On the Long-Run and Short-Run Demand for Money," *Journal of Political Economy*, pp. 111–131, April 1966.

———: "Reply: A Note on the Estimation of Long-Run Relationships in Stock-Adjustment Models," *Journal of Political Economy*, pp. 932–936, November–December 1969.

DE LEEUW, F.: "A Model of Financial Behavior" in Duesenberry et al., (eds.), *The Brookings Quarterly Econometric Model of the United States* (New York: Rand McNally, 1965a).

———: "The Demand for Money, Speed of Adjustment, Interest Rates, and Wealth," *Staff Economic Studies*, Board of Governors of the Federal Reserve System, October 1965b.

DE LEEUW, F., and E. GRAMLICH: "The Federal Reserve–MIT Econometric Model," *Federal Reserve Bulletin*, pp. 1–32, January 1968.

DUESENBERRY, J.: "The Portfolio Approach to the Demand for Money and Other Assets," *Review of Economics and Statistics*, pp. 9–24, February 1963.

———: *Money and Credit: Impact and Control* (Englewood Cliffs, N.J.: Prentice-Hall, 1967).

FEIGE, E.: *The Demand for Liquid Assets: A Temporal Cross-Section Analysis* (Englewood Cliffs, N.J.: Prentice-Hall, 1963).

———: "Estimations and Adjustments in the Monetary Sector," *American Economic Review*, pp. 462–473, May 1967.

FRIEDMAN, M.: "The Quantity Theory of Money: A Restatement," in M. Friedman (ed.), *Studies in the Quantity Theory of Money* (Chicago: The University of Chicago Press, 1956), pp. 3–21.

———: "The Demand for Money: Some Theoretical and Empirical Results," *Journal of Political Economy*, pp. 327–351, August 1959

———: "Interest Rates and the Demand for Money," reprinted in Friedman, M., *The Optimum Quantity of Money and Other Essays* (Chicago: Aldine, 1969), pp. 141–156.

GILBERT, J. C.: "The Demand for Money: The Development of an Economic Concept," *Journal of Political Economy*, 1953.

GURLEY, J. G.: "Liquidity and Financial Institutions in the Postwar Period," *Study Paper No. 11*, Joint Economic Committee, 1960.

KAUFMAN, G. G.: "The Demand for Currency," Staff Economic Studies, Board of Governors of the Federal Reserve System (mimeo.), 1966.

LATANÉ, H.: "Cash Balances and the Interest Rate: A Pragmatic Approach," *Review of Economics and Statistics*, pp. 456–460, November 1954.

LAIDLER, DAVID, E. W.: "Some Evidence on the Demand for Money," *Journal of Political Economy*, pp. 55–68, February 1966.

———: *The Demand for Money: Theories and Evidence* (Scranton, Pa: International Textbook, 1969), chaps. 3–9.

LYDALL, H. F.: "Income, Assets, and the Demand for Money," *Review of Economics and Statistics*, pp. 1–14, February 1958.

MARKOWITZ, H.: "Portfolio Selection," *Journal of Finance*, pp. 77–91, March 1952.

———: *Portfolio Selection* (New York: Wiley, 1959).

MATTHEWS, R. C. O.: "Expenditure Plans and the Uncertainty Motive for Holding Money," *Journal of Political Economy*, pp. 55–68, February 1966.

MCCALL, J. J.: "Differences between the Personal Demand for Money and the Business Demand for Money," *Journal of Political Economy*, pp. 358–369, 1960.

MCDONALD, S. K.: "Some Factors Affecting the Increased Use of Currency Since 1939," *Journal of Finance*, September 1956.

MELTZER, A.: "The Demand for Money: The Evidence from the Time Series," *Journal of Political Economy*, pp. 219–246, June 1963.

———: "The Demand for Money: A Cross-Section Study of Business Firms," *Quarterly Journal of Economics*, pp. 405–422, August 1963. See February 1965 issue for "Comments" by Vogel and Maddala and "Reply" by Meltzer.

MILLER, M. H., and D. ORR: "A Model of the Demand for Money by Firms," *Quarterly Journal of Economics*, pp. 413–435, August 1966.

SPRENKLE, C. M.; "Large Economic Units, Banks, and the Transactions Demand for Money," *Quarterly Journal of Economics*, pp. 436–442, August 1966.

STEDRY, A. C.: "A Note on Interest Rates and the Demand for Money," *Review of Economics and Statistics*, pp. 303–307, August 1959.

———: "An Aggregated Quarterly Model of the U.S. Monetary Sector," in K. Brunner (ed.), *Targets and Indicators of Monetary Policy* (San Francisco: Chandler, 1969).

TEIGEN, R. L.: "Demand and Supply Functions for Money in the United States: Some Structural Estimates," *Econometrica*, pp. 476–509, October 1964.

———: "The Demand for and Supply of Money," in W. L. Smith and R. L. Teigen (eds.), *Readings in Money, National Income, and Stabilization Policy* (Homewood, Ill.: Irwin, 1965), pp. 44–60.

TOBIN, J.: "Liquidity Preference and Monetary Policy," *Review of Economics and Stastitics*, pp. 124–131, May 1947.

———: "The Interest-Elasticity of the Transactions Demand for Cash," *Review of Economics and Statistics*, 1956.

———: "Liquidity Preference as Behavior toward Risk," *Review of Economic Studies*, pp. 65–86, February 1958.

————: Unpublished manuscript on "Monetary Economics" (mimeo, 1959).

TSIANG, S. C.: "The Rationale of the Mean-Standard Deviation Analysis, Skewness Preference, and the Demand for Money," *American Economic Review*, vol. 62, pp. 354–371, June 1972.

TURVEY, R.: *Interest Rates and Asset Prices* (London: G. Allen, 1960), chap. 3.

WHALEN, E. L.: "A Rationalization of the Precautionary Demand for Cash," *Quarterly Journal of Economics*, vol. 80, pp. 314–324, May 1966.

10

THE SUPPLY OF MONEY AND
THE FINANCIAL SECTOR EQUILIBRIUM

The supply side of the financial sector used in the basic models of Chapter 3 took the form

$$M_s = m\overline{H} \qquad (3\text{-}8)$$

The supply of money was assumed to be some multiple m (a constant) of the stock of "high-powered money" $\overline{H}$. In this chapter, this basic equation is refined and expanded, so that the effects of the policies of the central bank (the Federal Reserve System) and the Treasury on m and $\overline{H}$ are clearly spelled out. In addition, an alternative to the $M_s = M_d$ structuring of the financial sector is considered.

The following section explains those factors affecting the monetary base or high-powered money ($\overline{H}$). The second section expands the money supply equation to explore forces operating on m, and summarizes the resulting new version of an M_s function. The final section looks at the alternative way of structuring the financial sector—sometimes called the "weak approach"—which stresses the supply of and demand for the monetary base.

FACTORS AFFECTING THE MONETARY BASE

To derive an equation for the monetary base we must look at the balance sheets of the monetary system. (While United States accounts are used here, the basic principles remain the same.) Consider first the balance sheet of the central bank, the Federal Reserve System. Table 10-1 shows items in a condensed balance sheet for the Federal Reserve System, where some unimportant items have been combined to highlight these accounts of interest to us here. Each item in the balance sheet will be denoted in our discussion by the symbol following it in Table 10-1. Generally the convention followed is that the *issuer* of a security (the debtor) is shown by the *subscript* and the *holder* (or creditor) by the superscript (e.g., B_g^F represents the government securities held by the Federal Reserve).

The Federal Reserve System holds as assets (1) claims on the Treasury [United States government securities (B_g^F), gold certificates (U_c), and Treasury currency (X_T^F)]; (2) claims against commercial banks [discounts and advances (B_b^F)]; (3) claims on the private sector [acceptances, shown as (B_p^F)]; and (4) some miscellaneous assets Z^F (mainly the "float" and foreign exchange holdings).[1] Liabilities of the Federal Reserve include its currency issues outstanding (X_F) and deposits of the Treasury (D_F^T), commercial banks (D_F^b), and foreign central banks (D_F^f). It also has miscellaneous capital accounts and liabilities (L^F).

Now let us look at the items in the balance sheet of the Treasury. This is given in Table 10-2.

The Treasury's accounts seem a little strange at first glance, and indeed they do not fit easily into the categories of the conventional balance sheet. Treasury currency outstanding (X_T) is counted as an asset of the Treasury, but a liability arises when it is held either by banks (X_T^b), by the Federal Reserve System (X_T^b), or by the

Table 10-1 MAJOR ITEMS IN THE BALANCE SHEET OF THE FEDERAL RESERVE SYSTEM

Assets	Liabilities and capital accounts
Cash (Treasury currency), X_T^F	Federal Reserve notes*, X_F
Gold certificates, U_c	Member bank reserves, D_F^b
Discounts and advance, B_b^F	U.S. Treasury deposits, D_F^T
U.S. government securities, B_g^F	Foreign deposits, D_F^f
Acceptances, B_p^F	Other deposits
Float and $\Big\}Z^F$	Other liabilities, $\Big\}L^F$
Other assets	Capital accounts
Total assets	Total liabilities and capital accounts

* Federal Reserve notes outstanding *less* those held by the Federal Reserve; the latter are subtracted from both sides of the balance sheet.

[1] The "float" represents checks credited to one bank but not yet cleared against another.

public ($X_T{}^p$). The Treasury's gold stock is also counted as an asset, but an offsetting liability arises when the Treasury issues gold certificates against the gold stock (U_c) to be held by the Federal Reserve. Another asset of the Treasury is its holdings of Federal Reserve notes ($X_F{}^T$). The balancing item on the liability side is "Treasury cash" (J). This is the counterpart of the capital accounts for a firm or bank. Alternatively, solving for J from the balance sheet, we get $J = U - U_c + X_T{}^T + X_F{}^T$. This is a measure of the Treasury's "vault cash"; i.e., the Treasury has "money in its pocket" equal to free gold ($U - U_c$), for which it can issue gold certificates, plus its holdings of its own currency ($X_T{}^T$) and currency issued by the Federal Reserve ($X_F{}^T$).

The items in the combined balance sheet for the commercial banking system are shown in Table 10-3, along with the appropriate symbols. If we consolidate the balance sheet of the commercial banking sector, claims of one bank on another are eliminated (e.g., domestic interbank deposits cancel with "Balances with domestic banks"). Those items which are eliminated by consolidation are starred. After consolidation, what remains on the asset side are the banking sector's claims on other sectors—the central bank and Treasury ($X^b + D_F{}^b$ and $B_g{}^b$), state and local governments ($B_{gs}{}^b$), and private individuals and businesses ($B_p{}^g$)—and what remains on the liabilities and capital accounts side are the claims of other sectors on the banking sector and its ownership accounts.

The Equation for the Monetary Base and Adjusted Monetary Base

The monetary base of an economy is its stock of "ultimate money." This may be gold, silver, or paper claims on the central bank or treasury, depending on the monetary standard in use. The monetary base consists of those assets banks use as reserves for their monetary liabilities, whether they are actually being held by banks or not. These assets serve as the base for multiple expansion of deposits by banks, and include all those assets which banks can use to satisfy the public's desire to convert deposits to legal tender. In the United States at present, the monetary base therefore includes bank reserves (vault cash and deposits at the Federal Reserve) plus currency

Table 10-2 MONETARY ACCOUNTS OF THE TREASURY
(December 1965)

Assets	Liabilities and capital
Treasury currency outstanding, X_T	Gold certificates, U_c
Treasury gold stock, U	Treasury currency in banks, $X_T{}^b$
Federal Reserve notes, $X_F{}^T$	Treasury currency held by the Federal Reserve, $X_T{}^F$
	Treasury currency outside banks, $X_T{}^p$
	Treasury cash, J
Total assets	Total liabilities

held by the public.[2] As we shall see, the monetary base is ultimately under the control of the central government (including the central bank).

Let us denote the monetary base by H. Then, as defined,

$$H = R + X^p \tag{10-1}$$

or

$$H = D_F{}^b + X_T{}^b + X_F{}^b + X^p$$

Substituting from the Treasury's balance sheet (Table 10-2) for $X_T{}^b$ and from the balance sheet of the Federal Reserve System (Table 10-1) for $X_F{}^b$, we obtain

$$H = D_F{}^b + (X_T - X_T{}^T - X_T{}^p - X_T{}^F) + (X_F - X_F{}^p - X_F{}^T) + X^p \tag{10-2}$$

Since $X_T{}^p + X_F{}^p = X^p$, we get

$$H = D_F{}^b + (X_T - X_T{}^T - X_T{}^F) + (X_F - X_F{}^T)$$
$$= (D_F{}^b + X_F) + (X_T - X_T{}^T) - X_T{}^F - X_F{}^T \tag{10-3}$$

From the Federal Reserve accounts in Table 10-1, we obtain an expression for deposits of banks at the Federal Reserve plus Federal Reserve currency (notes) outstanding:

$$D_F{}^b + X_F = U_c + B_b{}^F + B_g{}^F + B_p{}^F + Z^F + X_T{}^F - D_F{}^T - D_F{}^f - L^F \tag{10-4}$$

Table 10-3 BALANCE SHEET FOR COMMERCIAL BANKS

Assets	Liabilities
Cash assets	Demand deposits
Vault cash, X^b	Domestic interbank*
Deposits at Federal Reserve banks, $D_F{}^b$	Foreign interbank, L^b
Balances with domestic banks*	U.S. government, DD^g
Balances with foreign banks, Z^b	State and local government, DD^{gs}
Cash items in process*	Certified and officer's checks, DD^p
Loans (except federal funds and loans to banks), $B_p{}^b$	IPC† DD^p
Federal funds*	Time deposits
Loans to banks (except federal funds)*	Domestic interbank*
U.S. government securities, $B_g{}^b$	U.S. government, DT^g
State and local government securities, $B_{gs}{}^b$	State and local government, DT^{gs}
Private securities, $B_p{}^b$	IPC† DT^p
Other assets, Z^b	Borrowings
	From Federal Reserve banks, $B_b{}^F$
	From other banks*
	Capital accounts, L^b
Total assets	Total liabilities and capital accounts

* Denotes items which cancel in consolidation.
† Individuals, partnerships, and corporations.

[2] Another term widely used to describe the monetary base is "high-powered money." Cf. Friedman and Schwartz (1963). Also see Cagan (1965).

As we saw earlier, from the monetary accounts of the Treasury in Table 10-2, we can write Treasury cash (J) as

$$J = (U - U_c) + X_F^T + X_T^T \qquad (10\text{-}5)$$

so that

$$X_T^T = J - (U - U_c) - X_F^T$$

and

$$-X_T^T = U - J - U_c + X_F^T$$

and

$$X_T - X_T^T = X_T + U - J - U_c + X_F^T \qquad (10\text{-}6)$$

Thus, substituting (10-4) and (10-6) into (10-3), we can write the monetary base as

$$H = (U_c + B_b^F + B_g^F + B_p^F + Z^F + X_T^F - D_F^T - D_F^f - L^F)$$
$$+ (X_T + U - J - U_c + X_F^T) - X_F^T - X_T^F \qquad (10\text{-}7)$$

Eliminating terms, we obtain

$$H = B_g^F + B_p^F + B_b^F + Z^F + X_T + U - J - D_F^T - D_F^f - L^F \qquad (10\text{-}8)$$

That is, the monetary base consists of Federal Reserve credit (discounts and advances, government security holdings, and acceptances); *plus* other Federal Reserve assets (mainly float and foreign exchange); *plus* the gold stock and Treasury currency outstanding; *less* Treasury cash, foreign and Treasury deposits at the Federal Reserve, and miscellaneous Federal Reserve liability and capital accounts. The Federal Reserve operates directly on B_g^F, and indirectly on B_p^F and B_b^F (by setting the rediscount rate and the discount rate on acceptances). The Treasury operates directly on X_T, J, and D_F^T, although in the case of the last one, it must operate within the constraint imposed on it by the need to maintain a satisfactory working balance at the Federal Reserve and on the budget deficit or surplus condition generated by the tax structure and government spending. U and D_F^f reflect the international monetary situation and policies of foreign governments and central banks and Z^F reflects the host of forces producing variations in the float.[3] In effect, the Federal Reserve operates, primarily on B_g^F but also indirectly on B_b^F and B_p^F, to offset all the other forces affecting H to achieve the amount it desires.

For our purposes, it is more convenient to use the *adjusted* monetary base, defined as the monetary base (H) *minus* bank borrowing and rediscounts at the Federal Reserve (B_b^F). The adjusted monetary base Ha is therefore given by (10-9):

$$Ha = B_g^F + B_p^F + Z^F + X_T + U - J - D_F^T - D_F^f - L^F \qquad (10\text{-}9)$$

Using data from the *Federal Reserve Bulletin* (September 1973 issue), the dollar value of the adjusted monetary base in the United States, December 1972, averaged $89.7 billion:

$$89.7 = 71.1 + 0.1 + 4.6 + 8.3 + 10.8 - 0.4 - 1.5 - 0.3 - 3.0$$

---

[3] U includes the special drawing rights (SDR) certificate account.

Since the central bank directly controls only B_g^F—its holdings of government securities—it must engage in open market purchases or sales to *offset* movements in the other factors affecting the adjusted monetary base. These are called *defensive* open market operations. On the other hand, even if movements in the factors other than B_g^F canceled themselves out, the central bank would normally be changing B_g^F to adjust the level of Ha. Such open market operations are *offensive*. Since both defensive actions and offensive actions in B_g^F are going on continuously, it is difficult to read the *direction* of Federal Reserve policy by observing its open market operations. A flurry of purchases of B_g^F may simply reflect action to offset the effect of a rise in Treasury deposits at the Federal Reserve (D_F^T) on the base rather than an attempt to increase the base (or increase it at a faster rate).

However, by observing the rate of growth of Ha over several months, it is possible to infer more about the general direction of monetary policy. Here we treat Ha as exogenous and put a bar over it ($\overline{Ha}$).

THE MONEY SUPPLY EQUATION

From the above discussion of the adjusted monetary base, we know that in its simplest form the base is

$$Ha = H - B_b^F$$
$$= R + X^P - B_b^F \qquad (10\text{-}10)$$

The most commonly used definition of money (see Chapter 9) is currency plus demand deposits by the public (or M_1):

$$M = X^P + DD^p \qquad (10\text{-}11)$$

From our knowledge of the balance sheets of the monetary system, we can use (10-10) and (10-11) to expand the simple expression for the money supply ($M_s = m\overline{H}$) used until now. First, let us define the currency, time deposit, and government deposit ratios:

$$\text{Currency ratio} = k = X^p/DD^p \qquad (10\text{-}12)$$

$$\text{Time deposit ratio} = t = DT/DD^p \qquad (10\text{-}13)$$

$$\text{Government deposit ratio} = d = DD^g/DD^p \qquad (10\text{-}14)$$

Next, we can divide the total reserves of commercial banks into *required reserves* and *excess reserves*:

$$R = R^r + R^e \qquad (10\text{-}15)$$

as well as into borrowed and unborrowed reserves:

$$R = R^b + R^u$$
$$= B_b^F + R^u \qquad (10\text{-}16)$$

Rewriting (10-16), we get, for R^u,

$$R^u = R - R^b \qquad (10\text{-}17)$$

Substituting for R from (10-15), we obtain

$$R^u = R^r + (R^e - R^b) \qquad (10\text{-}18)$$

Equation (10-18) notes that unborrowed reserves of commercial banks are equal to required reserves (R^r) plus *free reserves* ($R^e - R^b$), the latter representing the difference between excess reserves and borrowings of reserves from the Federal Reserve by commercial banks.

Now we define the *average* required reserve ratio—the ratio of required reserves to total deposits:

$$r^r = \frac{R^r}{D} = \frac{R}{DD^p + DD^g + DT} \qquad (10\text{-}19)$$

Since the required reserve ratio may vary as between demand and time deposits and for different banks, r^r is a weighted-average reserve ratio.

Similarly, we may define the desired excess reserves ratio r^e and borrowed reserves ratio b of the banking system:

$$r^e = \frac{R^e}{DD^p + DD^g + DT} \qquad (10\text{-}20)$$

$$b = \frac{B_b^F}{DD^p + DD^g + DT} \qquad (10\text{-}21)$$

and from these two, the desired *free* reserves ratio of the banking system:

$$r^f = r^e - b = \frac{R^e - B_b^F}{DD^p + DD^g + DT} \qquad (10\text{-}22)$$

Using Eqs. (10-10), (10-15), (10-18), (10-20), and (10-21), we get an expression for the adjusted monetary base:

$$\bar{H}a = R + X^p - B_b^F \qquad (10\text{-}10)$$
$$= R^u + X^p$$
$$= R^r + (R^e - R^b) + X^p$$
$$= [r^r + (r^e - b)](DD^p + DD^g + DT) + X^p$$
$$= (r^r + r^f)DD^p(1 + d + t) + DD^p k$$
$$= DD^p[(r^r + r^f)(1 + d + t) + k] \qquad (10\text{-}23)$$

Solving (10-23) for $DD,^p$ we get

$$DD^p = \bar{H}a/[(r^r + r^f)(1 + d + t) + k]$$

Since $X^p = kDD^p$, we get for M [Eq. (10-11)]:

$$M_s = DD^p + X^p = \left[\frac{1 + k}{(r^r + r^f)(1 + d + t) + k}\right]\bar{H}a \qquad (10\text{-}24)$$

Equation (10-24) is the money supply function, where the bracketed expression is the expanded money multiplier m. Substituting for $\bar{H}a$ from (10-9), we get, for the expanded money supply function,

$$M_s = \left[\frac{1+k}{(r^r + r^f)(1 + d + t) + k}\right](B_g{}^F + B_p{}^F + Z^F + X_T + U - J - D_F{}^T - D_F{}^f - L^F)$$

(10-25)

Equation (10-25) thus reflects all the major factors affecting the supply of money, whether through the money multiplier m or through the adjusted monetary base Ha. Over time, the rate of growth of the money stock (assuming $M_s = M_d$) will equal (approximately)

$$\frac{dM}{M} = \frac{dHa}{Ha} + \frac{dm}{m} \qquad (10\text{-}26)$$

or the sum of the rates of growth of the adjusted base and m.

Since the forces affecting Ha are straightforwardly shown in Eq. (10-25), consider the variables affecting the money multiplier m [the bracketed expression in Eq. (10-25)].

The free reserve ratio r^f is not exogenous and certainly not a constant. The *desired free* reserve ratio can be viewed as determined by a bank's comparison of risk versus return, in the vein of the Tobin-Markowitz model discussed in the previous chapter. By lowering their free reserve ratio, banks can earn more interest (by increasing their loans). At the same time, a lower free reserve ratio makes a bank more exposed to reserve shortages which will entail borrowing reserves from the Federal Reserve or in the open market. In this setting, the desired free reserve ratio $r_d{}^f$ can be expressed as a function of the interest rate (which the loan rate moves with) and the discount rate charged by the Federal Reserve when a bank runs short of reserves and is forced to borrow:

$$r_d{}^f = f(i, \rho) \qquad f_i < 0 \qquad f_\rho > 0 \qquad (10\text{-}27)$$

A rise in i increases the marginal return from reducing $r_d{}^f$ and lending more; hence it causes a *fall* in the desired free reserve ratio. A rise in the Federal Reserve's discount rate ρ increases the price that has to be paid if a bank runs short and has to borrow reserves; hence it induces a rise in $r_d{}^f$ to reduce the probability of a reserve shortage occurring.

Substituting (10-27) into (10-24)—assuming the actual free reserve ratio equal to the desired ratio—we see that the money supply is a positive function of the interest rate. As i rises, the desired free reserve ratio falls; this decreases the denominator in the expression for m and causes M_s to rise, given $\bar{H}a$.

In addition, the t ratio may also depend on i. As i rises, there is a shift from demand deposits DD^p to securities. This alone would tend to *raise* $t(= DT/DD^p)$. But there may also be a shift from time deposits DT to securities, if the rate paid on time deposits is not raised by banks by enough to offset the rise in i or if they are constrained by controls on their rates. In general, however, we may assume that $t_i > 0$, that a rise in i will decrease demand deposits demanded more than time deposits demanded.

While the currency ratio k can be argued to depend on interest rates, we assume here that it is not. In addition, the d ratio is assumed to be determined exogenously by the Treasury.

Thus, we may write the M_s function as

$$M_s = m(i, \rho, r^r)Ha \qquad (10\text{-}28)$$

where m_i may be positive or negative depending on the relative size of t_i and f_i. We assume that it is positive, that the supply of money is a positive function of i. The effect of the discount rate ρ is unambiguous; it clearly *increases* the free reserve ratio r^f and *reduces* M_s, as does an increase in the average required reserve ratio r^r.

With the demand-for-money function from Chapter 9 and the market equilibrium condition

$$\frac{M_d}{p} = L\left(Y^L, i, i_s, i_t, \frac{A}{p}\right) \qquad (9\text{-}21)$$

$$M_d = M_s$$

the financial sector is complete. Discussion of i_s and i_t is best held over to the following section.

In terms of the basic models discussed in Chapter 3, the major change is the dependence of the money multiplier on the rate of interest, which makes the supply of money an endogenous variable. Estimates put the elasticity of M_s with respect to i in the neighborhood of 0.2. The theoretical implication of this is that the fiscal multipliers are somewhat larger than when M_s was exogenous, while the money multipliers are reduced. If we compare the Keynesian-case government purchases and Ha multipliers[4] with these in Chapter 3, this is clear:

Old Multiplier	*New Multiplier*

$$\frac{dY}{d\bar{G}} = \frac{1}{1 - C_{Y_d}(1 - \tau) + \dfrac{I_i L_y}{L_i}} \qquad \qquad \frac{dY}{d\bar{G}} = \frac{1}{1 - C_{Y_d}(1 - \tau) + \dfrac{I_i L_y}{L_i - m_i \bar{H}a}}$$

$$\frac{dY}{d\bar{H}a} = \frac{m}{[1 - C_{Y_d}(1 - \tau)]\dfrac{L_i}{I_i} + L_y} \qquad \frac{dY}{d\bar{H}a} = \frac{m}{[1 - C_{Y_d}(1 - \tau)]\dfrac{(L_i - m_i \bar{H}a)}{I_i} + L_y}$$

The logic is quite simple. An increase in $\bar{G}$ causes Y and thus M_d to rise; before, this required i to rise, given $\bar{H}a$. Now, the rise in i induces a rise in m, which makes the required rise in i less and the offsetting effect on I less than before. In the case of an increase in $\bar{H}a$, the fall in i that ensues is not as large as before and the "kick"

---

[4] Note that if $\bar{H}a$ is used instead of $\bar{H}$, there is a difference in the size of m.

on I not as great; part of the effect is dissipated by the fall in m, and thus M_s, which occurs when i falls.

Thus, the more endogenous the supply of money is (the larger the effect of i on m and M_s), the less potent monetary policy is and the more potent fiscal policy is.

The reader may also now derive multipliers for changes in the discount rate and reserve requirements, using the earlier models modified by Eqs. (10-28). Thus the financial sector is expanded to allow for discussion of the effects of the range of tools of monetary policy.

THE DEMAND FOR AND SUPPLY OF THE MONETARY BASE: THE "WEAK APPROACH"

An alternative to putting the financial sector in terms of the supply of and demand for *money* is to construct a demand function for the *adjusted monetary base* and then center attention on the relation between the supply of and demand for this "high-powered money."

The Demand for *Ha*

When the public seeks to hold claims on banks—demand or time deposits—it gives rise to an indirect demand for the monetary base. Since banks hold a portion of the monetary base as reserves against demand and time deposits, they will desire more of the monetary base as their deposits increase. We can visualize each bank accepting all deposits made subject to the conditions and interest rates applying at the time. The supply of deposits at each bank is perfectly elastic at the going market rate and other conditions. Each dollar of deposits demanded by the public gives rise to a *derived demand* for the monetary base.

When the public decides to hold a dollar of currency, this is a direct demand for the monetary base; as we saw earlier in this chapter, the monetary base consists of bank reserves and currency in the hands of the public.

Let us then develop a demand function for the monetary base. From (10-15), *desired* total reserves of banks (R^d) is equal to

$$R^d = R^r + R^e \quad (10\text{-}15a)$$

i.e., the sum of required reserves R^r and desired *excess* reserves R^e. Required reserves in turn are given by

$$R_r = r_d^r DD + r_t^r DT \quad (10\text{-}29)$$

the sum of a weighted-average reserve ratio required for demand deposits times the public's holdings of demand deposits *plus* a weighted-average required reserve ratio for commercial bank time deposits times the public's holdings of time deposits.

From the discussion in the previous section, we may write desired excess reserves of the banking system in the following general form:

$$R^e = R^e(i, \rho, DD, DT) \quad (10\text{-}30)$$

Clearly, desired excess reserves are positively related to demand deposits DD and time deposits DT; as total deposits increase, so does the probable reserve loss through a drain to other banks. The rate of interest i is the opportunity cost of holding no-yield assets—reserves—so that we may expect desired excess reserves to vary inversely with i. The discount rate ρ is taken as a measure of the cost of obtaining reserves if the bank is caught short, so that we would expect desired excess reserves to vary directly with ρ.

Suppose we separate excess reserves into those held against demand deposits and those held against time deposits, and write the desired excess reserves functions as

$$R_{DD}{}^e = R_{DD}{}^e(i, \rho, DD) \quad (10\text{-}31a)$$

$$R_{DT}{}^e = R_{DT}{}^e(i, \rho, DT) \quad (10\text{-}31b)$$

Assume also that $(10\text{-}31a)$ and $(10\text{-}31b)$ are homogeneous to degree one in DD and DT, respectively. Then we may write

$$R_{DD}{}^e = e_d(i, \rho)DD \quad (10\text{-}31c)$$

$$R_{DT}{}^e = e_t(i, \rho)DT \quad (10\text{-}31d)$$

where e_d is the desired excess reserve *ratio* against demand deposits and e_t is the desired excess reserve *ratio* against time deposits. The total desired stock of excess reserves of the banking system is then

$$R^e = e_d(i, \rho)DD + e_t(i, \rho)DT \quad (10\text{-}32)$$

By assumption

$$\frac{\partial R^e}{\partial i} < 0 \qquad \frac{\partial R^e}{\partial \rho} > 0 \qquad \frac{\partial R^e}{\partial DD} > 0 \qquad \frac{\partial R^e}{\partial DT} > 0$$

For simplicity we assume banks adjust instantaneously any discrepancy between their desired stock of excess reserves and the actual stock, so that the stock of excess reserves at any time equals the desired stock.

We can now write the demand for total reserves by substituting $(10\text{-}29)$ and $(10\text{-}32)$ into $(10\text{-}15)$:

$$R = R^r + R^e \quad (10\text{-}15)$$

$$R = r_d{}^r DD + r_t{}^r DT + e_d(i, \rho)DD + e_t(i, \rho)DT$$

$$R = [r_d{}^r + e_d(i, \rho)]DD + [r_t{}^r + e_t(i, \rho)]DT \quad (10\text{-}33)$$

Since the demand for the monetary base, or high-powered money, is the sum of the demand for reserves by banks and the demand for currency by the nonbank public, we get

$$H_d = R + X^P = [r_d{}^r + e_d(i, \rho)]DD + [r_t{}^r + e_t(i, \rho)]DT + X^P \quad (10\text{-}34)$$

To get the demand for the *adjusted* monetary base we subtract the demand by banks for borrowed reserves from the demand for the monetary base. Reasoning along lines parallel to the demand function for excess reserves, we may write the demand-for-borrowed-reserves function as

$$R^b = b_d(i, \rho)DD + b_t(i, \rho)DD \qquad (10\text{-}35)$$

If for simplicity we assume $b_d = b_t$ and $e_d = e_t$, then subtracting (10-35) from (10-34), we get the demand for the adjusted monetary base:

$$Ha_d = [r_d^r + e(i, \rho) - b(i, \rho)]DD + [r_t^r + e(i, \rho) - b(i, \rho)]DT + X^p \qquad (10\text{-}36)$$

Now consider DD, DT, and X^p in (10-36). If we assume again, for simplicity, that there are no lags, the real stocks of these assets held by the private nonfinancial sector at any time, from the discussion in the previous chapter, are given by Eqs. (9-23), (9-25), and (9-22). Let us assume for simplicity that holdings of DD and DT by the federal government and by saving institutions depend on the same variables as private holdings. We may therefore rewrite (10-36) as follows:[5]

$$Ha_d = [r_d + e(i, \rho) - b(i, \rho)]p\lambda\left(Y^L, i, i_s, i_t, \frac{A}{p}\right)$$

$$+ [r_t + e(i, \rho) - b(i, \rho)]p\theta\left(Y^L, i, i_s, i_t, \frac{A}{p}\right)$$

$$+ p\mu\left(Y^L, i, i_s, i_t, \frac{A}{p}\right) \qquad (10\text{-}37)$$

If both sides of (10-37) are divided by p, the demand for the *real* adjusted monetary base may be written

$$\frac{Ha_d}{p} = H\left(r_d^r, r_t^r, i, \rho, i_s, i_t, Y^L, \frac{A}{p}\right) \qquad (10\text{-}38)$$

By assumptions made during the construction of Ha_d/p, we have the following signs of its partial derivatives with respect to r_d^r, r_t^r, Y^L, and ρ:

$$H_{r_d^r} > 0 \qquad H_{r_t^r} > 0 \qquad H_\rho > 0 \qquad (10\text{-}39)$$

$$H_{YL} > 0 \qquad H_{A/p} > 0$$

The relation between the demand for Ha/p and interest rates on securities, savings shares, and time deposits is complex, primarily because i_t and i_s, the rates of return

---

[5] Alternatively, we could write (10-37) using the desired *free reserve ratio* against demand and time deposits:

$$Ha_d = [r_d + r^f(i, \rho)]p\lambda\left(Y^L, i, i_s, i_t, \frac{A}{p}\right) + [r_t + r^f(i, \rho)]p\theta$$

$$\left(Y^L, i, i_s, i_t, \frac{A}{p}\right) + p\mu\left(Y, i, i_s, i_t, \frac{A}{p}\right)$$

on time deposits and savings shares, are related to the rate of interest on securities i. During any period in time, we may write the relation between i_s and i_t and i as

$$i - f_s = i_s \quad (10\text{-}40a)$$

$$i - f_t = i_t \quad (10\text{-}40b)$$

f_s and f_t represent gross profits per dollar of savings shares and time deposits, respectively, or the "unit profit of intermediation." This is determined by the legal framework under which financial institutions operate—restrictions on the number of firms, investment policies of firms, etc.—and market forces. f_s and f_t would generally decline if economies of scale were prevalent, if there were reductions in the cost of intermediation, or if entry provisions were eased for new firms. Changes in i_s and i_t thus occur with changes in the general level of interest rates on securities i, or with changes in f_s and f_t, in which case i_s and i_t change *relative to i*.

With this in mind, we may rewrite (10-38) as

$$\frac{Ha_d}{p} = H\left(r_d^r, r_t^r, i, \rho, f_s, f_t, Y^L, \frac{A}{p}\right) \quad (10\text{-}38a)$$

and consider the partial derivatives

$$\frac{\partial Ha_d/p}{\partial i}, \frac{\partial Ha_d/p}{\partial f_s}, \frac{\partial Ha_d/p}{\partial f_t}$$

If i changes with f_s and f_t remaining constant, we have $di = di_s = di_t$. The partial of Ha_d/p with respect to $i(H_i)$ will then be

$$
\begin{aligned}
H_i = {} & [r_d^r + e(i, \rho)](\lambda_i + \lambda_{i_s} + \lambda_{i_t} + \lambda_A A_i) \\
& + (e_i - b_i)\lambda + [r_t^r + e(i, \rho) \\
& - b(i, \rho)][(\theta_i + \theta_{i_s} + \theta_{i_t}) + \theta_A A_i] + (e_i - b_i)\theta \\
& + (\mu_i + \mu_{i_s} + \mu_{i_t} + \mu_A A_i)
\end{aligned}
\quad (10\text{-}38b)
$$

Clearly $e_i - b_i$ is negative; the desired excess reserve ratio against demand or time deposits *falls* when i rises and the desired borrowed reserve ratio *rises* when i rises. $\lambda_A A_i$ and $\theta_A A_i$ are negative; a fall in i *increases* A (for convenience we assume $p = 1$). By the analysis of the previous chapter, λ_i, λ_{i_s}, λ_{i_t}, θ_i, θ_{i_s}, μ_i, μ_{i_s}, and μ_{i_t} are also negative, but θ_{i_t} is positive; the partial derivative of the demand for time deposits with respect to the rate of return on time deposits is positive. We assume θ_{i_t} is absolutely small enough so that

$$\frac{\partial Ha_d/p}{\partial i} < 0$$

Thus on a graph with i plotted on the ordinate and Ha on the abscissa, the Ha_d curve has a negative slope, as shown in Figure 10-1.

What happens to Ha_d when f_s or f_t changes, i.e., when rates of return on savings shares and time deposits change *relative* to the interest rate on securities? Let us take changes in f_s first. A fall in f_s (a rise in i_s alone) *decreases* the amounts demanded of

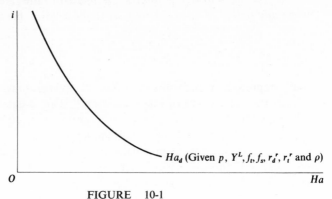

FIGURE 10-1
The demand curve for the adjusted monetary base.

DD, DT, and X^p. Clearly, in this case the demand for Ha_d *falls*. A fall in f_t (a rise in i_t is given levels of i and i_s) *decreases* the demand for DD and X^p but *increases* the demand for DT. The net effect on Ha_d depends on which of these effects is stronger. If time deposits are close substitutes for savings shares and securities and not for demand deposits and currency, it may well be that a fall in f_t (a rise in i_t) will *increase* the demand for the adjusted monetary base. On the other hand, a close substitute relationship between time deposits and demand deposits and currency may mean the demand for *Ha falls*, since X^p and DD have larger "multiplier" terms in front of them (since $r_d^r > r_t^r$ and the multiplier for X^p is unity). We will make no a priori judgment on this point.

Looking at the Ha_d curve in Figure 10-1, then, we can expect it to shift *rightward* when (1) real labor income Y^L rises, (2) r_d^r rises, and/or r_t^r rises, (3) ρ rises, (4) p rises,[6] or (5) f_s rises (i_s falls). It will shift leftward when these changes in Y^L, r_d^r, r_t^r, ρ, p, and f_s are reversed. When f_t changes, the effect on the Ha_d curve is ambiguous.

Equilibrium in the Market for the Adjusted Monetary Base

We can now combine the demand and supply functions for the adjusted monetary base and discuss equilibrium in the markets for financial assets. For any period, suppose the Federal Reserve System has control over the supply of the adjusted monetary base Ha_s. The demand for that base depends, as we have seen, on certain monetary policy variables—minimum reserve ratios against demand and time deposits and the discount rate—the rate of interest on securities, the price level, and the "unit

---

[6] The demand for *nominal Ha* rises when p rises because the premultiplicative p when Ha_d/p is converted to Ha_d "swamps" the negative affect of the A/p term. In short, a rise in p *reduces* the demand for *real Ha*, but not by as much as the proportion that p rises.

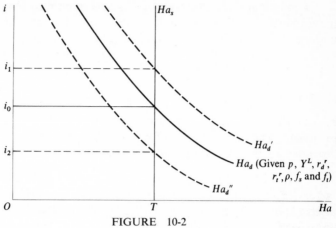

FIGURE   10-2

Equilibrium in the market for the monetary base.

profit of intermediation" in time deposits and savings shares. The market for Ha is thus in equilibrium in any period when $Ha_s = Ha_d$. This is shown graphically in Figure 10-2. Given Y^L, p, r_d^r, r_t^r, ρ, f_s, f_t, and the supply of Ha ($= OT$), the market for Ha is in equilibrium at an interest rate on securities of i_0. Anything *increasing* the demand for Ha, say to Ha_d', will *increase* the rate of interest required for equilibrium (given Ha_s). Forces decreasing Ha_d, for example to Ha_d'', will *decrease* the interest rate needed for $Ha_d = Ha_s$. Clearly, also any increase in Ha_s will *lower* the interest rate needed for market equilibrium and vice versa for a *decrease* in the supply of Ha. But given Y^L, p, r_d^r, r_t^r, ρ, f_s, f_t, and Ha_s, there is, for any period only *one* interest rate that equilibrates the market for high-powered money.

Equilibrium in the market for Ha means, conveniently, equilibrium in the markets for all financial assets *except* securities. When the market for Ha is in equilibrium, the public is holding the desired amounts of DD, DT, S, and X^p. This implies that it must also be holding the desired (net) amount of securities B^p. Since the banking system is in equilibrium when $Ha_d = Ha_s$, it must also be holding the desired amount of securities B^b, and the same holds for savings institutions B^s. The total demand for the stock of securities outstanding is composed of demands by the public, commercial banks, and savings institutions ($B = B^p + B^b + B^s$). We thus have equilibrium in the markets for claims on intermediaries ($DD + DT + S$) and currency (X^p). This does not mean that the rate of interest (i_s, i_t, i), the level of income (Y^L) and price level (p), and the monetary policy variables (Ha_s, ρ, r_d^r, and r_t^r) which "clear" the markets for DD, DT, S, and X^p also necessarily "clear" the securities market. Even if the desired holdings of securities by financial intermediaries (which equals $DD + DT + S + X^p$) and the public at the given set of values of the independent variables just equal the desired stock of claims on intermediaries and securities held by the public, there is no assurance that the desired holding of B by intermediaries *and* the public will just equal the desired *supply* of securities by firms, consumers, and government.

Equilibrium in the market for Ha thus implies equilibrium in the market for intermediary claims and currency; it does not imply equilibrium in all financial markets. However, if the commodity market is also cleared, then by Walras' law (Patinkin, 1965), clearing the market for Ha also implies clearing the market for B.

SUMMARY

In this chapter, we have explored the factors affecting the supply side of the market for money. The supply function for money was seen to depend on interest rates, the discount rate, reserve requirements, and the supply of the adjusted monetary base:

$$M_s = m(i, \rho, r^r)Ha \quad (10\text{-}28)$$

Factors affecting Ha were discussed in detail. If we assume that the central bank offsets the other forces affecting Ha, Ha can be considered exogenous. However, the money supply multiplier—m—is in part endogenous. Increases in the rate of interest, by lowering the desired free reserve ratio of commercial banks, *increase M_s* for a given value of Ha. This endogenous characteristic of M_s makes monetary policy (in terms of the basic Keynesian-case multipliers) less potent and fiscal policy more potent.

An alternative approach to the financial sector was also considered. A demand function for the adjusted monetary base can be derived and the financial sector can be approached in terms of equilibrium in the market for Ha.

READINGS FOR CHAPTER 10

FRIEDMAN, MILTON, and ANNA JACOBSON SCHWARTZ: *A Monetary History of the United States, 1867–1960* (Princeton, N.J.: Princeton, 1963), app. B.

BIRCH, ELEANOR M. and JOHN M. HEINEKE: "Stochastic Reserve Losses," *The American Economist*, vol. XI, pp. 20–28, Spring 1967.

BOORMAN, JOHN T.: "Stochastic Reserve Losses: Comment," *The American Economist*, vol. XI, pp. 28–35, Spring 1967.

BRUNNER, KARL: "A Schema for the Supply Theory of Money," *The International Economic Review*, vol. II, pp. 79–109, January 1961.

BRUNNER, KARL, and ALLAN H. MELTZER: "Some Further Investigations of Demand and Supply Functions for Money," *The Journal of Finance*.

BRUNNER, KARL: "Some Major Problems in Monetary Theory: Bank Reserves and the Money Supply Mechanism," *The American Economic Review*, vol. LI, pp. 47–56, May 1961.

BRUNNER, KARL and ALLAN H. MELTZER: "A Credit Market Theory of the Money Supply and an Explanation of Two Puzzles in U.S. Monetary Policy," *Rivista Internazionale di Scienze Economiche e Commerciali*, vol. XIII, pp. 405–432, May 1966.

BURGESS, ALFRED: *The Money Supply Process* (Belmont, Calif.: Wadsworth, 1971).

BRYAN, WILLIAM R.: "The Response of Banks to Changes in Aggregate Reserves: Comment," *The Journal of Finance*, vol. XXI, pp. 539–541, September 1966.

CAGAN, PHILLIP: "The Demand for Currency Relative to the Total Money Supply," *The Journal of Political Economy*, vol. LXVI, pp. 303–328, August 1958.

————: *Determinants and Effects of Changes in the Stock of Money, 1875–1960*, National Bureau of Economic Research (Princeton, N.J.: Princeton, 1965), chaps. 1–2.

COLLERY, A. P.: "A Graphic Analysis of the Theory of the Determination of the Money Supply," *The Journal of Finance*, vol. XI, pp. 328–331, September 1956.

CRAMP, A. B.: "Control of the Money Supply," *The Economic Journal*, pp. 278–287, June 1966.

DEWALD, WILLIAM G.: "Free Reserves, Total Reserves, and Monetary Control," *The Journal of Political Economy*, vol. LXXI, pp. 141–153, April 1963.

FAND, DAVID I.: "Some Implications of Money Supply Analysis," *The American Economic Review*, vol. LVII, pp. 380–400, May 1967.

GRAMLEY, L. E., and S. B. CHASE: "Time Deposits in Monetary Analysis," *Federal Reserve Bulletin*, October 1965.

JORDAN, JERRY L.: "Elements of Money Stock Determination, *Review of Federal Reserve Bank of St. Louis*, vol. 51, no. 10, pp. 10–19.

MEIGS, A. JAMES: *Free Reserves and the Money Supply* (Chicago: The University of Chicago Press, 1962).

MELTZER, ALLAN H.: "The Behavior of the French Money Supply: 1938–54," *The Journal of Political Economy*, vol. LXVII, pp. 275–296, June 1959.

————: "Money Supply Revisited: A Review Article," *The Journal of Political Economy*, vol. LXXV, pp. 169–182, April 1967.

————: "Some Implications of Money Supply Analysis: Comment," *The American Economic Review*, vol. LVII, pp. 426–428, May 1967.

MILLER, H. LAURENCE: "Stochastic Reserve Losses and Expansion of Bank Credit: Comment," *The American Economic Review*, vol. III, pp. 1118–1120, December 1962.

ORR, D., and W. G. MELLON: "Stochastic Reserve Losses and Expansion of Bank Credit," *American Economic Review*, September 1961.

————: "Stochastic Reserve Losses and Expansion of Bank Credit: Reply to Comment by H. Laurence Miller," *The American Economic Review*, vol. LII, pp. 1120–1122, December 1962.

PATINKIN, D.: *Money, Interest, and Prices* (New York: Harper and Row, 1965).

RANGARAJAN, C., and ALAN K. SEVERN: "The Response of Banks to Changes in Aggregate Reserves," *The Journal of Finance*, vol. XX, pp. 651–664, December 1965.

ROSS, MYRON H.: "Some Implications of Money Supply Analysis: Comment," *The American Economic Review*, vol. LVII, pp. 428–432, May 1967.

TEIGEN, RONALD L.: "Demand and Supply Functions for Money in the United States: Some Structural Estimates," *Econometrica*, vol. XXXII, pp. 476–509, October 1964.

TIEGEN, RONALD L.: "The Demand and Supply of Money," in Warren L. Smith and Ronald Teigen (eds.), *Income and Stabilization Policy* (Homewood, Ill.: Irwin, 1965).

TOBIN, JAMES: "Commercial Banks as Creators of Money," in Dean Carson (ed.), *Banking and Monetary Studies* (Homewood, Ill.: Irwin, 1963), pp. 408–419.

WALTERS, A. A.: "Monetary Multipliers in the U.S.," *Oxford Economic Papers*, vol. XVIII, pp. 270–283, November 1966.

YOHE, WILLIAM P.: "The Derivation of Certain Financial Multipliers," *The Southern Economic Journal*, vol. XXIX, pp. 26–32, July 1962.

11

THE GOVERNMENT SECTOR:
THE BUDGET CONSTRAINT

The government sector used in the simple models discussed in Chapter 3 was represented by the following equations:

$$G = \bar{G}$$

$$T = \frac{\bar{T}}{p} + \tau(Y) \qquad (3\text{-}7)$$

Real government expenditures (G) were assumed to be exogenous and determined according to "needs"; real taxes (T) were assumed to be a function of real GNP (Y) and prices (p).

In the real world, the government sector is immensely more complicated. First, the sector (at least for the United States) can be split in two—separate expenditure and tax equations can be identified for the federal government and for state and local governments. Second, within each of these two government sectors, separate functions can be developed for each of the major types of taxes—personal and corporate income taxes, sales and excise taxes (IBT), and social insurance (payroll) taxes —and for different types of expenditures.

Most large-scale econometric models do attempt to refine the government sector in both of these directions.[1] However, detailed analysis of separate tax and spending functions for the taxes and expenditures of each of the two parts of the government sector involves an enormous effort and detracts somewhat from the central skeleton of macroeconomic theory. Therefore, in this book, we shall continue to assume that the simplified tax and expenditure functions are "real."

There is yet a third simplification made in the basic models of Chapter 3 which has fundamental consequences and cannot be ignored—no equation was specified for the *budget constraint* of the government sector, i.e., the means used to finance its deficit or surplus. Adding the budget constraint has important ramifications for the fiscal and monetary policy multipliers, and this chapter is devoted to the subject.

THE NATURE OF THE BUDGET CONSTRAINT

The basic equation and rationale for the constraint on the government sector are quite simple. In each time period, the government sector's deficit (or surplus) must just equal the sum of (1) the change in government bonds held by the public (including commercial banks); (2) the change in high-powered money (if the central bank buys government bonds); and (3) the change in the Treasury's own balances—deposits at the central bank and Treasury cash. Since item 3 is not likely to be of lasting importance over any length of time, then in terms of the first two, we may write the constraint as follows:

$$p\bar{G} - \bar{T} - \tau p Y = d\bar{H}a + dB_g^p \qquad (11\text{-}1)$$

or

$$\bar{G} = \frac{\bar{T}}{p} + \tau Y + \frac{d\bar{H}a}{p} + \frac{dB_g^p}{p} \qquad (11\text{-}2)$$

The significance of the budget constraint is apparent from (11-1) and (11-2). At least *one* of the five policy variables—$\bar{G}$, $\bar{T}$, τ, $\bar{H}a$, and B_g^p—is endogenous. Suppose we pick the most likely candidate for this category, namely, government bonds held by the public (B_g^p). It is clear that a fiscal action, say an increase in purchases $\bar{G}$, could be financed in several ways. On the one hand, the Federal Reserve could finance any deficit not covered by the induced rise in taxes. At another extreme, the Federal Reserve could leave Ha unchanged, and let B_g^p rise (have the government sell bonds to the public) to the extent that tax revenues do not rise to cover the deficit. The results will be quite different in the two cases, all because we now recognize that whatever policy actions are carried out, they must satisfy the government's budget constraint.

---

[1] For example, de Leeuw and Gramlich (1968). For a model of the state and local sector, see Gramlich and Galper (1973).

THE BUDGET CONSTRAINT AND THE MULTIPLIERS

A simplified case will highlight the importance of this added equation: Let us take the basic Keynesian model of Chapter 3 and modify it to reflect the budget constraint. The relevant equations are shown as (11-3) to (11-5):

$$Y_t = C[(1 - \tau)Y_t] + I(i_t) + \bar{G}_t \qquad (11\text{-}3)$$

$$m\bar{H}a_t = L(Y_t, i_t) \qquad (11\text{-}4)$$

$$\bar{H}a_t = \bar{H}a_{t-1} + \bar{G}_{t-1} - \tau Y_{t-1} \qquad (11\text{-}5)$$

Equation (11-5) is the budget constraint, where it is assumed that (with a lag) all government deficits are financed by the central bank which buys government bonds, thus increasing Ha. For simplicity we assume that $\bar{T} = 0$, that the money supply multiplier m is constant, and p (which is a constant in the basic Keynesian model) equals unity, and that all the behavioral equations are linear in the variables.

Now assume we begin in equilibrium at time $t = 0$, with the government's budget in balance, and that at the beginning of time $t = 1$, $\bar{G}$ is raised permanently to a higher level. Solving for the behavior of Y over time, we get

$$\Delta Y_t = C_{Y_d}(1 - \tau)\Delta Y_t + I_i \Delta i_t + \Delta \bar{G}_t \qquad (11\text{-}6)$$

Substituting for Δi_t from (11-4) and (11-5), we get

$$\Delta Y_t = C_{Y_d}(1 - \tau)\,\Delta Y_t + I_i\left[\frac{m}{L_i}(\bar{G}_{t-1} - \tau Y_{t-1}) - \frac{L_Y}{L_i}\,\Delta Y_t\right] + \Delta \bar{G}_t$$

Collecting terms in ΔY_t we get

$$\Delta Y_t\left[1 - C_{Y_d}(1 - \tau) + \frac{I_i L_Y}{L_i}\right] = \frac{I_i m}{L_i}(\bar{G}_{t-1} - \tau Y_{t-1}) + \Delta \bar{G}_t$$

or $\quad Y_t\left[1 - C_{Y_d}(1 - \tau) + \dfrac{I_i L_Y}{L_i}\right] = Y_{t-1}\left\{\left[1 - C_{Y_d}(1 - \tau) + \dfrac{I_i L_Y}{L_i}\right] - \dfrac{I_i m\tau}{L_i}\right\}$

$$+ \bar{G}_t - \left(1 - \frac{I_i m}{L_i}\right)\bar{G}_{t-1}$$

For simplicity, write $[1 - C_{Y_d}(1 - \tau) + I_i L_Y/L_i]$ as D. Then we have

$$Y_t = \left(1 - \frac{I_i m\tau}{L_i D}\right)Y_{t-1} + \frac{\bar{G}_t}{D} - \left(\frac{1 - \dfrac{I_i m}{L_i}}{D}\right)\bar{G}_{t-1} \qquad (11\text{-}7)$$

Since we are interested in the new equilibrium position, we solve for Y_t for $t > 1$ and $\bar{G}_t = \bar{G}_{t-1}$. Equation (11-7) then becomes

$$Y_t = \left(1 - \frac{I_i m\tau}{L_i D}\right)Y_{t-1} + \frac{I_i m}{L_i D}\,\bar{G}_t \qquad (11\text{-}8)$$

The solution to the difference equation (11-8) is

$$Y_t = \left(Y_o - \frac{\bar{G}_t}{\tau}\right)\left(1 - \frac{I_i m\tau}{L_i D}\right)^t + \frac{\bar{G}_t}{\tau} \qquad (11\text{-}9)$$

The term $(Y_o - \bar{G}_t/\tau)$ is a measure of the difference between the old equilibrium income Y_o and the new equilibrium; $\bar{G}_t/\tau$ is the new equilibrium income.

Let us denote the term $(1 - I_i m\tau/L_i D)$ as A. The sign and value of A is not definite. It depends on the sign and values of τ, I_i, L_i, m, and D. We know only that $0 < D < 1$. We assume $0 < A < 1$, and it follows that as $t \to \infty$, income approaches $\bar{G}_t/\tau$ without oscillation.

The new equilibrium income $\bar{G}_t/\tau$ is the long-run static equilibrium with a balanced budget. *The interesting feature of this result is that the long-run government purchases multiplier is equal to $1/\tau$ when tax rates are fixed (the long-run tax receipts multiplier is $-1/\tau$ when government purchases are fixed)*. The expenditure multiplier —the reciprocal of the marginal propensity to tax—is considerably larger than the same multiplier calculated from similar models where government deficits or surpluses are ignored. The logic of this result is simple. Because changes in private holdings of money due to surpluses or deficits affect private behavior through money demand and expenditures equations, real income cannot reach a long-run equilibrium level until budget surpluses or deficits have ceased and Ha and the money supply have stopped changing.

In short, the simple textbook version of the Keynesian government purchases multiplier—$1/[1 - C_{Y_d}(1 - \tau) + I_i L_Y/L_i]$—is incorrect as a general case. It emerges as a special case where the deficit is financed by issuing bonds and where the change in bonds outstanding does not affect the demand for money and hence private spending, which effectively drops Eq. (11-5)—the budget constraint—out of the model.

Graphically, the point can be put in terms of the *IS-LM* curve analysis. In Figure 11-1, let Y_B define that level of income where the budget is balanced. Let this also be the initial equilibrium described above. Let $\bar{G}$ increase permanently in the amount $(Y_L - Y_B)/[1 - C_{Y_d}(1 - \tau)]$. Given τ, the new balanced budget income level will be $\{(Y_L - Y_B)/[1 - C_{Y_d}(1 - \tau)]\}/\tau$, to the right of Y_L, at (say) Y'_B. From the above analysis, we know that as long as a deficit exists (where $Y < Y'_B$), then Ha and M increase, shifting the *LM* curve to the right. Finally, long-run equilibrium will be where the budget is again balanced, at Y'_B. On the other hand, if the increase in $\bar{G}$ is all debt-financed and the increase in government bonds outstanding does not affect the *LM* curve (or *IS* curve), the new equilibrium is given by the conventional multiplier—at point A where the "new" *IS* curve intersects the "old" *LM* curve. But notice that this implies a continuous deficit in the budget $(Y_c < Y'_B)$ and a continuous accumulation of bonds by the private sector at the constant interest rate i_2 even though their money holdings are unchanged. Since the money demand equation [Eq. (11-4)] does not contain a wealth or portfolio variable, the model yields this rather nonsensical result. More appropriately, wealth effects should be included in the consumption function and the money demand function, as noted in Chapters 4 and 9,

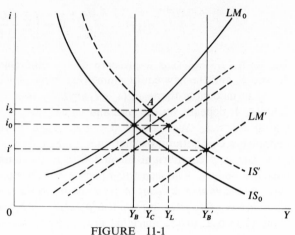

FIGURE 11-1
The revised result of $\Delta \bar{G}$ with wealth effect.

respectively. In keeping the exposition simple, we have left ambiguous the question of what the fiscal multipliers are when financing by debt issues is used exclusively.

To expand the analysis somewhat further, suppose we allow for a "portfolio effect" on the demand for money; i.e., instead of (11-4) we write

$$m\bar{H}a = L(Y_t, i_t, P_t) \quad (11\text{-}4a)$$

where P, the financial portfolio of the private sector, is defined as holdings of government bonds and money

$$P_t = B_{gt}^{P} + M_t \quad (11\text{-}10)$$

and

$$\Delta P_t = G_{t-1} - \tau Y_{t-1} \quad (11\text{-}11)$$

and the central bank is free to vary $\bar{H}a$ by choosing the parameter α:

$$\Delta Ha_t = \alpha \Delta P_t \quad (11\text{-}12)$$

where α can take on any positive or negative value. Under these conditions, we again solve for ΔY_t; but the change in i in any period now is

$$\Delta i_t = -\frac{L_Y}{L_i} \Delta Y_t + \frac{m\alpha - L_P}{L_i} (\bar{G}_{t-1} - \tau Y_{t-1}) \quad (11\text{-}13)$$

Substituting (11-13) into (11-6), we get

$$\Delta Y_t = C_{Y_d}(1 - \tau) \Delta Y_t - \frac{I_i L_Y}{L_i} \Delta Y_t + \frac{I_i(m\alpha - L_P)}{L_i} (\bar{G}_{t-1} - \tau Y_{t-1}) + \Delta \bar{G}_t$$

Collecting terms and simplifying, we obtain an expression for Y_t as before,

$$\Delta Y_t D = \frac{I_i(m\alpha - L_P)}{L_i} (\bar{G}_{t-1} - \tau Y_{t-1}) + \Delta \bar{G}_t$$

And
$$\Delta Y_t = \frac{I_i(m\alpha - L_P)}{L_i D} DEF_{-1} + \frac{\Delta \bar{G}_t}{D} \qquad (11\text{-}14)$$

where $DEF_{-1} = \bar{G}_{t-1} - \tau Y_{t-1}$, the initial government deficit.

Now we can ascertain what will happen to income under different assumptions regarding α—the ratio of $\Delta Ha/\Delta P$. First, consider the case where α takes on a value such that $m\alpha = L_P$. In this case, looking at Eq. (11-13), we see that the increase in Ha and thus M_s is just sufficient, *at the initial levels of i and Y*, to satisfy the increase in the *demand* for M due to ΔP. In other words, the money supply increases just enough (at given values of i and Y) to "feed" the increased demand for it. The result is that Y will increase by *only* the usual multiplier—$1/D$—the system will lodge at point A in Figure 11-1. While the government will show a continuous deficit, the money stock increases only enough to keep Y at Y_c; the LM curve never lets Y reach Y'_B where the budget would again be balanced with the higher level of expenditures. In terms of Eq. (11-14), the initial $\Delta \bar{G}$ in $t = 1$ causes ΔY_1 to be $\Delta \bar{G}_1/D$. In period 2, the higher G (and the higher revenues from the rise in Y_1 over Y_0) causes DEF_{-1}— the lagged deficit—to be larger. But with $m\alpha = L_p$, the coefficient of DEF_{-1} is zero. There is no further change in Y other than by the basic amount given by the standard multiplier.

It is now clear that if α is large enough so that $m\alpha > L_P$, the system will reach the long-run equilibrium described above, i.e., where $\Delta Y = \Delta \bar{G}/\tau$. If $\alpha = 0$, the coefficient of DEF_{-1} will be $-I_i L_P/D$, which is negative. In this case, the LM curve will shift leftward over time as the money supply remains constant while the demand for money increases. Income could *fall* as a result of an expansive fiscal action.

The second result of the budget constraint is that, in the long-run, monetary actions, which affect the LM curve via Ha or m, have no effect on equilibrium Y unless they are continued. If (say) Ha is increased, then income rises, a surplus occurs in the budget, and this shifts the LM curve leftward as the demand for money rises. As long as the surplus continues, the rising demand for money will tend to eventually offset the initial expansive monetary action. Thus to permanently "move the LM curve" requires not a once-and-for-all change in Ha, but a continuous one.

Actually, as we have seen in Chapter 4, the change in the net assets of the private sector produced by budget deficits or surpluses affects private spending via the wealth effect on consumption (including housing and durables). Thus an unbalanced budget will affect both the LM *and IS* curves. Furthermore, net assets also change when interest rates change, when there is a balance of payments deficit or surplus, and when there is net investment. Thus a more complete analysis of the short- and long-run effects of monetary and fiscal policy, with allowance for the budget constraint, should incorporate at least the most important of these other effects.

In addition, focusing on long-run multipliers is not particularly helpful. As Hansen (1973, p. 533) put it: "It would be entirely unrealistic ... to assume that the authorities should remain passive during a process toward a long-term stationary state (that may not exist). It is more likely that they would continuously work on rectifying the short-term position."

Chapter 13, where we attempt to pull together the main threads of the refined and expanded model we have been developing in these last eight chapters, will deal with short-run multipliers, and we will incorporate the government's budget constraint into the analysis.

SUMMARY

In this chapter, we have looked briefly at the budget constraint of the government sector, a feature missing from many macromodels. We showed that when the budget constraint is added, the basic textbook multipliers for fiscal policy are not, in general, correct. The long-run multiplier for government purchases and taxes become $1/\tau$—much larger than as developed in Chapter 3. The basic logic is simple—a change in G (or $\overline{T}$) causes the government budget to run a surplus or deficit. This shifts the LM curve. If high-powered money is used to finance a deficit, for example, then the LM curve shifts rightward as long as the deficit persists, or until income rises enough to cause taxes to rise enough to eliminate the deficit. Other outcomes are possible, depending on the method by which the government deficit is financed.[2]

Monetary policy must work continuously to change Y if the budget constraint is recognized. Increasing Ha causes income to rise, but this increases the surplus, which increases the demand for money and necessitates continuous injections of Ha to keep the LM curve where desired.

[2] For a complete discussion of the budget constraint, especially when government deficits are financed by bonds, see Solon and Blinder (1974), pp. 3–56.

READINGS FOR CHAPTER 11

BLINDER, ALAN S., and ROBERT M. SOLON: "Analytical Foundations of Fiscal policy," in *The Economics of Public Finance*, Essays by Alan S. Blinder and Robert M. Solon; George F. Break; Petr O. Steiner; and Dick Netzer (Washington, D.C.: The Brookings Institution, 1974).

CHRIST, C.: "A Short-Run Aggregate Demand Model of the Interdependence of Monetary and Fiscal Policies with Keynesian and Classical Interest Elasticities," *American Economic Review*, vol. 57, pp. 434–443, May 1967.

DE LEEUW, F., and E. GRAMLICH: "The Federal Reserve–MIT Econometric Model," *Federal Reserve Bulletin*, pp. 1–32, January 1968.

GRAMLICH, E., and H. GALPER: "State and Local Fiscal Behavior and Federal Grant Policy," *Brookings Papers on Economic Activity*, vol. 1, pp. 15–58, 1973.

HANSEN, BENT: "On the Effects of Monetary and Fiscal Policy: A Taxonomic Discussion," *American Economic Review*, vol. 63, pp. 546–571, September 1973.

LERNER, A. P.: "Functional Finance and the Federal Debt," *Social Research*, vol. 10, pp. 38–51, February 1943.

OTT, DAVID J., and ATTIAT F. OTT: "Budget Balance and Equilibrium Income," *Journal of Finance*, vol. 20, pp. 71–77, March 1965.

RITTER, L. S.: "Some Monetary Aspects of Multiplier Theory and Fiscal Policy," *Review of Economic Studies*, vol. 23 (2), no. 61, pp. 126–131, 1955–1966.

SILBUR, W. L.: "Fiscal Policy in IS-LM Analysis: A Correction," *Journal of Money, Credit, and Banking*, vol. 2, pp. 461–473, November 1973.

12

PRODUCTION FUNCTIONS, THE LABOR MARKET, AND AGGREGATE SUPPLY

In the previous chapters, we have explored the determinants of aggregate demand. In terms of the economy's production statement (Chapter 2), we have examined the variables explaining the right, or expenditures, side of the GNP accounts. In many early econometric models, as well as in many forecasting models currently in use, this is as far as the analysis is taken. However, it is also necessary to explain *aggregate supply*, for two reasons: (1) aggregate demand depends on the *distribution* of gross national income (for example, consumption depends on labor versus nonlabor income), which in turn reflects the manner in which inputs are combined to produce total output; and (2) *prices* (of both products and factors of production) and employment (or unemployment) reflect conditions of aggregate supply in the economy. In short, aggregate supply is examined in order to explain factor shares in income and to provide a basis for explaining prices, wages, and unemployment.

PRODUCTION FUNCTIONS

We begin by discussing the relation between total output and inputs used to produce aggregate supply—the aggregate production function. Since GNP is based on value-added (Chapter 2), "intermediate" inputs cancel out. It is thus convenient to consider

Y, total output, as a function of two inputs—(1) capital services K and man-hours of labor N and (2) time t—with the general form[1]

$$Y = f(K, N, t) \qquad (12\text{-}1)$$

where t is used to incorporate technical change.

The Cobb-Douglas Production Function

The most commonly used specific form of the aggregate production function has been the Cobb-Douglas function, which we have already briefly considered in examining business fixed investment (Chapter 5). This is written

$$Y = AN^\alpha K^\beta e^{\gamma t} \qquad (12\text{-}2)$$

or for estimating purposes,

$$\log Y = \log A + \alpha \log N + \beta \log K + \gamma t \qquad (12\text{-}2a)$$

The Cobb-Douglas function arose out of the observation that over long periods of time the share of output of capital and labor tended to be constant (Cobb and Douglas, 1928; Douglas, 1948). Under conditions of profit maximization by firms and perfect competition, the share of labor is α and the share of capital is β. First, take the marginal products of capital and labor, respectively,

$$\frac{\partial Y}{\partial N} = \frac{\alpha Y}{N} \qquad \frac{\partial K}{\partial Y} = \frac{\beta Y}{K} \qquad (12\text{-}3)$$

Then, under perfect competition, the cost-minimization conditions are

$$\frac{\partial N}{\partial Y} = \frac{\alpha Y}{N} = \frac{w}{p} \qquad (12\text{-}3a)$$

and

$$\frac{\partial K}{\partial Y} = \frac{\beta Y}{K} = \frac{p_K}{p} \qquad (12\text{-}3b)$$

where p is the price level, w is the money wage rate, and p_K is the price of capital services. Manipulation of (12-3a) and (12-3b) yields

$$\alpha = \frac{wN}{pY} \qquad (12\text{-}3c)$$

$$\beta = \frac{p_K K}{pY} \qquad (12\text{-}3d)$$

In short, the Cobb-Douglas function assumes *constant factor shares*.

If we assume that total payments to factors just exhausts total private product, or $pY = wN + p_K K$, then $\alpha + \beta = 1$. This implies *constant returns to scale*, in that

[1] Actually, the variables Y and N should have some notation to indicate that they refer to *private* output and private man-hours of labor. For the sake of notational simplicity, we ignore this distinction in the first part of the chapter.

an equiproportionate change in K and N yields a proportionate change in Y. Multiplying N and K by a scale factor λ, we obtain

$$Y = A(\lambda N)^{\alpha}(\lambda K)^{\beta}e^{\gamma t} = \lambda^{\alpha+\beta}Y = \lambda Y \qquad (12\text{-}4)$$

Finally, the Cobb-Douglas function imposes another constraint—the ratio of the two inputs K and N is strictly proportional to their respective prices, p_K and w —the elasticity of substitution is unity. Given the ratio of the marginal products of K and N and the cost-minimization condition, we have

$$\frac{\beta Y/K}{\alpha Y/N} = \frac{p_K/p}{w/p}$$

or, rearranging terms,

$$\frac{N}{K} = \frac{p_K}{w}\left(\frac{\beta}{\alpha}\right) \quad \text{and} \quad \frac{K}{N} = \frac{w}{p_K}\left(\frac{\alpha}{\beta}\right) \qquad (12\text{-}5)$$

Since the elasticity of substitution σ is

$$\sigma = \frac{\%\Delta(K/N)}{\%\Delta(w/p_K)} \qquad (12\text{-}5a)$$

then, from (12-5) we get

$$\log\frac{K}{N} = \log\frac{\alpha}{\beta} + \log\frac{w}{p_K} \quad \text{and} \quad d\log\frac{K}{N} = d\log\frac{w}{p_K}$$

and so

$$\sigma = \frac{d\log(K/N)}{d\log(w/p_K)} = 1 \qquad (12\text{-}6)$$

Thus, for the Cobb-Douglas production function, the elasticity of substitution between the inputs (σ) is constrained to be unity.

The CES Production Function

The three constraints imposed by assuming the production function is Cobb-Douglas —constant factor shares, constant returns to scale, and unitary elasticity of substitution—led to the development of a more general class of production functions. The CES (constant elasticity of substitution) production functions, as they are called, allow variable factor shares, increasing or decreasing returns to scale, and any (constant) value for the elasticity of substitution. They were developed out of the empirical observation that the average productivity of labor in different industries could be explained by the equation

$$\log\frac{Y}{N} = \log a + \sigma\log w \qquad (12\text{-}7)$$

where σ is the elasticity of substitution. From this equation came the specific form of the CES production function

$$Y = \gamma[\delta K^{-\rho} + (1-\delta)N^{-\rho}]^{-1/\rho} \qquad (12\text{-}8)$$

where γ = scale factor
δ = distribution parameter
ρ = substitution parameter = $1/\sigma - 1$

The derivation of (12-8) from (12-7) is somewhat complex and is not given here.[2] It can be shown that the CES production function reduces to the Cobb-Douglas production function as $\sigma \to 1$ (as $\rho \to 0$), that it reduces to the simple linear production function as $\sigma \to \infty$ (as $\rho \to -1$), and that it becomes a "fixed proportions" production function as $\sigma \to 0$ (as $\rho \to \infty$).[3] To show that σ is the elasticity of substitution defined in (12-6), we write the CES production function as

$$Y = \gamma S^{-1/\rho} \qquad (12\text{-}8a)$$

where S is the bracketed expression in (12-8). Then, solving for the marginal product of capital, we get

$$\frac{\partial Y}{\partial K} = \gamma \left(\frac{\partial Y}{\partial S} \frac{\partial S}{\partial K} \right)$$

$$= \gamma \left\{ -\frac{1}{\rho} [\delta K^{-\rho} + (1-\delta)N^{-\rho}]^{(-1/\rho-1)} \left[-\rho\delta \frac{K^{-\rho}}{K} \right] \right\}$$

$$= \gamma \left\{ [\delta K^{-\rho} + (1-\delta)N^{-\rho}]^{(-1/\rho-\rho/\rho)} \frac{\delta}{K^{1+\rho}} \right\}$$

$$= Y[\delta K^{-\rho} + (1-\delta)N^{-\rho}]^{-1} \frac{\delta}{K^{1+\rho}}$$

$$= \frac{Y}{K^{1+\rho}} \frac{Y^{\rho}}{\gamma^{\rho}} \delta = \left(\frac{Y}{K} \right)^{1+\rho} \gamma^{-\rho} \delta \qquad (12\text{-}8b)$$

Following the same technique, for Y/N we get

$$\frac{\partial Y}{\partial N} = (1-\delta)\gamma^{-\rho} \left(\frac{Y}{N} \right)^{1+\rho} \qquad (12\text{-}8c)$$

Using the cost-minimization conditions and taking the ratios of the two marginal product expressions and solving for K/N, we get

$$\frac{(1-\delta)\gamma^{-\rho}(Y/N)^{1+\rho}}{\delta\gamma^{-\rho}(Y/K)^{(1+\rho)}} = \frac{w/p}{p_K/p}$$

$$\frac{(1-\delta)(Y/N)^{1+\rho}}{\delta(Y/K)^{1+\rho}} = \frac{w}{p_K}$$

$$\frac{(1-\delta)}{\delta} \left(\frac{K}{N} \right)^{1+\rho} = \frac{w}{p_K}$$

$$\left(\frac{K}{N} \right)^{1+\rho} = \frac{\delta}{1-\delta} \frac{w}{p_K}$$

[2] See, for example, Evans (1969, pp. 256–258).
[3] Again, a good reference is Evans (1969, chap. 10).

Taking logarithms, we obtain

$$(1 + \rho) \log \frac{K}{N} = \log \frac{\delta}{1 - \delta} + \log \frac{w}{p_K}$$

Since $\sigma = \dfrac{1}{1 + \rho}$,

$$\log \frac{K}{N} = \sigma \left(\log \frac{\delta}{1 - \delta} + \log \frac{w}{p_K} \right)$$

and

$$\frac{d \log (K/N)}{d \log (w/p_K)} = \sigma \qquad (12\text{-}8d)$$

which is the same as (12-6).

The CES production function suffers from one major defect for business-cycle analysis. For values of the elasticity of substitution between zero and unity $(0 < \sigma < 1)$, *factor shares move in the same direction as the average productivity of the factor*. This can be seen by setting the marginal products of capital and labor equal to the real implicit rental values of capital and real wages, respectively, and solving for factor shares:

$$\frac{p_K}{p} = \left(\frac{Y}{K} \right)^{1+\rho} \gamma^{-\rho} \delta \qquad \frac{w}{p} = (1 - \delta) \gamma^{-\rho} \left(\frac{Y}{N} \right)^{1+\rho}$$

Then

$$\frac{p_K K}{pY} = \left(\frac{Y}{K} \right)^{\rho} \gamma^{-\rho} \delta \qquad \frac{wN}{pY} = \left(\frac{Y}{N} \right)^{\rho} \gamma^{-\rho} (1 - \delta) \qquad (12\text{-}8e)$$

For $\rho > 0$ $(0 < \sigma < 1)$, the share of capital or labor increases with the average productivity of the factor $(Y/N$ or $Y/K)$ and vice versa. Yet an often-cited feature of business cycles is that the share of labor *rises* in recessions when Y/N *falls*, and when an expansion occurs, labor's share falls while Y/N is rising.

Thus, the CES production function, like the Cobb-Douglas production function, is unsatisfactory in explaining factor incomes.

An Explanation of the Factor Shares Problem

As we shall see later, in Part 4, the most plausible explanation for the behavior of factor shares and average productivity is that at less than full employment, employers in effect are operating "off" their equilibrium demand-for-labor curves—in *disequilibrium* models the apparent inconsistency of the behavior of the factor share of labor and output per man-hour can readily be explained. In the present setting, the usual explanation for the inconsistency between actual factor shares over the business cycle and those predicted by the CES or Cobb-Douglas production functions is that firms "hoard" labor during a downturn. That is, the price of labor relative to capital *falls* when the potential costs of searching out and possibly training new workers during the ensuing expansion are taken into account.[4] Thus, while considerations of

---

[4] See the discussion in Evans (1969, pp. 249–251).

real wages and costs of capital may not indicate any change in factor prices, allowance for the costs of hiring and firing makes labor less expensive during a reduction in output and causes man-hours to fall more slowly than output so that output per man-hour *falls* as labor's share rises. This apparent "hoarding" is probably most pronounced for "overhead" workers, but may also apply to production workers.[5]

Thus the particular production function chosen must be modified to reflect the observed behavior of factor shares over the cycle. We will discuss how this might be done after considering the choice of a production function to be used.

Cobb-Douglas or CES?

While the CES production function avoids the constraints imposed by the Cobb-Douglas (C-D) production function, recent empirical work suggests that we may take advantage of the basic simplicity of the C-D function without as much loss of realism as might be supposed. (This also has the advantage that it simplifies the form of the investment function in Chapter 5).

Several arguments can be given in support of assuming Cobb-Douglas production functions. First, as pointed by Griliches (1967, p. 297) in a survey of the literature[6]:

Given our data we cannot reject the hypothesis that the Cobb-Douglas is an adequate representation up to a second-order approximation.

Furthermore, Nelson (1965) has shown that, in the short-run, the value of σ makes little difference in predicting output for reasonable values of α and β.[7] Finally, we

---

[5]For a model of hoarding behavior, see Branson (1972, pp. 122–126.)

[6]This article is in M. Brown (edited), *The Theory and Empirical Analysis Production*, 1967, copyright by the National Bureau of Economic Research. Acknowledgment is made to the author and NBER. Also see the discussion and references cited in Jorgenson and Stephenson (1969).

[7]His point is demonstrated by first writing the general expression for the percentage change in output, whether or not the production function is Cobb-Douglas.

$$\frac{\dot{Y}}{Y} = \frac{\dot{A}}{A} + b\frac{\dot{N}}{N} + (1-b)\frac{\dot{K}}{K}$$

In the C-D function, b and $(1-b)$ are α and β, respectively, and are also the elasticities of output with respect to labor and capital. But if the production function is not Cobb-Douglas, then b and $(1-b)$ will not necessarily be constants. In fact, if the elasticity of substitution is a constant (but not necessarily equal to 1), it can be shown that

$$b = Y_N\frac{N}{Y} = \frac{(Y_N/Y_K)NY_K(K/N)}{Y(K/N)} = \frac{r(1-b)}{(K/N)}$$

where $r = Y_N/Y_K$, i.e., the marginal rate of substitution. Taking logarithms and then time derivatives of the above, it can be shown that

$$\frac{db}{dt} = b(1-b)\frac{\sigma-1}{\sigma}\left(\frac{\dot{N}}{N} - \frac{\dot{K}}{K}\right)$$

Differentiating the first expression with respect to time and substituting in the second expression for db/dt, we get

$$\frac{d(\dot{Y}/Y)}{dt} = b(1-b)\frac{\sigma-1}{\sigma}\left(\frac{\dot{N}}{N} - \frac{\dot{K}}{K}\right)^2$$

have seen that the CES production function is no improvement over the Cobb-Douglas function in predicting the behavior of factor shares. In either case, some modification of the function has to be made to account for this cyclical problem.

Therefore, we will use the Cobb-Douglas production function for private output. To allow for the cyclical variation of factor shares, we define a capacity variable Cp:

$$Cp = \frac{Y}{Y^*} \qquad (12\text{-}9)$$

where Y^* is a measure of maximum potential real GNP. Since α and β in the Cobb-Douglas production function vary with the cycle, we may account for this by rewriting the C-D production function to be

$$Y = AN^{1-\alpha Cp} K^{\beta Cp} e^{\gamma t} \qquad (12\text{-}10)$$

Thus, when the economy operates below capacity $\left(Cp = \dfrac{Y}{Y^*} < 1\right)$, then the share of labor in output ($= 1 - \alpha Cp$) rises, and vice versa for the share of capital.

Total output is the sum of gross private product Y^p and government product Y^g. Strictly speaking, the production function should only apply to Y^p, but for simplicity we shall continue to use it to explain total output. The demand for labor, assuming competition, is given by solving (12-11):

$$\frac{\partial Y}{\partial N} = (1 - \alpha Cp)\frac{Y}{N} = \frac{w}{p} \qquad (12\text{-}11)$$

or

$$N_d = \frac{pY(1 - \alpha Cp)}{w} \qquad (12\text{-}12)$$

In terms of the usual labor market graph, where w is treated as the dependent variable:

$$w_d = \frac{pY(1 - \alpha Cp)}{N} \qquad (12\text{-}13)$$

From this, it is clear that the value of σ is important to the value of the percentage rate of change of Y only if the rate of growth of capital and labor differs. If $\sigma > 1$, the sign of $d(\dot{Y}/Y)/dt$ will be positive; if $\sigma < 1$, it will have a negative sign. For a small but finite period, the percentage change in Y is thus the percentage change in Y *ignoring* the effect of σ on $Y(\Delta Y/)/\Delta t$ *plus* an allowance for this effect (i.e., for $d(\dot{Y}/Y)/dt$). If the latter effect is linearized around the initial values, we get

$$\frac{\Delta Y}{\Delta t} \Big/ Y \simeq \frac{\dot{Y}}{Y} + \frac{1}{2}\frac{d}{dt}\left(\frac{\dot{Y}}{Y}\right)\Delta t$$

We apply this to the initial equation in this footnote, the percentage change in Y is

$$\frac{\Delta Y}{Y} = \frac{\dot{A}}{A} + b_0 \frac{\dot{N}}{N} + (1 - b_0)\frac{\dot{K}}{K} + \frac{1}{2}b_0(1 - b_0)\frac{\sigma - 1}{\sigma}\left(\frac{\dot{K}}{K} - \frac{\dot{N}}{N}\right)^2$$

Suppose $\sigma = \frac{1}{2}$, $\delta = \frac{1}{3}$, and $\dot{K}/K - \dot{N}/N = 0.03$. Then if we assumed $\sigma = 1$, the error introduced in estimating $\Delta Y/Y$ would be

$$\frac{1}{3} \times \frac{2}{3}\left[-\left(\frac{\frac{1}{2}}{\frac{1}{2}}\right) \times (0.03)^2\right] = -0.0002$$

compared to a growth rate of about 0.04.

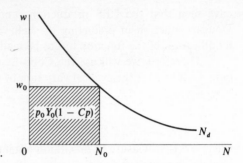

FIGURE 12-1
The demand for labor.

the labor demand curve N_d is a rectangular hyperbola (as long as p and Y are fixed) where the area under the curve for any combination $w_0 N_0$ is $p_0 Y_0(1 - \alpha Cp)$, as shown in Figure 12-1.

THE SUPPLY OF LABOR

In Chapter 3, we wrote the supply of labor, in terms of the supply price of labor w_s, as

$$w_s = h(N, p) \quad (3\text{-}58)$$

where h_p and h_N were both positive. With the labor market equilibrium condition,

$$w_s = w_d$$
$$pf(N) = h(N, p) \quad [f(N) = F_N] \quad (3\text{-}61)$$

then the case where $h_p = f(N)$ was the neoclassical case—the labor supply and demand curves shift upward equally for any change in p so that the labor market remains in equilibrium at the initial labor input N_0 [and with prices and wages higher by the proportion $f(N)$]. To produce variation in labor input with changes in p, it was necessary to assume $f(N)$ was greater than $h(p)$—that price changes were not fully reflected in labor supply [in the extreme case of $h(p) = 0$, labor supply would depend *only* on money wages and would not be affected by prices at all].

However, it is not really necessary to rely on "imperfectly perceived" price changes to produce variation in labor input as p changes.

The basis for the life-cycle model of consumption discussed in Chapter 4 is that an individual of a given age will maximize an intertemporal utility function with consumption in each period as arguments. However, theory suggests this utility function should also include consumption of *leisure* as an argument, *viz.*:

$$U = U(c_0, c_t, \ldots, c_T; \quad j_0, j_t, \ldots, j_T) \quad (12\text{-}14)$$

where the c's as before represent real consumption in each period from now (period 0) to T, the instant before he dies, and the j's are the leisure time "consumed" in these periods. In each period Eq. (12-14) is maximized subject to the constraint that the discounted value of total consumption not exceed the discounted value of total after-tax earnings by more than the amount of assets:

$$A_0 \geq \sum_{t=0}^{T} \frac{p_t c_t - (1 - \tau) w_t \eta_t}{(1 + i)^t} \qquad (12\text{-}15)$$

where p is the *price of consumption*, w_t the wage rate, τ the tax rate, and η the individual's supply of labor. The other constraint is that total time just be used up between work and leisure:

$$z_t = \eta_t + j_t \qquad (12\text{-}16)$$

where z_t is the total time available, η_t is labor (man-hours) supplied, and j_t is hours of leisure. Solving (12-16) for η_t and substituting into (12-15), the constraint may be written

$$A_0 = \sum_{t=0}^{T} \frac{p_t c_t - (1 - \tau) w_t (z_t - j_t)}{(1 + i)^t} \qquad (12\text{-}17)$$

Now $\sum_{t=0}^{T} \dfrac{(1 - \tau) w_t Z_t}{(1 + i)^t}$ can be interpreted as a *potential human wealth* and can be combined with assets A_0 to get total wealth V_0 of the individual:

$$V_0 = A_0 + \sum_{t=0}^{T} \frac{(1 - \tau) w_t z_t}{(1 + i)^t} = \sum_{t=0}^{T} \frac{p_t c_t + (1 - \tau) w_t j_t}{(1 + i)^t} \qquad (12\text{-}18)$$

Thus V_0 represents total resources to be allocated in determining the optimal time paths of consumption (c) *and* "consumption of leisure" (j).

Maximizing (12-14) subject to (12-18) is complex. However, by assuming a "double" Cobb-Douglas utility function for (12-14), Christensen and Jorgenson (1968) obtained the following consumption, leisure, and labor functions for a given period:

$$pc = \alpha c (1 - i) V_0 \qquad (12\text{-}19)$$

$$w(1 - \tau) j = \alpha j (1 - i) V_0 \qquad (12\text{-}20)$$

$$w(1 - \tau) N = w(1 - \tau) Z - \alpha j (1 - i) V_0 \qquad (12\text{-}21)$$

The similarity of (12-19) with the Ando-Modigliani and Friedman consumption functions is obvious. Current c is proportional to total resources (given i). However, the difference lies in the definition of total resources, which includes the present value of the potential labor supply over future time periods, $\sum_{0}^{T} \dfrac{w_t (1 - \tau) z_t}{(1 + i)^t}$ in addition to the present value of future earnings and existing nonhuman assets.

Equation (12-21)—an equation for the individual's labor income after taxes—

"drops out" of the maximization process. Aggregating and dividing Eq. (12-21) by p we get *real* aggregate labor income after taxes:

$$\frac{w(1 - \tau)N}{p} = \frac{w(1 - \tau)}{p} Z - \alpha j(1 - i) \frac{V_0}{p}$$

or

$$\frac{w(1 - \tau)N}{p} = \frac{w(1 - \tau)}{p} Z - \gamma\left(i, \frac{V_0}{p}\right) \qquad (12\text{-}22)$$

Labor hours supplied are, then,

$$N = Z - \frac{p}{w(1 - \tau)} \gamma\left(i, \frac{V_0}{p}\right) \qquad (12\text{-}23)$$

If real potential human wealth is a function of real *current* potential human income, then (12-23) can be written

$$N = Z - \frac{p}{w(1 - \tau)} \beta\left[\frac{w(1 - \tau)Z}{p}, \frac{A}{p}, i\right]$$

$$\beta_1 > 0 \qquad \beta_2 > 0 \qquad \beta_3 < 0 \qquad (12\text{-}23a)$$

An increase in Z, labor hours available (via increase in the working-age population), clearly increases the supply of labor hours. An increase in the interest rate i clearly decreases labor hours supplied ($\beta_3 < 0$). Now consider a doubling of prices and money wages, so that the *real wage* rate is unchanged. Whereas previously this would have had no effect on labor supplied unless the change in prices was "imperfectly perceived" (Chapter 3), now the reduction in the real value of nonhuman wealth—A/p—will decrease the demand for leisure and increase the supply of labor hours. Thus, hours of labor supplied depends not only on real wages, but on the *level* of prices in the real wage equation.

Now consider the effect of a change in real wages. Suppose money wages rise and prices are constant. The demand for the *real value* of leisure will rise [the β function in (12-23a)] as the real value of potential human wealth $\left[\dfrac{w(1 - \tau)Z}{p}\right]$ rises.

But as w rises, the real value of each hour of leisure (in terms of work and real income and consumption foregone) also rises proportionately. That price (per hour of leisure) is the (after-tax) real wage rate, $\dfrac{w(1 - \tau)}{p}$. If, say, w doubles, the real value of existing leisure doubles. The effect on *hours* of leisure (and thus labor) depends upon this price rise per hour of leisure and the increased demand for real leisure. If a doubling of w *less* than doubles the real value of leisure demanded, *hours* of leisure will be reduced (and hours of labor increased). If a doubling of w causes the demand for the real value of leisure to *more* than double, hours of leisure will be increased and hours of labor supplied reduced. The price effect working opposite to the wealth effect on leisure *hours* demanded is reflected in the premultiplicative $p/(1 - \tau)w$ in front of the β expression in (12-23a). We shall assume that the price effect predominates—

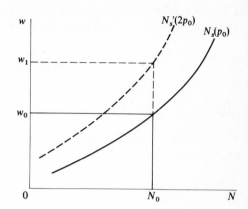

FIGURE 12-2
A rise in supply wage when the price level
is doubled.

a rise in w produces an *increase* in hours of *labor supplied*, a reduction in hours of leisure demanded. Note that an increase in the tax rate on labor income (τ) is perfectly analagous to a *fall* in the money wage.

Suppose the price level is halved. All the arguments above hold as to the outcome depending on the relative strengths of the price and wealth effects. But one thing is different: a fall in p *also increases nonhuman wealth.* Thus in this case, there is a stronger possibility that labor hours supplied will fall and the demand for leisure hours will increase.

Let us rewrite (12-23a) in the form of the labor supply price w_s:

$$w_s = \frac{\beta\left[\dfrac{w(1 - \tau)Z}{p}, \dfrac{A}{p}, i\right]p}{(Z - N)(1 - \tau)} \qquad (12\text{-}24)$$

In terms of Figure 12-2, for given values of Z, A, i, and τ, an increase in the price level will increase the supply wage w_s by a smaller proportion (at any given level of N). At N_0, for example, doubling of p from p_0 to $2p_0$ will shift the labor-hours-supplied curve up so that at N_0 the supply price of labor will be w_1—less than twice the old supply price of w_0.

LABOR MARKET EQUILIBRIUM AND THE AGGREGATE SUPPLY CURVE

From Eq. (12-13), the labor demand function was seen to be

$$w_d = \frac{pY(1 - \alpha Cp)}{N} \qquad (12\text{-}13)$$

Given the labor supply function from Eq. (12-24) and the labor market equilibrium condition $w_d = w_s$, we get, for equilibrium in the labor market,

$$\frac{pY(1 - \alpha C p)}{N} = \frac{\beta\left[\dfrac{w(1 - \tau)Z}{p}, \dfrac{A}{p}, i\right]p}{Z(1 - \tau) - N(1 - \tau)} \qquad (12\text{-}25)$$

Solving (12-25) for N, we obtain

$$N = \frac{Z}{\left\{\dfrac{\beta\left[\dfrac{w(1 - \tau)Z}{p}, \dfrac{A}{p}, i\right]}{(Y - \alpha C p)(1 - \tau)} + 1\right\}} \qquad (12\text{-}26)$$

Since the slope of the aggregate supply curve dp/dY is given by

$$dY = F_N N_p\, dp \qquad \frac{dp}{dY} = \frac{1}{F_N N_p}$$

then clearly dp/dY is positive if the partial N_p is positive. When we observe (12-26), it is clear that N_p is positive; an increase in p *reduces* the β term in the denominator. Since a rise in p causes the denominator to fall, it increases labor input N. N_p is positive, and so the aggregate supply curve has a positive slope. And, as we noted above, the wealth term in the labor supply function causes the aggregate supply curve to shift upward less than in proportion to the rise in p, and thus employment and output increase, as in Figure 12-3. Thus a positively sloped aggregate supply curve requires no reliance on ignorance, irrational behavior, or "wage stickiness" for its explanation. The theory of consumer behavior, when expanded to the labor-leisure choice, is sufficient to this end. Indeed, if one believes that consumption is affected by wealth, it follows that wealth operates also on the simultaneous work-leisure choice! At the same time, note that this model does *not* explain unemployment in the theoretical sense that workers are receiving less employment than they want at a given wage. In this world, the labor market is always cleared, and workers always find the amount of work they desire—they are always on their supply curves. Thus, variations in the rate of unemployment require further explanation. Since it is essentially a disequilibrium phenomenon, it is a major concern in Part 4, where we deal explicitly with disequilibrium models. Note that the aggregate supply curve is now affected by many variables other than the price level. Growth of the labor force (Z), the rate of interest (i), nonhuman wealth (A), the tax rate (τ), the wage rate (w), and capacity utilization all enter into the employment and output function. The reader may satisfy himself that the signs of the partials of N with respect to these variables are as follows: $N_Z > 0$, $N_w < 0$, $N_i < 0$, $N_{Cp} < 0$, $N_\tau < 0$, and $N_A < 0$.

For the aggregate supply curve, we now write

$$Y = F[\phi(Z, A, p, N, i, Cp), K, t] \qquad (12\text{-}27)$$

where ϕ is the N that satisfies the labor market equilibrium condition that $w_s = w_d$.

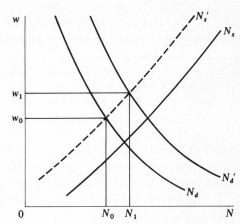

FIGURE 12-3
Increase in equilibrium labor when prices rise.

SUMMARY

In this chapter, we have expanded our basic model of Chapter 3 by looking in some detail at forces affecting aggregate supply. The Cobb-Douglas and CES production functions were analyzed, and neither was found satisfactory in explaining factor shares over the business cycle. A remedy was to use the Cobb-Douglas function with variable exponents for capital and labor, the variation being explained by a capacity utilization variable which raises labor's share of output when utilization falls and raises capital's share when capacity approaches higher utilization rates. The resulting production function was then used to derive the demand for labor.

Next, we saw that carrying through the theory of the household used in both the permanent and life-cycle versions of the consumption function substantially modifies the labor supply function. The supply of labor now also becomes a function of real net assets, with labor supply increasing when real wealth declines and decreasing when it rises. This provides a rationale for an aggregate supply curve where supply responds positively to a rise in the price level; the fall in real wealth induces a greater supply of labor. The theory also makes aggregate supply a function of the interest rate and the tax rate, among other things.

READINGS FOR CHAPTER 12

ARROW, K. J., H. B. CHENERY, B. S. MINHAS, and R. M. SOLOW: "Capital-Labor Substitution and Economic Efficiency," *Review of Economics and Statistics*, vol. 43, pp. 225–230, August 1961.

BRANSON, W. H.: *Macroeconomic Theory and Policy* (New York: Harper & Row, 1972).

CHRISTENSEN, L., and D. W. JORGENSON: "Intertemporal Optimization and the Explanation of Consumer Behavior," (mimeo.), 1968.

COBB, C. W. and P. H. DOUGLAS: "A Theory of Production," *American Economic Review*, vol. 18, pp. 139–165, March 1928.

DOUGLAS, P. H.: "Are There Laws of Production?" *American Economic Review*, vol. 38, pp. 1–41, March 1948.

EVANS, M. K.: *Macroeconomic Activity: Theory, Forecasting, and Control* (New York: Harper & Row, 1969), chap. 10.

GRILICHES, Z.: "Production Functions in Manufacturing: Some Preliminary Results," in M. Brown (ed.), *The Theory and Empirical Analysis of Production*, Studies in Income and Wealth, no. 31 (New York: Columbia, 1967), pp. 275–322.

JORGENSON, D., and J. A. STEPHENSON: "Issues in the Development of the Neoclassical Theory of Investment Behavior," *Review of Economics and Statistics*, August 1969.

NELSON, R. R.: "The CES Production Function and Economic Growth Projections," *Review of Economics and Statistics*, vol. 47, pp. 326–328, August 1965.

PESEK, B., and T. SAVING: *Money, Wealth and Economic Theory* (New York: Macmillan, 1967)

13

THE SUMMARY OF THE EXPANDED MODEL

We have reached the end of our discussion of refinements in and expansion of the basic model. At this point, it seems worthwhile to attempt to bring the major strands together and see what implications the extensions and refinements have in evaluating the impacts of fiscal and monetary actions.

In Chapter 3, the intermediate-case model was given by four equations:

Aggregate demand:
$$Y = C\left[Y(1 - \tau) - \frac{\overline{T}}{p}\right] + I(i) + \overline{G} \quad (3\text{-}12)$$

Money market equilibrium:
$$m\overline{H} = pL(Y, i) \quad (3\text{-}13)$$

Production function:
$$Y = F(N, K_0) \quad (3\text{-}51)$$

Labor market equilibrium:
$$pF_N = h(N, p) \quad (3\text{-}61)$$

with the endogenous variables Y, i, p, and N. Alternatively, in terms of aggregate supply and demand, the model was reduced to two equations in the two endogenous variables p and Y:

Aggregate demand:
$$Y = C\left[Y(1 - \tau) - \frac{\overline{T}}{p}\right] + I[\phi(\overline{H}_a, Y, p)] + \overline{G} \quad (3\text{-}16)$$

Aggregate supply:
$$Y = F[e^{\lambda t}q(p, L), K] \quad (3\text{-}72)$$

It was shown that the increment or decrement in Y per period (dY) reflected the (horizontal) shifts in the aggregate demand curve (dX) and the aggregate supply curve (dR), as well as the slopes of these two curves $(dp/dY|_D$ for aggregate demand and $dp/dY|_S$ for aggregate supply), so that to a linear approximation dY was

$$dY = \frac{\left|\dfrac{dp}{dY}\right|_D \left|dX\right| + \left|\dfrac{dp}{dY}\right|_S \left|dR\right|}{\left|\dfrac{dp}{dY}\right|_D + \left|\dfrac{dp}{dY}\right|_S}$$

Now consider the model developed in Chapters 4 and 5 and 8 to 12.[1] The basic structure of the model is given by these equations:

Real aggregate demand: $\qquad\qquad\qquad\qquad\qquad Y = C + I + \bar{G} \qquad$ (13-1)

Real consumption function: $\qquad\qquad C = C\left[Y(1 - \tau) - \dfrac{\bar{T}}{p}; \dfrac{A}{p}\right] \qquad$ (13-2)

Real investment demand: $\qquad\qquad\qquad\qquad\qquad I = I(i, Y) \qquad$ (13-3)

Net real nonhuman assets: $\qquad\qquad\qquad \dfrac{A}{p} = \dfrac{M}{p} + \dfrac{B_g^{\,p}}{ip} + K \qquad$ (13-4)

Capital stock: $\qquad\qquad\qquad\qquad\qquad\qquad K = \bar{K} + I \qquad$ (13-5)

Money demand: $\qquad\qquad\qquad\qquad M_d = pL\left(Y, i, \dfrac{A}{p}\right) \qquad$ (13-6)

Money supply: $\qquad\qquad\qquad\qquad\qquad M_s = m(i, \bar{p})\bar{H}a \qquad$ (13-7)

Money market equilibrium: $\qquad\qquad\qquad\qquad M_s = M_d \qquad$ (13-8)

Government budget constraint: $\qquad \dfrac{d\bar{H}a}{p} = \dfrac{\overline{DEF}}{p} + d\bar{G} - \dfrac{dBg}{ip} \qquad$ (13-9)

Production function: $\qquad Y = F(Ne^{\lambda t}, K) = (Ne^{\lambda t})^{\alpha}K^{1-\alpha} \qquad$ (13-10)

Labor market equilibrium: $\qquad\qquad pF_N = h\left(N, \dfrac{A}{p}, p, \bar{Z}\right) \qquad$ (13-11)

The eleven endogenous variables are Y, C, I, A, p, M_s, M_d, i, K, $B_g^{\,p}$, and N. The interest rate is assumed to be the rental price of capital in Eq. (13-3) by assuming there is no corporate income tax and no depreciation, and Y is defined as output *net* of depreciation.

---

[1] We abstract from the complexities of separate equations for consumer durables, housing and inventories, and the foreign sector in making this summary, since our purpose is not to develop a full-blown econometric model but to get a feeling for the general effect of the major refinements to the basic model. Variable factor shares are also ignored in the production function.

p = discount rate

$\bar{H}$ = high power money

THE DEFINITION OF WEALTH

Real wealth of the private sector is written [Eq. (13-4)] as the sum of the sector's (1) real money balances M/p, (2) real government bond holdings $B_g{}^p/ip$, and (3) physical capital K. Given the emphasis placed on wealth in the consumption function [Eq. (13-2)], the demand-for-money equation (13-6), and the supply-of-labor equation (13-11)—based on the theory explored in Chapters 4, 9, and 12—it is time to stop and define more precisely what we mean by real nonhuman assets or wealth. This issue has been debated at some length in relatively recent literature (Pesek and Saving, 1967 and 1968; Friedman and Schwartz, 1969; Patinkin 1969; and Johnson, 1969).

Consider the combined balance sheet of the private sector, as shown in Table 13-1 (in what follows we ignore the i term in the bond expressions). Consolidating the balance sheet of the private sector and solving for net worth (A), we get

$$A = X^p + DD^p + DT + B_g{}^p + (B_p{}^p - B_p) + pK$$

However, if the balance sheet of the banking system is considered (Table 13-2), and we solve for $DD^p + DT$, we get

$$DT + DD^p = X^b + D_F{}^b + B_p{}^b + B_g{}^b$$

and substituting this into A, we get

$$A = X^p + X^b + D_F{}^b + B_p{}^b + B_p{}^p - B_p + B_g{}^p + pK$$

But $B_p{}^b + B_p{}^p = B_p$—total private debt outstanding is held by either the private sector or the banking system. Furthermore, $X^p + X^b + D_F{}^b = Ha$ (we ignore the bank's borrowings from the Federal Reserve), so that

$$A = Ha + B_g{}^p + pK$$

and

$$\frac{A}{p} = \frac{Ha}{p} + \frac{B_g{}^p}{p} + K$$

Table 13-1   COMBINED BALANCE SHEET OF PRIVATE SECTOR

Money Currency, X^p	Private sector bonds, B_p
Demand deposits, DD^p	
Time deposits, DT	
Government bonds, $B_g{}^p$	
Private sector bonds, $B_p{}^p$	
Capital, pK	Net worth, A

Table 13-2   CONSOLIDATED BALANCE SHEET OF BANKING SYSTEM

Currency in vault, X^b	Demand deposits, private sector, DD^p
Deposits at the Federal Reserve, $D_F{}^b$	
Private bonds, $B_p{}^b$	Time deposits, DT
Government bonds, $B_g{}^b$	

This expression is the same as Eq. (13-4), except that Ha/p—the real monetary base—replaces M/p. Conventional accounting thus leads to the exclusion of a part of M from wealth—that part of DD^p not backed by bank holdings of claims on the government $(X^b + B_g{}^p + D_F{}^b)$. This part of money not included in wealth is termed "inside money," while the portion in wealth is called "outside money" (Gurley and Shaw, 1961).

However, recent literature (see especially Johnson, 1969, and Patinkin, 1971) has provided powerful arguments for putting most of M into wealth. The basic argument is that M provides a stream of services to its holders without diminishing the wealth of nonholders. Thus wealth is effectively increased dollar for dollar as M is increased. We have thus included M/p as real wealth.

Now we solve the first nine equations for dY and dp. For convenience, the only exogenous variables assumed to change are $\bar{G}$ and $\bar{H}a$, and we assume that $p = 1$. The result is rather tedious in its detail, but the final expression may be summarized as

$$dY = \frac{1}{\Delta} \quad \text{(a multiplicand)} \quad (13\text{-}12)$$

The terms in the multiplicand are

1 The impact of price changes on aggregate demand:

$$dp\, \Phi_1$$

2 The impact of changes in the adjusted monetary base (open market operations) on aggregate demand:

$$dHa\, \Phi_2$$

3 The direct impact of budgetary measures on aggregate demand:

$$dG$$

4 The impact of discretionary budget changes and initial budget deficit via the implied increase in the stock of bonds held by the private sector:

$$(d\bar{G} + \overline{DEF})\Phi_3$$

The multiplier $1/\Delta$ is given by

$$\frac{1}{\Delta} = \frac{1}{1 - C_{Y_d}(1 - \tau) - I_Y(1 + C_A) - \left\{ \dfrac{[C_A(m_i\bar{H}a - B_g{}^p/i^2) + I_i](L_Y + L_A I_Y)}{(m_i\bar{H}a)(1 - L_A) + \dfrac{L_A B_g{}^p}{i^2} - L_i} \right\}} \quad (13\text{-}13)$$

Assuming $1 - C_{Y_d}(1 - \tau) - I_Y(1 + C_A) > 0$, let us examine the expression in braces in the denominator of (13-13). Since $0 < L_A < 1$ and $L_i < 0$, the denominator of the braced expression is positive-definite. The numerator of it is likely to be negative, since $B_g{}^p/i^2$ is (absolutely) very large and $m_i\bar{H}a$ is not. Thus, we assume $1/\Delta$ is positive. Note also that without wealth effects and the effect of i on the supply of money, $1/\Delta$ collapses to the familiar Keynesian multiplier

$$\frac{1}{\Delta} = \frac{1}{1 - C_{Y_d}(1 - \tau) - I_Y + \dfrac{I_i L_Y}{L_i}}$$

The terms Φ_1, Φ_2, and Φ_3 are weights for the terms in the multiplicand. Their signs are not definite, as can be seen below [$COFi/DOMi$ is the expression in braces in (13-13)]:

$$\Phi_1 = C_{Y_d}\overline{T} - C_A\left(m\overline{H}a + \frac{B_g^{\,p}}{i}\right) - \frac{COFi}{DOMi}\left[m\overline{H}a(1 + L_A) + L_A\frac{B_g^{\,p}}{i}\right] \qquad (13\text{-}14)$$

$$\Phi_2 = -C_A(1 - m) - \frac{COFi}{DOMi}[L_A + m(1 - L_A)] \qquad (13\text{-}15)$$

$$\Phi_3 = C_A + \frac{COFi}{DOMi}L_A \qquad (13\text{-}16)$$

However, the size of the terms suggests that Φ_1 is negative and Φ_2 and Φ_3 are positive, as we shall see shortly.

Using estimates culled from the previous chapters, we can produce numerical estimates for Φ_1, Φ_2, Φ_3, and $1/\Delta$. First, consider the multiplier $1/\Delta$ [Eq. (13-13)]. We assume the values for the parameters (1972 data, all slopes in billions of dollars unless otherwise indicated) shown in Table 13-3. Then $1/\Delta$ is

$$\frac{1}{\Delta} = \cfrac{1}{1 - 0.7(0.71) - 0.16(1.06) - \left\{\cfrac{[0.06(0.078 \times 87 - 558.8] - 17.5(1 + 0.06)[0.23 + (0.06)(0.16)]}{[0.078(87)](1 - 0.06) + 0.06(558.8) + 17.0 + (0.06)(17.5)}\right\}}$$

$$= \cfrac{1}{0.33 - \cfrac{-12.4}{57.93}} = \frac{1}{0.33 - (-0.214)} = \frac{1}{0.544} = \underline{\underline{1.838}} \qquad (13\text{-}17)$$

Using the same values for the parameters as above, we get for the value of Φ_1, the first weight in the multiplicand.

$$\Phi_1 = 0.7(51) - 0.06[(2.82)(87) + 402]$$
$$+ (0.214)\,[(2.82)(87)(1 + 0.06) + 0.06(402)]$$
$$= -35.7 - 38.8 + (0.214)(284.18) = -35.7 - 38.8 + 60.8$$
$$= -13.7 \qquad (13\text{-}18)$$

It should be stressed that both results—for $1/\Delta$ and Φ_1—are not meant to precisely represent the "real world." Many of the assumed elasticities in Table 13-3 are subject to question, which makes the "slopes" (for example, I_Y, L_i, $\bar{\tau}$, L_A) subject to question. In particular, the calculations for Eq. (13-7) are especially sensitive to the assumed elasticity of taxes T with respect to Y. (An elasticity of unity, for example, would make Φ_1 *positive*). Thus the effort here is meant to give some "feel" for the numbers and not to forge a model with good forecasting characteristics.

Therefore, setting $d\overline{H}a$, $d\overline{G}$, and $d\overline{G} + \overline{DEF}$ equal to zero, we get for the slope of the aggregate demand curve

$$\left.\frac{dp}{dY}\right|_D = \frac{0.544}{-13.7} = -0.040 \qquad (13\text{-}19)$$

A rise of \$1 billion in Y thus corresponds to a fall of 0.04 in p. A doubling of p reduces aggregate demand by \$25 billion.

For the other weights, we obtain these values:

$$\Phi_2 = -0.06(1 - 2.82) + (0.214)[0.06 + (2.82)(0.94)]$$
$$= -0.06(-1.82) + (0.214)[0.06 + 2.65]$$
$$= 0.11 + (0.214)(2.71)$$
$$= 0.11 + 0.58 = 0.69 \tag{13-20}$$

$$\Phi_3 = 0.06 + (0.214)(0.06)$$
$$= 0.06 + 0.013$$
$$= 0.19 \tag{13-21}$$

As noted above, Φ_2 and Φ_3 are both positive. Thus $d\bar{H}a$ and $d\bar{G} + \overline{DEF}$ will have positive initial impacts on Y, given that $1/\Delta$ is also positive.

Table 13-3   ASSUMPTIONS FOR NUMERICAL CALCULATIONS

$Y = \$1,050$ billion
$C = \$726$ billion
$I = \$173$ billion
$G = T = \$255$ billion
$M = \$245$ billion
$K = \$3,153$ billion
$C_{Y_d} = 0.7$ (based on Chapter 4)
$\tau = 0.291$ (based on assumption that elasticity $\eta_{T,Y} = 1.2$ and 1972 T/Y)
$I_Y = 0.16$ (based on the elasticity of $\eta_{I,Y} = 1$ and 1972 I/Y)
$I_i = -\$17.5$ (based on the elasticity of $\eta_{I,i} = -0.7$ and 1972 I/i)
$C_A = 0.06$ (based on Chapter 4)
$m_i = 0.078$ (based on $\eta_{Ms,i} = 0.2$ and 1972 value of m)
$\bar{H}_a = \$87$ billion (1972 data)
$m = 2.82$ (1972 data)
$B_g{}^p/i = \$402$ billion (1972 data) $[B_g{}^p = (402)(7.2) = 2894.4]$
$100(i) = 7.2\%$ (1972) data
$\alpha = 0.67$ (1972 data)
$B_g/100(i^2) = 2,894.4/5.18 = \$558.8$ billion
$L_Y = 0.23$ (based on $\eta_{Md,Y} = 1$ and 1972 value of M/Y)
$L_A = 0.06$ (based on $\eta_{Md,A} = 1$ and 1972 value of A/Y)
$L_i = -17.0$ (based on $\eta_{Md,i} = -0.5$ and 1972 value of M/i)
$\bar{T} = 0.51$ (based on $\eta_{T,Y} = 1.2$ and 1972 values for T and Y)
$\bar{\tau} = 0.29$ (same basis as $\bar{T}$)
$p = 1$ (an index number)
$F_N = \alpha Y/N$ (from the Cobb-Douglas production function)
$N = 172.7$ billion man-hours
$\alpha = 0.67$
$h_N = \$0.12$ (1972 data, assuming $\eta_{N,w/p=0.2}$)
$h_p = \$3.72$ (1972 data, assuming $\eta_{N,w/p} = 0.2$, and $N_{A/p} = 0.2$)
$w = \$4.10$

SOURCE: *1973 Economic Report of the President's Council of Economic Advisors.* (Data only; 1972 values.)

Consider the slope of the aggregate supply curve, obtained (as in Chapter 3) by solving Eq. (13-11) for dN and inserting this in the production function [Eq. (13-10)]. We assume $dA = dt = d\bar{Z} = 0$ since changes in these variables have to do with *shifts* in the aggregate supply curve. Also, for convenience, we index $t = 0$, and so $E = N$. The slope of the aggregate supply curve is then

$$\left.\frac{dp}{dY}\right|_{s} = \frac{pF_{NN} - h_N}{F_N(h_p - F_N)} \qquad (13\text{-}22)$$

as in Chapter 3, except now h_p includes the real wealth effect on the supply wage w_s in addition to the effect through the impact of dp on w/p, the real wage rate. Using the assumptions shown in Table 13-3—in particular that the elasticity of the supply of labor with respect to both real wages and real assets is 0.2—we obtain the necessary slopes and substitute these into (13-22) to get

$$\left.\frac{dp}{dY}\right|_{s} = \frac{-0.024 - 0.12}{(4.10)(3.72 - 4.10)} = 0.0923 \qquad (13\text{-}23)$$

The result suggests that a rise of 9.2 percent in prices is required to induce a \$1 billion rise in the aggregate supply of output, that a doubling of p will cause the amount supplied to rise by only some \$10.8 billion.

THE FISCAL AND MONETARY MULTIPLIERS

From the equation for dY cited above (from Chapter 3), we now have

$$dY = \frac{(0.04)dX + (0.0923)dR}{0.132} \qquad (13\text{-}24)$$

where dX and dR are the horizontal shifts in the aggregate demand and supply curves measured at the initial price level. For shifts in the demand curve alone, the multipliers are

$$dY_{dX} = 0.302dX \qquad (13\text{-}25)$$

and for shifts in the supply curve alone, they are

$$dY_{dR} = 0.70dR \qquad (13\text{-}26)$$

Now consider the fiscal and monetary multipliers, assuming for the moment that the supply curve is *not* shifting ($dR = 0$). These are given by

$$dY_{dX} = (0.302)(1.838)(0.69)d\bar{H}a + (0.302)(1.838)(0.19)(d\bar{G} + \overline{DEF})$$
$$+ (0.302)(1.838)d\bar{G} \qquad (13\text{-}27)$$

The multipliers reflect the values of $1/\Delta$, Φ_2, and Φ_3 developed above. Combining terms, we obtain

$$dY_{dX} = 0.383d\bar{H}a + 0.105(d\bar{G} + \overline{DEF}) + 0.555d\bar{G}$$

or for $t = 0$ and $\overline{DEF} = 0$,

$$dY = 0.383d\overline{H}a + 0.660d\overline{G} \qquad (13\text{-}28)$$

Thus the *impact* multipliers for $\overline{G}$ and $\overline{H}a$ are positive, with the $\overline{G}$ multiplier almost double that for $\overline{H}a$. Both are much smaller than in the basic Keynesian model because the rise in p damps down the total impact.

Now consider shifts in the aggregate supply curve. If employment N grows at the same rate as the labor force $\overline{Z}$ (as defined in Chapter 12),

$$dR = \frac{dY_s}{dt} = \frac{\alpha Y}{E}\left(\lambda e^{\lambda t}N_t + e^{\lambda t}\frac{d\overline{Z}}{dt}\right) + \beta Y\frac{I}{K}$$

$$= \alpha Y(\lambda + g_{\bar z}) + \beta Y\frac{I}{K} \qquad (13\text{-}29)$$

Equation (13-29) considerably complicates matters, since the shift in the supply depends on the level of investment I, and I in turn depends on all the forces operating on the interest rate i and the level of income Y. In short, aggregate demand policies which affect i and Y shift not only the demand curve but the supply curve.

For expository purposes, we abstract from this interdependence between the two curves. It is clearer in the context of equilibrium growth models (Chapter 15) than in the "one-period-shift" analysis pursued here. However, we can express the shift (dR) in the aggregate supply curve as

$$dR = dY = d\left(\frac{Y}{N}\right)N + dN\left(\frac{Y}{N}\right) \qquad (13\text{-}29a)$$

where the rate of growth of output per man-hour Y/N—call it λ'—reflects the effects of *both* technical change and increased capital per worker (K/N). Then the rate of growth of output is

$$\frac{dY}{Y} = \frac{d(Y/N)}{Y/N} + \frac{dN}{N} = \lambda' + g_{\bar z} \qquad \left(\text{since } \frac{dN}{N} = \frac{d\overline{Z}}{\overline{Z}}\right)$$

i.e., the rate of growth of output is the sum of the rates of growth of output per man-hour (λ') and the labor force ($g_{\bar z}$). The long-term rate of growth of output per man-hour is about 2.7 percent, and available man-hours grow at about 1.5 percent per year. The shift in the supply curve is then

$$dR = dY = Y(0.027 + 0.015) = 0.042Y \qquad (13\text{-}30)$$

Substituting back into (13-24), we get for the change in real output per period

$$dY = 0.383d\overline{H}a + 0.555(d\overline{G} - 0.7d\overline{T}) + 0.105(d\overline{G} + \overline{DEF}) + 0.029Y$$

(We have added the term $-C_{Y_d}d\overline{T}$ to allow for tax changes).

CHANGES IN THE PRICE LEVEL

The change in the price level in each period can also be expressed in terms of the slopes of and shifts in the aggregate supply and demand curves:

$$dp = \frac{\left|\dfrac{dp}{dY}\right|_S \left|\dfrac{dp}{dY}\right|_D (dX - dR)}{\left|\dfrac{dp}{dY}\right|_S + \left|\dfrac{dp}{dY}\right|_D} \qquad (13\text{-}31)$$

In terms of our numerical estimates,

$$dp = \frac{(0.0037)(dX - dR)}{0.132} = 0.028(dX - dR) \qquad (13\text{-}32)$$

The price level responds to the difference between the shifts in aggregate demand and supply (measured at the initial price); the more the shift in the demand curve exceeds the shift in the supply curve, the greater the increase in prices, and vice versa. For example, a \$10.5 billion "overshoot" in the increase in aggregate demand relative to aggregate supply in a period (1 percent of the initial output) causes prices to rise by about 3 percent over their previous level.

Given the changes in Y and p, we can solve for the change in *nominal* GNP (pY):

$$d(pY) = p\,dY + Y\,dp \qquad (13\text{-}33)$$

$$= \frac{0.04dX + 0.0923dR + Y[0.0037(dX - dR)]}{0.132}$$

or using our estimate of Y,

$$d(pY) = 29.7dX - 28.7dR \qquad (13\text{-}34)$$

Because the slope of the supply curve is greater in absolute value than that of the demand curve, increases in real supply cause nominal GNP to fall. That is, given the demand curve, a rightward shift in the supply curve causes prices to fall proportionately more than Y rises. On the other hand, a rightward shift in the demand curve causes p *and* Y to rise, thus increasing nominal GNP. The numbers used here indicate that equal increases in X and R increases nominal GNP—the effect of the shift in the demand curve dominates in this respect.

THE MONETARIST-FISCALIST CONTROVERSY

Since the late 1960s a running debate has been carried on in economic literature over the relative potency of fiscal and monetary policy in affecting aggregate demand and thus real output and prices. While the conventional estimates of the relative elasticities, as used in this chapter, suggest that both fiscal and monetary actions affect

Y and pY, with the "impact multiplier" somewhat larger for fiscal than for monetary actions, several empirical studies show monetary policy to be very potent in its effect on pY while fiscal actions, at least over a period of several quarters, tend to have little if any impact, regardless of which measures of fiscal policy are used [$d\overline{G}$, $d\overline{T}$, of the "full-employment" surplus (or deficit)]. (See, especially, Andersen and Jordan, 1968). How can these findings be reconciled with the results here?

The basic equation set forth by the monetarists (Andersen and Jordan, 1968) takes the form

$$d(pY) = \alpha_0 + \alpha_1 \, d\overline{H} + \alpha_2 \, dg_F - \alpha_3 \, dREV_F \qquad (13\text{-}35)$$

where $\overline{H}$ is the unadjusted monetary base, g_F is *federal* expenditures measured at full employment, and $dREV_F$ a measure of changes in high-employment federal government receipts. Over a period of one year, Andersen and Jordan found the coefficients α_2 and α_3 to be not significant (statistically) from zero, while the coefficient α_1 was large and statistically significant. The size of α_1—16.4—suggests that a \$1 billion change in the unadjusted monetary base changes nominal GNP by \$16.4 billion over a period of one year, while over the same period changes in federal purchases and full-employment receipts and expenditures have no effect on nominal GNP.

There is similarity between (13-35) and (13-34). Substituting for dX in (13-34), we get

$$d(pY) = (0.04 + 0.0037Y)(0.383d\overline{H}a + 0.660d\overline{G} - 0.388d\overline{T} - 0.388d\tau Y + 0.105\overline{DEF})$$
$$+ (0.07 - 0.028Y)dR \qquad (13\text{-}36)$$

However, important differences in the two equations stand out. First, the Andersen-Jordan equation does not include the second part of (13-36); it is, in effect, an equation only for the $p \, dY$ part of $d(pY)$. Second, the Andersen-Jordan equation does not include real output Y, which appears as a multiplicative term in both parts of (13-36). Third, the variables are defined differently: their monetary variable is the *unadjusted* base H instead of the adjusted base Ha; their fiscal variables are for the federal government only; federal expenditures are *total* expenditures (including net interest, transfers, and grants-in-aid) net purchases, and federal taxes are gross rather than net (of transfers, etc.) and do not represent pure discretionary changes in taxes ($d\overline{T}$ and $d\tau Y$) but a mix of discretionary changes and changes induced by changes in pY. Finally, the initial deficit of the government sector is not included as a variable.

Thus it is very difficult to evaluate this monetarist interpretation of changes in nominal GNP when, at least on the basis of the structural equations used here [Eqs. (13-1 to 13-11)], it is misspecified as a reduced-form equation [where the complete model is solved for $d(pY)$]. On the other hand, the point of our exercise here is not to suggest what the multipliers may in fact be, but rather to highlight, the key parameters that determine their size. Whether one estimates structural equations (as we have done casually here) or chooses to estimate reduced-form equations is partly a statistical question, but if reduced forms are estimated, they should be consistent with the solution of a structural model which is theoretically defensible.

SUMMARY

In this chapter, we have attempted to breathe some life into the theory covered in much of Chapters 4 to 12 by "plugging" outside estimates of key elasticities and parameters into the model suggested by the theoretical modifications previously discussed, and solving for the reduced-form equations for dY, dp, and $d(pY)$. The numbers that result are suggestive only of what happens when disparate estimates from many separate empirical studies are put together, not of estimates derived from a complete model where the equations are estimated over consistent periods with consistent definitions of the variables and appropriate forms for the equations. We have, to put it another way, taken great liberty with numbers to aid us in putting together the main threads of the discussion in the theoretical chapters.

Finally, we briefly evaluated the monetarist-fiscalist controversy with the results of our somewhat simplistic model. Even at this level, the monetarist reduced-form equations are open to question as to specification of the variables to be included and their definition, so much so that it is difficult to draw any conclusion from their empirical efforts.

READINGS FOR CHAPTER 13

ANDERSEN, L. C., and J. L. JORDAN: "Monetary and Fiscal Actions: A Test of Their Relative Importance in Economic Stabilization," *Review—Federal Reserve Bank of St. Louis*, pp. 11–12, November 1968.

———: "Monetary and Fiscal Actions: A Test of Their Relative Importance in Economic Stabilization: Reply," *Review—Federal Reserve Bank of St. Louis*, pp. 12–16, April 1969.

DE LEEUW, F., and J. KALCHBRENNER: "Monetary and Fiscal Actions: A Test of Their Relative Importance in Economic Stabilization: Comment," *Review—Federal Reserve Bank of St. Louis*, pp. 6–11, April 1969.

FRIEDMAN, M., and A. L. SCHWARTZ: "The Definition of Money: Net Wealth and Neutrality as Criteria," *Journal of Money, Credit and Banking*, vol. 1, February 1969.

GURLEY, J. G., and E. S. SHAW: *Money in a Theory of Finance* (Washington, D.C.: The Brooking Institution, 1961).

JOHNSON, H.: "Inside Money, Outside Money, Income Wealth and Welfare in Monetary Theory," *Journal of Money, Credit and Banking*, vol. 1, pp. 1–14, February 1969.

PATINKIN, D.: "Money and Wealth: A Review Article," *Journal of Economic Literature*, vol. 7, pp. 1140–1160, December 1969.

PESEK, B. P., and T. R. SAVING: *Money, Wealth and Economic Theory* (New York: Macmillan, 1967), chap. 9.

———: *The Foundations of Money and Banking* (New York: Macmillan, 1967).

PART THREE

Economic Growth

14

INFLATION, PRODUCTIVITY, AND THE PHILLIPS CURVE

In Parts 1 and 2, we developed models that determined real output and prices in a comparative-statics setting. That is, assuming initial equilibrium at the intersection of the aggregate supply and demand curves, we investigated the effects of "one-time" shifts in the demand and supply curves on prices and wages by comparing the new equilibrium p and Y with the old. This chapter starts us into the dynamics of equilibrium macromodels, where one is concerned not just with a one-time change in aggregate supply or demand, but with the movement of the two over time and the resulting *paths* traced out by prices and output. This chapter is concerned with *inflation*—the behavior of prices over time. Chapters 15 and 16 deal with the time paths of prices *and* output.

The following section deals with the nature of inflation in the static model and discusses "demand-pull" versus "cost-push" inflation. The next section deals with the general relation between prices, productivity, and wages over time. The third section attempts, with the basic models used in macromodels, to explain price behavior: the now-famous "Phillips curve" approach and the more recent arguments of the "accelerationist" theorists.

THE NATURE OF INFLATION IN THE STATIC MODEL

Consider the static model outlined in Chapter 13. Given all the exogenous variables affecting supply and demand, for any period it can be depicted in terms of the familiar aggregate supply and demand graphs shown in Figure 14-1. The aggregate demand curve has a negative slope because a fall in prices increases A/p and $\overline{T}/p$, thus directly adding to aggregate demand via the wealth and tax effects on consumption. A fall in p also increases the real money stock M/p. This may or may not indirectly add to aggregate demand. The rise in A/p causes the *demand* for real balances to rise ($L_{(A/p)} > 0$), and this rise in the *demand* for real money balances works against the rise in the *supply* of real balances. If $(M/p)_d$ rises by the same amount as $(M/p)_s$, there is no indirect *monetary* effect on aggregate demand from a fall in the price level. If $(M/p)_d$ rises by *less* than $(M/p)_s$, the excess supply of real balances shifts the LM curve "out" and adds a monetary effect to the direct real wealth and real tax effects on aggregate demand. And if the demand for real balances rises by more than the supply when p falls, the indirect monetary effects cut against the direct wealth and tax effects of a fall in p—the fall in p induces a downward pressure on total demand from the monetary sector.[1]

On the supply side, a rise in p unambiguously increases the real amount supplied—the slope of the S curve in Figure 14-1 is positive. A rise in p reduces real nonhuman wealth, which *increases* the amount of labor supplied at each real wage rate.

In Figure 14-2, where the labor supply curve is drawn in the (w, N) space, for given values of p and A, a rise in p shifts the N_s curve *upward* for any value of N—the supply wage (w_s) increases. From Chapter 12, we have

$$w_s = \phi\left(p, N, \frac{A}{p}\right) \qquad (14\text{-}1)$$

Given N, the effect on the supply wage (the upward shift in the supply wage w_s) is

$$dw_s = \phi_p \, dp + \phi_{A/p} d\left(\frac{A}{p}\right)$$

$$= \phi_p \, dp - \phi_{A/p}\left(\frac{A}{p^2}\right) dp$$

$$= \left[\phi_p - \phi_{A/p} \frac{A}{p^2}\right] dp$$

$$(\phi_p > 0 \qquad \phi_{A/p} > 0)$$

---

[1] Notice that in Chapter 13 we implicitly assumed the monetary effects of price changes on aggregate demand to be zero since we assume the elasticity of M/p with respect to A/p was unity (the percentage increase in the two are thus the same). Note also that real *net exports* increase when p falls in an open economy, which would add to the (absolute) value of $(dp/dY)|_D$ in Chapter 13.

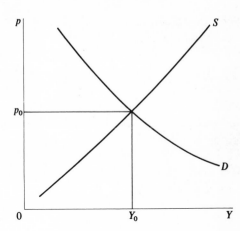

FIGURE 14-1
Aggregate equilibrium.

The sign of dw_s is not unambiguous; a rise in p shifts the N_s curve up through the real wage effect, but the accompanying fall in A/p works to reduce w_s.[2] The demand for labor in the (w, N) space is

$$w_d = F_N p \qquad (14\text{-}2)$$

where the VMP of labor ($F_N p$) equals the price of labor (Chapter 12). Thus the demand curve for labor is positively related to labor productivity and the price level. A change in p causes the demand curve for labor to shift up by

$$dw_d = F_N \, dp \qquad (14\text{-}3)$$

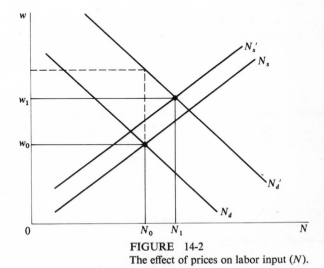

FIGURE 14-2
The effect of prices on labor input (N).

---

[2] Whether dw_s is positive or negative, a rise in p will always result in a rise in the equilibrium quantity of labor. This will be shown below.

Even in the neoclassical case where $\phi_p = F_N$, the supply curve for labor now shifts up by less than the demand curve:

$$dw_d = F_N \, dp > dw_s = \left[\phi_p - \phi_{A/p}\left(\frac{A}{p^2}\right) \right] dp \qquad \text{if } F_N = \phi_p$$

This is shown in Figure 14-2 by the shift in the N_s and N_d curves to N_s' and N_d', respectively. The result is the rise in employment from N_0 to N_1. From the production function

$$Y = F(N, K)$$

the sign of $\dfrac{dY}{dp} = F_N \dfrac{dN}{dp}$ is positive,[3] assuming that K is fixed.

"Demand-Pull" and "Cost-Push" Inflation

An increase in the price level in the static model can reflect shifts in either the aggregate demand or supply curve. Conceptually then we can divide inflation into two categories: (1) inflation caused by shifts in the demand curve (demand-pull) and (2) inflation caused by shifts in the supply curve (cost-push). We consider each in turn.

Suppose, as shown in Figure 14-3, there is a rightward shift in the aggregate demand curve, due to any (or some combination) of the forces acting on the IS curve and/or LM curve, from D to D'. At the initial price level p_0, aggregate demand is now Y_1, and with aggregate supply unchanged at Y_0, there is now excess demand (in real terms) of $Y_1 - Y_0$. The effect of this excess demand is to cause prices to rise. As we saw above, the rise in prices reduces aggregate real demand through the wealth and tax effects on consumption and (possibly) through the induced fall in the real supply of money. On the supply side, the rise in prices induces an increased amount supplied of real output; the demand for labor input rises and the fall in real net assets increases the supply of labor. Equilibrium is restored at a higher price level p_1 with greater output Y_2.

Obviously a leftward (or upward) shift in the aggregate supply schedule also can cause excess demand and inflation. In Figure 14-3, the same rise in price brought

---

[3] From the production function

$$dY = F_N \, dN$$

and in equilibrium

$$F_N \, p = \phi(p, N, A/p)$$

Differentiating totally, we get

$$dN[F_{NN} \, p - \phi_N] = [\phi_p - F_N - \phi_{A/p} \, A/p^2] \, dp$$

Where $\phi_p = F_N$, $\dfrac{dY}{dp}$ becomes

$$\frac{dY}{dp} = F_N \frac{dN}{dp} = F_N \frac{-\phi_{A/p}\dfrac{A}{p^2}}{F_{NN}p - \phi_N} > 0$$

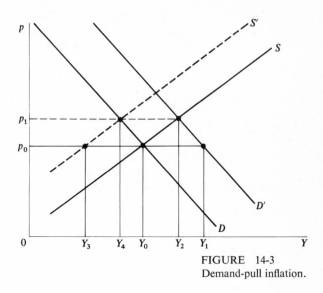

FIGURE 14-3
Demand-pull inflation.

about by demand-pull inflation could have been caused by a leftward shift in the aggregate supply curve to S'. Again, the excess demand ($Y_0 - Y_3$) drives prices up, reducing the amount demanded and increasing the amount supplied until equilibrium is restored at the higher price level p_1 and a *lower* level of real output Y_4.

What can cause the leftward shift in the aggregate supply curve? There are several possibilities. First, there may be an exogenous shift in the labor supply function (Figure 14-2), caused by an increased desire for leisure versus real income, by pressure for higher wages in a highly unionized economy, or by past or expected price increases. It could also be caused by a *reduction* in the marginal productivity of labor [Eq. (14.2)], which reduces the *demand* for labor at any wage rate. Whatever the cause, it increases costs (the wage rate) at the old output level, and this effect on aggregate supply (a higher p is now required for any given supply of real output) can produce cost-push inflation.

While it is easy to theoretically put the causes of a price increase into two "boxes" —demand-pull and cost-push—in practice it is very difficult, if not impossible, to identify the cause of an inflation. The data show only an increase in prices and wages. If one starts with the price side, demand-pull is suggested; looking at the wage increases suggests "cost-push" as the explanation. Often, both may be involved. A demand-pull inflation may create a cost-push inflation later, in that even though prices rise enough to eliminate the excess demand caused by the demand curve shift, the higher price level feeds with a lag into the labor-leisure choice or union wage demands to induce the supply curve of labor and the aggregate supply curve to shift leftward, creating more excess demand and a further rise in price. Furthermore, if a policy of *validation* is followed on the demand side, then to avoid the fall in output from the upward shift in the aggregate supply curve, fiscal and monetary policies may be used to increase aggregate demand and prices further, thus inducing another upward shift in the labor supply curve, and so on.

WAGES, PRICES, AND PRODUCTIVITY

In the previous section, it was noted that a fall in labor productivity (the marginal productivity of labor) would shift the labor demand curve leftward, thus shifting the aggregate supply curve leftward. Clearly an *increase* in labor productivity increases the demand for labor at any money wage rate w, thus offsetting to some extent the tendency for the supply curve to shift leftward and prices to rise. With the appropriate increase in labor productivity, the labor supply curve can shift up, the money wage rate w can rise, and prices can remain stable. Let us discuss the relation between rates of change in wages, prices, and labor productivity, with particular emphasis on the arithmetic of the nexus between *stable prices*, wage increases, and productivity.

From the demand function for labor [Eq. (14-2)], we have in equilibrium (where $w_d = w_s$)

$$w = F_N p$$

or solving for p,

$$p = \frac{w}{F_N} \qquad (14\text{-}4)$$

Taking logs, we get

$$\log p = \log w - \log F_N \qquad (14\text{-}5)$$

The derivatives of logarithms are percentage changes. Thus differentiating (14-5), we can see the basic arithmetic relating wages, prices, and productivity:

$$d \log p = d \log w - d \log F_N$$
$$\%\Delta p = \%\Delta w - \%\Delta F_N \qquad (14\text{-}6)$$

Equation (14-6) says that prices will increase at a percentage rate (per period) equal to the percentage increase in money wages *less* the percentage increase in productivity. Thus, for stable prices ($\%\Delta p = d \log p = 0$), the rate of increase of money wages must equal the rate of increase of labor productivity. If wages grow faster than productivity, prices rise, and if wages grow slower than productivity, prices fall.

How fast will *real wages* grow? Writing out the expression for real wages (ω), we have

$$\omega = \frac{w}{p}$$

Taking logarithms, we obtain

$$\log \omega = \log w - \log p$$

From (14-5) this equals

$$\log \omega = \log w - \log p = \log F_N$$

and so real wages grow at the same rate as labor productivity

$$d \log \omega = d \log w - d \log p = d \log F_N \qquad (14\text{-}7)$$

and money wages (w) grow as fast as real wages if prices are stable.

This relationship can be put in terms of output per man-hour (average productivity) using the Cobb-Douglas production function.

$$Y = N^\alpha K^{1-\alpha} \qquad (14\text{-}8)$$

As we saw in Chapter 12, the marginal product of labor (F_N) is

$$F_N = \frac{\alpha Y}{N} \qquad (14\text{-}9)$$

And from the profit-maximization condition (14-2),

$$p = \frac{w}{F_N}$$

$$p = \frac{w}{\alpha(Y/N)} \qquad (14\text{-}10)$$

Taking logs of (14-10) and differentiating we again see the basic wage-price-productivity relationships

$$d \log p = d \log w - d \log \frac{Y}{N} \qquad (14\text{-}11)$$

where Y/N is output per man-hour.

Finally we see that the share of labor and capital in total output remain constant if prices are stable and wages rise with productivity. The share of labor S_N is, by definition,

$$S_N = \frac{wN}{pY} = \frac{w/p}{Y/N} \qquad (14\text{-}12)$$

Taking logs of (14-12) and differentiating, we have

$$d \log S_N = d \log (w/p) - d \log (Y/N) \qquad (14\text{-}13)$$

and from (14-7) we know that if prices are stable, money wages rise as fast as real wages and productivity, so that under these circumstances

$$d \log S_N = 0 \qquad (14\text{-}14)$$

Since labor share is constant, capital share is also constant.

MODELS OF PRICE BEHAVIOR

We have seen that price changes reflect excess demand, whether the excess demand exists because of shifts in the aggregate demand curve or the aggregate supply curve. With this as a starting point, we can look at two models of price behavior current in the literature. The first approach we consider is the familiar Phillips curve model, because it is closely tied to the wage-price-productivity nexus discussed in the previous section. Next, we look at the "accelerationists" model.

The Phillips Curve

We have just seen that if money wages rise as fast as productivity, the equilibrium price level can be stable, but that if money wages rise faster than productivity, the price level will rise, and if money wages lag behind productivity growth, the price level will fall. These results reflect the behavior of the aggregate supply curve, whether it remains stable or shifts to the left or right.

Put another way, the issue is: How fast *will* money wages rise? Will the labor supply curve shift upward *more* than the upward shift in the demand curve brought about by productivity increases or not? A model of wage behavior thus can be "fed into" the wage-price-productivity arithmetic to determine the rate of increase in the equilibrium price level.

The Phillips curve approach starts with a model of wage behavior. In 1958, A. W. Phillips found a significant historical relation between the rate of money wage change and the rate of unemployment in the United Kingdom, and the concept of the Phillips curve has become a standard part of the professional vocabulary. Lipsey (1960) provided the basic theoretical foundation for the Phillips curve. The fundamental hypothesis is that the rate of increase in money wages (dw/w) is a function of relative excess supply (or demand) in the labor market:

$$\frac{dw}{w} = f\left(\frac{N_s - N_d}{N_s}\right) \qquad f' < 0 \qquad (14\text{-}15)$$

That is, the greater the excess supply in the labor market is (the less the excess demand is) the less the rate of change of money wages is to be; and the smaller the excess supply of labor is (the greater the excess demand for labor is), the greater the rate of growth of money wages is. This is shown graphically in Figure 14-4. Note that dw/w is drawn to have a lower limit at A: it is assumed that regardless of the amount of excess labor supply, wage rates can be reduced only at a limited rate.

The next step is the critical assumption in the Phillips curve approach, the one made by Phillips which gave the approach its name—*the global unemployment rate u is taken as a measure of the excess demand for or supply of labor.* More precisely, we assume

$$N_e = \frac{N_s - N_d}{N_s} = j(u) \qquad j_u > 0 \qquad (14\text{-}16)$$

Such a relationship is shown in Figure 14-5. Notice that when the excess supply of labor is zero, the unemployment rate is not zero. Zero excess supply does not mean there are no persons unemployed; it means the number of unemployed is equal to the number of vacant jobs. The unemployment rate u_0 then represents the frictional unemployment discussed in Chapter 2.

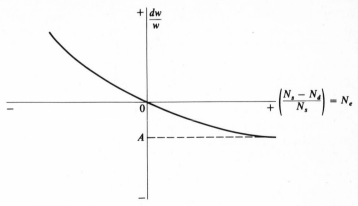

FIGURE 14-4
Relation between rate of change of wages and excess supply of labor.

We notice also that j_u increases as N_e falls—the rate of change in relative excess supply gets larger the lower the unemployment rate—$j_{uu} < 0$. Finally, as N_e becomes more negative past $N_e = 0$ (as the excess *demand* for labor rises), there is little or no effect on the unemployment rate, which is to say that *vacancies* rise but there are still the frictionally unemployed. For all practical purposes, $j_{uu} \to \infty$ as u reaches and then falls below u_0, and if we assume a lower limit to the fall in dw/w, the Phillips curve will be convex.

Substituting (14-16) into (14-15), we get the basic Phillips curve relationship

$$dw/w = f[j(u)] \qquad (14\text{-}17)$$

or

$$dw/w = q(u) \qquad (14\text{-}17a)$$

Since $q_u = f'j_u$ and $f' < 0$ while $j_u > 0$, then $q_u < 0$.

Figure 14-6 shows the Phillips curve linking wage increase and the unemployment rate. It has the negative slope suggested by (14-17), and from (14-16) we know

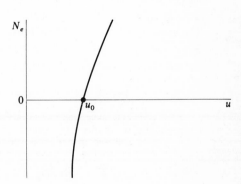

FIGURE 14-5
Excess supply of labor as a function of the
unemployment rate.

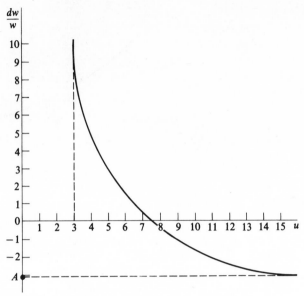

FIGURE 14-6
The Phillips curve linking wage increases and the unemployment rate.

that since j_{uu} approaches infinity for $u < u_0$, the curve asymptotically approaches a vertical line at u_0.

Most Phillips curve studies "throw in" other variables besides u to explain the rate of growth of wages. It is common to find among these added variables:

1 Current or past rates of change in prices (dp/p). The justification is that wage demands will reflect inflationary trends, as workers seek to keep up with the cost of living.

2 The rate of growth of productivity (output per man-hour). The basis for this variable is that higher productivity, given the unemployment rate, means higher wages as the demand curve for labor shifts "out."[4]

3 The rate of corporate profits. The higher the corporate profits–equity ratio, the greater, it is assumed, the pressure by unions for higher wages.

4 A measure of the monopoly power of unions. Presumably, the greater their power (or the more they exercise it), the greater the upward pressure on wages.

---

[4] Actually, the inclusion of productivity as a variable has been based on an alternative view of wage determination which stresses change in productivity as the main variable influencing excess demand. This essentially represents a denial that u is a proxy for relative excess demand. However, in these models u still enters as a variable determining supply-side elements—the lower u is, the greater dw/w, either because productivity increases will be translated more into wage than employment changes, or because a low u means greater bargaining power for employees, or because a low u means the labor supply is inelastic. See Hymans (1970) and Kuh (1967).

5 *"Dummy variables"* which *"switch on"* for periods when the wage-price guideposts were in effect (or for the 1971–1974 periods of wage-price freeze and controls).

6 *A variable for social insurance contributions.* The theory here is that an increase in payroll taxes induces higher wages as workers seek to recoup their after-tax labor income.

Thus, the form of the Phillips curve equation for estimation can be written

$$dw/w = \alpha_0 + \alpha_1 \frac{1}{u} + \sum_{i=1}^{n} \alpha_i Z_i \quad (14\text{-}18)$$

Since dw/w is assumed to have a convex relation to u, but not to the other variables, writing the wage rate increase in terms of $1/u$ rather than u is appropriate. The Z_i's are the other variables included.

Clearly Eq. (14-18) can be substituted into (14-11) to convert it to an expression for the rate of change of prices.

$$\frac{dp}{p} = \alpha_0 + \alpha_1 \frac{1}{u} + \sum_{i=1}^{n} \alpha_i Z_i - \frac{dPROD}{PROD} \quad (14\text{-}19)$$

where $PROD$ is output per man-hour. This assumes factor shares are constant over time—as we saw to be true in Chapter 15.

How does this analysis fit into the "excess demand framework" in explaining inflation? The Phillips curve approach to explaining price changes can be looked at in two ways, and it is not always clear which is in the minds of those using it. On the one hand, it can be interpreted as a model which explains shifts in the aggregate supply curve, with, presumably, the assumption that such shifts dominate movements in the price level. To put it another way, the Phillips curve can be interpreted as explaining price movements on the assumption that the aggregate supply curve is virtually horizontal, as in the simple Keynesian model, so that, as shown in Figure 14-7, shifts in aggregate supply (as explained via the Phillips curve) explain price changes, while shifts in aggregate demand and supply explain the change in real and nominal output. For example, given equilibrium at p_0 and Y_0, a new price p_1 is generated by the Phillips curve equation. Simultaneously the demand curve shifts out to D' from D. Since this does not enter the Phillips curve equation, the result is that at the new price p_1, output will be greater (Y_1) than before (Y_0) and less (Y_2) than if there had been no shift in the demand curve.

However, we have seen (Chapters 3 and 13) that a horizontal supply curve is not very plausible; thus this "supply-dominates" interpretation of Phillips curve analysis is not very appealing. A more appealing interpretation is that *both* aggregate supply and demand are reflected in the Phillips curve equation. From "Okun's law" (Okun, 1962) we have the familiar relationship

$$Y^* - Y = \sigma(u - u_0)Y \quad (14\text{-}20)$$

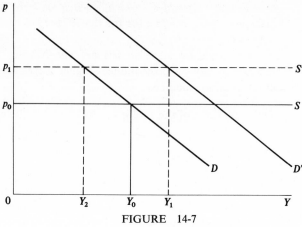

FIGURE   14-7
An interpretation of the Phillips curve.

i.e., the "gap" between potential real output (supply) and actual real output (demand) is some constant σ (Okun uses $\sigma = 3$) times the difference between the actual unemployment rate u and some rate u_0 that measures "full employment" (assume by Okun to be 0.04) times actual real output Y. Solving for u we obtain

$$u = \left(\frac{Y^* - Y}{Y}\right)\frac{1}{\sigma} + u_0 \qquad (14\text{-}21)$$

Thus u can be interpreted as reflecting relative excess supply in the market for real output rather than a proxy for relative excess supply in the labor market, and the Phillips curve equation can be interpreted as containing a variable $(1/u)$ reflecting excess demand as well as other variables (the Z_i's) which somehow "improve the fit."

Empirical Studies of the Phillips Curve

Empirical studies of the Phillips relationship are reaching the magnitude of those done on the consumption function and the demand for money, and we will not attempt to do more here than deal with the findings in the more recent studies by Perry (1964, 1966, and 1970), who has become perhaps the leading authority on the subject. In his earlier studies (1964, 1966), Perry estimated the rate of change of wages as

$$\frac{dw}{w} = -4.3 + 0.04\left(\frac{dp}{p}\right)_{-1} + 14.7\frac{1}{u} + 0.4R + 0.8(dR) \qquad (14\text{-}22)$$

where R is the rate of corporate profits (profits/equity) and the other variables are as used before. When we take into consideration the constant factor shares assumption that $dp/p = dw/w - dPROD/PROD$ and the long-run, steady-state situations where the rate of change of all variables is roughly constant, we can solve (14-22 (where all variables are in percentage units) to get

$$\frac{dw}{w} = -4.3 + 0.4\left(\frac{dw}{w} - \frac{dPROD}{PROD}\right) + 14.7\frac{1}{u} + 0.4R$$

or factoring out dw/w on the right-hand side and collecting terms, we obtain

$$\frac{dw}{w} = -7.2 - 0.7\frac{dPROD}{PROD} + 24.5\frac{1}{u} + 0.7R \qquad (14\text{-}23)$$

The percentage change in prices per period will be

$$\frac{dp}{p} = \frac{dw}{w} - \frac{dPROD}{PROD}$$

$$\frac{dp}{p} = -7.2 - 1.7\frac{dPROD}{PROD} + 24.5\frac{1}{u} + 0.7R \qquad (14\text{-}24)$$

Thus given $dPROD/PROD$, we obtain different rates of growth of prices for various combinations of u and R. $PROD$ has tended to grow over the long term at about 3 percent a year. Thus, for example, for a profit rate of 11 percent prices would be stable if the unemployment rate were about 5.2 percent. For an unemployment rate of 4 percent and for R of 11 percent, the rise in prices would be about 1.5 percent a year.

$$\frac{dp}{p} = -7.2 - 5.1 + 6.125 + 7.7 = 1.5$$

or for $R = 11.6$ percent,

$$\frac{dp}{p} = -7.2 - 5.1 + 6.1 + 8.1 = 2.0$$

This relationship assumes that the structural relationships underlying the equation are stable.

In more recent work Perry (1970) has found the price-unemployment rate relationship to have deteriorated—the Phillips curve has shifted to the right. Basically, he finds that a 4 percent unemployment rate would produce $1\frac{1}{2}$ percentage points more inflation per year than was the case in the mid-1950s, or a rate of inflation of about 3 percent per year. Two explanations are given for the shift. First, a larger proportion of the employed are women and teenagers, who have historically higher unemployment rates than married males. Thus a given unemployment rate in 1973, with its heavier weight of those prone to high unemployment rates, means overall labor market (or output market) conditions are "tighter" than the same unemployment rate of the mid-fifties. (The United States government, in fact, estimated that a 4.8 percent unemployment rate in 1973 is equivalent to a 4 percent unemployment rate with a mid-1950s work force composition. See the *Annual Report of the Council of Economic Advisers*, January 1974, p. 60). Second, *given* the work force composition, the unemployment rates for women and teenagers have risen relative to the rate for prime-age male workers, thus causing the overall unemployment rate to be higher for any degree of market "tightness."

Before leaving the Phillips curve literature, one additional point should be made. Theoretically, the unemployment rate may not be a good surrogate for excess demand or supply in the labor market, whether or not it is adjusted for changes in the composition of the work force and changing relative unemployment rates of different groups of workers. This can be put as follows (see Phelps, 1968). Excess demand for labor (call it X) is usually defined as

$$X = N_d - N_s \qquad (14\text{-}25)$$

where N_d refers to the *number* of workers demanded and N_s to the number offering themselves for work. The labor supply N_s is equal to those employed (N^e) and those wanting work but unemployed (U):

$$N_s = N^e + U \qquad (14\text{-}26)$$

Labor demand N_d is equal to the number of workers employed plus the number of vacant jobs V:

$$N_d = N^e + V \qquad (14\text{-}27)$$

When we substitute (14-26) and (14-27) into (14-25), the excess demand for labor is seen to be

$$X = V - U \qquad (14\text{-}27a)$$

i.e., the excess of vacancies over people looking for work. The *excess demand rate* X/N_s is then

$$x = v - u \qquad (14\text{-}28)$$

i.e., the difference between the vacancy rate and the unemployment rate. The Phillips curve relation, which posits that dw/w is proportional to X, is then viable only if it is assumed that $V = f(u)$ with $f_u < 0$, so that the unemployment rate is a good surrogate for X. Schultze (1971) has estimated Phillips curves using *quit rates* and *layoff rates* rather than the unemployment rate, and he obtained generally satisfactory results.

The Accelerationist School

Since 1968, a group of prominent economists has challenged the Phillips curve approach to wage and price movements. These economists, which we have labeled the "accelerationist school" (Friedman, 1968: Phelps, 1968; Lucas and Rapping, 1969; and Fellner, 1971, 1973), hold that there is no stable, *negative-sloped* Phillips curve. In essence, they argue that, at least over a period of years, the Phillips curve is *vertical* at some employment rate (sometimes called the "natural rate of unemployment"). This unemployment rate is thus consistent with *any* rate of inflation, and they argue that attempts to move the unemployment rate permanently below or above this "natural rate" by the use of aggregate demand policies will result in an *acceleration* of the rate of inflation or deflation.

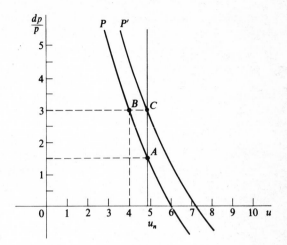

FIGURE 14-8
The accelerationist school,

Figure 14-8 provides a basis for exposition of the basic argument by this school. The curve P is a conventional Phillips curve for the initial period. We assume prices have been rising steadily over a considerable period at the 1.5 percent rate indicated on the graph at point A and that unemployment is around 4.8 percent, which we shall denote as u_n—the "natural rate" of unemployment. Suppose it is decided to reduce the unemployment rate to 4 percent, which on recent Phillips curves estimates (curve P) will cause an increase in the rate of inflation from 1.5 to 3 percent (a move to point B on the P curve). Since there is a history of prices rising at 1.5 percent, workers assume this will continue. Hence, when they are offered higher wages as employers respond to added demand by trying to hire workers, they view it as an increase in the *real* wage, and accept work. Now u falls toward 4 percent, and the increased demand causes the rate of inflation to increase to 3 percent as the Phillips curve tells us. We are, for the moment, at point B.

But now comes the essential element in the argument of the accelerationist school: employment increased because the workers hired responded to what they considered an increase in the *real* wage, based on their assumption that inflation would continue at its 1.5 percent historical rate. However, with prices now rising at a 3 percent rate, a 4 percent unemployment rate can be maintained only if wages rise faster, fast enough to continue to "trick" workers into continuing to work. That is, the Phillips curve shifts up to (say) P'. Without additional stimulus to demand and the rate of increase in wages, the rate of unemployment will slip back toward 4.8 percent, which, since prices are rising at a 3 percent rate, is now consistent with the new Phillips curve. If the government persists in trying to hold unemployment at 4 percent, the result will be short-run Phillips curves that shift upward continuously and prices and wages that rise at an *ever-increasing rate*. Note that, at point C, to return to the old inflation rate of 1.5 percent requires a substantial interim increase in employment. which will persist until the *actual* fall in the rate of inflation brings about reduced *expectations* of inflation. Inflation has to be brought down to a 1.5 percent rate and held there while this feeds into inflation expectations and shifts the short-run Phillips curve back down to *P*.

The accelerationist view is difficult to test empirically, largely because it is difficult to know how to construct an appropriate model of how *expectations* about wages and prices are formed. For example, Lucas and Rapping (1969) tested a model of the form

$$u_t = \beta_0 + \beta_1 \, d \log p_t + \beta_2 \, d \log p_{t-1} + \beta_3 \, d \log p_{t-2} + \text{(other terms)}$$

In this equation, a short-run Phillips curve exists when $\beta_1 < 0$. The accelerationist view that rates of inflation are *not* a function of the unemployment rate (the long-run Phillips curve is vertical) is supported if the *sum* $(\beta_1 + \beta_2 + \beta_3)$ is not significantly different from zero. In this case, a steady rate of inflation ($d \log p_t = d \log p_{t-1} = d \log p_{t-2}$) would be consistent with any value of u_t; the equation in this case collapses to $u_t = \beta_0 + \text{other terms}$. Lucas and Rapping found Phillips curves to exist for the subperiods tested (1904–1929, 1930–1945, 1946–1965), but their results for the long run were inconclusive. In addition to the conceptual problems of measuring expected rates of change, they note that one other problem may be that the "natural rate of unemployment" itself varies over time, thus making it difficult to find a *stable*, vertical long-run Phillips curve.

CONCLUSIONS

The introduction to the Phillips curve moves us into the realm of the dynamics of the economy. The wage-price-productivity nexus gives us, for any rate of unemployment and productivity increase, the rate of growth of prices and wages. Productivity growth and growth in the labor force determine the growth of real GNP, and this, together with the growth of prices, gives us the rate of growth of money GNP.

In the next two chapters, we use this entrée to survey formal models of economic growth.

READINGS FOR CHAPTER 14

BODKIN, RONALD G., ELIZABETH P. BOND, GRANT L. REUBER, and T. RUSSELL ROBINSON: *Price Stability and High Employment: The Options for Canadian Economic Policy: An Econometric Study*, Economic Council of Canada, Special Study No. 5. (Ottawa: Queen's Printer, 1967).

CORRY, BERNARD, and DAVID LAIDLER: "The Phillips Relation: A Theoretical Explanation," *Economica*, vol. 34, May 1967.

ECKSTEIN, O., and T. WILSON: "Determination of Money Wages in American Industry, "*Quarterly Journal of Economics*, pp. 370–414, August 1962.

FELLNER, W.: "Phillips-Type Approach or Acceleration?" *Brookings Papers on Economic Activity*, vol. 2, pp. 469–483, 1971.

———: "Employment Goals and Monetary-Fiscal Overexpansion," in Cagan et al. (eds.), *A New Look at Inflation* (Washington: The American Enterprise Institute, 1973), pp. 139–172.

FRIEDMAN, M.: "The Role of Monetary Policy," *American Economic Review*, pp. 1–17, March 1968.

GORDON, R. J.: "The Recent Acceleration of Inflation and Its Lessons for the Future," *Brookings Papers on Economics Activity*, vol. 1, 1970.

HYMANS, S. H.: "The Trade-off between Unemployment and Inflation: Theory and Measurement," in W. L. Smith and R. L. Teigen, *Money, National Income and Stabilization Policy*, 2d ed. (Homewood, Ill.: Irwin, 1970).

KUH, E.: "A Productivity Theory of Wage Levels:—An Alternative to the Phillips Curve," *Review of Economic Studies*, October 1967.

LIPSEY, R. G.: "The Relation between Unemployment and the Rate of Change of Money Wages in the United Kingdom, 1862–1957," *Economica*, vol. 28, pp. 1–31, 1960; reprinted in R. A. Gordon and L. R. Klein (eds.), *Readings in Business Cycles* (Homewood, Ill.: Irwin, 1965).

LUCAS, R. E., and L. A. RAPPING: "Price Expectations and the Phillips Curve," *American Economic Review*, vol. 56, 342–350, June 1969a.

———: "Real Wages, Employment, and Inflation," *Journal of Political Economy*, September–October 1969b.

OKUN, A.: "Potential GNP: Its Measurement and Significance," *American Statistics Association Proceedings*, 1962.

PERRY, GEORGE L.: "The Determinants of Wage Rate Changes and the Inflation-Unemployment Trade-off for the United States," *Review of Economic Studies*, August 1964.

———: *Unemployment, Money Wage Rates, and Inflation* (Cambridge, Mass.: The M.I.T., 1966), chaps. 1–3.

———: "Changing Labor Markets and Inflation," *Brookings Papers on Economic Activity*, vol. 3, pp. 411–441, 1970a.

———: "Inflation and Unemployment," in D. P. Jacobs (ed.), *Savings and Residential Construction: 1970 Conference Proceedings* (Chicago: U.S. Savings and Loan League, 1970b), pp. 30–45.

PHILLIPS, A. W.: "The Relation between Unemployment and the Rate of Change of Money Wage Rates in the United Kingdom, 1861–1957," *Economica*, N.S., Nov. 25, 1958.

PHELPS, E. S.: "Money-Wage Dynamics and Labor Market Equilibrium," *Journal of Political Economics*, pp. 687–711, August–September 1968.

RAPPING, L. A.: "The Trade-off between Employment and Prices," in Jacobs (ed.), op cit., pp. 11–29.

SCHULTZ, C. L.: "Has the Phillips Curve Shifted? Some Additional Evidence," *Brookings Papers on Economic Activity*, vol. 2, pp. 452–467, 1971.

SPENCER, R. W.: "The Relation between Prices and Employment: Two Views," *Bulletin of the Federal Reserve Bank of St. Louis*, March 1969.

15

EQUILIBRIUM GROWTH MODELS WITHOUT MONEY

In Part 2, the equilibrium conditions (the full-employment conditions) were analyzed in terms of aggregate demand and supply. The determination of output, prices, and employment was discussed assuming that the size of the labor force, the stock of capital, and the state of technology were fixed. These assumptions were reasonable and useful because the models we dealt with were mainly comparative-statics models, concerned with only a limited change within a short period of time. However, over a longer period of time, these assumptions must be relaxed, since the labor force, capital stock, and technology cumulatively increase. Figure 15-1 shows changes in productivity, the labor force, and capital stock in the United States during the period 1945–1965.

In this chapter, we will investigate the effect of growth in the labor force and productive capacity on output. We will also attempt to discuss the necessary conditions for full employment to be continuously maintained.

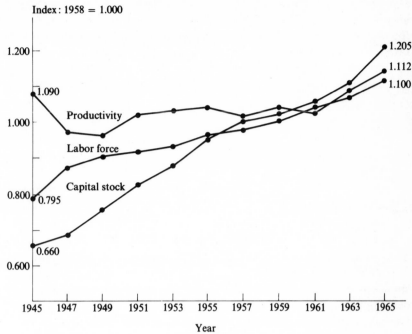

FIGURE 15-1

Change in productivity, capital stock, and labor force; 1945 to 1965. (*From Jorgenson and Griliches (1967), table VIII; Survey of Current Business, 1967; Brown (1968), p. 205;* figures after 1960 were estimated by the authors.)

CONCEPT OF ECONOMIC GROWTH, THE RATE OF GROWTH, AND THE EQUILIBRIUM RATE OF GROWTH

Before we present and analyze various growth models advanced in the literature we need to define the terms economic growth, the rate of economic growth, and the equilibrium growth rate. Economic growth is defined simply as the increase in national income or output over time; the rate of economic growth refers to the ratio of the increment in output to the total level of output in the previous period; and the equilibrium growth rate is that rate required to maintain full employment through-out a specific period of time.

Let Y = output in real terms
   N = labor force
   K = capital stock
   $Y = Y(K, N)$ = production function
   p = commodity price level
   w = money wage rate
   t = index of time

Economic growth during a period of time is then dY/dt, while the rate of economic growth rate is $\dot{Y} \equiv dY/dt/Y$. Note that from now on we use a variable with a dot on top of it as a percentage change per unit period of time. Since the equilibrium growth rate $\dot{Y}_e$ is the rate which is associated with full employment equilibrium in the economy, $\dot{Y}_e$ then requires that the change in the capital stock $dK/dt = I_t$ be equal to savings and that the demand for labor be equal to the supply of labor simultaneously:

$$\dot{Y}_e = \frac{dY}{dt} \bigg/ Y$$

$$\frac{dK}{dt} = S_t = I_t \qquad (15\text{-}1)$$

$$N_d = N_0 \, e^{nt}$$

where S_t denotes aggregate savings in period t, N_d is the demand for labor, and $N_0 \, e^{nt}$ is the supply of labor growing at the rate n.

The conditions for equilibrium growth can be shown in terms of the aggregate demand and supply curves. Since Eq. (15-1) represents a series of continuous equilibria over time, the locus of equilibria must constitute a long-run equilibrium path, TT as shown in Figure 15-2. The equation for the equilibrium path can be expressed by defining aggregate supply in terms of the labor force and the average productivity of labor (Chapter 14):

$$Y = \frac{Y}{N} N$$

or in terms of logarithms

$$\log Y = \log \frac{Y}{N} + \log N \qquad (15\text{-}2)$$

Differentiating (15-2) with respect to time, we have

$$\dot{Y} = \left(\frac{\dot{Y}}{N}\right) + \dot{N} \qquad (15\text{-}3)$$

that is, the rate of economic growth $\dot{Y}$ is composed of two parts: the growth rate of labor productivity Y/N and the growth rate of the labor force $\dot{N}$. If we assume that relative shares of capital and labor are constant over time, then we know from Chapter 14 that the rate of change in the price level is equal to the rate of change in the money wage rate less the rate of growth of labor productivity,[1]

$$\dot{p} = \dot{w} - \left(\frac{\dot{Y}}{N}\right) \qquad (15\text{-}4a)$$

From (15-3) we obtain $(\dot{Y}/N)$ and substitute it into (15-4a), and get

$$\dot{p} = \dot{w} - \dot{Y} + \dot{N} \qquad (15\text{-}4b)$$

---

[1] The money wage rate is assumed to be equal to the value of the average product of labor: $w = p(Y/N)$, or $\log p + \log (Y/N) = \log w$.

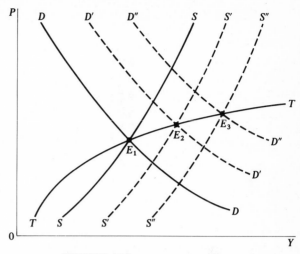

FIGURE 15-2
Shifts in aggregate demand and supply over time.

Equation (15-4b) together with the full-employment condition given in (15-1) characterizes the equation for the growth path depicted by the TT curve in Figure 15-2.

However, specifying the equilibrium growth path TT, in terms of the aggregate demand and supply curves, is not sufficient. A number of other variables must be incorporated into the equilibrium equation that are not included in (15-4b), such as the effect of changes in the stock of capital on Y/N and the effect of changes in the capital-labor ratio, the savings rate, the rate of monetary expansion, the money-output ratio, and the progress of technology embodied in each production factor. The ideal specification of the equilibrium growth path should be one that incorporates all or most of these variables simultaneously. Unfortunately, such a model does not exist at present. Rather, we have a number of different models, each concentrating on only a subclass of these additional variables. These models vary in that some utilize one set of variables which are not used in other models. Which model should be chosen to explain real world experience cannot be answered without more thorough and careful study of the various models.

In the following sections we analyze several prominent growth models. For convenience, these are summarized in Figure 15-3.[2] No attempt will be made here to review all models shown. The main focus of this chapter will be the models designated by an asterisk (*) in Figure 15-3, those models which have no monetary sector. Chapter 16 deals with certain growth models with monetary sectors; these are designated by a double asterisk (**) in Figure 15-3.

---

[2] The multisector model can be "branched out" further according to the type of technical progress. This work is left to the reader.

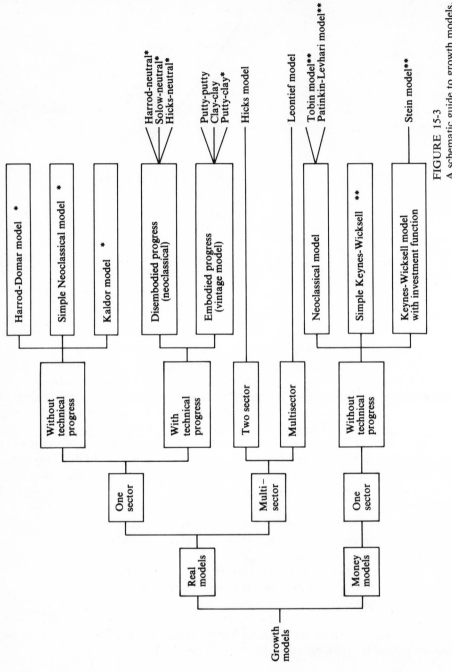

FIGURE 15-3
A schematic guide to growth models.

GROWTH MODELS

The Harrod-Domar Model

The Harrod-Domar model (Harrod, 1939, and Domar, 1947) was one of the earliest models to attempt to take into account the effect of investment on productive capacity and the requirement that labor and capital be fully employed as the economy grows. This model assumes that the labor force grows at a constant rate over time, that there is no technological change, and that the capital-output ratio also remains constant. It then derives the steady growth rate consistent, under this assumption, with the equilibrium growth path. Since the model is concerned mainly with the equilibrium growth path, Eqs. (15-3) and (15-4a) provide the necessary framework for the analysis —$\dot{Y} = (Y/N) + \dot{N}$ and $\dot{p} = \dot{w} - (Y/N)$. In addition, the Harrod-Domar model adds the flow equilibrium condition, that, in the absence of lags, planned investment I is equal to planned savings S.[3]

Consider year t. Let K, the full-capacity use of the capital stock, be defined as a multiple of output,

$$K = vY \qquad (15\text{-}5)$$

where v is a fixed coefficient denoting the capital-output ratio. The flow equilibrium between planned investment and savings can be written as

$$\frac{dK}{dt} = sY \qquad (15\text{-}6)$$

where s represents the average and marginal propensity to save. The labor force is assumed to grow at the constant proportional rate n.

$$N = N_0 e^{nt}$$

N_0 being an initial labor force. Using u as the labor-output ratio, uY represents the demand for labor. Labor market equilibrium can thus be written as

$$N_0 e^{nt} = uY \qquad (15\text{-}7)$$

From (15-5) and (15-6), we have a differential equation

$$\frac{dK}{dt} = v\frac{dY}{dt} = sY$$

or

$$\frac{1}{Y}\frac{dY}{dt} = \dot{Y} = \frac{s}{v} \qquad (15\text{-}8)$$

---

[3] The original basic Harrod-Domar model does not take an investment function into consideration. It is just based on a constant output-capital ratio $1/v$ and a fixed capital-labor ratio. In order to maintain full-employment equilibrium, the growth rate of output $\dot{Y}$ should match the growth rate of the labor force n; that is, $\dot{Y} = n$. Since $DY = DK/v = sY/v$, $\dot{Y} = DY/Y = s/v$. Therefore, the condition for equilibrium is $\dot{Y} = n = s/v$.

While Eq. (15-3) states the condition for the full-employment growth with regard to the labor force, Eq. (15-8) gives the equilibrium growth rate consistent with the full-capacity utilization of capital. For the labor force also to be fully employed, its growth rate n must be the same as the output growth rate,

$$n = \dot{Y} = \frac{s}{v} \qquad (15\text{-}9)$$

In other words, the natural rate of growth n must be equal to the warranted rate s/v for full employment in the labor market. If condition (15-9) is satisfied, the equilibrium growth paths in the product and factor markets are

$$Y = Y_0 \, e^{gt}$$
$$K = K_0 \, e^{gt} \qquad (15\text{-}10)$$
$$N = N_0 \, e^{gt}$$

where $g = s/v = n$. If we interpret the full-capacity condition in such a way that the increment in capital I is fully utilized at a constant capital-output ratio, I would replace K in condition (15-10):

$$Y = Y_0 \, e^{gt}$$
$$I = I_0 \, e^{gt} \qquad (15\text{-}11)$$
$$N = N_0 \, e^{gt}$$

where I is the addition to the capital stock. In equilibrium it is equal to savings (S),

$$I = sY \qquad (15\text{-}12)$$

The equilibrium growth path in the product and factor markets represented by Eq. (15-11) and the equilibrium condition for investment and saving equation (15-12) are depicted in Figure 15-4. They are related to the equilibrium path of $\dot{Y}$ and $\dot{p}$ given by (15-3) and (15-4), as shown in panel (e), Figure 15-4. Since the warranted rate of growth is equal to the natural rate of growth n, the aggregate supply curve shifts out to $S'S'$ [by an amount determined by the slope of uY in panel (d)] as shown in panel (c). The marginal propensity to consume ($1 - s$) implicitly guarantees that the aggregate demand curve will shift upward to $D'D'$ so that the equilibrium level of the price level and output always lies on the equilibrium growth path TT. In addition to the lagless assumption and the fixed production coefficient, the Harrod-Domar model rules out the possibility of technical change by assuming that the output-labor ratio is also constant,

$$\frac{Y}{N} = u = \text{constant}$$

or

$$\left(\frac{\dot{Y}}{N}\right) = 0$$

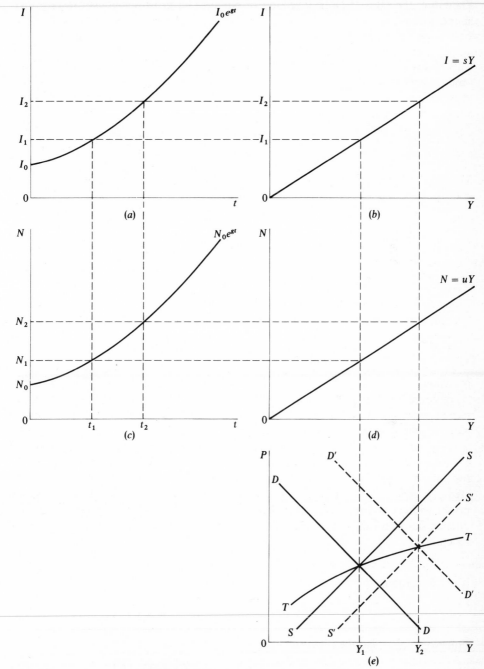

FIGURE 15-4a–e
Effect of growth in labor force and investment on equilibrium growth.

Therefore, the Harrod-Domar version of equilibrium growth models can be stated simply as

$$\dot{Y} = \dot{N} = \dot{K} \qquad (15\text{-}13)$$

This model is often criticized as being too inflexible. Nevertheless, it has often been used to determine an approximate value for the required propensity to save necessary to achieve the warranted rate of growth. For example, suppose the following values are ascribed to a given economy:

$$v = 3.5 \qquad \text{capital-output ratio}$$
$$n = 0.015 \qquad \text{rate of natural growth}$$

Then the required propensity to save for the equilibrium growth is obtained by substituting these values into Eq. (15-9),

$$n = s/v$$
$$nv = s$$
$$0.015(3.5) = s$$
$$0.052 = s$$

To achieve the equilibrium growth rate (the natural rate) of 1.5 percent in every period, the required savings rate out of income must be equal to 5.2 percent per period.

The Neoclassical Growth Model

Neoclassical growth theory, in general, is based upon three fundamental assumptions: (1) there are no fixed, nonaugmentable factors of production; (2) there exists a unique rate of growth of the labor force which is exogenously given; and (3) planned investment is always equal to planned savings (the savings ratio s being constant). An additional assumption is usually made (especially when a simple mathematical model is used), namely, that the production function is homogeneous of degree one in the two inputs K (capital) and N (labor). (The introduction of technical change is generated in a later section). For the moment, we shall confine ourselves to a real sector model without technical change. Given the assumption of homogeneity, the production function can be written in terms of the capital-labor ratio. If the production function is

$$Y_t = F(K_t, N_t)$$

it can be written

$$\frac{Y}{N} = y = y\left(\frac{K}{N}, 1\right) \qquad (15\text{-}14)$$

Equation (15-14) can be rewritten as

$$y = f\left(\frac{K}{N}\right) = f(k) \qquad (15\text{-}15)$$

The function $f(k)$ is the total product curve as varying amounts k of capital are used per unit of labor. Alternatively, it gives output per worker as a function of capital per worker. From the investment-saving relationship, we have

$$\frac{dK}{dt} = sY = I \qquad (15\text{-}16)$$

and assuming as before that the labor force grows at the rate n, we have

$$N_t = N_0 e^{nt} \qquad (15\text{-}17)$$

Equations (15-15) to (15-17) yield the solution for the equilibrium growth with respect to the factor ratio K/N. If there exists an equilibrium factor ratio (i.e., k^*), the economy will grow along a path which is consistent with k^*, provided that the equilibrium growth rate is always maintained.

Let $\dot{k}$ denote the proportional growth rate of the capital-labor ratio such that

$$\dot{k} = \frac{1}{k}\frac{dk}{dt} = \frac{d}{dt} \log k = \frac{d}{dt} (\log K - \log N) \qquad (15\text{-}18)$$

Writing Eq. (15-17) in log form we get

$$\log N_t = \log N_0 + nt$$

Differentiating this with respect to time, we get

$$\frac{d}{dt} \log N_t = n \qquad (15\text{-}19)$$

Substituting (15-19) into (15-18), we obtain

$$\dot{k} = \dot{K} - n \qquad (15\text{-}20)$$

$\dot{K}$ can be derived from (15-16) as

$$\dot{K} = \frac{1}{K}\frac{dK}{dt} = \frac{1}{K} sY = s\frac{Y/N}{K/N} = \frac{s}{k} f(k)$$

Substituting this value for $\dot{K}$ into (15-20), we get

$$\dot{k} = \frac{s}{k} f(k) - n \qquad (15\text{-}21)$$

Equation (15-21) is a differential equation involving the capital-labor ratio only. It states that the rate of change of the capital-labor ratio $\dot{k}$ is the difference of two terms, one representing the increment in capital and the other the increment of labor. Given an initial value $k = k_0$, the solution of this equation will result in the steady equilibrium path of the capital-labor ratio k^* over time, i.e., that k which makes $\dot{k}$ equal to zero ($K/N = $ constant). Thus, Eq. (15-21) becomes

$$0 = \frac{s}{k} f(k) - n$$

or

$$\frac{s}{k^*} f(k^*) = n \qquad (15\text{-}22)$$

Equilibrium output per worker, y^*, is given by

$$y^* = f(k^*) = \frac{n}{s} k^* \qquad (15\text{-}23)$$

This relationship is depicted graphically in panel (a) of Figure 15-5. As shown there, the system tends to converge to the equilibrium point A if the values of y and k are different from y^* and k^*, respectively. If $k \neq k^*$, then $\dot{k} \neq 0$. From Eq. (15-21) if $\dot{k} > 0$, the curve $f(k)$ is above the line $(n/s)k$ as at E in panel (a). Also from (15-21), $\dot{k} > 0$, and thus k is increasing toward k^*. Conversely, if $\dot{k} < 0$, k will decrease toward k^*. Thus the equilibrium value k^* is stable. Whatever the initial value of k, the system will move toward the equilibrium path indicated by point A.

To show the relationship between consumption and investment within the context of the neoclassical model, we refer to Eqs. (15-16) and (15-23). From (15-16), per capita investment can be written as

$$\frac{I}{N} = s \frac{Y}{N} = sy = sf(k) \quad (15\text{-}16a)$$

and from Eq. (15-23) we have the equilibrium condition

$$sf(k^*) = nk^* \qquad (15\text{-}24)$$

Therefore, in equilibrium, per capita investment is obtained at point C in panel (b), at the intersection between the straight line nk and the production function line $sf(k)$. The solution for k at C given by (15-16a) must be the same as the solution given by (15-23) as shown in panel (b) in Figure 15-5. The line nk must be "flatter" than $(n/s)k$ because s—the propensity to save—is usually less than unity. In the diagram, we have

$$Oy^* = k^*C + CB$$

where k^*C represents the level of per capita investment I/N and CB represents the level of per capita consumption C/N (i.e., per capita output minus per capita investment assuming a closed and private economy).

Varying the Savings Rate: Phelps' Golden Rule of Accumulation

The assumption of a constant savings ratio is dropped from the neoclassical model (while keeping all others), and instead we allow the saving ratio to vary.[4] At what level of k is consumption then maximized?

Let us look again at panel (b) in Figure 15-5. The value of consumption per capita C/N can be written as

$$\frac{C}{N} = y^* - \frac{I}{N}$$

$$= f(k^*) - sf(k^*) \qquad (15\text{-}25)$$

---

[4] It is still assumed that the growth rate of the labor force is the same and that the production function is homogeneous of degree one.

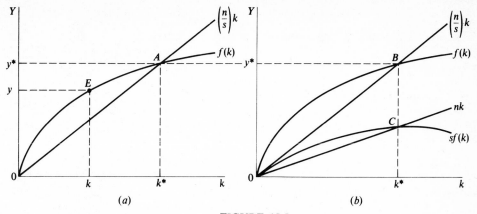

FIGURE 15-5
Equilibrium capital-labor ratio and per capita saving.

Since in the steady equilibrium $sf(k)$ is equal to nk, this gives

$$\frac{C}{N} = f(k) - nk \qquad (15\text{-}26)$$

To analyze the impact of a change in s on investment as well as on consumption, we introduce several different values for the savings ratio into Eq. (15-25). When $s = s_0$, the equilibrium value of consumption is obtained by

$$\left(\frac{C}{N}\right)_0 = f(k_0^*) - s_0 f(k_0^*) \qquad (15\text{-}27)$$

and the equilibrium value for k is obtained from

$$f(k_0^*) = \frac{n}{s_0} k_0^*$$

If the savings ratio increases from s_0 to s_1, as in Figure 15-6, the line $(n/s_0)k$ will rotate down to $(n/s_1)k$. At any given level of k, since s has risen, it would take less output to generate the investment needed to maintain that k. Since the slope of $(n/s_1)k$ is smaller than $(n/s_0)k$, the solution for k as s_1 increases will be larger.

The two savings functions $s_0 f(k)$ and $s_1 f(k)$ are drawn in Figure 15-6. Since $s_0 < s_1$, the savings function associated with s_0 lies below the one associated with s_1. Since the natural rate of growth (n) is still unchanged, the required growth of capital per capita (nk) can be used in both cases. In other words, both $s_0 f(k)$ and $s_1 f(k)$ intercept the line nk at their own solution level of k, as shown by points F and F', respectively.

At which value of k is equilibrium per capita consumption maximized? As we indicated earlier, consumption per capita was defined, given k, as the difference between output per capita and required per capita investment which moves the

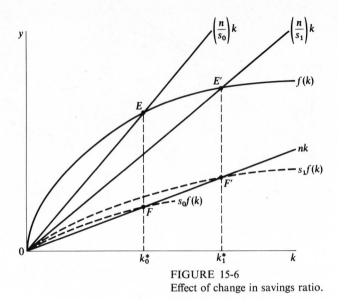

FIGURE 15-6
Effect of change in savings ratio.

economy along the equilibrium path. The greatest difference between these two—maximum consumption per capita—can be obtained at the point on the production function $f(k)$ where the slope of $f(k)$ is equal to the slope of the required investment curve. Since $f(k)$ is a diminishing function while nk is a straight line, the slope of $f(k)$ at that point (i.e., the marginal product) should be equal to n, the slope of nk. This is shown in Figure 15-7 at E^*. The curve C/N is obtained by the locus of points representing the vertical difference between $f(k)$ and nk, and its maximum value occurs at z.

Mathematically, let L be the difference between output and the required investment

$$L = f(k) - nk \qquad (15\text{-}28)$$

To maximize L with respect to k, we partially differentiate (15-28) with respect to k and set the result equal to zero:

$$\frac{\partial L}{\partial k} = f'(k) - n = 0$$

$$f'(k) = n \qquad (15\text{-}29)$$

The first term in (15-29), $f'(k)$, represents the slope of $f(k)$, and n indicates the slope of nk.

Thus, as noted above, point E^* on the production function in Figure 15-7 is in fact the solution guaranteeing the maximum consumption per capita under given

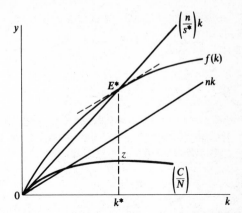

FIGURE 15-7
Equilibrium growth with consumption maximized.

$f(k)$ and n. Let s^* define a certain savings rate which is associated with the output-capital ray passing through point E^*. For consumption to be maximized the required savings rate must be equal to s^*, given values of k and n. This is *Phelps' golden rule of accumulation*. The golden rule path describes the long-run equilibrium growth path that maximizes consumption per capita for all periods, once the economy has reached the correct level of k. This is the k^* point where the slope of the production function is equal to the slope of the line nk. To attain this k, the savings rate may be used as a control variable.

Savings as a Function of Profits: Kaldor's Model

Kaldor decomposes savings S into two components: savings by "capitalists" (S_p) and savings by "workers" (S_w). The total savings ratio s is now a function of the distribution of income between "capitalists" and "workers." Defining national income or output as the summation of gross quasi-rent or profits P and aggregate wages W, total savings can be written as

$$S = s_p P + s_w W \qquad (15\text{-}30)$$

where s_p is the marginal (and average) propensity to save of capitalists and s_w is that of workers, and where $s_p > s_w$ so that S/Y depends on the distribution of income $(0 \le s_w \le s_p \le 1)$. The aggregate savings rate s is then

$$s \equiv \frac{S}{Y} = s_p \frac{P}{Y} + s_w \frac{Y - P}{Y} = s_w + (s_p - s_w) \frac{P}{Y} \qquad (15\text{-}31)$$

Multiplying the second term of Eq. (15-31) by K/K, this equation can be written as

$$s = s_w + (s_p - s_w) \frac{P}{K} \frac{K}{Y} \qquad (15\text{-}32)$$

Substituting (15-32) into (15-21), we get

$$k = \left[s_w + (s_p - s_w) \frac{P}{K} \frac{K}{Y} \right] \frac{y}{k} - n$$

or
$$k = s_w \frac{y}{k} + (s_p - s_w) \frac{P}{K} - n \qquad (15\text{-}33)$$

Equation (15-33) is a differential equation involving both the output-capital ratio and the profit-capital ratio. The solution of this equation gives the equilibrium growth path which makes $k = 0$. Therefore,

$$s_w \frac{y}{k} + (s_p - s_w) \frac{P}{K} = n \qquad (15\text{-}34)$$

Since P/K represents the profit-capital ratio and y/k the output-capital ratio in Eq. (15-34), $P/K < y/k$; the profit-capital ratio cannot exceed the output-capital ratio. In other words,

$$0 \le \frac{P}{K} \le \frac{y}{k} = \frac{1}{v} \qquad (15\text{-}35)$$

where v is the capital-output ratio. Substituting the term $1/v$ into Eq. (15-34) we get

$$\frac{s_w}{v} + (s_p - s_w) \frac{P}{K} = n \qquad (15\text{-}36)$$

As the value of the profit-capital ratio P/K varies from 0 to $1/v$, the left-hand side of (15-36) varies correspondingly from s_w/v to s_p/v. Therefore, the range of variation of the rate of growth is

$$\frac{s_w}{v} \le n \le \frac{s_p}{v} \qquad (15\text{-}37)$$

In the special case where $s_w = 0$, $n = s_p(P/K)$,[5] the required rate of growth of capital only depends on the profit-capital ratio. The Kaldor model thus represents an improvement over the Harrod-Domar model in the sense that the equilibrium growth rate could vary freely between the limits s_w/v and s_p/v, while the Harrod-Domar model restricts that equilibrium to the single value s/v.

The Kaldor model is often called a basic Keynesian model. The reason is that the model takes explicitly into account the distribution of income between labor and capital and the fact that the determination of the income distribution is mainly influenced by the investment decisions made by firms. This Keynesian idea can be depicted by a linear relationship between the investment-income ratio (I/Y) and the profit share (P/Y). From Eq. (15-31), the aggregate savings ratio is

$$s \equiv \frac{S}{Y} = s_p \frac{P}{Y} + s_w \frac{W}{Y} \qquad (15\text{-}38)$$

[5] In this case the overall propensity to save, s, is equal to s_p. This is the classical savings function.

where W represents wage income. Since saving must equal investment ex post, and since an equilibrium growth requires ex ante equality as well, (15-38) can be written as

$$s = \frac{I}{Y} = (s_p - s_w)\frac{P}{Y} + s_w$$

$$\frac{P}{Y} = -\frac{s_w}{s_p - s_w} + \frac{1}{s_p - s_w}\frac{I}{Y}$$

(15-39)

or

Equation (15-39) shows the profit share as depending on the investment-income ratio only, given the constant saving propensities. This relationship is shown in Figure 15-8.[6]

Kaldor's model has implications similar to those of the Harrod-Domar model in that equilibrium growth is obtained when the warranted growth rate is equal to the natural rate, the equilibrating force being the change in factor shares. This can be illustrated within the context of the Harrod-Domar model. Let g^w denote the warranted growth rate, where

$$g^w = \frac{s}{v}$$

Using the savings rate shown in (15-39), we can rewrite g^w as

$$g^w = \frac{(s_p - s_w)(P/Y) + s_w}{v} \qquad (15\text{-}39a)$$

If v, the capital-output ratio, is assumed constant as in the Harrod-Domar case, g^w would then depend only upon P/Y, since the savings ratios are also assumed to be constant. Suppose, for some reason or another, that the natural rate of growth g^n exceeds the warranted rate g^w at a full-employment situation. In this case, investment is encouraged and, according to (15-39), the profit share P/Y will be increased. As P/Y rises, with s_w, s_p, and v constant, g^w must rise according to Eq. (15-39a). This process will continue until g^w reaches g^n. In the reverse case, i.e., when $g^w > g^n$, g^w will decrease until it equals g^n. Once equilibrium between g^w and g^n is attained, there is no further incentive to increase or reduce investment, and thus factor shares will remain unchanged.

Kaldor's model is thus based on two fundamental hypotheses: first, as in the Harrod-Domar model, the economy is always at a full-employment state associated with a corresponding amount of income or output, and second, the rate of growth can be adjusted by changing relative factor shares by changes in the distribution of income.

---

[6] Joan Robinson's relationship between the profit share and the investment-income ratio is also based on the same ground, but she takes rather the very special case in which workers consume their entire income. In her case, $s_w = 0$ and $s_p = 1$. That is, the function is the 45° line passing through the origin. See Robinson (1956, pp. 73–84).

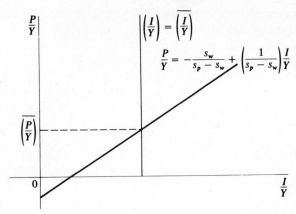

FIGURE 15-8
Relation between profit share and investment-income ratio.

Growth and Technical Progress: Disembodied Technical Progress

In a previous section, we discussed the neoclassical growth model where no technical change was allowed. In such a model the steady growth solution can be generated only by a certain rate of capital accumulation, a rate equal to the rate of growth of the labor force. However, this assumption is too restrictive. Technical progress does occur and in fact has been one of the major sources of economic growth. Technical progress, i.e., increase in productivity efficiency, takes two forms: disembodied and embodied. Increases in efficiency which are reflected in the increased productivity of all existing capital regardless of its age are called disembodied. Embodied technical progress implies technical improvement only in certain kinds of capital (new capital) and in the associated labor force.

Let us start with disembodied technical progress. Although we define this type of progress as an overall equal improvement of technology, it is necessary to investigate how it enters the production function and how it affects the variables derived from the production function. Its effect is different as we define "neutrality" of technical progress differently. Three different types of neutral technical change are prominent in the literature: Harrod-neutral, Solow-neutral, and Hicks-neutral. Technical change is Harrod-neutral if it augments labor, and the marginal product of capital (or the rate of return to capital) stays the same over time at a constant output-capital ratio. Technical change is Solow-neutral if it augments capital, and the wage rate is invariant over time at a constant output-worker ratio. And technical change is Hicks-neutral if the ratio of marginal products remains unaltered at a constant capital-labor ratio. These are elaborated in the following sections.

Harrod-neutral Harrod defines a technical change to be neutral, if, at a constant capital-output ratio, it does not disturb the value of the capital coefficient. The introduction of a Harrod-neutral technical change into the neoclassical growth model will have several effects. The production function in each time period t is now written

$$Y = F(K, N; t) \qquad (15\text{-}40)$$

As before, the function is assumed to be homogeneous of degree one, and we may write per worker output ($Y/N = y$) as

$$y = f(k; t)$$

Assume also that the production function is continuously differentiable with respect to K, N, and t and that the marginal rates of substitution are diminishing:

$$f_k > 0 \qquad (15\text{-}41)$$

and
$$f_{kk} < 0 \qquad (15\text{-}42)$$

where $f_k = \partial f / \partial k$ and $f_{kk} = \partial^2 f / \partial k^2$.

For a given rate of interest r, the optimum capital-labor ratio in year t call it $k^*(r, t)$—is the one at which the marginal product of capital is equal to the rate of interest (r):

$$f_k[k^*(r, t), t] = r \qquad (15\text{-}43)$$

The corresponding optimum output per worker $y^*(r, t)$ and capital-output ratio $v^*(r, t)$ are determined by

$$y^*(r, t) = f[k^*(r, t), t] \qquad (15\text{-}44)$$

$$v^*(r, t) = \frac{k^*(r, t)}{y^*(r, t)} \qquad (15\text{-}45)$$

Technical progress will then be termed Harrod-neutral if at a constant interest rate the optimum capital-output ratio given by (15-45) is independent of t,

$$v = v^*(\bar{r}) \qquad (15\text{-}46)$$

where $\bar{r}$ represents the constant rate of interest. This is shown graphically in Figure 15-9. The initial position, where $y(\bar{r}, t_1) = f[k(\bar{r}, t_1), t_1]$ is denoted by a. For the technical progress to be Harrod-neutral, the production function must shift in such a way that the slope at the intersection between the new production function and the capital-output ratio $v^*(\bar{r})$ is the same as that at point a.

It is useful at this point to introduce Robinson's theorem in connection with Harrod-neutral technical progress. The theorem reads:

Technical progress represented by $Y(K, N; t)$ is Harrod-neutral if and only if the production function $Y(K, N; t)$ is of the form $Y(K, N; t) = G[K, A(t)N_0]$ with a positive function $A(t)$.[7]

To illustrate this theorem, we may use a production function such that

$$Y = F[K, e^{(n + \lambda)t}N_0] \qquad (15\text{-}47)$$

---

[7] For formal proof, see Uzawa (1961, pp. 149–151).

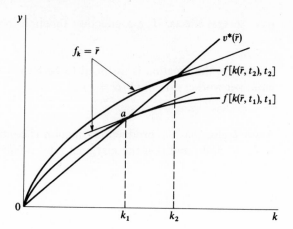

FIGURE 15-9
Harrod-neutral technical change.

which is homogeneous of degree one and where

$$A(t) = e^{(n+\lambda)t}$$
$$A(t) = 1 \quad \text{at } t = 0$$
$$A(t) > 1 \quad A'(t) > 0 \quad \text{for } t > 0 \quad (15\text{-}48)$$

Equation (15-48) implies that the labor force grows not only due to the natural growth rate but also due to the neutral technical progress denoted by λ.

Again we define $k = K/N$ and $y = Y/N$. The growth rate of capital per worker thus is

$$\dot{k} = \frac{d}{dt} \log k = \frac{d}{dt} (\log K - \log N) \quad (15\text{-}49)$$

and referring to (15-47) and (15-48), we have

$$\log N = \log N_0 + (n + \lambda)t$$

Differentiating this with respect to time, we get

$$\frac{d}{dt} \log N = n + \lambda$$

Therefore, $\dot{k}$ in (15-49) can be rewritten by

$$\dot{k} = \dot{K} - (n + \lambda) \quad (15\text{-}50)$$

Since

$$\dot{K} = \frac{1}{K} \frac{dK}{dt} = \frac{1}{K} sY = s \frac{Y/N}{K/N} = \frac{s}{k} f(k)$$

k in (15-50) is now rewritten as

$$k = \frac{s}{k} f(k) - (n + \lambda) \qquad (15\text{-}51)$$

The equilibrium value of k, k^*, is again obtained by setting k in (15-51) equal to zero as we did before, so that at k^*

$$\frac{sf(k^*)}{k^*} = n + \lambda \qquad (15\text{-}52)$$

The interpretation and analyses of Eq. (15-52) are the same as in the case where no technological progress exists, except that the equilibrium value of k is now equal to the rate of growth of labor plus the rate of technical progress. Rewriting the equilibrium condition given by (15-52) as

$$f(k^*) = \frac{n + \lambda}{s} k^*$$

the equilibrium k^* can be located as shown in Figure 15-10. As compared to the previous case, with no technical progress (Figure 15-5), the ray from the origin now has a slope $(n + \lambda)/s$ instead of n/s. The point of intersection of $f(k)$ and $(n + \lambda)k/s$ in Figure 15-10 gives us the equilibrium values for k and $\dot{y}$.

The effect of technical progress on per capita consumption is given by

$$\frac{C}{N_r} = \frac{C}{Ne^{-\lambda t}} = \frac{1}{e^{-\lambda t}} \left(\frac{Y - sY}{N} \right) = e^{\lambda t}[f(k) - sf(k)] \qquad (15\text{-}53)$$

where the actual number of workers N_r is discounted by the rate of technical progress λ. Using (15-53) we can find the solution for the optimum k^* which guarantees both equilibrium and the maximum consumption. Since in equilibrium

$$sf(k^*) = (n + \lambda)k^*$$

substituting this condition into (15-53), we get

$$\left(\frac{C}{N} \right)^* = e^{\lambda t}[f(k^*) - (n + \lambda)k^*] \qquad (15\text{-}54)$$

Equation (15-54) is the long-run condition for equilibrium consumption. Given n and λ, per capita consumption can be maximized and maintain its maximum level if

$$\frac{\partial (C/N_r)^*}{\partial k^*} = e^{\lambda t}[f'(k^*) - (n + \lambda)] = 0 \qquad (15\text{-}55)$$

that is,

$$f'(k^*) = n + \lambda \qquad (15\text{-}56)$$

This implies that the growth path that yields the highest level of per capita consumption is the one where the profit rate $f'(k^*)$ is equal to the growth rate $n + \lambda$. This is shown in Figure 15-10.

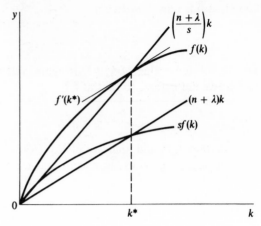

FIGURE 15-10
Equilibrium with technical change in
the neoclassical model.

Comparing Figure 15-10 with Figure 15-7, we now find that with the Harrod-neutral technical change the optimum capital-output ratio is given by $(n + \lambda)\ k/s$, where it is nk/s in the neoclassical model with no technical progress.

Solow-neutral   Technical progress is Solow-neutral if it augments capital, and the wage rate w is invariant over time at a constant output-worker ratio y. Thus,

$$\bar{w} = \phi(\bar{y}) \qquad (15\text{-}57)$$

where

$$\phi(y) = y - ky_k \qquad (15\text{-}58)$$

Integrating (15-57), we get

$$y(k;\, t) = y[B(t)k;\, t]$$

or

$$Y(K, N;\, t) = Y[B(t)K, N;\, t] \qquad (15\text{-}59)$$

where $B(t)$ is a capital-augmenting factor. Equation (15-59) has the same shape of the isoquant map as $Y(K, N)$ except the output number attached to each isoquant is multiplied by $B(t)$.

The Cobb-Douglas production function explains Solow-neutral in a simpler way. Take $B(t) = e^{\lambda t}$, and then the basic differential equation becomes

$$k = \dot{K} - n$$

$$= \frac{dK/dt}{K} - n$$

$$= \frac{sy}{k} - n$$

$$= \frac{se^{\lambda t}k^{\alpha}}{k} - n \qquad (15\text{-}60)$$

Multiplying both sides of (15-60) by k and rearranging, we get

$$\frac{dk}{dt} + nk = se^{\lambda t}k^{\alpha} \qquad (15\text{-}61)$$

This is a nonlinear differential equation with Bernoulli's form. Using a shorthand variable Z, $Z = k^{1-\alpha}$, instead of (15-61) we get

$$\frac{dZ}{dt} + n(1-\alpha)Z = (1-\alpha)se^{\lambda t} \qquad (15\text{-}62)$$

The solution for $Z(t)$ can be obtained by solving (15-62) directly:

$$Z(t) = e^{-\int n(1-\alpha)\,dt}[C + \int (1-\alpha)se^{\lambda t}e^{\int n(1-\alpha)\,dt}\,dt]$$

$$= Ce^{-n(1-\alpha)t} + \frac{s(1-\alpha)}{\lambda + n(1-\alpha)}\,e^{\lambda t} \qquad (15\text{-}63)$$

where the constant C is
$$C = k_0^{1-\alpha} - \frac{s(1-\alpha)}{\lambda + n(1-\alpha)} \qquad (15\text{-}64)$$

From (15-63) and (15-64), we can find the equilibrium time path of k. Converting k to K, we get

$$K(t) = \left(K_0^{1-\alpha} - \frac{s\beta}{\lambda + n\beta}\,N_0^{\beta} + \frac{s\beta}{\lambda + n\beta}\,N_0^{\beta}e^{(\lambda + n\beta)t}\right)^{1/\beta} \qquad (15\text{-}65)$$

where $\beta = 1 - \alpha$ and K_0 is the initial capital stock. As t becomes large, $K(t)$ grows eventually as much as

$$\left(\frac{s}{n + \lambda/\beta}\right)^{1/\beta} N_0\, e^{[n + (\lambda/\beta)]t} \qquad (15\text{-}66)$$

that is, it increases at the relative rate $n + \lambda/\beta$, compared with n in the case of no technical change. The eventual rate of increase of real output is $n + \alpha\lambda/\beta$, and specially, it is even faster than $n + \lambda$. The reason is that higher real output means more savings and investment, which accelerate the growth rate still more.

Note that, unlike Harrod-neutral, no steady-state capital-labor ratio exists in this case. The ever-increasing investment capacity is never matched by any growth rate of labor force. The eventual growth rate of k is

$$\dot{k} = \dot{K} - \dot{N} = n + \lambda/\beta - n = \lambda/\beta \qquad (15\text{-}67)$$

and the output-capital ratio must diminish at rate

$$\dot{Y} - \dot{K} = n + \alpha\lambda/\beta - n - \lambda/\beta = -\lambda$$

For example, suppose the following values are given to an economy:

$$\lambda = 0.02$$
$$n = 0.015$$
$$\alpha = \tfrac{1}{3}$$
$$\beta = \tfrac{2}{3}$$

so that the Solow-neutral production function is

$$Y = e^{(0.02)t}K^{1/3}(N_0 e^{(0.015)t})^{2/3}$$
$$= e^{(0.03)t}K^{1/3}N_0^{2/3}$$

and the eventual growth rate of k is

$$k = \frac{\lambda}{\beta} = 0.020/\tfrac{2}{3} = 0.03$$

The output-capital ratio will be eventually diminishing at 2%.

Hicks-neutral Technical progress can be said to be Hicks-neutral if, and only if, the output elasticity of capital, and hence the output elasticity of labor, remains constant (Ferguson, 1969, p. 219). This definition of neutrality differs from that given by both Harrod and Solow. Instead of comparing labor-augmenting to capital-augmenting change, Hicks uses the marginal rate of technical substitution as a yardstick to determine whether the change in technology is capital-using, neutral, or labor-using. If the marginal rate of technical substitution of capital for labor decreases, technology is said to be capital-using; it is neutral if it remains unchanged, and labor-using if the marginal rate of substitution is increasing.

This can be shown graphically. Suppose that the ratio of input price and the capital-labor ratio are fixed. If the original output denoted by isoquant I requires K_0 of capital and N_0 of labor (Figure 15-11), technical progress reduces the capital-labor requirements for that level of output, or higher output can be obtained from the same amount of inputs K_0, N_0. To present the effect of technical progress on input use given the same level of output, in Figure 15-11 we show the isoquant I moving downward (or inward) toward the origin. If it shifts from I to I_C, then

$$\text{MRTS}_{K:N} = \frac{\text{MP}_N}{\text{MP}_K} = \left(-\frac{dK}{dN}\right)_{I_C} < \left(\frac{dK}{dN}\right)_{I} \qquad (15\text{-}68)$$

where MP_N and MP_K denote the marginal product of labor and capital. That is, the marginal rate of technical substitution (MRTS) decreases, implying that technical progress is capital-using. Hicks neutrality, on the other hand, is represented by the shift from I to I_N, where

$$\text{MRTS}_{K:N} = \frac{\text{MP}_N}{\text{MP}_K} = \left(-\frac{dK}{dN}\right)_{I_N} = \left(-\frac{dK}{dN}\right)_{I} \qquad (15\text{-}69)$$

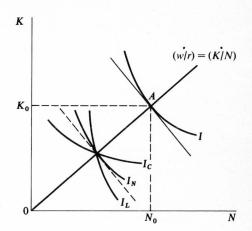

FIGURE 15-11
Types of technical change as defined by
Hicks.

The marginal rate of technical substitution is unchanged. A shift to I_L, where the marginal rate of technical substitution increases, portrays labor-using technical change.

In terms of the output elasticity of capital, Hicks neutrality can be illustrated by Figure 15-12. As shown in the graph, at a given capital-labor ratio k, the marginal rate of technical substitution remains the same when the production function shifts from $f(k, t_1)$ to $f(k, t_2)$:

$$(\text{MRTS}_{K:N})_{t_1} = (\text{MRTS}_{K:N})_{t_2} \qquad k = k_1 \qquad (15\text{-}70)$$

Using the production function $y = f(k)$, the relationship in Eq. (15-70) can be expressed in terms of the output elasticity ϵ_k, defined by

$$\epsilon_k = \frac{kf'(k)}{y} \qquad (15\text{-}71)$$

The marginal product of labor can be obtained from writing the production function as

$$Ny = Nf(k)$$

The marginal product of labor is

$$\text{MP}_N = \frac{\partial Ny}{\partial N} = f(k) - kf'(k)$$

Substituting for the marginal product terms, the marginal rate of technical substitution is

$$\text{MRTS}_{K:N} = \frac{f(k) - kf'(k)}{f'(k)}$$

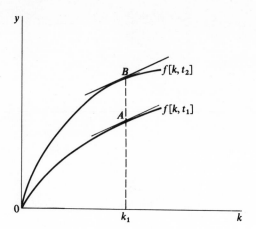

FIGURE 15-12
Hicks-neutral in output-capital plane.

Using the neutrality definition given by (15-70), we get

$$\frac{(\mathrm{MRTS}_{K:N})_{t_1}}{(\mathrm{MRTS}_{K:N})_{t_2}} = \frac{[f(k, t_1) - kf'(k, t_1)]/f'(k, t_1)}{[f(k, t_2) - kf'(k, t_2)]/f'(k, t_2)}$$

$$= \frac{[y_1/f'(k, t_1)] - k}{[y_2/f'(k, t_2)] - k}$$

$$= 1$$

Therefore,

$$\frac{y_1}{f'(k, t_1)} = \frac{y_2}{f'(k, t_2)} \qquad (15\text{-}72)$$

or multiplying both sides of (15-72) by $1/k$, and getting the inverse, we have

$$\frac{kf'(k, t_1)}{y_1} = \frac{kf'(k, t_2)}{y_2} \qquad (15\text{-}73)$$

that is,

$$\epsilon_{k_1} = \epsilon_{k_2} \qquad (15\text{-}74)$$

where ϵ_k is the output elasticity defined by (15-71). Consequently, Hicks-neutral technical progress is characterized by a constant output elasticity when technical progress leaves the capital-labor ratio unchanged. In Figure 15-12, the output elasticity must be the same at points A and B.

In Figure 15-13, the Harrod-neutral technology is compared to that of Hicks. The Hicks-neutral case is illustrated by the shift from A to B, *isoelastically*, whereas the Harrod-neutral case is represented by the shift from A to C *isomarginally*. In the former case k remains unchanged, while in the latter case k varies. A technical change

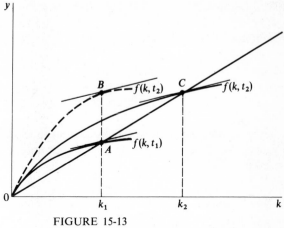

FIGURE 15-13
Comparison between Harrod- and Hicks-neutral.

may be said to be both Hicks- and Harrod-neutral if, and only if, the production function is characterized by constant output elasticities at all points, as is the case with the Cobb-Douglas production function.

Embodied Technical Progress

As defined earlier, embodied technical progress involves improvements only in capital which is newly introduced and in the labor force associated with the new capital. This type of new capital can be introduced only by scrapping old capital equipment. In this section we discuss a growth model with embodied technology commonly called the *vintage model.*

The vintage model can be classified into three categories, based on three assumptions about the substitutability of labor and capital. The *putty-putty model* is a vintage model with *smooth* substitution as in the Cobb-Douglas production function. In this case it is assumed that capital of a particular vintage can be used forever, but its price and associated labor decline toward zero as time goes on. The *putty-clay model* allows substitution of labor for capital only when new machines are installed. Once they are installed, the capital-labor ratio remains the same until another new technology is introduced. Finally, the *clay-clay model* rules out substitution altogether. The capital-labor ratio in this case is always the same no matter what kind of new technology is introduced. The last version is somewhat extreme, and in general, the actual description of any technical progress may be something between the putty-putty and putty-clay models (Allen, 1968, p. 282). Available empirical evidence seems to indicate that the putty-clay model performs better than the other model in the sense that capital once brought into production usually continues to be used with a fixed amount of labor until it is scrapped. (Allen, 1968, p. 292; Boddy, 1967; Gapinski, 1973; and Nerlove, 1967).

In this section, we shall introduce the putty-clay model as a representation of the vintage model. Since this model takes obsolescence of capital into account, the economic life of a unit of capital becomes an important factor.

The vintage putty-clay model   In the putty-clay model, one must first distinguish between two types of decisions a firm must take: (1) when the new investment should be made and (2) when machines should be scrapped due to obsolescence.

NEW INVESTMENT   Assume the production function to be of the Cobb-Douglas form. Machines with vintage τ at the time of adoption will contribute to the production in such a way that

$$Y_\tau = e^{m(1-\alpha)\tau} K_\tau^{\alpha} N_\tau^{1-\alpha} \qquad (15\text{-}75)$$

where m denotes the Harrod-neutral rate.[8]   Up to time t, total labor used and total output are

$$N = \int_{-\infty}^{t} N_\tau \, d\tau \qquad (15\text{-}76)$$

and

$$Y = \int_{-\infty}^{t} Y_\tau \, d\tau \qquad (15\text{-}77)$$

respectively.

The equilibrium conditions at the time the new investment was made are

$$K_\tau = \overline{K}_\tau \qquad \text{(fixed)}$$
$$N_\tau = \overline{N}_\tau \qquad \text{(fixed)}$$
$$Y_\tau = e^{m(1-\alpha)\tau} \overline{K}_\tau^{\alpha} \overline{N}_\tau^{1-\alpha} \qquad \text{(fixed)}$$
$$\text{for all } \tau \leq t$$

given $I = sY$ (investment = savings) and $N = N_0 e^{nt}$ (full employment). From (15-75) and (15-77), we get

$$\frac{dY}{dt} = Y_t = e^{m(1-\alpha)t} K_t^{\alpha} N_t^{1-\alpha}$$

and, knowing that the labor force grows at the rate n, we get

$$\frac{dN}{dt} = N_t = nN_0 e^{nt}$$

Hence,

$$\frac{dY}{dt} = e^{m(1-\alpha)t} (sY)^{\alpha} (nN_0 e^{nt})^{1-\alpha}$$

or

$$\frac{dY}{dt} = s^{\alpha} n^{1-\alpha} N_0^{1-\alpha} e^{(m+n)(1-\alpha)t} Y^{\alpha} \qquad (15\text{-}78)$$

---

[8] According to the Harrod neutrality, $Y_\tau = e^{\lambda t} K_\tau^{\alpha} N_\tau^{1-\alpha}$, $\lambda > 0$ and $0 < \alpha < 1$. Here, however, we assume the constant returns to scale and the constant rate of growth, m. Therefore, $\lambda = m(1-\alpha)$. The following derivations draw with minor changes on Allen (1968).

The growth equation (15-78) is now given in terms of the time change in output, rather than in terms of the capital stock, as was the case in the neoclassical growth model shown earlier [Eq. (15-23)]. Also, the constant multiple in the dY/dt equation differs by having s^α rather than s, and nN_0 rather than the simple N_0 seen earlier.

Equation (15-78) gives an equilibrium growth path of the economy in terms of output which converges to the steady-state path as time goes on. If the initial value of Y is assumed to be

$$Y_0 = nN_0\left(\frac{s^\alpha}{m+n}\right)^{1/(1-\alpha)} \qquad (15\text{-}79)$$

the steady-state solution of Y is

$$Y^* = Y_0\, e^{(m+n)t} \qquad (15\text{-}80)$$

TIME TO SCRAP MACHINES   Let us now consider the cost of labor as compared with the productivity of a machine. In this model the employment of an additional unit of labor with a new machine implies a continuous use of that labor as long as the machine is operative. Assuming the wage rate to be constant, the marginal product must be sufficient to cover the current wage rate. Assume now that the wage rate rises over time. In this case *the marginal product must cover not only the going wage rate but also the expected rise in the future* (Allen, 1968, p. 295). If, at any time, the marginal product of the machine is not sufficient to cover the increased wage rate, its use should be terminated and the machine discarded.

Let λ be the rate of growth of the wage rate. Consider a machine which is introduced at time t, and combined, until scrapped, with labor N_t to produce output Y_t. Let $\omega(t)$ represent the wage bill at time t. Then at time $t + T$ the wage bill is

$$\omega(t+T)N_t \qquad (15\text{-}81)$$

and the quasi-rent from the machine is

$$Y_t - \omega(t+T)N_t$$

The condition for obsolescence of this machine is

$$Y_t - \omega(t+T)N_t < 0 \qquad (15\text{-}82)$$

Since $\omega(t)$ grows at the rate λ, (15-81) can be rewritten as

$$\omega(t+T) = e^{\lambda t}\omega(t) \qquad (15\text{-}83)$$

From (15-82) and (15-83) we define the obsolescence condition as

$$\frac{Y_t}{N_t} < \omega(t+T) = e^{\lambda t}\omega(t) \qquad (15\text{-}84)$$

i.e., when the average product is less than the wage rate. The time of obsolescence, T, can be determined by the equation

$$T = \frac{1}{\lambda}\log\left[\frac{Y_t}{\omega(t)N_t}\right] \qquad (15\text{-}85)$$

From (15-85) the obsolescence time T depends on both the value of $1/\lambda$ and on the ratio of output to wage costs. The equilibrium conditions are, therefore,

$$K_\tau = \overline{K}_\tau \quad \text{(fixed)}$$
$$N_\tau = \overline{N}_\tau \quad \text{(fixed)}$$
$$Y_\tau = e^{m(1-\alpha)\tau}\overline{K}_\tau^\alpha\overline{N}_\tau^{1-\alpha} \quad \text{(fixed)}$$

for all $\tau \le t$

$$I_t = sY \quad \text{(investment = savings)}$$
$$N = N_0 e^{nt} \quad \text{(full employment)}$$
$$= \int_{t-T}^{t} N_\tau \, d\tau$$

The steady-state growth condition, assuming that the equilibrium conditions given above remain satisfied, can now be derived. Using the steady-state solution given by (15-80), the *optimum* increment in output during the time T is:

$$\frac{dY^*}{dt} = Y_t(1 - e^{-(m+n)T})$$

$$= e^{m(1-\alpha)t}(1 - e^{-(m+n)T})K_t^\alpha N_t^{1-\alpha}$$

$$= e^{m(1-\alpha)t}(1 - e^{-(m+n)T})s^\alpha Y^\alpha(nN_0)^{1-\alpha}\frac{e^{n(1-\alpha)t}}{(1 - e^{-nT})^{1-\alpha}}$$

This differential equation gives us the solution for Y such that

$$\frac{dY}{dt} = s^\alpha n^{1-\alpha}N_0^{1-\alpha}Ae^{(m+n)(1-\alpha)t}Y^\alpha$$

where
$$A = \frac{1 - e^{-(m+n)T}}{(1 - e^{-nT})^{1-\alpha}} \qquad (15\text{-}86)$$

Therefore, if the initial value of Y is exactly the same as

$$Y_0 = nN_0 s^{\alpha/(1-\alpha)}\left(\frac{A}{m+n}\right)^{1/(1-\alpha)} \qquad (15\text{-}87)$$

then $m + n$ is the steady-state growth rate in this model.

What value would T then have under the above steady-state specifications? Let us assume that the growth rate of the wage rate λ is equal to the technological growth rate m,

$$\omega(t + T) = e^{mt}\omega(t) \qquad (15\text{-}88)$$

Then, substituting in (15-85), we have

$$T = \frac{1}{m} \log \left[\frac{Y_t}{\omega(t)N_t} \right] \quad (15\text{-}89)$$

the term $Y_t/\omega(t)N_t$ in this case being a constant. The economic life of these machines is inversely related to the ratio m and directly to the constant output-labor cost ratio $Y_t/\omega(t)N_t$.

The following list summarizes the various ratios and values which give the steady-state growth solution in the putty-clay model.

Steady-state growth rate	$m + n$
Labor force growth rate	n
Utilization rate of labor increment	n
Technological growth rate	m
Wage-rate growth rate	m
Initial value of Y	$nN_0 s^{\alpha/(1-\alpha)} \left(\dfrac{A}{m+n} \right)^{1/(1-\alpha)}$
Length of economic life of machine	$\dfrac{1}{m} \log \left[\dfrac{Y_t}{\omega(t)N_t} \right]$

Implications of the vintage model   The model we have just outlined is only one of several different versions of vintage models. We chose the putty-clay model because in reality technical progress must always be accompanied by a new capital-labor ratio, and older machines are scrapped due to the profit ability of new technology. We actually observe many cases where older machines are discarded because of their inefficiencies, even though their marginal productivity is still positive. The criterion used by manufacturers with respect to the useful life of an old machine is usually based on the value of the quasi-rent (whether it is greater or less than zero), the very decision criterion implied by the putty-clay model.

Another reason for choosing the putty-clay model as a representative of the vintage model is that other versions have solutions not much different from the neoclassical disembodied growth model or the Harrod-Domar type of fixed-proportions growth model. The putty-putty case of vintage capital turns out to be almost identical in its steady-state solution as the simple neoclassical model with a Cobb-Douglas production function.[9] Also, the clay-clay model solution coincides with the case of the Harrod-neutral, disembodied technical progress model discussed earlier.[10]

However, substantial disagreement exists on the empirical performance of the vintage model. Some argue that the putty-clay model produces significantly different results from the disembodied models. Others assert that there are no substantial departures in the embodied model from net capital-stock models. For lack of conclusive evidence on the subject the choice between these two versions can perhaps be made according to the purpose of the investigation and the availability of data.

---

[9] For comparison of these solutions, see Brown (1966) and Jorgenson (1966).
[10] See Allen (1968, p. 302).

SUMMARY

In this chapter, we have discussed five major growth models. Looking at models with no technical change, we first considered the Harrod-Domar model, characterized by a constant savings rate as well as a fixed capital-output ratio, with the ratio between these two (s/v) being the warranted growth rate. For equilibrium growth, we derived the familiar proposition that the warranted rate must equal the natural rate. The condition for equilibrium growth in the neoclassical model without technical change is that per worker savings equal investment per worker, while for maximum consumption per worker, the marginal product of capital (the real rate of interest) must be equal to the rate of growth of the labor force. Finally, we found that the Kaldor model allows us to examine the importance of income distribution to economic growth.

Next, we considered various ways in which technical progress is introduced into growth models. Technical progress was classified into two categories: disembodied and embodied. We considered three cases of disembodied technical change: Harrod-neutral, Hicks-neutral, and Solow-neutral. The major conclusion drawn from putting technical change into growth models was that if the marginal product of capital is equal to capital accumulation, taking both natural growth and technical progress into account, an economy achieves maximum consumption. Embodied technical progress was considered with a putty-clay model. According to this model, steady-state growth can be obtained if an economy starts with the right initial output and if the length of the economic life of machines is correctly determined.

Multisector models will not be discussed, in part because this would take us too far afield and also because we maintain the basic assumption that national income and output are in aggregatable units, and that thereby all kinds of output are homogeneous regardless of whether they are consumption goods or investment goods, even though this limits the relationships between the variables we are able to analyze.

READINGS FOR CHAPTER 15

Trend of Economic Growth

ABRAMOVITZ, M.: "Review of Denison," *American Economic Review*, September 1962.

BROWN, M.: *On the Theory and Measurement of Technological Change* (New York: Cambridge, 1968), part III.

DENISON, E.: *The Sources of Economic Growth in the U.S.* (New York: Committee for Economic Development, 1962), chaps. 4 and 12.

JORGENSON, D. W., and Z. GRILICHES: "The Explanation of Production Change," *Review of Economic Studies*, July 1967.

KENDRICK, J.: *Productivity Trends in the U.S.* (Princeton, N. J.: Princeton, 1961), chaps. 3 and 4.

—— and R. SATO: "Factor Prices, Productivity, and Economic Growth," *American Economic Review*, December 1963.

KUH, E.: "The Measurement of Potential Output," *American Economic Review*, September 1966.

OKUN, A.: "Potential GNP: Its Measurement and Significance," *American Statistics Association Proceedings*, 1962.

THROW, L., and TAYLOR: "The Interaction between the Actual and Potential Rates of Growth," *Review of Economics and Statistics*, November 1966.

Harrod-Domar Model

DOMAR, E. D.: "Capital Expansion, Rate of Growth and Employment," *Econometrica*, April 1946.

HAHN, F. H., and R. C. O. MATTHEWS: "The Theory of Economic Growth: A Survey," *Economic Journal*, 1964.

HARROD, R. F.: "An Essay in Dynamic Theory," *Economic Journal*, March 1939.

——: *Toward a Dynamic Economics* (London: Macmillan 1948).

JORGENSON, D. W.: "On Stability in the Sense of Harrod," *Economica*, 1960.

Simple Neoclassical Model

ANDO, A.: "An Empirical Model of U.S. Economic Growth," in *Models of Income Determination, Studies in Income and Wealth*, (New York: National Bureau of Economic Research, 1964), vol. 28.

ARROW, A., H. B. MINHAS, and R. M. SOLOW: "Capital-Labor Substitution and Economic Efficiency," *Review of Economics and Statistics*, 1961.

EISNER, R.: "Growth and the Neoclassical Resurgence," *Economic Journal*, 1958.

HAHN, F. H., and R. C. O. MATTHEWS: "The Theory of Economic Growth: A Survey," *Economic Journal*, 1964.

JOHNSON, H. G.: "The Neoclassical One-Sector Growth Model: A Geometrical Exposition and Extension to a Monetary Economy," *Economica*, August 1966.

MEADE, J. E.: *A Neo-Classical Theory of Economic Growth*, (London: G. Aller., 1961), particularly chaps. 1–5 and the two appendices.

PHELPS, E. S.: "The Golden Rule of Accumulation," *American Economic Review*, September 1961.

SAMUELSON, P. A., and R. SOLOW: "Balanced Growth under Constant Return to Scale," *Econometrica*, 1953.

SOLOW, R.: "A Contribution to the Theory of Economic Growth," *Quarterly Journal of Economics*, February 1956.

STIGLITZ, J., and H. UZAWA (eds.): *Readings in the Theory of Economic Growth* (New York: Cambridge, 1970).

SWAN, T.: "Economic Growth and Capital Accumulation," *Economic Record*, 1956.

Kaldor's Model

KALDOR, N.: "Theories of Income Distribution," *Review of Economic Studies*, 1956.

———: "A Model of Economic Growth," *Economic Journal*, 1957.

———: "Capital Accumulation and Economic Growth," in Lutz and Hague (eds.), *The Theory of Capital* (International Economic Association, 1961).

KALDOR, N., and J. A. MIRLEES: "A New Model of Economic Growth," *Review of Economic Studies*, 1962.

ROBINSON, J.: *The Accumulation of Capital* (Homewood, Ill.: Irwin, 1956).

Disembodied Technical Progress

BURMEISTER, E., and A. R. DOBELL: *Mathematical Theories of Economic Growth* (New York: Macmillan, 1970).

CASS, D.: "Optimum Growth in an Aggregative Model of Capital Accumulation," *Review of Economic Studies*, July 1965.

DIAMOND, P. A.: "Disembodied Technical Change in a Two-Sector Model," *Review of Economic Studies*, April 1965.

DRANDAKIS, E. M., and E. PHELPS: "A Model of Induced Invention, Growth, and Distribution," *Economic Journal*, December 1966.

FEI, J. C. H., and G. RANIS: "Innovation Intensity and Factor Bias in the Theory of Growth," *International Economic Review*, May 1965.

FELLNER, W. J.: "Two Propositions in the Theory of Induced Innovations," *Economic Journal*, June 1961.

FERGUSON, C. E.: *The Neoclassical Theory of Production and Distribution* (New York: Cambridge, 1969), chap. 13.

HAHN, F. H., and R. C. O. MATTHEWS: "The Theory of Economic Growth: A Survey," *Economic Journal*, 1964.

HICKS, J. R.: *The Theory of Wages* (London: Macmillan, 1932), pp. 121–122.

JORGENSON, D.: "Embodied and Disembodied Progress," *Journal of Political Economy*, 1965.

KENNEDY, C. M.: "The Character of Improvements and of Technical Progress," *Economic Journal*, December 1962.

———: "Induced Bias in Innovation and the Theory of Distribution," *Economic Journal*, September 1964.

LEVHARI, D., and E. SHESHINSKI: "On the Sensitivity of the Level of Output to Savings: Embodiment and Disembodiment," *Quarterly Journal of Economics*, August 1967.

———: "The Relation between the Rate of Interest and the Rate of Technical Progress," *Review of Economic Studies*, July 1969.

ROBINSON, J.: "The Classification of Inventions," *Review of Economic Studies*, 1937–1938.

RONALD, J.: "Neutral Technological Change and the Isoquant Map," *American Economic Review*, September 1965.

SAMUELSON, P. A.: "Weizsacker-Kennedy Theories of Induced Innovation," *Review of Economics and Statistics*, November 1965.

SOLOW, R. M.: "Technical Change and the Aggregate Production Function," *Review of Economics and Statistics*, 1957.

UZAWA, H.: "Neutral Inventions and the Stability of Growth Equilibrium," *Review of Economic Studies*, February 1961.

Embodied Technical Progress

ALLEN, R. G. D.: *Macroeconomic Theory* (New York: St. Martin's, 1968), chap. 13.

BODDY, R.: "Comment on the Nerlove Paper," in M. Brown (ed.), *The Theory and Empirical Analysis of Production* (New York: Columbia, 1967).

BROWN, M.: *On the Theory and Measurement of Technological Change* (New York: Cambridge, 1966).

BURMEISTER, E., and A. R. DOBELL: *Mathematical Theories of Economic Growth* (New York: Macmillan, 1970).

FISHER, F. M.: "Embodied Technical Progress and the Existence of an Aggregate Capital Stock," *Review of Economic Studies*, April 1965.

FELLNER, W. J.: "Two Propositions in the Theory of Induced Innovations," *Economic Journal*, June 1961.

GAPINSKI, J. H.: "Putty-Clay Capital and Small-Sample Properties of Neoclassical Estimators," *Journal of Political Economy*, January–February 1973.

GLISS, C.: "On Putty Clay," *Review of Economic Studies*, April 1968.

GREEN, H. A. J.: "Embodied Progress, Investment and Growth," *American Economic Review*, March 1966.

GRILICHES, Z., and D. JORGENSON: "The Explanation of Productivity Change," *Review of Economic Studies*, July 1967.

JORGENSON, D.: "Embodied and Disembodied Progress," *Journal of Political Economy*, 1965.

———: "The Embodiment Hypothesis," *Journal of Political Economy*, February 1966.

LEVHARI, D., and E. SHESHINSKI: "On the Sensitivity of the Level of Output to Savings: Embodiment and Disembodiment," *Quarterly Journal of Economics*, August 1967.

MATTHEWS, R. C. O.: "The New View of Investment: Comment," *Quarterly Journal of Economics*, February 1964.

NERLOVE, M.: "Recent Empirical Studies of the CES and Related Production Functions," in Brown (ed.), op. cit.

PHELPS, E. B.: "The New View of Investment," *Quarterly Journal of Economics*, 1962.

———: "Substitution, Fixed Proportions, Growth and Distribution," *International Economic Review*, 1963.

SOLOW, R. M.: "Substitution and Fixed Propositions in the Theory of Capital," *Review of Economic Studies*, 1962.

———: *Capital Theory and the Rate of Return*, (Amsterdam: North Holland, 1963), chap. 2 and 3.

———: "Investment and Technical Progress," in K. J. Arrow et al. (eds.), *Mathematical Methods in the Social Sciences* (Stanford, Calif.: Stanford, 1959).

———, J. TOBIN, D. VON WEIZSACHER, and M. YAARI: "Neoclassical Growth with Fixed Factor Proportions," *Review of Economic Studies*, April 1966.

STIGLITZ, J., and H. UZAWA (eds.): *Readings in the Theory of Economic Growth* (New York: Cambridge, 1970).

16

MONEY AND GROWTH

The growth models discussed in the previous chapter specified all variables in real terms: real output, real rate of interest, real capital, real terms of trade (price), and so forth, thus ignoring the existence of money and its impact on the rate of growth. In this chapter, a money sector is introduced so that the analysis incorporates the effect of changes in the supply of and the demand for money on the real sector.

The first link between the money supply and the real sector is the price level. If output remains unchanged, then an increase in the supply of money will directly affect prices. The price change will in turn affect the equilibrium growth path because, as shown in the previous chapter (Figure 15-1), the growth path is defined in terms of both the rate of change in prices and the rate of change in output. Secondly, a change in the money supply and the demand for money affects the rate of capital accumulation. Capital accumulation is determined by the interactions between investment and saving. Changes in the money supply or in the demand for money, or both, may result in a different savings rate and thus a different rate of capital accumulation than that which otherwise would have prevailed.[1]

---

[1] Here we are dealing with the normal case rather than the special case of a liquidity trap.

These are but two of many examples which show the interrelationship between money and economic growth. In this chapter we present two growth models which explicitly acknowledge the role of money on the rate of growth. These are the neoclassical model (with a monetary sector) and the so-called Keynes-Wicksell model. The major difference between these two models lies in the way the investment-savings relation is stated. In the neoclassical model, the growth of capital per period, dK/dt, is always equal to planned savings, sY, whereas in the Keynes-Wicksell model real savings and investment are independent of each other and they are determined by the price-adjustment mechanism in the market.

NEOCLASSICAL MODEL WITH MONEY

Before introducing money into the model, let us review briefly the simple neoclassical growth model. Using the one-sector model, we have a production function

$$Y = Y(K, N) \qquad (16\text{-}1)$$

where we assume that

1 the production function is subject to constant returns to scale
2 the savings rate s is given
3 there is no technical progress
4 population is growing exogenously at a fixed rate n

From (16-1), we get

$$y = y\left(\frac{K}{N}, 1\right) \qquad \text{or} \qquad y = f(k) \qquad (16\text{-}2)$$

where $k = K/N$. The equilibrium condition (as shown earlier in Chapter 15) can be obtained by choosing the proper k satisfying

$$f(k) = \frac{n}{s} k \qquad (16\text{-}3)$$

This condition is presented graphically in Figure 16-1. At point E, where $f(k)$ intercepts $(n/s)k$ the equilibrium condition stated by (16-3) is satisfied with a given n and s, so that the equilibrium output per capita is y^*, and the equilibrium stock of capital per capita is k^*. Let us draw the capital requirement line nk. At the equilibrium capital-labor ratio k^*, the required change in capital (or investment) should be equal to savings in order for equilibrium to be maintained. The savings curve sy which lies below $f(k)$ must intercept nk at point F, as shown in Figure 16-1. If, for some reason, sy were to lie *below* nk, a solution may not exist for every level of k. On the other hand, a multiple solution might exist if sy intercepts the nk line more than once. If

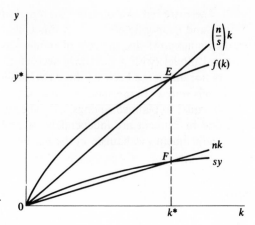

FIGURE 16-1
The equilibrium condition in the neoclassical model with no money.

at the equilibrium solution E the marginal product is equal to the rate of growth of the labor force n, then according to the golden rule of accumulation, point E also guarantees maximum per capita consumption.

Money as an Asset to Hold

Now let us introduce money into the neoclassical framework. From the quantity theory of money, we know that

$$MV = pY$$

or

$$\log M + \log V = \log p + \log Y$$

Assuming velocity V remains unchanged over time, we have the differential equation

$$\dot{M} = \dot{p} + \dot{Y}$$

and

$$\dot{p} = \dot{M} - \dot{Y} \qquad (16\text{-}4)$$

where $\dot{M} = \dfrac{1}{M}\dfrac{dM}{dt}$, $\dot{p} = \dfrac{1}{p}\dfrac{dp}{dt}$, and $\dot{Y} = \dfrac{1}{Y}\dfrac{dY}{dt}$. That is, the rate of price change is the difference between the rate of increase in nominal money and the rate of growth of output. If the money stock is not changed as output increases, the price level will fall at the rate $\dot{Y}$, and real money balances M/p will rise.

When these effects of money are incorporated into the growth model, the following modifications are made:

1   Real balances are part of private wealth (Chapter 13) so the *growth* in real balances should be added to real income.
2   Since real balances can be held as a form of asset, increments of real balances in each period must be deducted from savings available for investment in real capital.

The long-run impact of an increase in real balances on growth is then to reduce the per capita capital stock and per capita output. We will show this in what follows.

Let Y = real income
C = real consumption
M = nominal money stock
M/p = real balances

$b = \dfrac{M_d/p}{Y}$, the ratio of real balances held to output

$\hat{Y}$ = real output plus the change in real balances
$r = \partial Y/\partial K = F'(K, N)$, the real rate of return to capital (i.e., the marginal product of capital)
π = rate of return to real money balances
i = money rate of interest

We assume that the ratio b is inversely dependent on the difference between what could have been earned from the holding of a unit of physical capital and what will be earned from the holding of real money balances. The change in the real money stock held over time is

$$\frac{d\dfrac{M_d}{p}}{dt} = \frac{p\dfrac{dM_d}{dt} - M\dfrac{dp}{dt}}{p^2}$$

$$= \frac{M_d}{p}(\dot{M_d} - \dot{p}) \qquad (16\text{-}5)$$

Since an increase in real balances increases real income $\hat{Y}$, we have

$$\hat{Y} = Y + \frac{M_d}{p}(\dot{M_d} - \dot{p}) \qquad (16\text{-}6)$$

We now have two kinds of assets in the model: the real capital stock K and real balances M_d/p. In a perfectly competitive market, the rate of return to real capital is equal to the marginal product of capital.

$$r = \frac{\partial Y}{\partial K} = F'(K, N) \qquad (16\text{-}7)$$

The rate of return to real balances (assuming money pays no interest) is the rate of *price decrease*,

$$\pi = -\dot{p} \qquad (16\text{-}8)$$

The money rate of interest is equal to the real rate of return plus the rate of inflation,[2]

$$i = r - \pi = r + \dot{p} \qquad (16\text{-}9)$$

If the savings rate s is assumed to remain constant and the above changes are introduced into the neoclassical growth model, the solution for the equilibrium growth path can be investigated. In equilibrium, the model specifies that investment (capital formation) per period be equal to savings. Since real investment is equal to total output less consumption, from Eq. (15-16) we can write

$$I_t = \frac{dK}{dt} = Y_t - C_t \qquad (16\text{-}10)$$

Since consumption is a function of real income $C_t = (1 - s)\hat{Y}_t$, Eq. (16-10) can be written as

$$\frac{dK}{dt} = Y_t - (1 - s)\hat{Y}_t$$

$$= Y_t - (1 - s)\left[Y_t + \frac{M_{dt}}{p_t}(\dot{M}_d - \dot{p}) \right] \qquad (16\text{-}11)$$

Using b, the ratio of real balances to output, we can write real balances in terms of output units:

$$\frac{M_d}{p} = bY$$

or

$$\frac{M_d}{p} = bF(K, N) \qquad (16\text{-}12)$$

Substituting (16-12) into (16-11) and dropping the subscript t for simplicity, we get

$$\frac{dK}{dt} = Y - (1 - s)[Y + bY(\dot{M}_d - \dot{p})]$$

$$= sY - (1 - s)bY(\dot{M}_d - \dot{p})$$

$$= Y[s - (1 - s)b(\dot{M}_d - \dot{p})] \qquad (16\text{-}13)$$

Dividing both sides of equation (16-13) by K, we obtain

$$\frac{dK}{dt} \Big/ K = \dot{K} = \frac{Y}{K}[s - (1 - s)b(\dot{M}_d - \dot{p})]$$

In terms of output per unit of labor, we have

$$\dot{K} = \dot{k} + n = \frac{y}{k}[s - (1 - s)b(\dot{M}_d - \dot{p})]$$

---

[2] In fact, the monetary rate of interest (i) has the following relationship: $1 + i = (1 + \dot{p})$ $(1 + r)$, or $i = \dot{p} + r + \dot{p}r$. Since $\dot{p}r$ is likely to be very small, i can be approximated by (16-9).

Equilibrium and steady-state growth (i.e., $\dot{k} = 0$) for the neoclassical model with no technical change and no money [Eq. (15-24)] were given by

$$sf(k) = nk$$

In the present case the condition is

$$[s - (1 - s)b(\dot{M}_d - \dot{p})]f(k) = nk \quad (16\text{-}13a)$$

Equilibrium growth in this model requires that (1) the rate of capital accumulation ($\dot{k}$) be zero at the equilibrium point as in the simple neoclassical model without money and that (2) real balances per unit of labor must be constant if r is constant (and r is constant if both output and capital grow at the same rate). This is because the rate of capital accumulation (dK/dt) cannot be zero unless real balances also remain unchanged since real balances affect the savings rate and thus capital accumulation. The second requirement—that $(M_d/p)/N$ be constant—can be derived as follows: Let m denote the real per capita money stock. Then

$$m = \frac{M_d}{pN} \quad (16\text{-}14)$$

and

$$\dot{m} = \dot{M}_d - \dot{p} - n \quad (16\text{-}15)$$

where n represents the rate of growth of the labor force. For the second condition to be satisfied in equilibrium, $\dot{m}$ should be zero, or

$$\dot{M}_d - \dot{p} = n \quad (16\text{-}15a)$$

Substituting (16-15a) into the first equilibrium condition given by Eq. (16-13a), we have the final equilibrium-growth solution for the model as

$$nk = f(k)[s - (1 - s)bn] \quad (16\text{-}16)$$

As shown earlier, the solution of the neoclassical model with no money was

$$nk = f(k)s$$

In contrast, equilibrium growth in the money model depends, in addition to the rate of growth of the labor force, on the ratio of real balances to output, b. Since both b and n are positive,

$$s > s - (1 - s)bn \quad (16\text{-}17)$$

which means that for any given value for s the term is smaller than s. When money is introduced, the bracketed term replaces s in the equilibrium condition, and thus the equilibrium level for y and k will be less than when money was absent.

Graphically, the savings function $f(k)s$ lies above the money-savings function $f(k)[s - (1 - s)bn]$, as shown in Figure 16-2. As the ratio of real balances to output, b, gets larger, the smaller the available savings out of any output for capital formation will be, the lower the savings function with money will be, and consequently the smaller the equilibrium capital-labor ratio will be, as shown in Figure 16-2. Thus, real output will be reduced due to the increase in real money holdings.

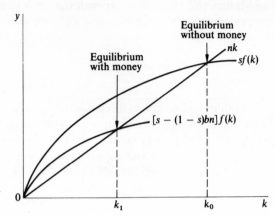

FIGURE 16-2
The effect of money on equilibrium output and capital.

The following hypothetical example illustrates such effects. The following function and values are given:

$$Y = \sqrt{KN}$$
$$s = 0.10$$
$$n = 0.02$$
$$b = 0.45$$

Then
$$f(k)[s - (1 - s)bn] = k^{1/2}[0.10 - (0.90)(0.45)(0.02)]$$
$$= k^{1/2} \times 0.092$$

For steady-state growth, $nk = f(k)[s - (1 - s)bn]$; that is,

$$k^{1/2} \times 0.092 = (0.02)k$$

and
$$k = 16.81$$

and the steady-state real income per worker is

$$y = f(k) = \sqrt{16.81} = 4.1$$

Substituting the above hypothetical values, we get for the no-money case,

$$f(k)s = nk$$
$$k^{1/2}(0.1) = (0.02)k$$
$$k = 25$$
$$y = 5$$

Introducing money into the neoclassical model, thus, reduces the value of real output in the steady-state solution.

The golden rule path What does money do to our earlier conclusion about conditions required for the golden rule position? Let k_g denote the golden rule capital-labor ratio and k_m denote the steady-state capital-labor ratio without money. If for some reason

$$k_m < k_g$$

k_m should be raised to achieve the maximum consumption level, i.e., to put the economy on the golden path. In a money economy, an inflationary policy by rapid expansion of nominal money supply will increase k toward k_g and a deflationary policy will lower it when $k_m > k_g$, so that the economy can always be moved to the golden path with monetary policy. The reason for this is as follows: From the definition of b,

$$b = \frac{M_d}{p} \bigg/ Y \quad (16\text{-}17a)$$

this ratio can be expressed as a function of the expected rate of inflation $\dot{p}$ and thus the rate of increase in the money supply. Differentiating (16-17a) with respect to time, we get

$$\frac{db}{dt} = \frac{Y\left(\dfrac{d(M_d/p)}{dt}\right) - \dfrac{M_d}{p}\dfrac{dY}{dt}}{Y^2}$$

$$= \frac{Y\left(\dfrac{\dfrac{pdM_d}{dt} - M\dfrac{dp}{dt}}{p^2}\right) - \dfrac{M_d}{p}\dfrac{dY}{dt}}{Y^2}$$

$$= \frac{M_d}{pY}(\dot{M}_d - \dot{p}) - \frac{M_d}{pY^2}\frac{dY}{dt}$$

$$= \frac{M_d}{pY}(\dot{M}_d - \dot{p} - \dot{Y}) \quad (16\text{-}18)$$

From (16-18), we see that b gets smaller, the larger the expected rate of inflation $\dot{p}$, as the supply of money is increased. As the rate of increase of the money stock $\dot{M}$ is increased, the opportunity cost of holding real balances will be higher due to the associated higher inflation rate, and thus the lower the ratio of real-balance holding to output will be. However, the lower value for b will eventually increase real savings and consequently the equilibrium capital-labor ratio k^*, and real output per worker y^* will be achieved. Monetary policy affecting the supply of money together with the demand for money is thus seen to affect the equilibrium growth path in this model.

However, the success of monetary policy in altering k_m to the desired level is assured only when the real savings function cuts nk to the right of the golden rule position, as shown in Figure 16-3. If the savings function sy cuts kn to the left of the

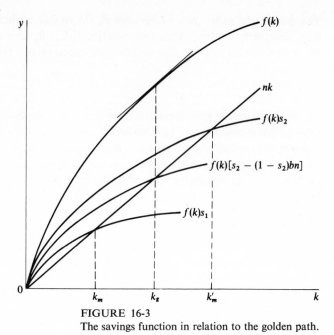

FIGURE 16-3
The savings function in relation to the golden path.

golden rule position k_g, the curve $f(k)[s - (1 - s)bn]$ cannot reach the golden rule point because it is impossible for it to be above the real savings function sy. On the other hand, if we are initially at k_m', then the savings function with money, $f(k)$ $[s - (1 - s)bn]$, through the change in b, may shift back and forth until the solution for k is equal to k_g. Again, an inflationary policy is needed when b is too high, while a deflationary policy is called for when b is too low.

Money as a Consumer's Good

In the previous model, we saw that equilibrium capital intensity, equilibrium income level, and thus consumption were lower in the monetary growth model than in the simple neoclassical model without money. A question must then arise: If money caused k, y, and c to be reduced, why should it be introduced? What is the advantage of a monetary economy? In this section we will extend the role of money, interpreting it not only as an asset but also as a consumer's good. That is, the services rendered by money balances will be an individual's objective of choice included in his utility function. Using this interpretation of money, monetary expansion policy can increase k and y. We will show this using the Levhari-Patinkin (1968) model.

The services rendered by money balances can be converted to real income units. Consider the alternative cost at the margin of holding money balances, $r + \dot{p}$ in

Eq. (16-9), as the value of the services rendered by a unit of real balances. Thus, Eq. (16-6) is revised to

$$\hat{Y} = Y + \frac{M}{p}(\dot{M} - \dot{p}) + \frac{M}{P}(r + \dot{p})$$

$$= Y + \frac{M}{p}(\dot{M} + r) \qquad (16\text{-}18a)$$

Y is thus defined as net national disposable income *plus* the real value of the increase in nominal money, $[\dot{M}(M/p)]$, *plus* the imputed real interest on real balances, $r(M/p)$. Note that $\dot{p}$ is eliminated from Eq. (16-18a) and the subscript d is removed from M. This implies that, in an economy in which everyone foresees with certainty a given price change and adjusts his money holdings accordingly, such a price change cannot generate the capital losses as it does in Eq. (16-6), and also the money market is always cleared.

Let us now find the conditions for steady-state growth. The rate of capital formation is

$$I = \frac{dK}{dt} = Y - C \qquad (16\text{-}18b)$$

Consumption to be deducted from total commodity output in (16-18b) is not total consumption but physical consumption (C_p). That is, the liquidity services should be deducted from total consumption:

$$C_p = \left\{ (1 - s)\left[Y + \frac{M}{p}(\dot{M} + r)\right] - \frac{M}{p}(r + \dot{p})\right\}$$

Substituting this for C in (16-18b), we get

$$\frac{dK}{dt} = Y - \left\{ (1 - s)\left[Y + \frac{M}{p}(\dot{M} + r)\right] - \frac{M}{p}(r + \dot{p})\right\} \qquad (16\text{-}18c)$$

Let us define the steady-state growth path as one in which both per capita physical capital k and per capita real money balances m stay constant. That is,

$$\dot{k} = \dot{K} - n = 0 \qquad (16\text{-}18d)$$

$$\dot{m} = \dot{M} - \dot{p} - n = 0 \qquad (16\text{-}18e)$$

Using the variable b [the ratio of holdings of real balances to output, i.e., $(M/p)/Y = b$], Eq. (16-18c) becomes, in equilibrium:

$$\frac{dK}{dt} = Y - \{(1 - s)Y[1 + b(\dot{M} + r)] - bY(r + \dot{p})\}$$

$$= Y\{s[1 + b(n + \dot{p} + r)] - bn\}$$

Dividing this by K, we get

$$\dot{K} = \frac{Y}{K}\{s[1 + b(n + \dot{p} + r)] - bn\}$$

or using Eq. (16-18d) in terms of per capita units, we get

$$n = \frac{f(k)}{k} \{s[1 + b(n + \dot{p} + r)] - bn\}$$

or
$$\{s[1 + b(n + \dot{p} + r)] - bn\}f(k) = nk \quad (16\text{-}18f)$$

The term in the bracket of Eq. (16-18f) can be interpreted in economic terms as the "physical savings ratio." Labeling this as σ, Eq. (16-18f) becomes

$$\sigma f(k) = nk \quad (16\text{-}18g)$$

Thus, for a steady state to be maintained, the amount of new physical capital through savings, $\sigma f(k)$, must be equal to the amount of new physical capital required to maintain a constant capital-labor ratio, nk. It is clear from this condition that if a steady state exists, then σ must be greater than zero, for since the labor supply is growing, there must be positive physical savings in order to maintain a constant k. We also find that σ is not necessarily less than s. In the previous model (i.e., where money did not enter the utility function), the equilibrium k must be less than the neoclassical equilibrium k^* without money. But in the present model, it can be greater than the neoclassical k^*, although it depends on the sign of the following:

$$s(n + \dot{p} + r) - n \gtrless 0$$

Even if the sign is negative so that σ is less than s, consumption including the services of money per capita may be larger than in the neoclassical case without money.

We now consider the conditions for golden-rule path of growth. Individuals want to maximize utility for all points in time, where the utility function in per capita terms is

$$U = U(c, m) \quad (16\text{-}18h)$$

By definition, per capita physical consumption c is

$$c(k) = f(k) - \sigma f(k) \quad (16\text{-}18i)$$

and in the steady state, this reduces to

$$c(k) = f(k) - nk \quad (16\text{-}18j)$$

Hence, the utility function is

$$U = U[f(k) - nk, m] \quad (16\text{-}18k)$$

Maximizing U, we need the condition that

$$dU = U_1[f'(k) - n] \, dk + U_2 \, dm = 0 \quad (16\text{-}18l)$$

Assuming nonsatiety of commodity consumption, i.e., $U_1 \neq 0$, the following must be simultaneously satisfied:

$$f'(k) - n = 0 \quad (16\text{-}18m)$$

$$U_2 = 0 \quad (16\text{-}18n)$$

This implies that, for golden rule path, (1) the real rate of interest $f'(k) = r$ must be equal to the natural rate of labor force growth and (2) real money balances must be at their satiety level. This level of balances can be achieved when the alternative cost of holding money, i, is also zero. Since $i = f'(k) + \dot{p}$, it follows that the optimum rate of price change should be

$$-\dot{p} = f'(k) = n$$

This and Eq. (16-18e) give us

$$\dot{M} = \dot{p} + n = 0$$

which implies that, in equilibrium, optimum monetary policy calls for a constant total quantity of money.

How does monetary policy affect real variables in this model? We know that this depends on variables s, b, n, $\dot{p}$, and r. Assume that s and n are fixed and that the ratio b is a function of the money rate of interest, $i = r + p = f'(k) + p$. Then, from the definition of σ in Eq. (16-18f), we get

$$\sigma = \sigma[b(i), \dot{p}, r]$$
$$\sigma = \sigma\{b[f'(k) + \dot{p}], \dot{p}, f'(k)\}$$

In a simpler form, σ is a function of k and $\dot{p}$:

$$\sigma = \sigma(k, \dot{p}) \quad (16\text{-}18o)^3$$

Using the steady-state condition, we get

$$\sigma f(k) = nk$$
$$\frac{f(k)}{k} = \frac{n}{\sigma(k, \dot{p})}$$

Since $f(k)/k = (Y/N)/(K/N)$, we can write

$$a(k) = \frac{n}{\sigma(k, \dot{p})} \quad (16\text{-}18p)$$

where $a(k) = Y/K$, or the output-capital ratio. Recall that in a steady state $\dot{M} - \dot{p} = n$. Thus, the effect of dm (a change in the ratio of money to output in per capita terms) on the steady-state value of $a(k)$ can be found by differentiating (16-18p) totally:

$$a'(k)\, dk = \frac{-n[\sigma_k\, dk + \sigma_{\dot{p}}\, d\dot{p}]}{[\sigma(k, \dot{p})]^2}$$

---

[3] Even if s is treated as a variable, Eq. (16-18o) remains the same, because we may assume that $s = s[f'(k), -\dot{p}]$, $s_1 > 0$, $s_2 > 0$.

Dividing both sides by $d\dot{p}$ and $a'(k)$, we get

$$\frac{dk}{d\dot{p}} = -\frac{n}{\sigma^2 a'(k)}\left[\sigma_k \frac{dk}{d\dot{p}} + \sigma_{\dot{p}}\right]$$

or

$$\frac{dk}{d\dot{p}} = -\frac{\sigma_{\dot{p}}}{\dfrac{\sigma^2 a'(k)}{n} + \sigma_k} \tag{16-18q}$$

Let us examine the sign of (16-18q). First, $a'(k) < 0$ because the average product is, in general, decreasing. Second, the sign of σ_k is given by

$$\frac{\partial\sigma}{\partial k} = \frac{\partial}{\partial k}\{s[f'(k), -\dot{p}][1 + b(n + \dot{p} + r)] - bn\}$$

$$= s_1 f''(k)[1 + b(n + \dot{p} + r)] + f''(k)bs\left[1 + \frac{b_i}{b}(\dot{p} + r)\right]$$

$$- f''(k)(1 - s)b_i n \tag{16-18r}$$

Since $0 < s < 1$ $\qquad s_1 > 0 \qquad f''(k) < 0 \qquad b_i < 0 \qquad$ and $\qquad (\dot{p} + r) > 0$

$\partial\sigma/\partial k$ is negative if $|b_i(\dot{p} + r)/b| < 1$. In other words if the elasticity of money holdings with respect to i (the money rate of interest) is less than unity, then $\sigma_k < 0$. Similarly,

$$\frac{\partial\sigma}{\partial\dot{p}} = s_2[1 + b(n + \dot{p} + r)] + bs\left[1 + \frac{b_i}{b}(\dot{p} + r)\right] - (1 - s)b_i n \tag{16-18s}$$

The sign of $\sigma_{\dot{p}}$ is thus ambiguous. If the change in the rate of increase in prices affects more significantly the composition of the two assets—physical capital and real money balances—than total physical savings, then $\sigma_{\dot{p}} > 0$.[4] From the assumptions about the elasticity of money holdings and the composition effect, we may conclude that

$$\frac{dk}{d\dot{p}} > 0$$

Money expansionary policy increasing $\dot{p}$ may be effective in increasing the capital intensity, and thereby, output under certain conditions. But the true effect of $\Delta\dot{p}$ on the capital-labor ratio depends on how the economy reacts to $\Delta\dot{p}$. The faster the change in asset compositions, the larger the impact of $\Delta\dot{p}$.

---

[4] The first term on the right-hand side of (16-18s), that is negative, is called the "overall-savings effect" because it reflects a change in total savings due to $\Delta\dot{p}$ corresponding to a given level of physical output. The last two terms, which are both positive, are the "composition effect" because they reflect the impact of $\Delta\dot{p}$ on savings through changing the composition of the two assets. See Levhari and Patinkin (1968, pp. 724–725).

KEYNES-WICKSELL MODEL WITH MONEY

In the neoclassical growth model with money, it was assumed that the economy is continuously in equilibrium and that real investment is always equal to real savings. Prices were assumed to change only when the supply of money changes. In contrast to the neoclassical model, a new model in the tradition of Keynes and Wicksell has been developed to remove some of these restrictions (Stein, 1969, 1970). The Keynes-Wicksell growth model (as it is called) assumes:

1 Consumption is a function of assets, where assets consist of the capital stock and real money.

2a Prices change in response to excess demand in the money market.

2b Prices change in response to excess demand in the commodity market.

3 Both consumption and investment plans are partially satisfied when markets are not cleared.

4 There is an independent investment function in the model, and the commodity market may not be equilibrated.

In this section we present two models of growth based on the Keynes-Wicksellian analysis. These are referred to as the "simple model" (or the model with the commodity market always equilibrated) where assumptions 1, 2*a*, and 3 are introduced and a second version where assumptions 1, 2*b*, 3, and 4—an independent investment function—are used.

The Simple Model

This model takes the money market as the source of disequilibrium-generating forces. Let us start with a production function homogeneous of degree one:

$$Y = F(K, N)$$

Per worker output is (again):

$$y = f(k) \qquad f' > 0 \qquad f'' < 0 \qquad (16\text{-}19)$$

We also assume as usual that the labor force grows at the rate n. Introducing the assumption that the community's total real wealth, A, at any point in time, consists of the real capital stock and real money balances, we write this, in per worker units, as

$$a = k + m \qquad (16\text{-}20)$$

where $m = M/pN$. Per worker real wealth a is assumed to affect the level of consumption and, therefore, the propensity to save. The rate of capital formation per worker is

$$\frac{I}{N} = \frac{dK/dt}{N} = f(k) - c(k + m) = S(k, m) \qquad (16\text{-}21)$$

where $c(k + m)$ and $S(k, m)$ represent the per capita consumption and savings function, respectively. In the simple neoclassical model, the time rate of change in capital, $\dot{k}$, was given by

$$\dot{k} = \frac{1}{k}\, sf(k) - n$$

Since in the Keynes-Wicksell model, savings is a function of assets—monetary as well as physical—$\dot{k}$ is now

$$\dot{k} = \frac{1}{k}\, S(k, m) - n$$

or
$$\frac{dk}{dt} = S(k, m) - kn \qquad (16\text{-}22)$$

Substituting (16-21) into (16-22), we get

$$\frac{dk}{dt} = f(k) - nk - c(k + m) \qquad (16\text{-}23)$$

Equation (16-23) is the capital growth function in the real sector when the real balance effect on consumption is allowed for. Introducing the monetary sector, we use the following simplified version of the money demand function:

$$L = L(K, \dot{p}) \qquad (16\text{-}24a)$$

where $\dot{p}$ denotes the expected rate of price change.[5] The aggregate demand for real balances per worker is

$$L = L(k, \dot{p}) \qquad (16\text{-}24b)$$

As we saw earlier with the neoclassical model with money, the rate of change in real balances, $\dot{m}$, can be written as

$$\dot{m} = \dot{M} - \dot{p} - n \qquad (16\text{-}25)$$

---

[5] The conventional Keynesian demand function for money must be $L = L(y, i; \bar{b}, \bar{c})$ where $\bar{b}$ and $\bar{c}$ denote the brokerage fee and the holding costs, respectively (Chapter 9). In this model we are interested in the relationship between money supply and capital formation. Thus, we assume b and c are fixed and convert y and i in such a way that

$$y = f(k)$$
$$i = \dot{p} + r$$
$$r = f'(k)$$

Therefore, $L = L(y, i; \bar{b}, \bar{c}) = L(k, \dot{p})$.

The expected rate of change in prices, or the price adjustment in the real sector, depends, according to assumption 2a, upon excess supply (or demand) in the money sector, while the commodity market is cleared. That is,

$$\dot{p} = \lambda[m - L(k, \dot{p})] \qquad (16\text{-}26)$$

where λ is the speed-of-adjustment coefficient. Moreover, in the neighborhood of equilibrium, the expected rate of price change $\dot{p}$ is equal to the equilibrium rate of price change $\dot{p}_e$,

$$\dot{p}_e = \dot{p} \qquad (16\text{-}27)$$

Substituting Eq. (16-27) into Eq. (16-26) and differentiating totally, we get

$$d\dot{p}_e = \lambda(dm - L_1 \, dk - L_2 \, d\dot{p}_e)$$

or

$$\left(\frac{1}{\lambda} + L_2\right) d\dot{p}_e = dm - L_1 \, dk \qquad (16\text{-}28)$$

Equation (16-28) implies that, in the neighborhood of equilibrium, $d\dot{p}$ can be written in terms of dm and dk, or

$$\dot{p} = \dot{p}(k, m) \qquad (16\text{-}29)$$

Substituting Eq. (16-29) into Eq. (16-25), we get

$$\dot{m} = \dot{M} - \dot{p}(k, m) - n$$

or

$$\frac{dm}{dt} = m\dot{M} - m\dot{p}(k, m) - mn \qquad (16\text{-}30)$$

Equation (16-23), the capital growth equation in the real sector, together with Eq. (16-30) depicting the change in real money balances per worker represents the Keynes-Wicksell "simple" growth model.

$$\frac{dk}{dt} = f(k) - nk - c(k + m) \qquad (16\text{-}23)$$

$$\frac{dm}{dt} = m\dot{M} - m\dot{p}(k, m) - mn \qquad (16\text{-}30)$$

These two equations can be approximated linearly in a sufficiently small neighborhood of equilibrium by Taylor series expansion. Thus,

$$\frac{dk}{dt} = a_{11}(k - k_e) + a_{12}(m - m_e)$$

$$\frac{dm}{dt} = a_{21}(k - k_e) + a_{22}(m - m_e)$$

where k_e and m_e are the equilibrium values of k and m, and the coefficients a_{ij} are given by

$$a_{11} = \frac{\partial f}{\partial k} - n - \frac{\partial c}{\partial k}$$

$$a_{12} = -\frac{\partial c}{\partial m}$$

$$a_{21} = -m\frac{\partial \dot{p}}{\partial k}$$

$$a_{22} = \dot{M} - m\frac{\partial \dot{p}}{\partial m} - n$$

Let

$$A = \begin{bmatrix} a_{11} & a_{12} \\ a_{21} & a_{22} \end{bmatrix}$$

Stability conditions require that the determinant of A be positive.[6] To find the stable solution, we put dk/dt and dm/dt equal to zero in Eq. (16-23) and (16-30). Differentiating these totally with respect to all variables, we obtain

$$\begin{bmatrix} a_{11} & a_{12} \\ a_{21} & a_{22} \end{bmatrix}\begin{bmatrix} dk_e \\ dm_e \end{bmatrix} = \begin{bmatrix} 0 \\ -d\dot{M} \end{bmatrix} \qquad (16\text{-}31)$$

or

$$\begin{bmatrix} a_{11} & a_{12} \\ a_{21} & a_{22} \end{bmatrix}\begin{bmatrix} dk_e/d\dot{M} \\ dm_e/d\dot{M} \end{bmatrix} = \begin{bmatrix} 0 \\ -1 \end{bmatrix}$$

The solution for $dk_e/d\dot{M}$ is

$$\frac{dk_e}{d\dot{M}} = \frac{a_{12}}{|A|} < 0 \qquad (16\text{-}32)$$

because $a_{12} < 0$ and $|A| > 0$. From Eq. (16-32), it is clear that a rise in $\dot{M}$ (the rate of increase in money supply) must lower the rate of capital formation. This is because, first, a rise in $\dot{M}$ causes real balances per worker to increase, and thus increases wealth and consumption, and, second, a rise in $\dot{M}$ accelerates $\dot{p}$ so that the quantity of real balances demanded per worker declines. To reduce their holdings of real balances to the desired level, individuals will further increase their consumption expenditures because the higher value for $\dot{p}$ increases the opportunity cost of holding real balances. The rise in consumption shifts the consumption function upward and absorbs more of the funds available for real capital.

This can be shown graphically in Figure 16-4. From Eq. (16-23) the equilibrium condition is where $dk/dt = 0$, or

$$f(k) - nk = c(k + m) \qquad (16\text{-}33)$$

The left-hand side of Eq. (16-33) is the difference between the output-per-worker function and required-investment-per-worker line. Since the consumption function

---

[6] The equilibrium is stable if and only if $[A]$ is the matrix of a negative definite quadratic form, i.e., only if all principal minors alternate in sign starting with $a_{11} < 0$. See Allen (1968, pp. 495–498).

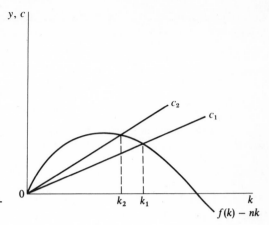

FIGURE 16-4
The effect of changes in money on capital function.

is an increasing function of k, the equilibrium solution for k is found at the intersection of $f(k) - nk$ and the consumption line $c(k + m)$. Let k_1 be the initial equilibrium solution for k where the consumption function is represented by c_1. If $\dot{M}$ rises, then real balances per worker (m) will increase, and this results in an upward shift of the consumption function to c_2, as in Figure 16-4. The equilibrium k would then move from k_1 to k_2. That is, the capital-labor ratio is decreased.

In short, the simple Keynes-Wicksell model completely reverses the first neoclassical proposition presented earlier—a rise in $\dot{M}$ (i.e., an inflationary policy) lowers rather than raises the equilibrium capital-labor ratio.

The Keynes-Wicksell Model with an Independent Investment Function

Keynes advanced the proposition that only in equilibrium does investment equal savings. Thus recognizing the possibility of disequilibrium—investment may not be equal to savings—the simple model discussed above is modified by introducing an independent investment function (assumption 4 in addition to 1, 2b, and 3). In other words, investment demand is now a function of variables other than those determining savings. Let bonds be considered as another form of asset in addition to money and capital. If these modifications are taken into account, the expected rise in prices now becomes a function of the difference between investment and saving rather than the excess demand and supply of money balances. Equation (16-26) is thus replaced by

$$\dot{p} = \lambda\left(\frac{I}{K} - \frac{S}{K}\right) \qquad (16\text{-}34)$$

where I and S are expressed in units of capital, for convenience. Assume that the actual growth of capital $\dot{K}$ is a linear combination of planned investment per unit of capital and planned savings per unit of capital. Then,

$$\dot{K} = \frac{dK}{dt}\bigg/ K = a(I/K) + (1 - a)(S/K)$$

$$1 > a > 0 \quad \text{when } \dot{p} > 0 \tag{16-35}$$

$$a = 0 \quad \text{when } \dot{p} \leq 0$$

Substituting (16-34) into (16-35), the actual rate of growth of capital can be written as

$$\dot{K} = \frac{a\dot{p}}{\lambda} + \frac{S}{K} \tag{16-36}$$

From Eq. (16-36), as $\dot{p}$ rises during an inflationary period, capital formation will take place over and above desired savings. This portion of the rate of capital growth $(a\dot{p}/\lambda)$ is the so-called *forced savings rate*. For the steady-state equilibrium, the following two conditions are needed:

$$\dot{K}_e = n \tag{16-37}$$

$$\dot{p}_e = \dot{M} - n \tag{16-38}$$

that is, capital and labor grow at the same rate, and the equilibrium rate of change in the price level $\dot{p}_e$ is equal to the rate of change of the money supply per worker. Substituting (16-37) and (16-38) into (16-36), we get

$$\dot{K}_e = n = \frac{a}{\lambda}(\dot{M} - n) + \frac{S}{K} \tag{16-39}$$

Equation (16-39) gives us the relation between monetary policy and the capital-labor ratio. Consider the inflationary case where $\dot{M} - n > 0$. The rate of monetary expansion raises the rate of inflation, $\dot{p}_e$ as specified by Eq. (16-38). This causes the first term on the right-hand side of Eq. (16-36)—the forced savings rate—to increase. However, since the rate of growth of the labor force, n, is exogenous, S/K must decline for the equality of both sides of the Eq. (16-39) to hold. Since S/K is in general negatively related to the capital-labor ratio,[7] a fall in S/K means an increase in the capital-labor ratio. This relationship is shown in Figure 16-5.

The rate of growth of the labor force is fixed at n_0, and S/K is drawn to be a decreasing function of k. If the rate of monetary expansion exceeds n, that is, $\dot{M} - n$ is positive, the equilibrium level of k will be greater than k_0. In short, the equilibrium capital-labor ratio which maintains steady-state growth is positively related to the rate of monetary expansion; the same result as in the neoclassical model, but opposite to that yielded by the simple Keynes-Wicksell model. Consider a numerical example, where

$$Y = \sqrt{KN}$$
$$s = 0.05$$
$$n = 0.02$$
$$a/\lambda = 0.50$$

[7] $S/K = \dfrac{S/Y}{K/Y} = \dfrac{s}{K/Y} = s\,\dfrac{Y/N}{K/N} = sy\,\dfrac{1}{k}$

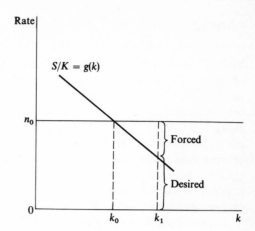

FIGURE 16-5
Monetary expansion and the capital-labor ratio.

Then, the equilibrium "k" is obtained as follows:

$$sf(k) = nk$$
$$(0.10)k^{1/2} = (0.02)k$$
$$k^{1/2} = 5$$
$$k = 25$$

The rate of monetary expansion associated with equilibrium steady-state growth in the example is found by substituting the values given above into Eq. (16-39):

$$0.02 = 0.50(\dot{M} - 0.02) + \frac{S}{K}$$

Writing S/K in terms of k, we get

$$\frac{S}{K} = \frac{sY}{K} = \frac{s\sqrt{KN}}{K} = s\sqrt{\frac{N}{K}} = \frac{s}{\sqrt{k}}$$

We get the rate of monetary expansion $\dot{M}$ as follows:

$$0.02 = 0.05(\dot{M} - 0.02) + \frac{0.05}{5}$$

$$\dot{M} = 0.04$$

In summary, the lower the savings rate, the greater the rate of growth of the money supply must be to achieve any desired k and output per worker. Forced savings can be used to fill the gap between the required savings and those forthcoming without monetary expansion.

CONCLUSION

In this chapter, we have examined four growth models with money: two neoclassical models, a simple Keynes-Wicksell model, and the Keynes-Wicksell model with an independent investment function. In neoclassical models we found that the effect of an increase in the rate of growth of money raises the capital-labor ratio although it becomes ambiguous when real balances enter into the utility function. On the other hand, in the simple Keynes-Wicksell model, an increase in the rate of growth of money causes the quantity of real balances per worker to increase, thus increasing wealth and consumption. The increase in consumption in turn reduces saving and thus the equilibrium capital-labor ratio. Finally, in the Keynes-Wicksell model with an independent investment function, greater monetary expansion, by increasing forced savings, increases the capital-labor ratio.[8]

Even though the direction of effect of monetary policy on output per worker (via the capital-labor ratio) is not unambiguous but depends on the specification of the model, it seems clear that money plays an important role in economic growth. Which model best fits the real world is still an open question.[9] In Table 16-1 the models and their implications are summarized for comparison.

Table 16-1   COMPARISON OF VARIOUS MONETARY GROWTH MODELS

Neoclassical models		Keynes-Wicksell models	
Tobin model	**Patinkin-Levhari model**	**Simple K-W model**	**K-W model with independent investment**
$[s - (1-s)bn]f(k)$ $= nk$	$\{s[1 + b(n + \dot p + r)] - bn\}f(k)$ $= nk$	$\dfrac{dk}{d\dot M} = \dfrac{a_{12}}{\mid A \mid}$	$\dot K = n = \dfrac{a}{\lambda}(\dot M - n) + \dfrac{S}{K}$
$\dot M \to \dot p \to b \to k$ $\uparrow \quad \uparrow \quad \downarrow \quad \uparrow$	$\dfrac{\partial k}{\partial \dot p} = \dfrac{-\sigma \dot p}{\dfrac{\sigma^2 a'(k)}{n} + \sigma_k}$	$\dot M \to k$ $\uparrow \quad \downarrow$	$\dot M \to \left(\dfrac{S}{K}\right) \to k$ $\uparrow \quad \downarrow \quad \uparrow$
	$\sigma \dot p = \mathrm{OSE}^* + \mathrm{CE}^{**}$		
	$\sigma_k =$ depends upon the interest-elasticity of money demand Assuming $\sigma \dot p > 0,\ \sigma_k < 0,$		
	$\dot M \to \dot p \to k$ $\uparrow \quad \uparrow \quad \uparrow$		

* Overall Savings Effect
** Composition Effect

[8] None of these models treats money as a factor of production. Money is held only by consumers for the transaction services it yields. The neoclassical model has been extended to cover this case by Levhari and Patinkin (1968).

[9] Recent critiques of monetary growth models challenge the view that money holdings are a substitute for holdings of physical capital. Stressing the importance of intermediation by financial institutions, they argue that inflation, by reducing the attractiveness of money holdings, *lowers* the rate of capital formation and rate of growth of output per capita. For details, see Shaw (1973) and McKinnon (1973).

READINGS FOR CHAPTER 16

ALLEN: *Mathematical Analysis for Economists* (New York: St. Martin's, 1968).

FOLEY, D. K., and M. SIDRAUSKI: "Portfolio Choice, Investment and Growth," *American Economic Review*, March 1970.

HAHN, F.: "On Money and Growth," *Journal of Money, Credit and Banking*, May 1969.

JOHNSON, H. G.: "The Neoclassical One-Sector Growth Model: A Geometrical Exposition and Extension to a Monetary Economy," *Economica*, August 1966.

————: "Money in a Neo-classical One-Sector Growth Model," in *Essays in Monetary Economics* (London: G. Allen, 1967).

LEVHARI, D., and D. PATINKIN: "The Role of Money in a Simple Growth Model," *American Economic Review*, September 1968.

MARTY, A. L.: "Notes on Money and Economic Growth," *Journal of Money, Credit and Banking*, May 1969.

MCKINNON, R. I.: *Money and Capital in Economic Development* (Washington: The Brookings Institution, 1973).

NEIHAUS, J.: "Efficient Monetary and Fiscal Policies in Balanced Growth," *Journal of Money, Credit and Banking*, April 1969.

PHELPS, E.: "Second Essay on the Golden Rule of Accumulation," *American Economic Review*, February 1965.

ROSE, H. B.: "Unemployment in a Theory of Growth," *International Economic Review*, September 1966.

SHAW, E. S.: *Financial Deepening in Economic Development* (New York: Oxford, 1973).

SIDRAUSKI, M.: "Inflation and Economic Growth," *Journal of Political Economy*, December 1967.

————: "Rational Choice and Patterns of Growth in a Monetary Economy," *American Economic Review*, 1957.

STEIN, J. L.: "Money and Capacity Growth," *Journal of Political Economy*, October 1966.

————: "Monetary Growth Theory in Perspective," *American Economic Review*, March 1970.

————: "Neoclassical and Keynes-Wicksell Monetary Growth Models," *Journal of Money, Credit and Banking*, May 1969.

TOBIN, J.: "A Dynamic Aggregate Model," *Journal of Political Economy*, April 1955.

————: "Money and Economic Growth," *Econometrica*, October 1965.

————: "Notes on Optimal Monetary Growth," *Journal of Political Economy*, 1968.

WALLICH, H. C.: "Money and Growth: A Country Cross-Section Analysis," *Journal of Money, Credit and Banking*, May 1969.

PART FOUR

Disequilibrium Macrotheory

17

LIMITATIONS OF EQUILIBRIUM MACROMODELS

The basic analytical framework in macroeconomic analysis is aggregate demand and supply. In Chapter 3, we discussed the aggregate demand function together with three different types of aggregate supply functions, those for the neoclassical, Keynesian, and intermediate cases. In the neoclassical- and intermediate-case models we have seen that prices must change if either the supply curve or the demand curve shifts. However, in the Keynesian model, a shift in the aggregate demand function alone cannot affect prices in the short run, because the supply curve is assumed to be horizontal—prices offered by suppliers are fixed in the short run.

The fixed-price hypothesis is the point of departure for macro disequilibrium theory. Although initiated by Keynes, the strength of this approach to macrotheory was not recognized until recently. Keynes's hypothesis of price rigidity together with his assumptions about the behavior of workers was interpreted by most economists to represent a special case of the real world. Recently, a more rigorous reinterpretation of Keynes's hypothesis has been made, and it has been argued that Keynes's propositions are not a special case but rather a general description of the aggregate market. Due to wage rigidity, monopoly elements, and like features pervasive in today's labor market, adjustment to full-employment equilibrium is not instantaneous but is delayed for a considerable period of time. Thus, although the ultimate equilibrium solution may be that suggested by the neoclassical- or intermediate-case models, if the adjustment is not instantaneous, then the whole body of macrotheory based upon the comparative-statics analysis must be revised, as well as the policy measures needed to achieve the targets of macropolicy.

Disequilibrium theory is mainly concerned with (1) the inability of prices— such as commodity prices, the interest rate, and the wage rate—to change freely in the short run, (2) modifications that should be made to the conventional general equilibrium theory of market adjustment with the hypothesis of such price rigidities, and (3) how this new model fits into the analysis of inflation and unemployment.

In this chapter, the conventional neoclassical general equilibrium model is briefly reviewed, and its limitations are discussed. The limitations shown in this chapter provide the theoretical foundation for the disequilibrium models to be presented thereafter. In Chapter 18, we will present Keynes's disequilibrium model of involuntary unemployment, concentrating on the relationship between the commodity and the labor market. In Chapter 19, the analysis will be extended to a multimarket model using the commodity, bond, and labor markets. Finally, in Chapter 20 we introduce some unique disequilibrium properties of the money demand function, and analyze how the real sector is affected by those properties of the money market, using the conventional *IS-LM* apparatus.

THE LIMITED-QUANTITY HYPOTHESIS

In the conventional general equilibrium macromodel two assumptions are usually made: (1) quantities are limited (or, in the extreme case, fixed) in the short run, while prices are completely flexible, and (2) transactions take place only at equilibrium prices.

The fixed-supply assumption dates back to Marshall, while the second is associated with the *tatonnement process* described by Walras. In this chapter, we will begin our discussion with a brief review of the Marshallian limited-quantity hypothesis. In the second section of the chapter, the Walrasian *tatonnement* process will be discussed. The final section outlines the limitations of conventional theory and the implication for disequilibrium models.

Marshall defines the short run to be a period of time during which the supply of specialized skills and ability of suitable machinery and appropriate industrial organization does not have time to be fully adapted to demand (Marshall, 1890, pp. 376ff.). During this period producers can only adjust their supply in response to increased demand by increasing the utilization of capital already at their disposal. However, at full capacity, the supply of the product cannot be increased to meet the increase in demand in the short run since capacity expansion can only be made in the long run.

In short, supply of commodities is thus limited in the short run—the supply curve is very inelastic. As aggregate demand increases, suppliers, in the absence of unused capacity, will react to this increase in demand by raising their prices on their own initiative to eliminate excess demand or leave it to consumers to bid up the price to clear the market. The length of time required to clear the market is assumed to be negligible.

Looking at the demand side, it is assumed that when excess demand exists, households realize that they cannot buy as much as they did at the previously prevailing prices. As a result they will bid up the price of the commodity until excess demand is eliminated. Assuming that households possess *perfect* and *immediate* information about the market, the time needed for reacting to the change in prices is therefore negligible.

Conventional theory thus assumes a fixed supply—full employment of capital —on the supply side and perfect information and knowledge on the demand side. The market is cleared by adjusting either prices or quantities demanded or both. Since quantities are assumed to be limited, the short-run market adjustment in the classical world depends entirely on the assumption of flexible prices.

Based on the fixed-quantity flexible-prices hypotheses, the equilibrium price can be determined using a simultaneous equation system where the quantity supplied is a given parameter and the quantity demanded is a function of the flexible prices. We have seen this simultaneous equation system in Chapter 3. Recall the neoclassical model with three markets: the commodity market, the money market, and the labor market. Reproducing Eqs. (3-12), (3-13), (3-51), and (3-56), we get in equilibrium

$$Y = C\left[Y(1 - \tau) - \frac{\overline{T}}{P}\right] + I(i) + \overline{G} \quad (3\text{-}12)$$

$$m\overline{H} = pL(Y, i) \quad (3\text{-}13)$$

$$Y = F(N, K_0) \quad (3\text{-}51)$$

$$f(N) = \phi(N) \quad (3\text{-}56)$$

This neoclassical system implies that the "real sector" equilibrium is determined first, thus providing us with the solutions for real output and employment [from Eqs. (3-51) and (3-56)]. Once the value for real output is found, equilibrium in the "demand sector" is determined. Since the quantity supplied is fixed, the variables to be adjusted are *prices* and the *interest rate*. Given N, Y, $\overline{G}$, $\overline{T}$, and τ, Eqs. (3-12) and (3-13) can be solved with respect to p and i. In other words, p and i must be flexible enough in order to guarantee instantaneously the full-employment general equilibrium in the system.

In Chapter 3 we discussed the effect of an exogenous disturbance, such as an increase in government purchases ($\overline{G}$), on p and i when it is introduced into the system already in equilibrium. Prices and the interest rate were presumed to change infinitely fast so that the full-employment equilibrium already obtained at Y and N can be maintained. Without repeating the derivation, we have

$$dp = \frac{-pL_i\, d\bar{G}}{C_{Y_d}\bar{T}pL_i/p^2 - m\bar{H}I_i}$$

$$di = \frac{-d\bar{G}(m\bar{H})}{C_{Y_d}\bar{T}pL_i/p^2 - m\bar{H}I_i}$$

The signs of both dp and di are positive. Therefore, according to the classical fixed-quantity hypothesis, the *flexibility of prices and the interest rate* is a necessary condition to keep the system always in general equilibrium.

THE TATONNEMENT HYPOTHESIS

Another important theoretical basis for conventional market-adjustment theory is the *tatonnement* process. Consider an *atomistic market* where many buyers and sellers competitively exist. There is no information center or price-announcing organization. Individuals are assumed to each have a preference function that sets the quantity-price relationships as they go to the marketplace. Their information is not perfect, and they do not know what prices other traders might ask for their commodities, and so the price they have in mind is not, in general, the equilibrium price. Therefore, they must "grope" for the market-clearing price by the process of trial and error. They do not actually trade until they reach the equilibrium price. Through the groping process households are led closer and closer to the general equilibrium. When the quantities of each good offered are equal to the quantities demanded, the equilibrium price is established and transactions are actually made. Prices and transactions once concluded by this process will remain constant until disturbed by exogenous forces.

The "groping process" has been called *tatonnement* by Walras. According to Walras, this process resembles that of a blindman feeling his way, since no one in the marketplace is presumed to know in advance the values of the parameters or the equilibrium solution (Jaffé, 1967).[1]

The market-clearing mechanism discussed by Walras can be shown by Figure 17-1, the Edgeworth-Bowley box diagram for the two-individual case. In Figure 17-1, $O_A GO_B$ is the contract curve, and curves EQ_A and EQ_B represent the offer curves of individuals A and B, respectively. Assume that individual A with endowment X_A of X and Y_A of Y believes that the prevailing price will be DE. In this case he would be willing to go to point U by supplying $X'_A X_A$ of X and demanding $Y'_A Y_A$ of Y. However, at this price, he will immediately find that individual B demands $X'_B X_B$ of

---

[1] Sometimes, a recontracting process is assumed where individuals keep revising their contracts (prices and quantities to be traded) until the market becomes cleared. Its result is the same as *tatonnement* since no actual transactions are made in the groping process.

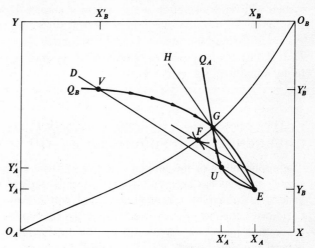

FIGURE 17-1
Illustration of the *tatonnement* process toward the general equilibrium solution.

X by supplying $Y'_B Y_B$ of Y. Since $X'_B X_B$ is greater than $X'_A X_A$ and $Y'_B Y_B$ is also greater than $Y'_A Y_A$, the market will have an excess demand for X and an excess supply of Y. This is the result of individual A's first "groping move." Realizing the market situation, individual A will revise his demand for Y and supply of X, probably by increasing both his supply of X and demand for Y. Individual B will react in the same way by curtailing both his demand for X and supply of Y.

Suppose both individual A and B meet at point F on the contract curve. At this point no transaction would be made. At the hypothetical price line drawn at this point with the mutual tangency between the indifference curves of both individuals, the market would not be cleared, because the price line would not go through the endowments (point E). Therefore, the two individuals, although they are continuously conjecturing and announcing their hypothetical prices, will meet at the general equilibrium point G, where transactions will actually be made for the first time. The *tatonnement* process can be represented in the graph by continuous movement from point U (for individual A) and point V (for individual B) to point G. In the process, prices will be revised repeatedly by trial and error until the equilibrium price is finally established.

A comparative-statics model needs the *tatonnement* hypothesis which provides a basis for assuming the solution for the new prices and quantities immediately obtained after an exogenous disturbance is introduced. For the limited-quantity–hypothesis case, discussed above, the *tatonnement* process implies that transition from one equilibrium state to a new equilibrium is made in a once-and-for-all fashion because no "intermediate transactions" are allowed to occur during the adjustment process. If we neglect analysis of what happens in between the two equilibria, the Walrasian system will yield a solution if the system is stable. However, if we are interested in the "in between"—the dynamic properties of the adjustment mechanism while the system is in disequilibrium—a model based upon *tatonnement* is of no help. *Tatonnement* is only a conceptual device to justify simplification of the real world's complexity in a comparative-statics model.

LIMITATIONS OF THE CONVENTIONAL MODEL AND THE EMERGENCE OF DISEQUILIBRIUM THEORY

The applicability of the limited-quantity and the *tatonnement*-hypothesis process to today's markets has been questioned in recent studies. In today's markets prices are, generally, quoted by manufacturers, and within limits it is the manufacturer who decides whether to raise or lower the initial offer price facing consumers. Since the production plan made by most firms for the current period is based on the market data of previous periods, it will remain the same for the entire period, and will only be revised at the end of the period if circumstances have changed. During the planning period, the manufacturer's planned prices (i.e., ex ante prices) may be treated as fixed. This planning period is generally referred to as the *short run*.

How would firms then react in the short run to a sudden unexpected increase in demand under the fixed-price policy? Because production is limited in the short run and the price is set by firms' ex ante plans, increased demand can only be met via adjustment in *inventories*. However, if inventory stocks are not sufficient to meet the increased demand, consumers will bid up the price until excess demand disappears. Thus, through changes in inventory positions and upward pressures on prices, firms are provided with ex post information upon which planning for the next period will be based.

The adjustment process of today's markets thus differs significantly from that implied by the Marshallian or Walrasian process. Ex ante prices may in effect be fixed during the planning period (the short run), but quantities are flexible through changes in inventory. The classical position is compared to the disequilibrium position in Figure 17-2. OP_0 is firms' ex ante price level and OQ_0 is their output at this price. Suppose that during the period, the price rises to a higher level than OP_0. At the higher price, firms will attempt to increase supply by using idle machines. This is the classical supposition depicted by a very inelastic supply curve RR.

Now consider the disequilibrium case. Prices, once determined (at the beginning of the period), will not be revised during the period. Prices can be adjusted and reannounced only by sellers at the beginning of the following period after they consider the ex post results of the current period. In Figure 17-2, the ex ante price is OP_0 and ex ante output is OQ_0. Consumers want to buy OQ_0' at the price of OP_0. $Q_0 Q_0'$ is the excess demand in this period, which may be satisfied by a reduction in inventories, assuming that firms carry sufficiently large amounts. Firms will increase the price only in the next period so that the long run supply curve may have a slope such as SS.

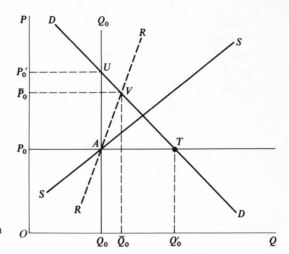

FIGURE 17-2
Comparison between the equilibrium
method and the disequilibrium method.

The disequilibrium theory also rejects the Walrasian proposition that transactions are not made until the short-run market equilibrium price is established.
Looking at today's market, it is not very convincing to argue that because individuals
are uncertain about what the equilibrium price will be, they simply sit and wait,
without buying or selling, until the price reaches the equilibrium level. In an atomistic
buyer's market where all buyers are price takers, it is very likely that individuals
would act in accordance with their presumptive "guess" as to the equilibrium price,
within the limits that their respective utility-maximization rules allow.

The possibilities of transactions being made in a disequilibrium state have been
recognized by Hicks (1939, pp. 192–202). He notes that actual transactions can occur
at "false prices" because individuals presume that the price they face is the best one
at the present situation. They will maximize their utility by purchasing some of the
product even if its price is not an equilibrium price. If this interpretation about the
market system is accepted, the *tatonnement* proposition should be replaced by a new
adjustment hypothesis, such that, even if a market is in disequilibrium, transactions
will take place at the disequilibrium price. These should occur in such a way that
only "one side" of the market, demand or supply—whichever is smaller—is satisfied.
If unsatisfied demands exist, prices tend to rise. If unsold supplies exist, prices tend
to fall, with no changes in prices made until firms can change their management
plans.

In sum, modern disequilibrium theory is mainly based on three suppositions:
(1) price is fixed during a planning period but quantity is flexible due to the existence
of inventories, (2) transactions are actually made even at disequilibrium prices, and
(3) either demand or supply will remain unsatisfied depending upon whether the
situation is one of excess demand or excess supply. These three propositions are
specially crucial in macromodel building because the adjustment system yielded by

these propositions is entirely different from that of the conventional general equilibrium system. First, disequilibrium models imply that, in the short run, the variable to be adjusted is not price but quantity. Second, due to false trading, *planned income* may be different from *realized income*. Third, in reaching the new equilibrium set of prices, individuals will take information costs into account. Information is no longer free, because the opportunity to be able to make trades must be given up while gathering information. Keynes's disequilibrium model focuses mainly on the first point. A new adjustment theory known as the *income-constrained process* (with distribution and spillover effects) is related to the second problem. The last proposition is discussed in the recent theory of resource unemployment. In the following chapters, these three propositions will be discussed more fully.

READINGS FOR CHAPTER 17

BAUMOL, W. J.: *Economic Dynamics*, 3d ed. (New York: Macmillan 1970).

BOLAND, L. A.: "Axiomatic Analysis and Economic Understanding," *Australian Economic Papers*, vol. 9, pp. 62–75, June 1970.

FRISCH, R.: "On the Notion of Equilibrium and Disequilibrium," *Review of Economic Studies*, vol. 3, pp. 100–105, 1935–1936.

HANSEN, B.: *Lectures in Economic Theory* (Lund, Sweden: studentlitteratur, 1969).

HAYEK, F. A.: *Individualism and the Economic Order* (London: Routledge, 1949).

HICKS, J.: *Value and Capital* (New York: Oxford, 1939).

———: *Capital and Growth* (New York: Oxford, 1965).

HOTELLING, H.: "Stability in Competition," *Economic Journal*, vol. 39, pp. 41–57, March 1929.

JAFFÉ, W.: "Walras' Theory of Tatonnement: A Critique of Recent Interpretations," *Journal of Political Economy*, vol. 75, pp. 1–19, February 1967.

KALDOR, N.: "A Classificatory Note on the Determinateness of Equilibrium," *Review of Economic Studies*, vol. 1, pp. 122–136, February 1934.

MACHLUP, F.: *Essays on Economic Semantics* (Englewood Cliffs, N.J.: Prentice-Hall, 1963).

MARSHALL, A.: *Principles of Economics* (London: Macmillan 1890).

MARTINDALE, D. (ed.): *Functionalism in the Social Sciences* (Philadelphia: American Academy of Political and Social Science, 1965).

NEWMAN, P.: "Approaches to Stability Analysis," *Economica*, vol. 28, pp. 12–29, February 1961.

NORTHROP, F. S. C.: *The Logic of the Sciences and Humanities* (New York: Macmillan, 1947), pp. 235–254.

RICHARDSON, G. B.: "Equilibrium, Expectations and Information," *Economic Journal*, pp. 223–237, June 1959.

SAMUELSON, P. A.: *Foundation of Economic Analysis* (Cambridge, Mass.: Harvard, 1947).

18

KEYNES'S DISEQUILIBRIUM MODEL:
THE TWO-MARKET CASE

The interrelationships between two separate markets during a disequilibrium period can best be explained by Keynes' model of the commodity and labor markets. Assuming that both the money and the bond market are always cleared, Keynes's adjustment mechanism can be described by the following propositions:

1 Firms, in the short run, always hold some inventory stock as a buffer to meet any unexpected change in demand.

2 Firms do not change the short-run price, even though excess demand exists, until the end of the planning period.

3 Firms offer the money wage rate that prevails in the labor market, but it is up to workers, depending upon their information and expectations, to accept it or reject it.

4 Firms' demand for labor depends upon the *real wage rate*—equal to the marginal product of labor—while the supply of labor depends upon the *money wage rate*. Workers are presumed to be ill-informed about the general price level but very sensitive to the absolute amount of their money income (money illusion exists).

$$N_d = f\left(\frac{w}{p}\right)$$
$$N_s = s(w)$$

5 The money wage rate is rigid downward but flexible in the upward direction.

We also assume no foreign sector or government sector.

Propositions 1 and 2 are the same as the disequilibrium hypothesis stated earlier in Chapter 17. In contrast to the classics, Keynes viewed the labor market as a disequilibrium-generating source and argued that the adjustment to equilibrium is not instantaneous or always guaranteed. Propositions 3, 4, and 5 are the kernel of the characteristics of the labor market adjustment that Keynes's model is based upon.

KEYNES'S LABOR MARKET DISEQUILIBRIUM MODEL

The aggregate relationships in the economy may be expressed in terms of the supply and demand equations in the *commodity, money, bond,* and *labor markets.* In the commodity market, the demand for commodities, consisting of the demand for consumer goods (C_{dc}) and working capital goods (C_{dk}), is given by

$$C_d = C_{dc} + C_{dk} \qquad (18\text{-}1)$$

Assume the demand for consumer goods in the current period, C_{dc}, is determined by real income and individuals' intertemporal preferences,

$$C_{dc} = C_{dc}(Y,i) \qquad (18\text{-}2)$$

where Y is real income and i represents the interest rate. The demand for working capital goods is also a function of real income and the rate of interest.

$$C_{dk} = C_{dk}(Y,i) \qquad (18\text{-}3)$$

When Eqs. (18-2) and (18-3) are substituted into (18-1), aggregate demand can be expressed as a function of Y and i:

$$C_d = C_d(Y,i) \qquad \frac{\partial C_d}{\partial Y} > 0 \qquad \frac{\partial C_d}{\partial i} < 0 \qquad (18\text{-}4)$$

The commodity supply function is given by the aggregate production function, which in the short run depends upon firms' labor employment. Thus, the aggregate supply of commodities can be written as a function of the demand for labor.

$$C_s = C_s(N_d) \qquad \frac{\partial C_s}{\partial N_d} > 0 \qquad \frac{\partial^2 C_s}{\partial N_d^2} < 0 \qquad (18\text{-}5)$$

The equilibrium condition in the commodity market is

$$C_d = C_s$$

or

$$C_d(Y,i) = C_s(N_d) \qquad (18\text{-}6)$$

In the money market, as we saw in Chapter 10, the money supply depends upon the money multiplier and the monetary base. We assume here that the multiplier is constant and the monetary base is an exogenous variable controlled by the central bank. Thus, the supply of money in real terms is

$$\frac{M_s}{p} = \frac{\overline{M}}{p} \qquad (18\text{-}7)$$

The demand for real money $(M/p)_d$ is assumed to be a function of real income and the interest rate as in the basic models of Chapter 3:

$$\left(\frac{M}{p}\right)_d = \left(\frac{M}{p}\right)_d (Y,i) \qquad \frac{\partial (M/p)_d}{\partial Y} > 0 \qquad \frac{\partial (M/p)_d}{\partial i} < 0 \qquad (18\text{-}8)$$

[handwritten: $i \uparrow \Rightarrow B_d \uparrow \Rightarrow \left(\frac{m}{p}\right)_d \downarrow$]

The equilibrium condition for the money market is

$$\left(\frac{M}{p}\right)_d = \frac{M_s}{p} \qquad (18\text{-}9)$$

The resources of households consist of actual holdings of money and bonds and current real income, and these initial resources are used for consumption and money balances and for purchasing bonds. The household budget constraint is then

[handwritten: Bond Purchasing]

$$Resources= \frac{M_0}{p} + \frac{B_0}{ip} + Y = \left(\frac{M}{p}\right)_d + \frac{B_d}{ip} + C_d$$

[handwritten: i is the interest rates.]

where B is the number of bonds, each bond being a perpetuity promising to pay \$1 per year. The demand for bonds in real terms (b^d) thus is

[handwritten: demand for bonds in real terms =]

$$b^d = \frac{B_d}{ip} = \frac{B_d}{ip}\left(Y, i, \frac{M_0}{p}, \frac{B_0}{ip}\right) \qquad (18\text{-}10)$$

$$\frac{\partial b^d}{\partial Y} > 0 \qquad \frac{\partial b^d}{\partial i} > 0 \qquad \frac{\partial b^d}{\partial (M_0/p)} > 0 \qquad \frac{\partial b^d}{\partial (B_0/ip)} < 0$$

Assuming that the real supply of bonds is exogenously given,

$$\frac{B_s}{ip} = \frac{\bar{B}}{ip} \qquad (18\text{-}11)$$

the equilibrium condition for the bond market is

$$\frac{B_d}{ip} = \frac{\bar{B}}{ip} \quad \text{[handwritten: } = \frac{B_0}{ip}\text{]} \qquad (18\text{-}12)$$

Finally, the labor market is specified in the following way. According to Keynes' proposition 4, the demand for labor is a function of real wage w/p,

$$N_d = N_d\left(\frac{w}{p}\right)$$

[handwritten: $\frac{w}{p} \Rightarrow Nd\downarrow$]

where

$$\frac{w}{p} = MP_N \quad \text{and} \quad \frac{\partial N_d}{\partial (w/p)} < 0 \qquad (18\text{-}13)$$

w denotes the money wage rate, and MP_N denotes the marginal product of labor. Since the supply of labor depends upon the individual's choice between income and leisure, the variables entering into the supply function are those included in the individual's utility function. The individual's first-hand information about what is going on in the labor market is the *money wage rate* (i.e., money income). On the basis of this information, he will decide on the amount of labor he will offer. Since he is subject to money illusion (proposition 4), the money wage rate rather than the real wage rate is relevant to his decision-making criterion.[1] The supply of labor, under money illusion, is

$$N_s = N_s(w) \qquad \frac{\partial N_s}{\partial w} > 0 \qquad (18\text{-}14)$$

The equilibrium condition for the labor market is

$$N_d = N_s \qquad (18\text{-}15)$$

In the above system of 12 equations—(18-4) to (18-15)—all 11 unknowns—C_d, C_s, M_d, $\overline{M}_s$, $\overline{B}_d$, $\overline{B}_s$, N_d, N_s, p, w, and i (one equation being redundant)—may be solved for using comparative statics. The Keynesian system, unlike that of the classics, does not, however, guarantee full-employment equilibrium; Keynes's model may contain disequilibrium-amplifying forces which prevent the system from adjusting itself to a stable equilibrium state. The disequilibrium forces are contained in his concepts of *involuntary unemployment* and the *expectation gap*.

Involunta ry Unemployment

Keynes's concept of involuntary unemployment is quite different from the classical frictional unemployment, and it plays a very crucial role in Keynes's macro adjustment process.[2] Although it is difficult to describe precisely the *norm* for judging voluntariness of individual behavior in the market, it may be defined with reference to behavior of an individual maximizing his utility under *normal* conditions (perfect competition, the normal income constraint, and prices that are normally determined). If some exogenous circumstance imposes an additional constraint on the individual, he is said to be acting involuntarily. Keynes's concept of involuntary unemployment is based upon this idea. As long as both the amount of labor demanded and supplied are located on the demand and supply curves, respectively, both parties are said to be acting voluntarily. Therefore, a state involving the voluntariness of both parties simultaneously is the general equilibrium state.

Involuntary unemployment is thus said to exist when an excess supply of labor

---

[1] The labor supply function is in this respect not homogeneous with the labor demand function. That is, the two functions depend upon totally different kinds of variables; the former depends upon the wage rate *perceived* by suppliers of labor services, whereas the latter depends upon the real wage rate that employers actually face.

[2] According to Keynes (1936, chap. 2), classical economists recognize only "voluntary" unemployment. Several kinds of unemployment are included in this category, such as frictional, seasonal, or institutional unemployment. Unemployment due to the lack of training and skills needed for jobs, or due to the cost of transferring from one job to another, or due to unions or minimum wage laws, is considered as voluntary by Keynes. It is because workers refuse or are unable to accept the jobs, and so they give up *a reward corresponding to the value of the product attributable to their marginal productivity*.

exists at the prevailing real wage rate, when the desires of both parties are not met. To illustrate, suppose that, due to some exogenous force, the labor market is disturbed so that either the demand side or the supply side (or both) is away from the original equilibrium position such that at the prevailing wage rate supply exceeds demand. If the adjustment in the labor market is made infinitely fast through the proper adjustment in wage rates, disequilibrium (involuntary unemployment) will be eliminated. According to Keynes, this will not be the case in the labor market because the money wage rate is rigid downward. There are three major behavioral reasons why the money wage rate may be inflexible downward. First, workers are assumed to resist any reduction in money wages, although they do not resist a reduction of real wages—due to money illusion. The assumption of "money illusion" on the part of workers presumes them to be ill-informed about the general price level while, on the other hand, they are very sensitive as to the absolute amount of their money income. Second, workers resist a reduction of money wages because they have inelastic expectations about wages. That is, they compare their reduced money wages with others' money wages and believe that there still exist many opportunities offering them the same money wage as before. They will thus reject the lower wage rate offered and remain unemployed until a new position offering the old wage rate is available. Third, wage bargaining, as Keynes points out, is carried on in terms of money wages. However, the money wage thus determined has different implications for the employer and the employee. The employer looks at the money wage deflated by the price level in relation to the marginal product of the worker, while the employee regards the money wage as his money income.[3]

These behavioral aspects make the supply side of the labor market very inflexible in adjusting when an excess supply of labor exists. Suppose a reduction in business activity during a recession period leads to a reduction in aggregate demand. Assume no monetary policy action is taken to offset this shift in demand (i.e., the money market and bond markets remain unaffected.) Firms' inventories must increase since production cannot be reduced in the short run. The continuous accumulation of unsold inventories will lead firms to revise their demand for labor. Two alternatives are open to business firms: (1) they may offer a real wage rate that is below the prevailing level for the same amount of labor input or (2) they may demand less input at the same real (and money) wage rate. The latter alternative is consistent with Keynes' proposition 5 stated earlier.

In spite of the reduction in the demand for labor, there is no change in the supply of labor. Since the money wage rate remains unaffected, workers are willing to supply the same quantity of labor that they supplied before. Using Equations (18-4)

$$C_d = C_d(Y, c)$$

[3] There is another justification for the inflexibility of the money wage rate recently made by A. A. Alchian (1969). He claims, "Workers' information-search progress gives rise to unemployment whenever they believe that the marginal benefit from it is greater than the marginal costs. He regards acquisition of information as an ordinary production activity, and thinks that faster acquisition (or greater acquisition within a given period) costs more. That is, the deeper the wage cut necessary to retain the old job, the greater the incentive to embark on a job information search while unemployed." Ibid., p. 118n.

to (18-6) and (18-13) to (18-15), we have the following two sets of equations depicting the initial and the new condition in the commodity and labor markets:

Initial equilibrium condition:

$$\text{(i)} \quad C_d(Y_1, i) = C_s(N_{d1}) \quad \textit{18-6}$$

$$\text{(ii)} \quad N_{d1} = N_d\left(\frac{w_1}{p_1}\right) \quad \textit{18-13}$$

$$\text{(iii)} \quad N_{s1} = N_s(w_1) \quad \textit{18-14}$$
$$\text{(iv)} \quad N_{d1} = N_{s1} \quad \textit{18-15}$$

Disequilibrium period:

$$\text{(i')} \quad C_d(Y_2, i) = C_s(N_{d2})$$

$$\text{(ii')} \quad N_{d2} = N_d\left[C_s(N_{d2}), \frac{w_1}{p_2}\right]$$

$$\text{(iii')} \quad N_{s2} = N_s(w_1)$$
$$\text{(iv')} \quad N_{d2} < N_{s2} \quad \textit{involuntary unemployment}$$

Equation (i') denotes the new equilibrium in the commodity market after the reduction in aggregate demand. Equation (ii') gives the revised demand for labor based on the new equilibrium level of supply in the commodity market. Equation (iii') is the same as (iii)—at the initial money wage rate w_1, N_{s2} is the same as N_{s1}. The last inequality (iv') implies that involuntary unemployment exists in the labor market,[4]

$$IU = N_{s2} - N_{d2}$$

where IU denotes the quantity of labor involuntarily unemployed.

The initial equilibrium condition and the disequilibrium position can be shown graphically. In Figure 18-1, the two systems of equations are represented in panels (a) to (e). In panel (a), the Keynesian aggregate demand curve is presented. C_{d1} is the initial aggregate demand curve, and C_1 and Y_1 are the full-employment equilibrium solutions for demand and output. The aggregate production function is depicted in panel (b). Y_1 in this panel represents the equilibrium output associated with $N_{s1}(=N_{d1})$ of labor shown in panel (c). In panel (d) the demand curve for labor is shown. Panel (e) is drawn for the convenience of converting the real wage rate to the money wage rate.

Let us start with the initial equilibrium condition. Points A to D in panels (a) to (d) indicate the initial equilibrium state where both the commodity and labor

---

[4] The last inequality characterizes Keynes's argument. In his system with *money*, the classical propositions such as Say's law are invalid because individual workers determine their notional plan for demand and supply in terms of their money income. Therefore, the sum of $n-1$ nonmoney excess demands in this monetary system is not necessarily identically zero. See Clower (1965) and Leijonhufvud (1968).

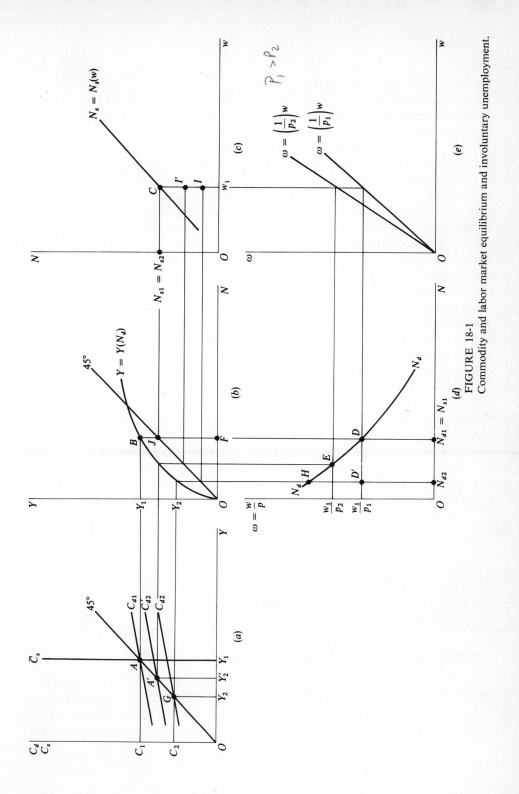

FIGURE 18-1
Commodity and labor market equilibrium and involuntary unemployment.

markets are cleared. The equilibrium real wage rate is w_1/p_1 [panel (d)], and the corresponding money wage rate is w_1. At these real and money wage rates the required amount of labor demanded to produce the equilibrium output Y_1 is equal to the amount of labor that workers are willing to supply. This is shown in panel (b). The 45° line was drawn in panel (b) to show equilibrium in the labor market; that is, $OF = FJ$, where FJ represents the equilibrium amount of labor supplied.

Now, assume that the full-employment equilibrium is disturbed by a downward shift in the aggregate demand function. In panel (a), C_{d1} shifts down to C_{d2}. Suppose that the money and bond markets remain in equilibrium so that the disturbance is geared only to the labor market.[5] Recall that, according to Keynes's propositions, prices are fixed during the short run and money wages are rigid downward. Firms are still paying the same real wage rate and accumulating inventory due to the reduction in demand. Firms, therefore, do not see any other short-run solution except to cut down production by reducing their demand for labor. In panels (a) and (b), Y_2 is the new production, and this is associated with N_{d2}, the new demand for labor shown in panel (d). Since Y_2 is less than the full-employment output Y_1, idle capacity as well as unemployed labor will exist. As long as the demand conditions in the commodity market continue to remain the same as described by C_{d2}, the corresponding demand schedule in the labor market will be given by the kinked curve N_dHD' instead of N_dHD in panel (d). But as long as w remains the same, the supply of labor will remain unaffected—$N_{s2} = N_{s1}$. The money wage rate will eventually adjust downward as workers realize that the downward shift in the aggregate demand is the general tendency (Keynes, 1936, p. 264; Leijonhufvud, 1968, pp. 95–97; Alchian, 1969), but will take time until workers take this general tendency for granted and accept a lower money wage rate. During this period of the rigid money wage rate, the amount of labor that workers are willing to supply is the same as the previous equilibrium supply:

$$N_{s2} = N_{s1}$$

The excess supply of labor is, therefore,

$$N_{d1} - N_{d2} = D'D$$

as shown in panel (d). This is Keynes's *involuntary unemployment*. Due to reduction in demand, workers are forced "off" their intended supply schedule. In panel (c) the involuntary point is point I, while at w_1 the intended supply is given by point C.

Adjustment from Involuntary Unemployment to Equilibrium

While both prices and money wages are assumed to be rigid in the short run, as time passes beyond the short run the price level cannot remain unchanged as firms cannot be expected to accumulate inventory indefinitely. Thus they are forced to offer a lower price in the next period. However, the money wage rate may or may not

---

[5] We will analyze the money and bond markets in Chapter 20 where the sticky disequilibrium state is produced due to the special characteristics of the money market.

adjust downward at the same rate as the price level. Money illusion or workers' inelastic expectations, or both, may cause the money wage rate to fall more slowly than the price level. In this section, we will examine the process of adjustment under three sets of assumptions regarding the relative rigidity of the money wage rate and the price level: (1) wages are assumed to be more rigid than prices but they are not absolutely rigid; (2) wages are absolutely rigid no matter what happens to the price level; and (3) both the money wage rate and prices are absolutely rigid.

In the state of involuntary unemployment, prices and wages will eventually fall unless some institutional restrictions, such as labor unions, exist, even if the fall is realized only after a long delay. If money wages are assumed to be more rigid than prices, as the price level falls, the real wage rate rises. Now suppose that the price level falls first, the money wage rate being the same. In panel (d) of Figure 18-1, the real wage rate rises from w_1/p_1 to w_1/p_2. Since real wage earnings are workers' real incomes, the aggregate demand for commodities will shift up from C_{d2} to C'_{d2} as the price level falls from p_1 to p_2. Because of this increased demand, firms are now willing to hire more workers by paying even a higher real wage rate, that is, w_1/p_2, because curve $N_d N_d$ is still the demand schedule for labor that firms are willing to be on. At this rate firms will be able to sell the full amount of their products, Y'_2, shown in panel (a). The commodity market has now restored equilibrium although the level of output is lower than the initial full-employment equilibrium output, Y_1. At point A' in panel (a) there is no excess of either actual or planned output. In the next round the money wage rate, which lags behind the price change, tends to fall. The new real wage rate is now less than w_1/p_2. At a lower real wage rate, firms will demand more labor, and hence the commodity supply curve will shift rightward causing (eventually) another fall in the commodity price. Workers' real income will further increase, and thereby C'_{d2} will shift further upward. If this process continues, the economy will move from A' to A in panel (a) and from E to D in panel (d), and so the same full-employment equilibrium will be reestablished with the money wage rate to its original level. The crucial point to remember is that the reestablishment of equilibrium in the Keynesian model is not instantaneous, as the classical economists presumed.

Now consider the case where money wages are absolutely rigid while prices are flexible. Since prices are permitted to fall, the first round of the real income effect will take place—the rise in the real wage rate again shifts the demand for output upward. The commodity market is equilibrated at A' and the labor market position moves from D' to E on the demand side while moving from I to I' on the supply side. The process is halted at this point with no further adjustment taking place. Because of the absolutely rigid money wage, the real wage rate cannot fall below w_1/p_2, and no further increment in the demand for labor would take place. At this wage rate, w_1/p_2, the labor market is not cleared—involuntary unemployment equal to $I'C$ in panel (C) exists. In the commodity market, the supply of output is below the original equilibrium level, a situation of an underemployment level of output. The system remains indefinitely in the state of *underemployment disequilibrium* as long as the real wage remains at w_1/p_2.

Finally, in the case where both prices and money wages are absolutely rigid, the system will not move at all toward full employment equilibrium. Points G, I, and D' in panels (*a*), (*c*), and (*d*), respectively, represent such situations. Firms will only produce OY_2 of output hiring ON_{d2} of labor with involuntary unemployment remaining at CI. Only when workers, realizing the disequilibrium situation, *voluntarily* accept a lower money wage rate will full equilibrium be restored.

The Expectation Gap

$$E(P_T) = f(P_z - 1) \quad (Firm)$$

Even in the absence of money illusion and wage rigidity, unemployment disequilibrium is still possible in the Keynesian system due to the "expectation gap." The expectation gap refers to the discrepancy between ex ante (planned) and ex post (realized) levels of income or prices of firms as well as individual consumers. Let us start with the firms. As we indicated earlier, a firm's production plan is made according to the ex post results of the previous period and expectations of the price and the quantity to be sold in the next period. Keynes (1936) classifies these expectations into two categories: short-term expectations and long-term expectations. Short-term expectations are concerned with "the price which a manufacturer can expect to get for his finished output at the time when he commits himself to starting the process which will produce it" (pp. 46–47). Long-term expectations are concerned with "what the entrepreneur can hope to earn in the shape of future returns if he purchases finished output as an addition to his capital equipment" (p. 47). In discussing the short-run market adjustment process, we will concern ourselves first type of expectation—short-run expectation.

A firm's short-run expectations with respect to the cost of output clearly determine the short-run quantity of labor demanded other factors being constant. However, a change in the firm's expectations in response to some unexpected changes in the market will only have its full effect on employment over a considerably long period of time. During an economic downturn, changes in expectations are not sufficiently rapid to cause a total cessation of production, while in an upturn, preparation time is needed before employment and output can reach the level the expectations dictate. Therefore, the effects of expectations on employment and on output must overlap each other over several periods so that the level of employment at any time depends not only upon the existing state of expectations but on the states of expectations which have existed over certain past periods (Keynes, 1936, p. 50).

$C = C(Sp)$ On the consumer side, short-run expectations are directly related to the individual's "dichotomized account of spending and saving decisions" (Clower, 1965, p. 117). That is, in deciding on how much to spend on current consumption, the individual has some perception of the income currently realized from the sale of his labor. Consumer spending is thus based upon the individual information-seeking behavior about this current income.

The individual's search for information about realizable income is similar to the *tatonnement* process. However, in Keynes's system, the search is not for price but for quantity. Since, as we noted earlier, prices and money wages are determined and announced by firms (and assumed to remain constant in the short run), the individual as a consumer and as a supplier of labor will react to these prices and determine the quantity demanded for commodities and the quantity of labor he is willing to supply. Assume that the commodity, money, and bond markets are in equilibrium. Now assume an excess supply of labor to exist in the labor market due to the lack of communication or the gap between successive expectations about the market situation. In this case what the income workers *realize* will be less than what they expected (ex ante), and consequently their demand for commodities will be reduced. A reduction in the demand for output will cause a contraction in production and subsequently a reduction in the demand for labor, and the system will be in disequilibrium.

In short, expectational errors may cause firms to overshoot or undershoot in their demand for labor, and thus they may end up away from the original demand curve for labor. Individuals' lack of correct information and their expectation gap also cause confusion on the supply side of the labor market, which together with demand errors, prevent the labor market from being cleared. Thus while the commodity, money, and bond markets are in equilibrium, the labor market is in disequilibrium.

Policies for Restoring Full-Employment Equilibrium

Disequilibrium in the labor market clearly will not remain isolated. Rather its effect is spread throughout the whole economy through its link to the commodity market. As we saw earlier, as labor income is reduced, aggregate demand for output will be reduced, and this reduces firms' derived level of output, and in turn, the demand for labor and further involuntary unemployment can be created. Therefore a tenacious disequilibrium state in the labor market will lead to further deterioration in the labor market unless policy measures are undertaken to remove the sources of disequilibrium. Both monetary and fiscal policy can be used for this purpose, but the effectiveness of these policies, as will be seen below, depends upon the degree of rigidity of prices and money wages.

First, consider the case where both prices and money wages are absolutely rigid. Assume that, for some reason, the aggregate demand curve shifts down from C_{d1} to C_{d2} in Figure 18-2. This results in involuntary unemployment in the labor market shown by $N_{d1} N_{d2}$ in panel (c) of Figure 18-2. This involuntary unemployment cannot be removed through market adjustments because of the assumption of absolutely rigid prices and money wages. To eliminate disequilibrium ($N_{d1} N_{d2}$) from the labor market, a monetary policy is adopted where the money supply is increased from the initial amount M_s to, say, $2M_s$. Since both prices and money wages are assumed to be perfectly rigid, the increase in the quantity of money will have no effect on either wages or prices. Instead, due to the increase in the stock of real money from M_s/p to $2M_s/p$, the interest rate will fall, and according to Eq. (18-4), aggregate demand will shift up toward its original position A. This process will continue until the equilibrium interest rate and output levels are reached. This is shown in Figure 18-2 using the

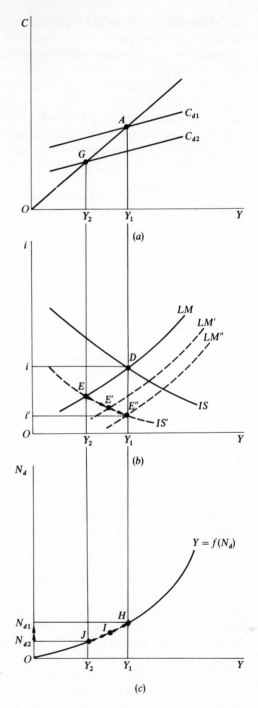

FIGURE 18-2
Effect of monetary policy on labor market adjustment.

IS-LM apparatus. In panel (*b*), the fall in aggregate demand shifts the *IS* curve down to *IS'* and the equilibrium level of output moves from *D* to *E*. However, the increase in the money supply shifts the *LM* curve rightward, causing the interest rate to fall and aggregate demand to increase, as manifested by a movement along the *IS'* curve toward *E"*. *E"* can only be reached if the expansion of the money supply is sufficiently large to push the interest rate down to *i'*. That is, the required change in the money supply must be large enough to shift the *LM* curve in a once-and-for-all fashion to *LM"* to restore equilibrium to the original position. At *E"*, employment is restored to the original level, and involuntary unemployment is eliminated.

Suppose that prices are less rigid than in the previous case, while money wages are absolutely rigid. In this case a partial adjustment toward equilibrium through the autonomous price mechanism takes place; the excess supply eventually forces down the price level (even if it is only after a long delay), and subsequently creates the real income effect even in absence of any policy action. This is shown in Figure 18-2 by the partial outward shift of the *LM* curve to *LM'* [panel (*b*)]. Through the price adjustment, involuntary unemployment is partly eliminated, because the economy is at *E'* in panel (*b*); the corresponding position on the production function is *I* in panel (*c*). But once the economy arrives at *E'*, there are no further autonomous adjusting forces because the money wage rate is absolutely fixed.[6] An increase in the supply of money will provide the needed stimulus to the system. In this case the monetary expansion required to restore equilibrium is not as large as in the previous case. Thus when prices are flexible but wages are absolutely rigid, monetary policy complements the price-adjustment mechanism, accelerating the speed of adjustment toward equilibrium.

Finally, consider the case where both prices and wages are not absolutely sticky but only adjust downward with lags. The automatic adjustment will work to restore the initial full-employment equilibrium, but it may be too slow. In this case, monetary policy can stimulate the adjustment, as in the previous case, through both prices and wages. It raises the speed of adjustment because both the production and the consumption sectors react promptly not only to the change in prices and wages but also to the change in the interest rate due to monetary policy. An appropriate monetary policy can therefore eliminate involuntary unemployment quickly.

The effectiveness of monetary policies discussed here depends of course upon elasticity of the demand for real balances with respect to the interest rate. As discussed in Chapters 3 and 9, the (absolutely) larger that this elasticity is, the less powerful monetary policy is in affecting aggregate demand and vice versa.

Fiscal policy may also be used to eliminate involuntary unemployment by shifting the *IS* curve up or down with the fixed *LM* curve. The analytical framework is much the same as in the case of monetary policy. In Chapter 20 the effectiveness of monetary and fiscal policy will be examined for cases where the system is bound by special elasticity conditions.

---

[6] Refer to the same case in the section on adjustment from involuntary unemployment characterized by point *E* in panel (*d*) of Figure 18-1.

READINGS FOR CHAPTER 18

ALCHIAN, A. A.: "Information Costs, Pricing, and Resource Unemployment," *Western Economic Journal*, vol. 7, pp. 107–129, June 1969.

ALLEN, R. G. D.: *Macro-Economic Theory—A Mathematical Treatment* (London: St. Martin's, 1968).

CLOWER, R. W.: "Keynes and the Classics: A Dynamical Perspective," *Quarterly Journal of Economics*, vol. 74, pp. 318–323, May 1960.

———: "The Keynesian Counterrevolution: A Theoretical Appraisal," in F. H. Hahn and R. P. R. Brechling (eds.), *The Theory of Interest Rates* (London: Institute of Economic Affairs, 1965), pp. 103–125.

DAVIDSON, P.: "A Keynesian View of Patinkin's Theory of Employment," *Economic Journal*, vol. 77, pp. 559–578, September 1967.

GROSSMAN, H. I.: " 'Was Keynes a Keynesian'?—A Review Article," *Journal of Economic Literature*, vol. 10, pp. 26–30, March 1972.

HANSEN, A. H.: *A Guide to Keynes* (New York: McGraw-Hill, 1953).

HICKS, J.: *Capital and Growth* (New York: Oxford, 1965).

KEYNES, J. M.: *The General Theory of Employment, Interest, and Money* (New York: Harcourt, Brace & World, 1936).

KURIHARA, K. K.: "Real Balances, Expectations, and Employment," *Economic Journal*, vol. 70, pp. 320–324, June 1960.

LEIJONHUFVUD, A.: *On Keynesian Economics and the Economics of Keynes* (New York: Oxford, 1968).

MISHAN, E. J.: "The Demand for Labor in a Classical and Keynesian Framework," *Journal of Political Economy*, vol. 72, pp. 610–616, December 1964.

PATINKIN, D.: "Involuntary Unemployment and the Keynesian Supply Function," *Economic Journal*, vol. 59, pp. 360–383, September 1949.

———: *Money, Interest, and Prices* (New York: Harper & Row, 1965), chap. 13.

PESEK, B. P., and T. R. SAVING: *Money, Wealth and Economic Theory* (New York: Macmillan, 1967).

RICHARDSON, G. B.: "Equilibrium, Expectations and Information," *Economic Journal*, pp. 223–237, June 1959.

TOBIN, J.: "Money Wage Rates and Employment," in S. E. Harris (ed.), *The New Economics: Keynes' Influence on Theory and Public Policy* (New York: Knopf, 1947), pp. 572–587.

19

DISTRIBUTION AND SPILLOVER EFFECTS

In the previous chapter we analyzed a disequilibrium model incorporating Keynes's propositions of rigidities in prices and money wages, suppliers of labor reacting to money wages rather than real wages, and the existence of inelastic expectations. These factors were shown to provide an explanation for involuntary unemployment. Attention was centered on the adjustment properties of the labor market with varying degrees of price flexibility in the commodity market.

In this chapter, we expand our analytical base to a multimarket model, which permits analysis of the interrelationships among markets where disequilibrium exists. For the moment, we restrict ourselves to the commodity, bond, and labor markets. The money market is put aside.

If we allow false trading and drop the *tatonnement* hypothesis, excess demand or excess supply in one market may affect prices in other markets.

Such intermarket pressures take two forms: *distribution effects* and *spillover effects*. Distribution effects arise if market excess demand functions depend on the *array* of assets, the amounts of commodities, bonds, or leisure held by each individual, not just on the *aggregate* amounts. With distribution effects, transactions at false prices cause the individual's holdings of each of those assets to change, thus causing the market excess demand functions to shift.

Spillover effects arise when the individual's demand for commodities, bonds, or leisure is a function of prices and *realized income*—the amount actually received—rather than *notional income*—the amount he would receive in an equilibrium situation. With spillover effects, the conventional equilibrium model must be revised so that the excess demand function for one good depends upon excess demands existing in other markets.

In the following sections we study the implications of distribution and spillover effects in a disequilibrium model. First, we examine how they change the equilibrium solution itself and then how they affect the movement of the price level, the wage rate, and the interest rate during the adjustment toward equilibrium.

DISTRIBUTION EFFECTS

If false trading is allowed to occur during disequilibrium, two fundamental changes must be made in conventional equilibrium theory: (1) Since the individual is now allowed to change his stock of commodities, bonds, and leisure through exchange in a disequilibrium state, his demand, which is a function of prices and the distribution of the three goods among individuals, will be successively revised; (2) when there is excess supply in a particular market, only the demand side is satisfied, and when excess demand exists, only the supply side is satisfied.

Consider a market in a disequilibrium state—excess demand exists at the prevailing price level. Even though excess demand exists, suppliers are satisfied because they can dispose of as much of their stocks as they desire through false trading. False trading produces a change in stocks of the three goods (commodities, bonds, and leisure) held by each individual. Since the demand for each good depends on prices and the array of holdings of stocks of the three goods, the change in distribution of them causes the demand functions to shift. The shift in the demand function for each good causes prices to change inversely with the aggregate stock of that good. This is what we call *distribution effects*. We proceed now to a more rigorous analysis of the properties and directions of macroadjustment when distribution effects are operative.

For convenience, let us label commodities, bonds, and leisure as commodities 1, 2, and 3, respectively. Now, we formulate the demand function for the *j*th commodity by the *i*th individual. Since demand is a function of prices and the *distribution* of commodities, we get

$$F_{ij}(p, \overline{Y}) = 0 \qquad (i = 1, \ldots, m) \qquad (19\text{-}1)$$
$$(j = 1, 2, 3)$$

where p is a positive price vector $p = (p_1, p_2, p_3)$ and $\overline{Y}$ is a matrix denoting the stock of commodities among individual participants; i.e.,

$$\overline{Y} = \begin{bmatrix} \overline{Y}_{11} & \overline{Y}_{12} & \overline{Y}_{13} \\ \vdots & \vdots & \vdots \\ \overline{Y}_{m1} & \overline{Y}_{m2} & \overline{Y}_{m3} \end{bmatrix}$$

The first subscript denotes the number of the individual, and the second subscript indicates the number of the commodity. For example, $\overline{Y}_{12}$ is holdings of bonds by individual 1. Equation (19-1) implies that the demand for the jth commodity by the ith individual depends upon the prices of all commodities and the stocks of all commodities held by all individuals.

Suppose that price adjustment is proportional to excess demand, and the nth commodity is used as the numeraire (i.e. $p_n = 1$), so that the amount of excess demand itself represents the change in price in terms of p_n. Thus,

$$\dot{p} = \frac{dp_j}{dt} = F_j(p, \overline{Y}) - \overline{Y}_j'$$

$$\dot{p} = \frac{dp_j}{dt} = Y_j - \overline{Y}_j \qquad (j = 1, 2, 3)$$

(19-2)

where Y_j is total demand for and $\overline{Y}_j$ is total stock (i.e., supply) of the jth commodity.[1]

Assume also that no production activity takes place during the period of disequilibrium so that the endowment of any commodity in the system as a whole is constant. Thus,

$$\sum_{i=1}^{m} F_{ij}(p, \overline{Y}) = 0 \qquad (j = 1, 2, 3) \qquad (19\text{-}3)$$

and

$$\sum_{i=1}^{m} \dot{\overline{Y}}_{ij} = 0 \qquad (j = 1, 2, 3) \qquad (19\text{-}4)$$

where

$$\dot{\overline{Y}}_{ij} = \frac{d\overline{Y}_{ij}}{dt} \qquad (i = 1, \ldots, m) \qquad (19\text{-}5)$$

Equations (19-3) and (19-4) imply that the stocks of commodity j held by different individuals in any period can only change in that period via the change of their demand for that commodity. Equation (19-5) implies that an individual's demand for the jth commodity in a period determines the change in his endowment of the jth commodity in that period.

Finally, let us introduce our *non-tatonnement* assumptions that when excess demand exists, only the supply side is satisfied, and when excess supply exists, only the demand side is satisfied. This means that if any supplier in any market is left unsatisfied, then the market as a whole is said to be in excess supply; with prices given, all possible exchanges are instantaneously effected in a "first come, first served" basis. This leads us to the following assumption:

If $Y_{ij} - \overline{Y}_{ij} \neq 0$, then the sign $(Y_{ij} - \overline{Y}_{ij}) = $ sign $(Y_j - \overline{Y}_j)$ for all i and j; and if $Y_j - \overline{Y}_j = 0$, then $Y_{ij} - \overline{Y}_{ij} = 0$ for all i.

That is, if the amount of good j that individual i wants, Y_{ij}, is less than the amount that he holds, $\overline{Y}_{ij}$, then $Y_{ij} - \overline{Y}_{ij} < 0$—the supply side is not satisfied. In this

---

[1] Put another way, we assume that the speed of adjustment is equal to unity.

case, there exists excess supply for the jth good, and while individuals on the demand side are satisfied, some suppliers are not [sign $(Y_{ij} - \overline{Y}_{ij}) = $ sign $(Y_j - \overline{Y}_j) < 0$].

In addition to the above assumption, we assume that for an individual to obtain something, he must offer, in return, something of equal value. Such an exchange will not alter the value of the commodity stocks held by an individual. That is

$$\sum_{j=1}^{3} p_j \dot{\overline{Y}}_{ij} = \sum_{j=1}^{3} p_j F_{ij}(p, \overline{Y}) = 0 \qquad (19\text{-}5a)$$

$$(i = 1, \ldots, m)$$

Using these assumptions, let us analyze what happens to "aggregate utility" in a state of disequilibrium with *non-tatonnement* false trading. From the individual's budget constraint, we have

$$\sum_{j=1}^{3} P_j(Y_{ij} - \overline{Y}_{ij}) = 0 \qquad (19\text{-}6)$$

that is, an individual's aggregate excess demand over *all* commodities $(j = 1, 2, 3)$ must be zero. In order to investigate a change in an individual's real income over time, we differentiate Eq. (19-6) with respect to time; that is, with n markets in general,

$$\sum_{j=1}^{n} p_j(\dot{Y}_{ij} - \dot{\overline{Y}}_{ij}) + \sum_{j=1}^{n} \dot{p}_j(Y_{ij} - \overline{Y}_{ij}) = 0 \qquad (19\text{-}7)$$

From Eq. (19-2), we know

$$\sum_{j=1}^{n} \dot{p}_j(Y_j - \overline{Y}_j) > 0 \qquad (19\text{-}8)$$

because $\dot{p}_j$ and $(Y_j - \overline{Y}_j)$ move in the same direction. From the "first come, first served" assumption above we know that

$$\text{Sign } (Y_j - \overline{Y}_j) = \text{sign } (Y_{ij} - \overline{Y}_{ij})$$

Therefore, the second term in Eq. (19-7) becomes

$$\sum_{j=1}^{n} \dot{p}_j(Y_{ij} - \overline{Y}_{ij}) > 0 \qquad (19\text{-}9)$$

Using Eqs. (19-7) and (19-9), the first term must be negative.

$$\sum_{j=1}^{n} p_j(\dot{Y}_{ij} - \dot{\overline{Y}}_{ij}) < 0 \qquad (19\text{-}10)$$

or

$$\sum_{j=1}^{n} p_j \dot{Y}_{ij} - \sum_{j=1}^{n} p_j \dot{\overline{Y}}_{ij} < 0 \qquad (19\text{-}11)$$

Considering Eq. (19-5a), Eq. (19-11) becomes

$$\sum_{j=1}^{n} p_j \dot{Y}_{ij} < 0 \qquad (19\text{-}12)$$

This is the *distribution effect*. Equation (19-12) says that in a disequilibrium period the change in the total value of transactions realized by an individual through

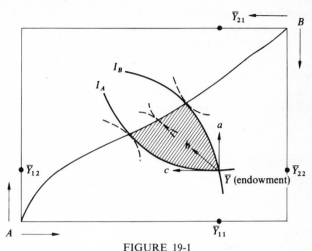

FIGURE 19-1
Effect of distribution effects on welfare.

false trading is negative. The individual's income is reduced in terms of the value of the numeraire if he was initially at the endowment point.

Thus, *non-tatonnement* false trading reduces the utility of at least one individual, and so society is unambiguously "worse off" than otherwise.[2] In the case of two individuals and two commodities, for example, they are most likely trading outside the shaded Pareto-efficiency region shown in Figure 19-1.

Let $\overline{Y}$ denote the society's total endowments of goods 1 and 2. I_B denotes the indifference curve of individual B passing through $\overline{Y}$. I_A is that of individual A. If both individuals, through their false trading, moved in a direction such as toward b, the aggregate utility would be greater than at $\overline{Y}$. However, as Eq. (19-12) indicates, they must have moved in the direction of a or c.

In summary, if false trading takes place in the market, it gives rise to *distribution effects* through changes in individuals' endowments. These distribution effects lead the economy to a worse position with respect to the utility of at least one individual and thus society as a whole may be worse off. This is a significant deviation from

---

[2] This can be shown as follows: Suppose that the society's aggregate utility is written as

$$V = \sum_{i=1}^{m} U_i(Y_{i1}, Y_{i2}, \ldots, Y_{in})$$

where Y_{ij} is the amount of consumption of the jth commodity by the ith individual. Differentiating this equation with respect to time, we have

$$\sum_{i=1}^{m} \sum_{j=1}^{n} \left(\frac{U_i}{Y_{ij}}\right) \dot{Y}_{ij} = \sum_{i=1}^{m} \lambda_i \sum_{j=1}^{n} p_j \dot{Y}_{ij} < 0$$

where λ_i is the marginal utility of income, a positive function of t. From Eq. (19-12), we get $\sum_{j=1}^{n} p_j \dot{Y}_{ij} < 0$. Therefore, the time differentiation above is negative.

neoclassical general equilibrium theory. Due to distribution effects that occur during the disequilibrium period, the economy may diverge forever from the conventional general equilibrium solution.

Either monetary or fiscal policy is inevitably needed in this case to achieve an efficient solution. To ensure that trading takes place *inside* the shaded area in Figure 19-1, monetary or fiscal policy must be used to *quickly* eliminate any disequilibrium and the false trading and distribution effects that follow.

SPILLOVER EFFECTS

When false trading is allowed to occur in disequilibrium, spillover effects also may occur.[3] A spillover effect is defined as an income effect transferred to different markets due to discrepancies between an individual's *planned* and *realized* transactions. Suppose there are three markets: A, B, and C. Suppose further that an individual plans to buy quantity Q_A of commodity A, Q_B of commodity B, allocating his planned or expected income from sales of Q_C, given his utility function. Assume that market C is disturbed for some reason or another and it is in an excess supply situation. An individual's planned (or expected) income now cannot be realized, because he cannot sell as much of commodity C as he planned to. In this case, individuals on the demand side are satisfied, but suppliers, such as this individual, are not. With less income than he expected, this individual must revise his purchasing plan. He can buy only Q'_A and Q'_B which must be less than Q_A and Q_B. Therefore, markets A and B are also disturbed, and they tend to be in excess supply in terms of *planned quantities* of demand and supply.

Spillover effects have two features that make it essential to revise the conventional general equilibrium macromodel. First, when they occur, we must reinterpret intermarket relationships. That is, if there are n markets in the system and one market is in excess supply, as illustrated above, the other $(n - 1)$ markets are also initially driven into an excess supply situation. And, in the aggregate, the excess demand function for any one commodity will have, as arguments, the *excess demands realized in the other markets*.

A Macromodel with Spillover Effects

Let us formulate a macromodel with spillover effects. From now on we use the term *notional* demand or supply for planned or expected demand and supply and the term *effective* demand or supply for the realized or actual quantities traded. Assume there are three markets: those for commodities, bonds, and labor (instead of leisure).[4]

Suppose there is an excess demand for commodities; households cannot satisfy

---

[3] This type of intermarket effect was originally recognized by Patinkin (1965) and reinterpreted by Clower (1965) and Leijonhufvud (1968). It was developed further by Barro and Grossman (1971) and Tucker (1972).

[4] For simplicity, we assume that changes in the price level have no effect on the community's real wealth. Thus, the money market is put aside in this chapter.

their notional demand for commodities at the prevailing price level. Therefore, they will spend their unused income either to buy bonds or to bid up the commodity price, or both. In the bond market an excess demand for bonds would occur due to the transferred demand from the commodity market (assuming the bond market to have been initially in equilibrium). Assume that bond prices are as inflexible as commodity prices. The excess demand arising in the bond market will only partly cause bond prices to rise. The large part of the excess purchasing power will then return to the commodity market. When we introduce the labor market, the spillover will affect all markets until a new equilibrium is established.

Excess demand in a given market can be divided into two components: *Primary excess demand* and *spillover excess demand.* Primary excess demand (or excess supply, if excess demand is negative) is the excess demand with which most equilibrium theory is concerned, which occurs due to the discrepancy between the prevailing and the equilibrium price *in that market.* Spillover excess demand is purchasing power transferred from other markets which are in disequilibrium, and thus must be a function of *all* price variables. Generally, spillover excess demand X^t can be written as

$$X^t = X^t(Y^d - Y^s)$$
$$= X^t[Y^d(\pi; \alpha) - Y^s(\pi; \beta)]$$
$$= X^t(\pi; \alpha, \beta)$$

where Y^d and Y^s are, respectively, notional demand for and realized supply of *other* commodities, π is a vector of price variables, and α and β are other (predetermined) variables.

Now let us spell out the macromodel with these concepts in mind. The following symbols will be used:

p = commodity price level
i = rate of interest
ω = real wage rate
M_0^H = initial money holdings of the household sector
M_0^F = initial money holdings of the production sector
$M_0 = M_0^H + M_0^F$

$\dfrac{M_0^H}{p}, \dfrac{M_0^F}{p} = M_0^H$ and M_0^F in real terms

C^d, B^d, N^d = notional demand for commodities, bonds, and labor
C^s, B^s, N^s = actual quantities demanded of commodities, bonds, and labor
$b^s, b^d = B^d, B^s$ in real terms (i.e., deflated by ip)
C^t, B^t, N^t = transferred demand spilled over to the commodity, bond, and labor markets
y = real income

The predetermined variables α and β in the general discussion above are the appropriate components of real money balances—M_0^H/p and M_0^F/p—and real income y.

When primary and spillover excess demands are combined, the following system of simultaneous aggregate excess demand functions is established:

$$ED_c = C^d\left(p, i, \omega; \frac{M_0{}^H}{p}, y\right) - C^s\left(p, i, \omega; \frac{M_0{}^F}{p}, y\right) + C^t(p, i, \omega) \qquad (19\text{-}13)$$

$$ED_b = b^d\left(p, i, \omega; \frac{M_0{}^H}{p}, y\right) - b^s\left(p, i, \omega; \frac{M_0{}^F}{p}, y\right) + b^t(p, i, \omega) \qquad (19\text{-}14)$$

$$ED_n = N^d\left(p, i, \omega; \frac{M_0{}^F}{p}, y\right) - N^s\left(p, i, \omega; \frac{M_0{}^H}{p}, y\right) + N^t(p, i, \omega) \qquad (19\text{-}15)$$

where ED_c, ED_b, and ED_n are the excess demands for commodities, bonds, and labor, respectively. In each equation above, the first two terms on the right-hand side represent the primary excess demand, and the last indicates the spillover excess demand transferred from other markets until the system arrives at general equilibrium. The difference between the conventional equilibrium model and the spillover model is this last term in the excess demand equations. The spillover forces are explicitly introduced in the spillover model as a function of price variables since it was assumed for simplicity that disequilibrium occurs only because of false prices.

Consider now the conditions under which the spillover demands are positive, negative, or zero. If the primary excess demand for commodities is positive, one of the following three cases must apply to the other markets:

(i) $b^t = 0$ $N^t > 0$ Spillover is to the labor market
(ii) $b^t > 0$ $N^t = 0$ Spillover is to the bond market
(iii) $b^t > 0$ $N^t > 0$ Spillover is to both markets

We can express the spillover demand functions as

$$C^t = C^t(p, i, \omega)$$
$$b^t = b^t(p, i, \omega)$$
$$N^t = N^t(p, i, \omega)$$

The sign properties of each spillover demand with respect to the price variables are[5]

$$\frac{\partial C^t}{\partial p} \leq 0 \qquad \frac{\partial C^t}{\partial i} \geq 0 \qquad \frac{\partial C^t}{\partial \omega} \leq 0$$

$$\frac{\partial b^t}{\partial p} \leq 0 \qquad \frac{\partial b^t}{\partial i} \geq 0 \qquad \frac{\partial b^t}{\partial \omega} \leq 0 \qquad (19\text{-}16)$$

$$\frac{\partial N^t}{\partial p} \leq 0 \qquad \frac{\partial N^t}{\partial i} \geq 0 \qquad \frac{\partial N^t}{\partial \omega} \leq 0$$

---

[5] In order to determine these nine signs, the following set of combinations of partial derivatives was used for the commodity market:

$$\underset{(+)\ \ (+)\ \ (-)}{\frac{\partial C^t}{\partial p} = \frac{\partial C^t}{\partial ED_o} \frac{\partial ED_o}{\partial ED_c} \frac{\partial ED_c}{\partial p}} < 0 \qquad \underset{(+)\ \ (+)}{\frac{\partial C^t}{\partial i} = \frac{\partial C^t}{\partial ED_b} \frac{\partial ED_b}{\partial i}} > 0$$

$$\underset{(+)\ \ (-)}{\frac{\partial C^t}{\partial \omega} = \frac{\partial C^t}{\partial ED_N} \frac{\partial ED_N}{\partial \omega}} < 0$$

and so on for the other markets. ED_o denotes the excess demands in *other* markets.

The equality sign denotes the possibility of a "one-to-one" spillover: the excess demand or supply in one market affects only one of the others.

Interaction between the Commodity and Bond Markets

Let us first investigate the direction of adjustment of prices and the rate of interest. Rewriting Eq. (19-13), we have

$$C^d\left(p, i, \omega; \frac{M_0^H}{p}, y\right) + C^t(p, i, \omega) = C^s\left(p, i, \omega; \frac{M_0^F}{p}, y\right) \qquad (19\text{-}17)$$

Let us assume that the labor supply is exogenous and that the demand for labor depends only upon the real wage rate ω so that the labor market is always cleared regardless of the price level. This assumption enables us to investigate the direction of adjustment of the price level in two cases: when the bond market has excess demand (EDB) and when it has excess supply (ESB).

Equation (19-17) implies the case of EDB, where the spillover demand for commodities from the bond market, i.e., the C^t function, is positive. In the case of ESB, C^t must have a negative sign. Differentiating both sides of Eq. (19-17) totally and dividing by dp, we have

$$C_p^{\,d} + C_i^{\,d}\left(\frac{di}{dp}\right) + C_\omega^{\,d}\left(\frac{d\omega}{dp}\right) - C_m^{\,d}\left(\frac{M_0^H}{p^2}\right) + C_y^{\,d}\left(\frac{dy}{dp}\right) + C_p^{\,t}$$

$$+ C_i^{\,t}\left(\frac{di}{dp}\right) + C_i^{\,t}\left(\frac{d\omega}{dp}\right)$$

$$= C_p^{\,s} + C_i^{\,s}\left(\frac{di}{dp}\right) + C_\omega^{\,s}\left(\frac{d\omega}{dp}\right) - C_m^{\,s}\left(\frac{M_0^F}{p^2}\right) + C_y^{\,s}\left(\frac{dy}{dp}\right) \qquad (19\text{-}18)$$

where $\qquad C_m^{\,d} = \partial C^d \big/ \partial\left(\dfrac{M_0^H}{p}\right) \qquad$ and $\qquad C_m^{\,s} = \partial C^s \big/ \partial\left(\dfrac{M_0^F}{p}\right)$

Since we have assumed that the labor market is independent of the price level, and the supply of labor is constant, we know $d\omega/dp = 0$ and $dy/dp = 0$. Consequently, we have

$$\frac{di}{dp} = \frac{(C_p^{\,s} - C_p^{\,d} - C_p^{\,t}) - C_m^{\,s}\left(\dfrac{M_0^F}{p^2}\right) + C_m^{\,d}\left(\dfrac{M_0^H}{p^2}\right)}{C_i^{\,d} - C_i^{\,s} + C_i^{\,t}} \qquad (19\text{-}19)$$

Let $\qquad\quad C_p^{\,s} > 0 \qquad C_p^{\,d} < 0 \qquad C_m^{\,s} < 0 \qquad C_m^{\,d} > 0$

$$C_i^{\,d} < 0 \qquad C_i^{\,s} > 0 \qquad C_i^{\,t} \geq 0 \qquad C_p^{\,t} \leq 0$$

Then $\qquad\qquad\qquad\qquad \dfrac{di}{dp} \gtrless 0 \qquad$ as $\ |C_i^{\,d} - C_i^{\,s}| \lessgtr C_i^{\,t} \qquad (19\text{-}20)$

and di/dp is indeterminate if $|C_i^{\,d} - C_i^{\,s}| = C_i^{\,t}$.

When the bond market is in an excess supply situation, the C^t function must be added to the supply side because it is negative. Therefore, di/dp, when ESB prevails, is given by

$$\frac{di}{dp} = \frac{(C_p^s - C_p^d) - C_m^s\left(\frac{M_0^F}{p^2}\right) + C_m^d\left(\frac{M_0^H}{p^2}\right) + C_p^t}{C_i^d - C_i^s - C_i^t} \qquad (19\text{-}21)$$

Since $C_p^t \le 0$ and the denominator is unambiguously negative,

$$\frac{di}{dp} \gtreqless 0 \qquad \text{as } (C_p^s - C_p^d) - C_m^s\left(\frac{M_0^F}{p^2}\right) + C_m^d\left(\frac{M_0^H}{p^2}\right) \gtreqless |C_p^t| \qquad (19\text{-}22)$$

because the left-hand side is unambiguously positive.

Conditions (19-20) and (19-22) have been derived where the *commodity market* is in equilibrium during the period while the bond market is in either excess demand or excess supply. Since there are two possibilities in (19-20) and three possibilities in (19-22), we can consider the six different combinations of those conditions as shown in Table 19-1. The sign of di/dp is depicted in Figure 19-2. To illustrate, let us take as cases (a), (c), and (f) in Table 19-1. In panel (a), the CC curve represents equilibrium in the commodity market, the sign of its slope indicating the sign of di/dp. The upper portion of the CC curve represents equilibrium in the commodity market when the bond market is in excess demand, due to an excessively high rate of interest. The lower portion of the CC curve depicts commodity equilibrium when the bond market is in excess supply because of too low an interest rate. According to Table

Table 19-1 COMPARISON BETWEEN PRIMARY AND SPILLOVER EXCESS DEMAND WHEN THE BOND MARKET IS DISTURBED

	Compared to primary forces	Sign of di/dp in EDB	Sign of di/dp in ESB	Remarks
(a)	C_i^t smaller C_p^t smaller	Negative	Negative	Classical case
(b)	C_i^t smaller C_p^t same	Negative	Zero	
(c)	C_i^t smaller C_p^t larger	Negative	Positive	p dominates
(d)	C_i^t larger C_p^t smaller	Positive	Negative	i dominates
(e)	C_i^t larger C_p^t same	Positive	Zero	
(f)	C_i^t larger C_p^t larger	Positive	Positive	Keynesian case

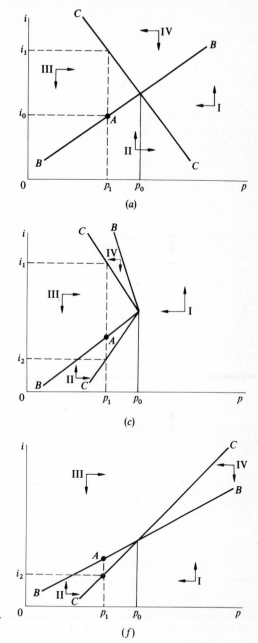

FIGURE 19-2
Equilibrium curves of the commodity
and bond markets.

19-1, the sign of di/dp in both EDB and ESB is negative in the first combination of C_i^t and C_p^t. Thereby, in panel (a) of Figure 19-2, the CC curve is negatively sloped throughout its length. In panel (c) which corresponds to combination (c) in Table 19-2, the CC curve is "kinked" at the general equilibrium point. This is because the sign of di/dp is negative when there is an EDB but positive when there is an ESB, as we see in the table. Finally, in panel (f) the CC curve is positively sloped throughout because in this case C_i^t (the spillover demand to the commodity market due to EDB) is larger than the primary demand for commodities and C_p^t (the spillover demand generated in the bond market due to an ESB) is also larger than the primary demand.

In similar fashion we can specify the equilibrium condition of the bond market when the commodity market is disturbed. Rewriting Eq. (19-14), we have

$$b^d\left(p, i, \omega; \frac{M_0^H}{p}, y\right) + b^t(p, i, \omega) = b^s\left(p, i, \omega; \frac{M_0^F}{p}, y\right) \qquad (19\text{-}23)$$

The spillover function b^t appears on the left-hand side of Eq. (19-23) if the commodity market has excess demand (EDC), but on the right hand side if the commodity market has excess supply (ESC). Differentiating Eq. (19-23) totally and dividing each term by dp, we get

$$b_p^d + b_i^d\left(\frac{di}{dp}\right) + b_\omega^d\left(\frac{d\omega}{dp}\right) - b_m^d\left(\frac{M_0^H}{p^2}\right) + b_y^d\left(\frac{dy}{dp}\right) + b_p^t + b_\omega^t\left(\frac{d\omega}{dp}\right) + b_i^t\left(\frac{di}{dp}\right)$$

$$= b_p^s + b_i^s\left(\frac{di}{dp}\right) + b_\omega^s\left(\frac{d\omega}{dp}\right) - b_m^s\left(\frac{M_0^F}{p^2}\right) + b_y^s\left(\frac{dy}{dp}\right) \qquad (19\text{-}24)$$

where $\qquad b_m^d = \partial b^d \left/ \partial\left(\frac{M_0^H}{p}\right)\right.$ and $\qquad b_m^s = \partial b^s \left/ \partial\left(\frac{M_0^F}{p}\right)\right.$

Employing the same assumption used above, that $d\omega/dp = 0$ and $dy/dp = 0$, we obtain

$$\frac{di}{dp} = \frac{(b_p^s - b_p^d - b_p^t) - b_m^s\left(\dfrac{M_0^F}{p^2}\right) + b_m^d\left(\dfrac{M_0^H}{p^2}\right)}{b_i^d - b_i^s + b_i^t} \qquad (19\text{-}25)$$

Let $\qquad b_p^s > 0 \qquad b_p^d < 0 \qquad b_p^t \leq 0 \qquad b_m^s < 0 \qquad b_m^d > 0 \qquad b_i^d > 0$

$$b_i^s < 0 \qquad b_i^t \geq 0$$

Then both the numerator and denominator of Eq. (19-25) are positive, so that the sign of di/dp for the bond equilibrium with EDC is unambiguously positive.

In the case of ESC the b^t function must be on the supply side (right side of Eq. 19-23) because firms will most likely issue more bonds to finance the sales gap in the commodity market. Thus,

$$\frac{di}{dp} = \frac{(b_p^s - b_p^d + b_p^t) - b_m^s\left(\dfrac{M_0^F}{p^2}\right) + b_m^d\left(\dfrac{M_0^H}{p^2}\right)}{b_i^d - b_i^s - b_i^t} \qquad (19\text{-}26)$$

The sign of di/dp in Eq. (19-26) is ambiguous because both numerator and denominator are ambiguous in sign. The sign depends upon the absolute magnitudes between

$$\left[b_p{}^s - b_p{}^d - b_m{}^s\left(\frac{M_0{}^F}{p^2}\right) + b_m{}^d\left(\frac{M_0{}^H}{p^2}\right) \right] \text{ and } b_p{}^t \qquad (19\text{-}27)$$

and between $(b_i{}^d - b_i{}^s)$ and $b_i{}^t$

Therefore

$$\frac{di}{dp} \gtreqless 0 \qquad (19\text{-}28)$$

Let us construct the same kind of table as that constructed for commodity market equilibrium. Since the sign of di/dp is unambiguously positive when an excess demand exists in the commodity market, the lower part of the bond equilibrium curve is positively sloped. For the upper part of BB associated with the region of excess supply in the commodity market, we may consider various combinations between the primary forces and the spillover forces as shown in Table 19-2.

Cases (a), (c), and (f) are relevant to the cases with the same labels in Table 19-1. Case (a) in Table 19-2 together with case (a) in Table 19-1 forms the classical case where the spillover forces are insignificant. Case (c) in both tables describes a system where the price adjustment dominates in the spillover effects. Case (f) can be called the Keynesian world where disequilibrium can be indefinitely amplified.[6] These are

Table 19-2 COMPARISON BETWEEN PRIMARY AND SPILLOVER EXCESS DEMAND WHEN THE COMMODITY MARKET IS IN EXCESS SUPPLY

Compared to primary forces		Sign of di/dp in ESC	Remarks
(a)	$b_i{}^t$ smaller $b_p{}^t$ smaller	Positive	Classical case
(b)	$b_i{}^t$ smaller $b_p{}^t$ same	Zero	
(c)	$b_i{}^t$ smaller $b_p{}^t$ larger	Negative	p dominates
(d)	$b_i{}^t$ larger $b_p{}^t$ smaller	Negative	i dominates
(e)	$b_i{}^t$ larger $b_p{}^t$ same	Zero	
(f)	$b_i{}^t$ larger $b_p{}^t$ larger	Positive	Keynesian case

[6] According to Keynes, the disequilibrium forces will be amplified if a feedback shock from an initial disequilibrium is greater than the original shock. For more details see Keynes (1936) and Leijonhufvud (1968, chap. II).

also drawn in Figure 19-2. First, in panel (a), in the same manner as that used in drawing the commodity equilibrium curve when the spillover forces are relatively weak, we draw the BB curve (the bond equilibrium curve). The lower portion of BB is invariably positive as shown by Eq. (19-25). The upper portion of BB is also positively sloped. Second, when b_p^t is larger but b_i^t is smaller than the primary forces, the upper portion of BB is negatively sloped as shown in panel (c). Third, when both b_p^t and b_i^t are greater than the primary forces, the upper BB is positively sloped. This is drawn in panel (f).

In each panel of Figure 19-2, the different combinations of disequilibrium are specified by Roman numerals I to IV. Each number represents a disequilibrium area, the combination of which is as follows:

Area I: *ESB* and *ESC*
Area II: *ESB* and *EDC*
Area III: *EDB* and *EDC*
Area IV: *EDB* and *ESC*

In each area of each panel also are drawn the directions of adjustment in prices and the interest rate. For example, in the region of *ESB* and *EDC* (i.e., area II), both prices and the rate of interest rise in general *no matter how the spillover forces influence each market*.

Why are the slopes of the equilibrium curves and the areas of disequilibrium so important? First, the slopes of CC and BB are important because different slopes provide us with different policy measures for restoring equilibrium. Suppose that the economy is at point A in panel (a) of Figure 19-2, i.e., with an excess demand for commodities while the bond market is in equilibrium. To achieve equilibrium in the commodity market, there is no alternative but to raise the interest rate to i_1, assuming that the price level is fixed at p_1. Since C_i^d (the primary effect on excess demand) is negative and C_i^t (the spillover effect) is positive but insignificant, in panel (a)—see case (a) in Table 19-1—the excess demand for commodities will fall and finally be eliminated. In panel (f), if the economy is at point A, the interest rate must be lowered to i_2 because the CC curve is upward-sloping. Due to the primary effect on excess demand, C_i^d, the demand for commodities will be further increased. But recall that panel (f) represents the case where the spillover effect dominates the primary effect. That is, C_i^t, which brings spillover effects into the commodity market, will more than offset the increased demand and will by itself remove excess demand from the commodity market. This is possible when firms face a very tight financial situation due to the excessively high price of bonds which leads to a sharp reduction in investment. Finally, in panel (c), when the economy is at point A, there are two alternative ways for restoring equilibrium in the commodity market, assuming that the price level remains the same: (1) raising the interest rate to i_1 or (2) reducing it to i_2. This is possible because of the two portions of the CC curve with an opposite slope. If we raise the rate of interest, commodity demand in terms of the primary effect on excess demand (C_i^d) will fall. The spillover force to the commodity market (C_i^t) is positive but it is smaller in absolute value than C_i^d—refer to case (c) in Table

19-1. Thereby, the excess demand for commodities can be eliminated. If we lower the interest rate, excess demand increases by the primary effect in the commodity market but an excess supply of bonds will be created in the bond market. Due to the spillover effects, however, the spilled-over demand from the bond market to the commodity market, C_i^t, will partly offset the increase in demand. Furthermore, the excess supply of bonds would prevent firms from investing more and selling less to households, although the lower interest rate induces them to do so. The only alternative left for them to finance new investment is to increase their supply of commodities, even at a lower price than they were willing to accept previously, such as p_1. Assuming that the interest rate policy has a greater impact on the bond market than on the commodity market, the increase in the supply of commodities together with the spillover effect C_i^t will exceed the increase in the household's commodity demand. Thus, excess demand for commodities at point A would tend to fall, and it would be eliminated if the interest rate fell far enough.

It is a significant modification to the classical general equilibrium model if there are two opposite policy measures that may be effective in bringing the economy to an equilibrium position. According to the analysis, an excess demand for commodities can be eliminated either by raising the interest rate or by lowering it, if the situation is as depicted in panel (c) of Figure 19-2. If an economy is experiencing a severe inflation, contraction of the money supply will be desirable because it has two effects: (1) the increase in prices will be tapered down, and (2) the interest rate will rise, and thereby the excess demand for commodities will be eliminated.

Different relationships between spillover effects and primary disequilibrium forces gave us different types of equilibrium curves. As the slope of the equilibrium curve varies, the counterdisequilibrium policies must be properly chosen; identifying the type of economy from various cases shown in Tables 19-1 and 19-2 is thus of greatest importance.

Thus, we turn next to analysis of the area of disequilibrium. For this purpose, we need to verify the types of price and interest rate adjustment. There are two types of dynamic adjustment patterns with respect to prices and the rate of interest: (1) a monotonic adjustment toward the equilibrium point and (2) an oscillatory adjustment toward the equilibrium level. As the shapes of areas I to IV in Figure 19-2 vary, the adjustment patterns of prices and the interest rate change accordingly. For example, consider panels (a) and (c) in Figure 19-2, which are reproduced in Figure 19-3. The economy is assumed to be at point A in area III in panel (a). Due to the adjustment directions indicated for p and i, the economy achieves bond equilibrium first at point D. Once the bond market is cleared, adjustment in the commodity market must be strong, and thus the price adjustment will predominate over the interest rate adjustment. The excess demand for commodities will raise prices up to point E on the lower portion of the CC curve. In the meantime the bond market is disturbed through the spillover process. At point E the interest rate adjustment will predominate over the price change. This spiraling adjustment will continue until the system reaches the general equilibrium point, Z. During this period of adjustment, the price level cuts the commodity market equilibrium price level p_0 several times, and in fact continuously approaches p_0. This is shown by path (a) in Figure 19-4. (We could show the same adjustment path for the rate of interest as well.)

In panel (c) of Figure 19-3, however, the adjustment path is not the same as in the previous case. Consider point A in area III in panel (c). Through the adjustment of p and i the economy moves to point D on the BB curve. Since the commodity market is still in an excess demand situation, the price adjustment dominates over the interest rate adjustment, and the economy will be at point E on the lower part of the CC curve. At point E the price level would not rise any further because the commodity market is temporarily in equilibrium. This prevents the price level from rising above the general equilibrium price level p_0. From point E the rate of interest will rise due to the new excess supply of bonds on the one hand and the spillover effects from the commodity market on the other which take place between points D and E. The dynamic path of this adjustment is shown by path (c) in Figure 19-4. Since path (c) represents the monotonic as well as the bounded adjustment process, the equilibrium of panel (c) may be restored more quickly than that of panel (a).[7]

Policy Implications

We have seen that the pattern of the dynamic adjustment of prices and the interest rate during a disequilibrium period depend upon the relative strength of the spillover excess demands, assuming false trading to occur. Prices and the rate of interest will oscillate around the equilibrium level when the magnitude of spillover effects is negligible. They will adjust monotonically without oscillation toward the equilibrium level if the spillover effect *due to the "false" price level* is larger than the primary effect, but the spillover effect *due to "false" interest rates* is smaller than the primary effect.

From the standpoint of policy makers, monotonic and prompt adjustment of prices and the rate of interest is much more desirable, since repetitive and prolonged false trading gives rise to reduced social welfare, as shown above. If the economy fits the description of the monotonic-adjustment case, there is therefore no need for government to use discretionary fiscal or monetary policy. On the other hand, fiscal or monetary policy (or both) must be undertaken to lead the adjustment in the right direction when spillover effects have a perverse effect.

It is very difficult to identify which adjustment pattern is most descriptive of the real world. Techniques for empirical estimation for markets in disequilibrium are not in general available. The general problem is that in the absence of an equilibrium condition the *notional* demand and supply quantities cannot in general be equal to the *observed* quantity traded in the market. Not knowing the notional demand and supply schedule, we cannot estimate either the primary excess demand effect or the spillover excess demand effect. A few studies have attempted to tackle this problem by using various probability likelihood functions, but they are not yet firm enough to use with confidence. Therefore, the multimarket disequilibrium model is essentially untested.[8]

---

[7] The path of adjustments for panel (f) in Figure 19-2 is left to the reader.
[8] For a discussion of these empirical problems, see Fair and Jaffee (1971).

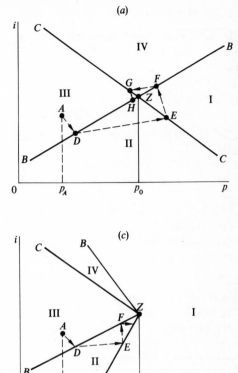

FIGURE 19-3
Adjustment of prices and the interest rate.

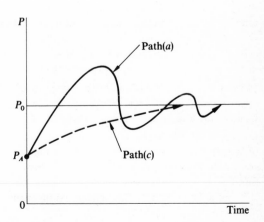

FIGURE 19-4
Two types of price adjustment over time.

SUMMARY

In this chapter, we have presented two typical cases of intermarket pressures in disequilibrium which make it essential to modify the conventional excess demand functions. *Distribution effects* arise when we assume that the market excess demand functions depend upon the stock of each commodity held by each individual. Such effects lead to a worsening of efficiency in the Pareto optimal sense. The policy implication is that fiscal and monetary policy should be used so that the economy will not deviate too much from the efficiency solution—disequilibrium should be avoided.

The *spillover effect* arises when an individual demand function depends upon realized (or effective) income rather than notional income. Effective income in a certain market is determined by realized transactions in other markets. Therefore, in analyzing the direction of adjustment of price variables, it is crucial to investigate the relative strength of the primary excess demand effects and the spillover effects from other markets. Various combinations of these forces can be formed which are associated with different types of equilibrium curves and disequilibrium areas, which suggest different policy measures to restore general equilibrium.

READINGS FOR CHAPTER 19

ARROW, K. J.: "Toward a Theory of Price Adjustment," in M. Abramowitz (ed.), *The Allocation of Economic Resources* Stanford, Calif.: Stanford, 1959), pp. 41–51.

BARRO, R. J., and H. I. GROSSMAN: "A General Disequilibrium Model of Income and Employment," *American Economic Review*, vol. 61, pp. 82–93, March 1971.

CLOWER, R. W.: "'Keynes and the Classics' A Dynamical Perspective," *Quarterly Journal of Economics*, vol. 74, pp. 318–323, May 1960.

———: "The Keynesian Counterrevolution: A Theoretical Appraisal," in F. H. Hahn and R. P. R. Brechling (eds.), *The Theory of Interest Rates* (London: Institute of Economic Affairs, 1965), pp. 103–125.

CROSS, J. G., and J. WILLIAMSON: "Patinkin on Unemployment Disequilibrium," *Journal of Political Economy*, vol. 70, pp. 76–81, February 1962.

DAVIDSON, P.: "A Keynesian View of Patinkin's Theory of Employment," *Economic Journal*, vol. 77, pp. 559–578, September 1967.

DIAMOND, P.: "A Model of Price Adjustment," *Journal of Economic Theory*, vol. 3, pp. 156–168, June 1971.

FAIR, R. C., and D. M. JAFFEE: "Methods of Estimation for Markets in Disequilibrium," *Econometrica*, July 1971.

GOGERTY, D. C., and G. C. WINSTON: "Patinkin, Perfect Competition, and Unemployment Disequilibria," *Review of Economic Studies*, vol. 31, pp. 121–126, April 1964.

GRAHAM, D. A., E. JACOBSON, and E. R. WEINTRAUB: "Transactions Costs and the Convergence of a Trade Out of Equilibrium Adjustment Process," *International Economic Review*, vol. 13, pp. 123–131, February 1972.

GROSSMAN, H. I.: "Money, Interest, and Prices in Market Disequilibrium," *Journal of Political Economy*, vol. 79, pp. 943–961, September–October 1971.

HAHN, F. H.: "A Stable Adjustment Process for a Competitive Economy," *Review of Economic Studies*, pp. 62–65, 1962.

—— and T. NEGISHI: "A Theorem on Non-Tatonnement Stability," *Econometrica*, vol. 30, pp. 463–469, July 1962.

——: "Some Adjustment Problems," *Econometrica*, vol. 37, pp. 1–17, January 1970.

HURWICZ, L.: "Optimality and Information Efficiency in Resource Allocation Processes," in *Mathematical Methods in Social Sciences* (Stanford, Calif.: Stanford, 1959), pp. 27–46.

KEYNES, J. M.: *The General Theory of Employment, Interest, and Money* (New York: Harcourt, Brace & World, 1936).

LEIJONHUFVUD, A.: *On Keynesian Economics and the Economics of Keynes* (New York: Oxford, 1968).

NEGISHI, T.: "A Note on the Stability of an Economy Where All Goods Are Gross Substitutes," *Econometrica*, vol. 25, pp. 635–669, 1958.

——: "The Stability of a Competitive Economy: A Survey Article," *Econometrica*, vol. 30, pp. 635–669, October 1962.

——: "*Market Clearing Processes in a Monetary Economy*," in F. H. Hahn and F. P. R. Brechling (eds.), *The Theory of Interest Rates* (London: Institute of Economic Affairs, 1965), pp. 152–163.

PATINKIN, D.: "Involuntary Unemployment and the Keynesian Supply Function," *Economic Journal*, vol. 59, pp. 360–383, September 1949.

——: *Money, Interest, and Prices* (New York: Harper & Row, 1965).

SAMUELSON, P. A.: *Foundation of Economic Analysis* (Cambridge, Mass.: Harvard, 1947).

SAVING, T. R.: "Transaction Costs, and Monetary Theory," *American Economic Review*, vol. 61, pp. 418–419, June 1971.

SOLOW, R. M.: "Short-Run Adjustment of Employment to Output," in J. N. Wolfe (ed.), *Value, Capital, and Growth* (Chicago: University of Edinburgh, 1968), pp. 481–484.

TUCKER, D. P.: "Macroeconomic Models and the Demand for Money under Market Disequilibrium," *Journal of Money, Credit, and Banking*, vol. 3, pp. 57–83, February 1971.

——: "Patinkin's Macro Model as a Model of Market Disequilibrium," *Southern Economic Journal* October 1972.

20

MONEY AND DISEQUILIBRIUM

In Chapters 18 and 19 we discussed two important disequilibrium models—Keynes's model with involuntary unemployment and a multimarket model with spillover and distribution effects. In Keynes's model the relationship between the commodity and labor markets was analyzed concentrating on the price level and the money wage rate. In Chapter 19, we introduced the bond market, analyzing the adjustment of prices, wages, and the interest rate. The next logical step is to build a "complete" disequilibrium model which includes the money market as well as the commodity, labor, and bond markets. This is the purpose of this chapter. First, however, we must deal with the question—recently raised in the literature on disequilibrium analysis—about whether adding the money market is necessary or even helpful.

THE MONEY MARKET IN A DISEQUILIBRIUM MODEL

There are several reasons to question the necessity of adding the money market to a general disequilibrium model. First, for the money market to play an important role in disequilibrium, there should be a definitional distinction between the *notional* and the *effective* demand for money. But households' decisions about money holdings are *always* notional, and they are always carried out. Thus, no spillover pressures are generated from the money market. Second, the excess demand for money—however it may be defined—is not *directly* related to the dynamic adjustment of the interest rate or of any other price variable. It is the disequilibrium in the *bond market* that pushes the interest rate around. Thus, as Tucker (1971, 1972) argues, adding the money market to a disequilibrium model does not contribute anything to understanding the dynamic adjustment path. Third, in a multimarket system with money, disequilibrium in the money market (in terms of *effective* demand, if this is possible) may be connected with excess supply for any one of the other commodities, through Walras's law.[1] For example, when the money market and the commodity market are in disequilibrium the price level and the interest rate adjust according to Eqs. (19-19), (19-21), (19-25), and (19-26) shown earlier. Thus, adding a money market does not give us any more significant information than what we already had. Finally, but not least in importance, the effect of interest rate changes on the *effective* money demand and supply is not known. Existing empirical studies (Chapters 9 and 10) show the interest elasticity of the demand for and supply of money, but these are based on and explain the behavior of actual balances, not effective money demand or supply. The interest elasticity of the effective demand for money is thus still open to question. For this reason we do not (and cannot) build a four-market model.

Does money then have to be completely ignored in disequilibrium analysis? The answer is "yes" as long as the money market is functioning "normally" so that its excess demand equation does not add any independent information implicitly included in the three-equation system in Chapter 19. However, there is one special case in which the system "sticks in the mud" due to a peculiar aspect of the money market. This is Keynes's *liquidity trap* based on households' speculative behavior with inelastic expectations. In Chapter 9 we found that the theory of the speculative demand for money is unsatisfactory in the usual interpretation, because of its assumption that an investor holds *either* all money *or* all earning assets (depending on the interest rate)—which is unlikely to be the case in reality. However, in the recent literature (Leijonhufvud, 1968), a strong defense has been mounted for Keynes's hypothesis about investors' inelastic expectations, and thereby for the existence of the speculative demand for money and the liquidity trap.

This exegetical controversy will not be discussed here. Instead, we will assume the speculative demand for money exists and consider the case with a "liquidity trap" and inelastic expectations, analyzing how these bring about a stable unemployment disequilibrium. For simplicity, we ignore distribution and spillover effects to concentrate on the liquidity trap. We examine in particular the Keynesian proposition that, in the presence of the liquidity trap, only fiscal policy can eliminate unemployment disequilibrium.

---

[1] The law states that if all but one of the markets in an economy are in equilibrium, then that other market also must be in equilibrium.

THE LIQUIDITY TRAP

In Chapter 3, we derived the simple Keynesian model using the following macro-equations:

$$Y = C\left[Y(1 - \tau) - \frac{\overline{T}}{P}\right] + I(i) + \overline{G} \quad (3\text{-}12)$$

$$m\overline{H} = pL(Y, i) \quad (3\text{-}13)$$

$$p = p_0 \quad (3\text{-}14)$$

where τ denotes the marginal tax rate, $\overline{T}/p$ denotes the intercept of the net real tax function, and $\overline{H}$ is the monetary base. For equilibrium in the real sector, differentiating (3-12) totally and setting the increments of the policy variables equal to zero, we get

$$dY = C_{Y_d} dY(1 - \tau) + I_i \, di$$

$$dY[1 - C_{Y_d}(1 - \tau)] = I_i \, di$$

$$\left.\frac{di}{dY}\right|_{IS} = \frac{1 - C_{Y_d}(1 - \tau)}{I_i} \quad (20\text{-}1)$$

$$0 < C_{Y_d} < 1 \qquad 0 < \tau < 1 \qquad I_i < 0$$

Thus, the slope of the commodity market equilibrium curve, the IS curve, is negative. When we differentiate (3-13), the equilibrium condition for the money market is

$$0 = L(Y, i) \, dp + p(L_y \, dY + L_i \, di)$$

and since p is assumed to be fixed at p_0:

$$p(L_y \, dY + L_i \, di) = 0$$

$$\left.\frac{di}{dY}\right|_{LM} = -\frac{L_y}{L_i} \quad (20\text{-}2)$$

$$L_y > 0 \qquad L_i < 0$$

Therefore, given the assumptions about the signs of the partials, the slope of the LM curve is positive.

The "steepness" of the slope of the IS curve depends upon the responsiveness of investment with respect to the rate of interest, I_i, given the marginal propensity to consume and the marginal tax rate. In terms of elasticities, the IS curve is steeper the more *inelastic* the interest elasticity of investment.

The steepness of the slope of the LM curve also depends upon the responsiveness of money demand with respect to the rate of interest, that is, L_i, and the effect of a change in income on the demand for money L_y. Given L_y, the LM curve is flatter as the demand for money becomes more *interest-elastic*.

As discussed in Chapter 3, fiscal policy is less effective the flatter the IS curve and the steeper the LM curve. On the other hand, monetary policy is less effective the steeper the *IS* curve and the flatter the *LM* curve. This is shown by reproduction of the "multiplier equations"—(3-25) to (3-28):

$$\frac{dY}{d\overline{G}} = \frac{1}{1 - C_{Y_d}(1 - \tau) + (I_i L_y)/L_i} \quad (3\text{-}25)$$

$$\frac{dY}{d\overline{T}} = \frac{- C_{Y_d}}{1 - C_{Y_d}(1 - \tau) + (I_i L_y)/L_i} \quad (3\text{-}26)$$

$$\frac{dY}{d\tau(Y)} = \frac{- C_{Y_d}}{1 - C_{Y_d}(1 - \tau) + (I_i L_y)/L_i} \quad (3\text{-}27)$$

$$\frac{dY}{d\overline{H}} = \frac{m(I_i/L_i)}{1 - C_{Y_d}(1 - \tau) + (I_i L_y)/L_i} \quad (3\text{-}28)$$

One of the special and extreme shapes of the *LM* curve is now the subject of our attention. As will be recalled from Chapter 3, there may be a case where the lower part of the *LM* curve is absolutely interest-elastic—where the curve is horizontal. This follows if the demand curve for money is "kinked" at some interest rate (i_0); below this rate the curve flattens out. That is,

$$M_d = pL(Y, i)$$

$$L_y > 0 \quad\quad\quad\quad\quad (20\text{-}3)$$

$$L_i < 0 \quad\quad \text{if } i > i_0$$

$$L_i = - \infty \quad\quad \text{if } i \leq i_0$$

The portion of the curve specified by the last condition is called the *liquidity trap*, and the interest rate i_0 is called the *critical rate*. The economic implications of this part of the curve are as follows. If the interest rate falls to i_0, the demand for money turns perfectly elastic with respect to the interest rate. That is, at this rate of interest, households will demand any increments in assets in the form of cash. If, for example, the real quantity of money increases due to a fall in the price level, households will not use the additional balances to purchase bonds because they are indifferent to holding their wealth in bonds or cash balances when the interest rate is equal to the critical rate. In the bond market, the interest rate cannot fall below the critical rate because no one wants to buy bonds (i.e., release cash holdings) at a higher bond price (or lower interest rate) than the price relevant to the critical rate.

When we have this type of the *LM* curve, there are two factors of special concern in dealing with a macro disequilibrium model. First, we have to check where the initial equilibrium was located on the *LM* curve. Second, we must consider the interest elasticity of the *IS* curve, because the shift in the aggregate demand curve as the *IS* curve shifts (due, say, to a fiscal action) depends upon the steepness of the curve. We will analyze various cases one after another.

First, suppose that aggregate demand is reduced exogenously. This will cause the system to have involuntary unemployment. The reader will recall, from Chapter 18 (Figure 18-2), that this unemployment disequilibrium can be removed by either fiscal or monetary policy. It can also be eliminated by the automatic adjustment process, so long as prices and wages are not absolutely rigid. However, this is only the case *where both the IS and the LM curves are of normal shape.* Assume that the *IS* curve is a downward-sloping curve throughout, but that the *LM* curve has a horizontal portion at the critical interest rate due to the liquidity trap in the money demand function. That is, if Y_u and i_0 denote the income and interest rate level associated with the "kinked point" of the *LM* curve, then

$$\frac{di}{dY} = 0 \quad \text{if } 0 < Y \le Y_0 \text{ and } i = i_0$$

$$\frac{di}{dY} > 0 \quad \text{if } Y > Y_0 \text{ and } i > i_0 \quad (20\text{-}4)$$

Assume further that full-employment equilibrium (before the fall in demand) was in the upward-sloping portion of the *LM* curve. Let the new *IS* curve after the downward shift in the aggregate demand curve be written as

$$Y_1 = C_1\left[Y_1(1 - \tau) - \frac{\overline{T}}{p}\right] + I(i) + \overline{G} \quad (20\text{-}5)$$

Combining (20-4) and (20-5), we can generate two different types of interaction between the real sector and the monetary sector: (1) the *IS* curve is originally *interest-elastic* (because investment is interest-elastic) so that the new *IS* curve cuts the horizontal line $i = i_0$ to the right of the full-employment income level Y_F; (2) the *IS* curve is originally *interest-inelastic* (because investment is interest-inelastic) so that the new *IS* curve cuts $i = i_0$ to the left of Y_F.[2]

The two cases are compared in Figure 20-1. Suppose that aggregate demand is reduced by ΔY due to a depression. In panel (a) IS_1' is the new *IS* curve after the shift from the interest-elastic (IS_1) curve, and IS_2' is the new one shifting from IS_2, which is relatively interest-inelastic. Since IS_1' is relatively interest-elastic, it cuts the horizontal line $i = i_0$ at point C_1. The same shift in the second case, however, has IS_2' cutting the i_0 line at C_2. The interest elasticity of the *original IS* curve makes the outcome different even if the initial shift in the *IS* curve is the same.

Consider the first case. If prices and the money wage rate were absolutely rigid, the economy would be caught at point B and there would be no autonomous adjustment forces at work. This causes involuntary unemployment to occur, and it cannot be removed unless fiscal or monetary expansion is implemented. If prices are relatively flexible compared to money wages (although not adjusting instantaneously), the price level will eventually fall due to the deficient demand. When it falls from the equilibrium price p_F to (say) p_2, the real quantity of money increases from M/p_F to M/p_2, the *LM* curve shifts outward, and the level of aggregate demand increases. If the *LM* curve keeps shifting outward due to further reductions in prices —to p_1—and passes through point A in panel (a) of Figure 20-1, the initial full-

---

[2] There is another possibility; the new *IS* curve cuts the horizontal portion of the *LM* curve. This case is considered later.

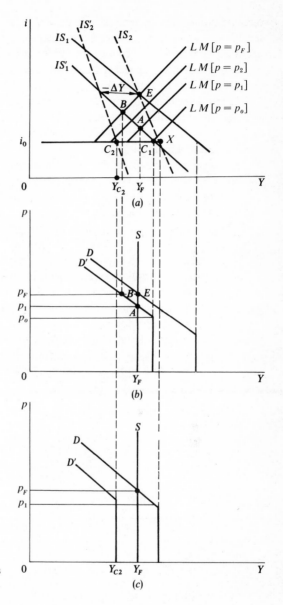

FIGURE 20-1a–c
Different aggregate demand curves as interest elasticity of investment varies.

employment equilibrium will be restored with a lower price level and interest rate. This can also be explained with the aggregate demand and supply curves. In panel (b) the intersections between various LM curves and the original IS curve give the aggregate demand curve D. As the IS curve shifts inward to IS'_1, the aggregate demand curve shifts in to D' as well. Both the original demand curve and the new demand curve become vertical where the original and the new IS curves hit the interest level $i = i_0$ in panel (a). The disequilibrium with underemployment was temporarily set at point B in panels (a) and (b). If the price level tends to adjust downward (even if it is only after a long delay in the disequilibrium model), the new full-employment equilibrium will be established at point A in the two panels.

Now suppose that the economy faces a depression characterized by interest-inelastic IS_2' in panel (a) in Figure 20-1. In this case, point C_2 is inside of Y_F. Even though the price level tends to fall and the LM curve shifts outward, the maximum attainable income is only at C_2 (i.e., Y_{c2}), which is short of the full-employment income. Unemployment in the labor market corresponding to $(Y_F - Y_{c2})$ of income cannot be eliminated.[3] The new aggregate demand curve for this case should be such that the vertical portion of it lies to the left of the vertical aggregate supply curve. The maximum attainable income is only Y_{c2}.

There is one more possibility for interaction between the IS and LM curves. If the new IS curve cuts the horizontal portion of the LM curve, then, regardless of the interest elasticity, the new aggregate demand curve will be vertical throughout and parallel to the supply curve, and so there will be no equilibrium at all. Therefore, there cannot be any improvement in income and employment. Flexibility of prices would not help the system remove unemployment disequilibrium.

So far, we have discussed the special condition in the money demand function that may produce different combinations between the IS and LM curves which in turn determine the shape and the location of the aggregate demand function. What about the shape of the aggregate supply curve? In the foregoing diagrams we simply assumed that it is a vertical line at the full-employment income level. However, this needs to be reconsidered. In the case where both prices and the money wage rate are equally flexible—when prices fall, the money wage rate also falls—the real wage rate remains the same. As long as the real wage rate remains unchanged, the quantity of labor demanded by firms must be the same. Therefore, the aggregate supply curve in the short run is vertical.[4] Consider next the case where prices are flexible but the money wage rate is rigid *downward*. As prices fall, the real wage rate must rise, and firms will reduce their amount of labor demanded. In this case the aggregate supply curve is "kinked" at the equilibrium point and positively sloped below that point. This is shown by the broken line FE in panel (b) in Figure 20-2. The new aggregate demand curve D' intersects the positively sloping part of the supply curve at point H. The adjustment in the system will be arrested at point H even if a further decrease in prices could shift the LM curve further to the right. This is because of the failure of the money wage rate to fall, and firms would have no inducement to expand input and hence output. In these circumstances there will exist involuntary unemployment which cannot be removed through the price-adjustment mechanism.

---

[3] That is, firms have expectations that are so pessimistic that they are not willing to increase investment even at a very low interest rate. Thus, workers involuntarily unemployed before cannot return to work.

[4] In the typical Keynesian case, however, the aggregate supply curve is horizontal, as discussed in Chapter 3. This is because prices are absolutely fixed in the short run. Here we allow prices to vary in order to see various cases in disequilibrium.

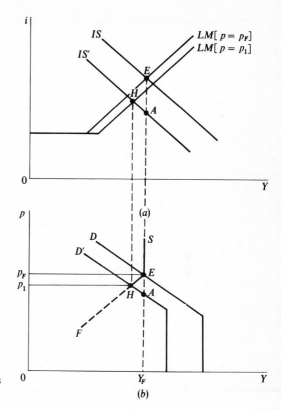

FIGURE 20-2
Aggregate supply when money wages
are rigid downward.

In summary, we have examined different combinations between the *IS* curve
and the *LM* curve with the *liquidity trap*: when investment is interest-elastic, the
income level on the *IS* curve when i is the critical rate is very likely greater than Y_F;
when investment is interest-inelastic, it is very likely less than Y_F. When both prices
and the money wage rate are flexible, full-employment equilibrium can be restored
in the first case through the price and wage adjustment. In the second case, a conventional equilibrium cannot exist at all in the commodity market. When both prices
and the money wage rate are fixed, no adjustment will occur. When prices are flexible
but the money wage rate is rigid downward, full-employment equilibrium cannot be
restored in any case, although unemployment disequilibrium exists in the system in
each case.

INSUFFICIENT INVESTMENT

There is yet another reason for the kinked aggregate demand curve, the vertical
portion of which may lie to the left of the full-employment income—the so-called
insufficient investment case. This is worth discussing here even though it is not directly

related to money market phenomena. From Eq. (20-1) the slope of the IS curve is

$$\frac{di}{dY}\bigg|_{IS} = \frac{1 - C_{Y_d}(1 - \tau)}{I_i} \qquad (20\text{-}1)$$

$$0 < C_{Y_d} < 1 \qquad 0 < \tau < i \qquad I_i < 0$$

Since the IS curve is negatively sloped, it was assumed in the previous section that it intersects the income axis at greater than full employment. Also, the IS curve was assumed to be negatively sloped throughout. These two assumptions will not hold if in reality investment becomes perfectly interest-inelastic even before investment reaches the required level for the full-employment level of output. Firms compare the rental price of capital, as affected by the interest rate and the marginal returns to investment. If firms' expectations are so pessimistic that they believe there will be no return to investment, they will not be willing to borrow funds however low the interest rate. This can happen when an excess capacity already exists and that excess capacity is not expected to be used in the near future.

As the return to capital becomes very small, the effect on investment of a change in the interest rate is immaterial. That is,

$$I_i \simeq 0$$

In Eq. (20-1) the slope of the IS curve must be infinite (or vertical) as I_i approaches zero. If this happens at a lower income level than Y_F, then

$$\frac{di}{dY} < 0 \qquad \text{when } 0 < Y < Y_c$$

$$\frac{di}{dY} = \infty \qquad \text{when } Y = Y_c < Y_F$$

where Y_c is the critical level of income—the maximum attainable aggregate income on the IS curve. This relationship is shown in Figure 20-3. In panel (a) the initial LM curve is $LM(p = p_F)$ and the initial IS curve is also drawn with a vertical segment. Assume that there was an initial full-employment equilibrium. In the commodity market [panel (b)] this is shown by point E. Now suppose that the IS curve shifts to IS' due to a depression so that the vertical portion of the curve lies to the left of Y_F. Then the aggregate demand curve shifts from D to D'. In this case the income level Y_c is the limit to the expansion in demand, because further reductions in the rate of interest as the LM curve continues to shift to the right due to the fall in prices will not induce any more net investment.

There can also be different combinations of the IS and LM curves due to differences in the interest elasticity of investment: (1) the IS curve shifts, but $Y_c > Y_F$; (2) it shifts, but the LM curve cuts it in the downward-sloping portion; (3) the LM curve cuts the vertical portion of the IS curve. Each case has different economic implications, but the fundamentals are the same as in Figure 20-1. When prices and money wages are flexible, the first case will eventually result in the full-employment equilibrium. But when the money wage rate is rigid downward, all three fall into unemployment disequilibrium with involuntary unemployment in the labor market.

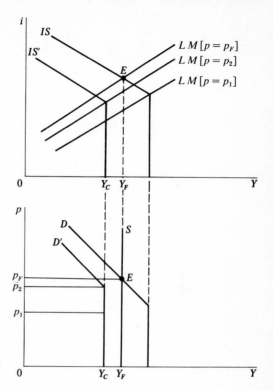

FIGURE 20-3
Aggregate demand curves when investment is insufficient.

ECONOMIC POLICIES FOR THE LIQUIDITY TRAP

In the previous sections we found that the aggregate demand curve would become vertical at the "critically low" rate of interest when there exists either an interest-elastic demand for money or insufficient investment. Furthermore, the aggregate supply curve may have the lower portion which is positively sloping if the money wage rate is rigid downward. With this kinked aggregate supply curve, full-employment equilibrium cannot be restored regardless of the position of the point at which the new IS curve is associated with the critical interest rate. The price-adjustment mechanism is no longer effective in these circumstances, and therefore monetary or fiscal policy actions are required in order to reestablish full-employment equilibrium.

Monetary Policy

Traditional Keynesian theory asserts that monetary policy is an inefficient, if not ineffective, policy tool, and the only effective tool that can lead the economy to full-employment equilibrium is fiscal policy.[5] In this section we will examine this

---

[5] Recall Figure 3-6 in Chapter 3 where an increase in government expenditure has a maximum effect on the income level.

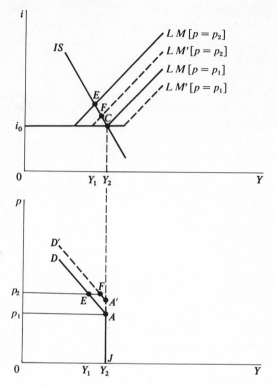

FIGURE 20-4
Shift in aggregate demand due to a
change in the money supply.

proposition in light of our two different IS curves (in terms of the interest elasticity
of investment I_i).

Before we examine the Keynesian proposition, let us first analyze the effect of
monetary policy on the aggregate demand curve when the money demand function
has a liquidity trap segment. In Figure 20-4 the initial aggregate demand curve
$DEAJ$ is drawn in panel (b) using the LM curves associated with different prices, for
example, p_2 and p_1. Segment AJ is vertical because a liquidity trap is present at
income level Y_2 and interest rate i_0, and the price level at which the aggregate demand
curve becomes vertical is p_1 because the LM curve when $p = p_1$ is kinked at the critical
point C in panel (a). Now suppose the money supply is increased from M to M'
but the price level remains at p_2. This will have the effect of shifting the real money
supply curve to the right, and thereby shifting the LM curve from $LM[p = p_2]$ to
$LM'[p = p_2]$ as shown in panel (a). At the price level p_2, the IS curve intersects
the LM curve at point F instead of E due to the increase in the money supply. This
point corresponds to point F in panel (b), which is still associated with p_2. When the
price level is p_1, which is lower than p_2, the initial LM curve should be $LM[p = p_1]$
as shown in panel (a). If the money supply is increased from M to M', then the LM

curve will shift to $LM'[p = p_1]$. The shift in the LM curve beyond the critical point C, however, will not affect aggregate demand. Therefore, the curve is kinked at point A' in panel (b). A set of points such as F and A' gives us the new curve $D'FA'J$. This is the aggregate demand schedule with expansion of the money supply. Thus, an increase in the nominal money supply causes the aggregate demand curve to shift upward, with its rightward shift being limited by the liquidity trap.

Let us now examine the efficacy of monetary policy in the following two typical *Keynesian* cases: (1) investment is interest-elastic, the money wage rate is rigid downward, and the liquidity trap exists; (2) investment is interest-inelastic, the money wage rate is rigid downward, and the liquidity trap exists.

Case 1 This case can be explained by using panels (a) and (b) in Figure 20-5. In panel (a) a depression disequilibrium exists at point B, where the IS_1 and LM curves intersect each other. Although the financial market is in equilibrium, the commodity market is at a less-then-full-employment situation. It was shown in the previous section that in this case the price-adjustment mechanism alone can bring about the full-employment equilibrium even if it takes a considerably long time. If monetary policy is properly used, the speed of adjustment can be increased so that the involuntary unemployment corresponding to the reduction in income ($Y_1 Y_F$) in panel (b) can be eliminated more rapidly. That is, as the nominal money supply is continuously increased, curve DAJ will shift upward until it reaches point E where full-employment equilibrium exists. This is possible because, first, investment is interest-elastic so that a fall in the interest due to monetary expansion leads to new investment which is sufficiently large to raise the economy to full employment. Second, a rise in the price level due to a policy of monetary expansion produces a decline in the real wage rate, thus increasing employment and output. Therefore, monetary policy is effective in this case *even if* a liquidity trap is present.

Case 2 Since investment is interest-inelastic, the IS curve is so steep that the vertical portion of the aggregate demand curve lies on the left side of the full-employment income. As shown in panel (c) in Figure 20-5, the intersection of DAJ and SEF occurs in the less-than-full-employment region. Even though expansionary monetary policy can increase the level of income by shifting DAJ up to $D'GJ$, the maximum attainable income is only Y_2; further increases in the nominal money supply cannot continue to expand output and employment beyond the level characterized by point G.[6]

In summary, under wage rigidity, if a liquidity trap exists, the efficacy of monetary policy depends upon the interest elasticity of investment. If investment is relatively interest-elastic so that the aggregate demand curve is price-elastic in a wide range,

---

[6] Consider the extreme case where the IS curve initially cuts the horizontal portion of the LM curve. In this case, the demand curve is vertical, and monetary policy is *completely* ineffective.

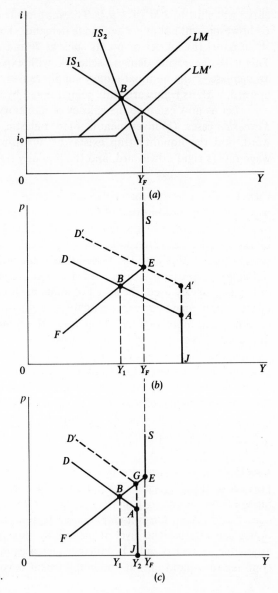

FIGURE 20-5a–c
Efficacy of monetary policy in two cases.

monetary policy is effective and accelerates the autonomous price adjustment. Conversely, if investment is interest-inelastic, monetary policy is incapable of restoring the economy to full-employment equilibrium although it can increase income to short of full employment. The Keynesian argument that monetary policy is likely to be ineffective in a depression is valid only when the investment schedule is interest-inelastic. Even with a liquidity trap, monetary policy *can* be effective and successful in restoring full-employment equilibrium if investment is interest-elastic.

Fiscal Policy

According to the Keynesians, fiscal policy is effective and powerful in generating aggregate demand in a depression situation and the system can always be lead to the full-employment equilibrium with this policy tool. In this subsection we examine this proposition, again with the focus on the interest elasticity of investment.

In Figure 20-6 we present the two *IS* curves used in the two cases studied in the previous subsection. Let us investigate the efficacy of fiscal policy in each case.

Case 1   Less-than-full-employment disequilibrium is set at point *B* in panels (*a*) and (*b*); IS_1 cuts the *LM* curve at an income level less than Y_F. Since investment is interest-elastic in this case, the vertical portion of the aggregate demand curve is likely to be on the right of Y_F. We assume that the aggregate supply curve does not cut the vertical portion of the demand curve.

In order to achieve full-employment equilibrium, the IS_1 curve must be shifted to IS_1'; that is, income must be increased by ΔY_1 for any price level, as indicated in panels (*a*) and (*b*). This increase in income can be achieved by an increase in government expenditures (prices constant) $\Delta \bar{G}$ in the amount

$$\Delta Y_1 = \frac{1}{D} \Delta \bar{G} \qquad (20\text{-}6)$$

where *D* is the denominator of Eq. (20-3). However, the *actual* increase in income that will be realized is less than ΔY_1, that is, $Y_F - Y_1$. As we saw in Chapter 3, the increase in government expenditures raises prices, reduces the real money supply, and raises the interest rate. This increase in the rate of interest causes net investment to decline because, in this case, it is assumed that investment is interest-elastic. The decrease in investment offsets a part of the expansionary effect of $\Delta \bar{G}$ on income. In panel (*b*) the final effect of $\Delta \bar{G}$ is $Y_F - Y_1$ although the immediate multiplier effect of $\Delta \bar{G}$ is ΔY_1.

Case 2   As in the previous case, the initial less-than-full-employment disequilibrium is set at point *B* in panels (*a*) and (*c*) of Figure 20-6. IS_2 cuts the *LM* curve at *B*. IS_2 is assumed to reflect interest-inelastic investment demand, and so the aggregate demand curve never cuts the full-employment income level Y_F. The goal is to shift IS_2 to IS_2' in panel (*a*) through an increase in government expenditures in order to shift the aggregate demand curve to D' in panel (*c*). The necessary increase in $\bar{G}$ is less than in the previous case. Since investment is assumed now to be interest-inelastic, a horizontal shift of IS_2 only by ΔY_2 will be sufficient to achieve full-employment equilibrium.

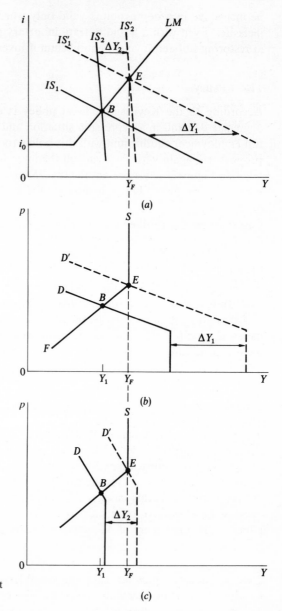

FIGURE 20-6a–c
Efficacy of fiscal policy as interest
elasticity varies.

Since the required increase in $\Delta\bar{G}$ is less than the interest-elastic case, the effect of $\Delta\bar{G}$ on prices will be less, and the decrease in real money balances will not be as great as before. Thus, the rise in the rate of interest is less and the decline in net investment is not as great, and for any given rise in the interest rate, investment will not be affected as much as before because it is assumed to be interest-inelastic. In panel (c) ΔY_2 is the initial "kick" from $\Delta \bar{G}$ needed to restore full-employment equilibrium, and the ultimate rise in Y will be $Y_F - Y_1$, shown in panel (c).

Now compare cases 1 and 2. First we saw that when investment is interest-elastic, a large increase in $\bar{G}$ is needed to restore equilibrium. The decrease in net investment due to the rise in interest rates will retard the expansionary impact. Thus the Keynesian proposition about the efficacy of fiscal policy in a depression should be reevaluated in the light of the interest elasticity of investment. Fiscal policy is effective in increasing the level of income, but it is "efficient" and "powerful" only if investment is interest-inelastic.

POLICIES FOR THE INSUFFICIENT INVESTMENT CASE

So far we have analyzed cases associated with the liquidity trap, putting aside the other Keynesian special case of *insufficient investment*. However, the analytical framework in this case parallels that for the liquidity trap. Monetary expansion shifts the aggregate demand curve strictly upward, whereas fiscal expansion moves the curve upward and to the right. Detailed analysis of this case is left to the reader as an exercise.

CONCLUSION

In this chapter we presented disequilibrium models of the Keynesian special cases. These differ from Keynes's own disequilibrium model (Chapter 18) in that Keynes treats disequilibrium with involuntary unemployment as a *general* phenomenon when the economy is experiencing a depression, whereas the Keynesians interpret unemployment disequilibrium as a special state taking place only when either a liquidity trap or insufficient investment prevails.

Two cases were examined here where a liquidity trap exists and the money wage rate is rigid. We saw that if investment is interest-elastic, the autonomous price-adjustment mechanism will gradually work and restore the general full-employment equilibrium although it would take a considerable period of time. Monetary policy is effective in this case, and it is complementary to the price adjustment. On the other hand, we found that when investment is interest-inelastic, monetary policy will likely be unable to reestablish full-employment equilibrium.

Fiscal policy was found to be efficient and powerful in restoring full employment only if investment is interest-inelastic. If investment is interest-elastic, large-sized fiscal actions are required. Therefore, monetary policy is more desirable when investment is interest-elastic, whereas fiscal policy is more efficient in the other case.

The conclusion by Keynesians that fiscal policy is the only effective method for curing a *sticky* unemployment disequilibrium is not fully supported by our analysis. The interest elasticity of investment is the crucial yardstick involved in making a choice between monetary and fiscal policy.

READINGS FOR CHAPTER 20

BAILEY, M. J.: *National Income and the Price Level*, 2d ed. (New York: McGraw-Hill, 1971).

BRONFENBRENNER, M., and T. MAYER: "Liquidity Functions in the American Economy," *Econometrica*, vol. 28, pp. 810–834, October 1960.

FRIEDMAN, M. (ed.): *Studies in the Quantity Theory of Money* (Chicago: The University of Chicago Press, 1956).

———— and A. J. SCHWARTZ: *A Monetary History of the United States, 1867–1960* (New York: National Bureau of Economic Research, 1963).

HABERLER, G.: *Prosperity and Depression* (Geneva: League of Nations, 1941).

HANSEN, A. H.: *A Guide to Keynes* (New York: McGraw-Hill, 1953).

HELLER, H. R.: "The Demand for Money: The Evidence from the Short-Run Data," *Quarterly Journal of Economics*, May 1965.

HICKS, J. R.: "Mr. Keynes and the 'Classics': A Suggested Interpretation," *Econometrica*, April 1937.

JOHNSON, H. G.: "Monetary Theory and Policy," *American Economic Review*, June 1962.

————: *Macroeconomics and Monetary Theory* (Chicago: Aldine, 1972).

KEYNES, J. M.: *The General Theory of Employment, Interest, and Money* (New York: Harcourt, Brace & World, 1936).

KLEIN, L. R.: *The Keynesian Revolution* (New York: Macmillan, 1960).

KUENNE, R. E.: *The Theory of General Economic Equilibrium* (Princeton, N.J.: Princeton, 1963), especially pp. 354–361.

LAIDLER, D.: *The Demand for Money* (Scranton, Pa.: International Textbook, 1969).

LEIJONHUFVUD, A.: *On Keynesian Economics and the Economics of Keynes* (New York: Oxford, 1968), chaps. 4 and 5.

MALKIEL, B. G.: "Expectations, Bond Prices, and the Term Structure of Interest Rates," *Quarterly Journal of Economics*, May 1962.

MODIGLIANI, F.: "Liquidity Preference and the Theory of Money," *Econometrica*, vol. 12, pp. 74–105, January 1944.

PATINKIN, D.: *Money, Interest, and Prices* (New York: Harper & Row, 1965), especially chap. 14.

PESEK, B. P., and T. R. SAVING: *Money, Wealth and Economic Theory* (New York: Macmillan, 1967).

PIGOU, A. C.: "The Classical Stationary State," *Economic Journal*, vol. LIII, pp. 343–351, 1943.

SAMUELSON, P. A.: "A Brief Survey of Post-Keynesian Developments," in J. E. Stiglitz (ed.), *The Collected Scientific Papers of Paul A. Samuelson* (Cambridge, Mass.: 1966).

SPIRO, A.: "Wealth and the Consumption Function," *Journal of Political Economy*, August 1962.

TOBIN, J.: "Liquidity Preference and Monetary Policy," *Review of Economics and Statistics*, vol. 29, pp. 124–131, May 1947.

————: "Liquidity Preference as Behavior towards Risk," *Review of Economic Studies*, February 1958.

TUCKER, D.: "Macroeconomic Models and the Demand for Money under Market Disequilibrium," *Journal of Money, Credit, and Banking,* pp. 57–83, February 1971.
———: "Patinkin's Macromodel as a Model of Market Disequilibrium," *Southern Economic Journal,* October 1972.

NAME INDEX

NAME INDEX

Abramovitz, M., 130, 133
Ackley, G., 63
Aftalion, A., 107
Alchian, A., 106, 335, 338
Allen, R. G. D., 97, 289, 291, 293, 314
Andersen, L. C., 242
Ando, H., 64, 180, 182
Arena, J. J., 83

Bailey, M. J., 94
Ball, R. J., 90
Barro, R. J., 350
Baumol, W. J., 40, 163
Bird, C., 80
Bischoff, C. W., 94, 103, 104
Boddy, R., 289
Bodkin, R., 79, 80
Bowley, 326
Branson, W. H., 224
Bronfenbrenner, M., 155, 179, 181, 182

Brown, E. C., 138
Brown, M., 265, 293
Brown, T. M., 138
Brumberg, R., 81
Brunner, K., 180, 181

Cagan, P., 182, 198
Chase, S. B., Jr., 167, 168, 180
Christiansen, L., 227
Clark, J. M., 107
Clower, R., 340, 350
Cobb, C. W., 220

Darling, P., 130, 133, 136, 138
DeLeeuw, F., 161, 181, 183, 213
Dernberg, J., 40
Dernberg, T., 40
Domar, E. D., 269, 278, 279
Douglas, P. H., 220
Drake, P. S., 90
Duesenberry, J., 64, 168

Edgeworth, 326
Eisner, R., 103
Evans, M. K., 90, 91, 127, 222

Fair, R. C., 360
Feige, E., 183
Fellner, W., 260
Ferber, R., 63
Friedman, M., 66, 79, 80, 155, 161, 176, 179–
    181, 198, 235, 260
Frisch, R., 107

Galper, H., 213
Gapinski, J. H., 289
Goldsmith, R., 64, 78
Gramlich, E., 125, 183, 213
Griliches, E., 224, 265
Grossman, H., 350
Gurley, J. G., 161, 236

Hansen, B., 217
Harrod, R. F., 269, 278–280, 285, 288
Hicks, J. R., 280, 286–288, 329
Hirshleifer, J., 94, 106
Houthakker, H. S., 147
Hymans, S. H., 256

Jaffé, W., 326
Jaffee, D. M., 360
Johnson, H., 235, 236
Jordan, J. L., 242
Jorgenson, D. W., 94, 103, 227, 265, 293

Kaldor, N., 277
Kaufman, G. G., 182
Keynes, J. M., 3, 106, 299, 311, 313, 315, 316,
    318, 330–343, 345, 357
Klein, L. R., 130, 133, 135, 136, 138
Kreinin, M. E., 79
Kuh, E., 256
Kuznets, S., 64, 84

Laidler, D. E. W., 180
Latané, H., 161
Leijonhufvud, A., 338, 350, 357, 365
Levhari, D., 306, 318
Lipsey, R. G., 254
Lovell, M., 130, 133, 136–138

Lucas, R. E., Jr. 260, 262
Lundberg, E., 133
Lydall, H. F., 180

McDonald, S. L., 182
McGouldrick, P., 138
Magee, S. P., 147
Markowitz, H., 175, 185, 202
Marshall, A., 324
Mayer, T., 179, 181, 182
Meltzer, A. H., 179–182
Metzler, L., 130, 133–136, 138, 179
Milles, E., 130
Modigliani, F., 64, 81, 155, 181, 182
Mosak, J., 61
Mundell, R. A., 145, 153

Nadiri, M. I., 103
Nelson, R. R., 224
Nerlove, M., 289

Okun, A., 258
Ott, A. F., 153, 155
Ott, D. J., 153, 155

Patinkin, D., 235, 236, 306, 318,
    350
Perry, G. L., 258, 259
Pesek, B. P., 235
Phelps, E. S., 260, 274
Phillips, A. W., 254

Rapping, L. A., 260, 262
Reid, M., 79
Robinson, J., 279

Saving, T. R., 235
Schultze, C. L., 260
Schwartz, A., 198, 235
Shaw, E. S., 236
Smithies, A., 62
Smyth, D., 133, 136, 138
Solow, R. M., 138, 280, 284
Spiro, A., 86
Stanback, T., 130
Stedry, A. C., 180, 181
Stein, J., 311
Stephenson, J. A., 103

Stigler, G., 21
Suits, D. B., 59

Teigen, R. L., 180, 181, 183
Tobin, J., 163, 171, 175, 180, 185, 190, 202
Tsiang, S. C., 175
Tucker, D. P., 350, 365
Turvey, R., 167

Uzawa, H., 281

Walras, L., 324, 326, 327
Watts, H., 80
Whalen, E. L., 169
Whitin, I., 131
Wicksell, K., 299, 311, 313, 315, 316, 318
Witte, J., 94

SUBJECT INDEX

SUBJECT INDEX

Absolute income hypothesis, 60–62, 80, 89
Absorption approach, 142
Accelerationist approach, 247, 260–262
Accelerator model:
  of inventory, 133, 135
  on investment, 107–110
Actual income, 330, 341, 346, 362
  (*See also* Realized income)
Adjusted monetary base, 204, 236
  impact on aggregate demand, 236
Aggregate demand, 6, 233, 234, 332, 336
Aggregate demand curve (function), 27, 248,
    267, 370
  "kinked," 371
  simultaneous, 352
Aggregate supply curve (function), 27, 233, 239,
    240, 248, 257, 267, 270, 332, 370
  horizontal ("Keynesian"), 27, 29, 251, 323
  "kinked," 370, 373
  positively sloped ("intermediate"), 27, 47,
    323
  shift in, 52
  vertical ("neoclassical"), 27, 42, 323
  when wages and prices are flexible, 27
Aggregate utility, 334, 335

Anticipation error, 138
Asset:
  categories of, 160–161
  financial, 159
  nonhuman, 234
Asset demand for money, 175, 176
Asset portfolio, 172, 173
Automatic market, 326, 329
Autonomous price adjustment, 376
Average cash balance, 165
Average productivity of labor, 221, 223, 266
Average propensity to consume (APC), 60–62,
  76

Backlog of demand, 132
Balance of payment:
  deficit in, 147
  equation of, 140, 144
  equilibrium of, 144, 147
  surplus in, 147
Balance sheet:
  of commercial banks, 198, 235
  of monetary system, 196, 197, 200
  of private sector, 233

Bank reserves, 197
Behavioral equation, 5
Bond holdings:
  average, 166
  cost of, 166
  initial, 166
Bond market equilibrium, 357, 358
Brokers fee, 164–166, 179, 312
Brookings-SSRC model, 161
Budget constraint, 213, 234
  with multipliers, 214
Buffer motive, 132
Buffer stock, 132, 331
Business cycle, 231
Business transfer payment in national income
    account, 17

Capacity utilization, 230, 270
Capital:
  definition of, 93
  desired stock of, 94–100, 107
  gain and loss of, 11, 188
  human, 176, 177
  optimum stock of, 95–103
  physical, 177
  stock of, 94, 264, 270
Capital account equation, 140
Capital accumulation (or formation), 308, 309,
    311, 314, 315
Capital consumption allowance, 17
Capital goods, price of, 99, 100
Capital intensity, 310
Capital-labor ratio, 104, 267, 269, 272, 273, 285,
    287, 308, 310, 316, 318
  equilibrium, 275, 299, 303, 315, 318
  optimum, 281
Capital movement:
  autonomous, 144
  induced, 144
Capital-output ratio, 269, 272, 285
  constant, 270, 280
  optimum, 281
Capital services, price of, 100
Capital share, 253
Certificate of deposit, 125
CES production function, 99, 221–223,
  231
Characteristic equation, 41
Chicago school, 175, 179, 180, 182, 184
Clay-clay model, 289, 293
Closed economy, 140, 142
Cobb-Douglas production function, 220–223,
  225, 227, 231, 253, 284, 289, 290, 293
Coefficient of adjustment, 313

Coefficient of anticipation, 137
Commodity endowment, 347
Commodity market equilibrium, 343, 354, 452
Comparative static multiplier, 34
Comparative statics, 7, 247, 264, 324, 327
Composition effect, 310
Constant factor shares, 220
Constant returns to scale, 220, 221
Consumer durables, 234
Consumer price index (CPI), 21
Consumption:
  definition of, 59
  maximized, 275, 276, 283, 300, 305
  price of, 227
Consumption expenditures:
  personal, 16
  real, 29
Consumption function:
  with absolute income hypothesis, 60–62
  Ackley's, 63
  Ando-Modigliani's, 64, 80, 227
  Friedman's, 66–71, 227, 231
  including money, 314
  Keynesian, 60
  with life-cycle hypothesis, 80, 226, 227, 231
  long-run properties of, 84, 124
  with permanent income hypothesis, 66–71,
    227, 231
  real, 234
  with relative income hypothesis, 64–66
  shape of, 74
  shift over time, 77
  short-run, 60
Corner maximum, 189
Corporate bond, 183
Corporate income tax, 212, 234
Correspondence principle, 39–43
  dynamic property in, 39
Cost:
  of holding bonds, 166
  of holding cash, 169, 305, 314
  opportunity, 99
Cost minimization, 221
Credit market, imperfect, 170
Credit unions, 161
Critical interest rate, 172, 367
Cross-section study, 81
Currency, demand for, 182
Currency account:
  deficit in, 142
  equation, 140
  surplus in, 142
Currency appreciation, 153, 157
Currency depreciation, 153
Currency ratio, 200

Debt-financed expenditure, 215
Deficient demand, 368
Deflation, 21, 260
  in money growth model, 305
Demand for currency, 182
Demand deposit, 30
  demand for, 182, 203
Demand for labor, 43, 226
Demand for money, 159–184, 234, 235
  asset, 175, 176
  Chicago school approach to, 175
  effective, 365
  empirical studies of, 167, 180
  function of, 161–184
  income elasticity of, 181
  interest elasticity of, 38, 181
  inventory-theoretic model of, 165
  Keynesian, 162–175
  long-run fraction of, 182
  national, 364
  precautionary, 162, 168–170, 184
  risk in, 174
  short-run function of, 182
  speculative, 162, 170–175, 184, 185, 365
  stability of, 162
  transaction, 31, 162–170, 184
  transaction elasticity of, 165
  variables in, 161
Demand for security, 183
Demand for time deposit, 183
Depreciation:
  in expanded model, 234
  in investment decision, 94, 99
  in national income account, 12
Differential equation, 273, 278, 284
Direct taxation, 267
Discount rate, 102, 107, 179, 202, 203, 208
Disembodied technical progress, 280–289, 294
Disequilibrium, 323–379
  less-than-full-employment, 377
  policy measures in, 358
  underemployment, 340, 365, 367, 370–372,
    379
Disequilibrium-amplifying force, 334
Disequilibrium theory (model), 3, 223, 230,
    323–376
  empirical test of, 360
  foundation of, 323
  Keynes', 331–343
  major concerns of, 324
  money, 364–379
  multimarket, 345–362
Disinvestment, 163
Distribution effects, 345–350, 362, 364, 365
  demand function with, 346

Distribution parameter, 221
Dividend yield, 177
Dummy variable, 257
Durable goods, 79
  demand for, 176
  expenditure for, 88
  in permanent income hypothesis, 79
Dynamics, 7, 247

Economic Report of the President's Council,
    238
Edgeworth-Bowley box, 326
Effective demand (supply), 350, 362
Elasticity of substitution, 102, 104, 221, 223,
    224
Embodied technical progress, 280, 289–294
Endogenous variables, 4, 234
Equation:
  concept, 5
  definitional, 6
  equilibrium, 6
  institutional, 5
  reduced-form, 7
  structural, 6
  technological, 5
Equilibria over time, 266
Equilibrium:
  long-run, 215, 217
  long-run static, 215
  short-run, 47
Equilibrium growth model, 7, 264–294
Equilibrium growth path, 266, 269, 270, 272,
    294
Equilibrium in the labor market, 226, 229–230
Equilibrium in the money market, 31
Equilibrium output overtime, 273
Equity, 176, 177, 183
  return to, 177
Euler conditions, 97
Ex ante value, 328, 340
Excess demand, 253, 257, 311, 315, 324, 329,
    345–347, 350
  for labor, 260
  primary, 351, 352, 354
  spillover, 351, 352, 354
Excess purchasing power, 350, 351
Excess supply, 254, 258, 313, 315, 329, 346,
    347, 350
  of labor, 260
Exchange rate, 141, 147
  equilibrium, 154
  fixed, 149–153
  flexible, 149, 153–154
Excise tax, 212

Exogenous variables, 4
Expanded macro models, 233–243
Expectation, 134, 138, 262
  long-term, 340
  short-term, 340
Expectation elasticity, 134, 138, 335
Expectations gap, 334, 340–341
Expected consumption, 72
Expected income, 82, 83, 88, 350
Expected utility function, 185
Expenditure-receipt gap, 163, 164
Export, 141
  effect on IS curve, 142
  net, 16
Ex post value, 279, 328, 340
External balance, 147
  adjustment to, 152–153
  fiscal policy for, 150, 152
  monetary policy for, 150, 152

False price, 329
False trading, 330, 346, 349, 350, 360
Federal Reserve assets, 199
Federal Reserve credit, 199
Federal Reserve-MIT model, 125
Federal Reserve notes, 197
Federal Reserve System (FED), 195–210
  balance sheet of, 196
FHA loan, 124
Financial institution, 123
  operation frameworks of, 207
Fiscal multipliers, 34–36, 49
Fiscal policy:
  in disequilibrium, 341, 350, 379
  effect on aggregate demand, 28
  effect on the interest rate, 36
  with a new multiplier, 204
  as the shapes of IS and LM vary, 37–38
Fixed coefficient, 269
Fixed exchange rate, 149–153
Fixed price hypothesis, 323, 324
Fixed proportions production function, 222
Flexible accelerator model, 135
Flexible exchange rate, 149, 153–154
Flexible price, 325
Float, 196, 199
Flow, 4
Flow equilibrium, 269, 270
Forced savings, 309, 310, 318
Foreign exchange:
  demand for, 154
  as a reserve asset, 199
  supply of, 154

Foreign trade balance equation, 140
Foreign trade multiplier, 143
Frictional deposit rate, 177
Full employment, 45, 66, 264, 269, 325, 334,
    338–340, 368, 371–373, 375, 377
  adjustment to, 323

General equilibrium approach, 324, 329, 350
Gold:
  certificate, 196
  points, 150
  role of, in fixed exchange rate system, 150
Golden Rule of accumulation, 274, 300
  with money, 305–306, 308, 309
Government budget constraint, 213, 234
Government deposit ratio, 200
Government income in GNP, 19
  disposable, 19
Government sector, 212–218
  in national income account, 12
  purchases of goods and services, 16
Government securities, 183, 196, 213, 235
  federal, 183
  local, 183
  long-term, 183
Groping process (*see* Tatonnement)
Gross national income:
  classification, 18–19
  definition, 16
  implicit GNP deflator, 21
Gross national product (GNP), 12
  actual GNP, 258
  definition, 12
  full-employment GNP, 24
  money GNP, 22
  potential GNP, 24, 225, 258
  real GNP, 22
Growth:
  concept of, 265–268
  equilibrium, 240
    and MPC, APC, 85, 87
  full-employment, 270
Growth models:
  basic Keynesian, 279
  clay-clay, 289, 293
  disembodied, 280
  embodied, 280, 289–293
  Harrod-Domar, 269–272, 278, 279, 293, 294
  Kaldor's, 278–279
  Keynes-Wicksell, 299
  Levhari-Patinkin, 306, 310
  with money, 298–318
  multisector, 294

Growth models:
  neoclassical, 272–277, 291, 294
  putty-clay, 289–294
  putty-putty, 289
  real sector, 272
  schematic guide to, 268
  with technical progress, 280–282
  vintage, 289
Growth rate, 240
  equilibrium, 265
  natural, 270, 272, 279, 294
  warranted, 270, 279, 294

Harrod-Domar model, 269–272, 278, 279, 293, 294
Harrod-neutral, 280–285, 289, 290
Hicks-neutral, 281, 285–289, 294
High-powered money, 51, 195, 198, 204, 205, 209, 213, 218
  effect on aggregate demand, 51
  equilibrium in the market for, 209
  multiplier of, 51
Homogeneous of degree one, 272, 281, 311
Housing:
  characteristics of, 122–123
  counter-cyclical aspect of, 123, 126
  demand for, 120–122
  demand curve for, 120
  investment in, 120–128
  mortgage availability for, 123
  multifamily, 123, 127
  neoclassical interpretation of, 123
  relative price of, 120–121
  single-family, 127
Housing stock, 121
  desired, 122
  optimum, 122
Human capital, 176
  return to, 177, 183
Hypothetical price, 327

Illegal transaction, 182
Illiquidity, 169
  opportunity cost of, 169, 179
  probability of, 169
Impact multiplier, 242
Imperfect credit market, 170
Import, 141
  effect on IS curve, 142
Income:
  actual, 330, 341, 346, 362
  balanced-budget, 215

Income:
  definition of, 8
  imputed, 10
  measuring, 12–18
  national, 9, 16, 18
  net, 9
  notional, 346
  permanent, 9, 67
  potential, 9
  realized, 330, 341, 346, 362
  stream of, 170
Income-constrained process, 330
Income distribution, 279, 294
Income effect, 350
Income elasticity:
  of consumption, 71, 78
  of money demand, 181
  of taxes, 237
Income-leisure choice, 230, 251, 333
Income tax:
  corporate, 212
  personal, 212
Independent investment function, 207, 315, 318
Indifference curve, 187–189, 191
  concave downward, 187, 189
  concave upward, 187, 189
  intertemporal, 95
  in portfolio choice, 187
  (See also Utility function)
Inelastic expectation, 339, 365
Inflation, 21, 247
  cost-push, 247, 250–252
  demand-pull, 247, 250–252
  effect on labor demand, 249
  effect on labor supply, 248
  money growth model, 305
Inflow of foreign capital, 144
Information cost, 330, 335
Input of production, 219
Inside money, 236
Insufficient investment, 371, 379
Interest elasticity of capital movements, 153
Interest elasticity of demand for bonds, 191
Interest elasticity of demand for money, 38, 181, 310, 343, 365
  effect on monetary policy, 38
  as the shape of LM varies, 38
Interest elasticity of investment, 38, 366, 368, 371, 373, 375–377, 379
  effect on fiscal policy, 38
  as the shape of IS varies, 38
Interest elasticity of supply of money, 203, 365

Interest rate:
  bond, 169, 179
  critical, 172, 367
  effect on demand for money, 31, 181
  effect on supply of money, 202
  equilibrium, 32
  future, 155, 174
  money, 169
  real, 294
Intermarket pressure, 350
Intermediate case:
  in demand and supply, 47–54, 233
  equilibrium conditions in, 47, 49, 233
  response of labor to prices, 47, 233
Internal equilibrium, 147
Internal-external equilibrium, 147, 155
  fiscal rule for, 154–157
  monetary rule for, 154–157
Inventory, 13
  actual stock of, 131
  at book value, 13
  desired stock of, 131
  in the physical value, 13
  speculative demand for, 132, 133
  transaction demand for, 131, 133
Inventory adjustment, 328
Inventory adjustment coefficient, 135
Inventory investment, 130–139
  empirical estimation of, 133
  errors-in-anticipating sales model of, 136–137
  expectations model of, 134–135
  flexible accelerator model of, 135
  variable accelerator model of, 136
Inventory/sales ratio, 131
Investment:
  concept of, 93
  ex post, 279
  net, 93
  planned, 269, 272, 316
  private domestic, 16
  real private domestic, 29
Investment function, 6
  aggregate, 94
  real, 234
  required, 275, 314
Investment-income ratio, 279
Investment model:
  accelerator, 107–110
  Keynes', 105–107
  neoclassical, 94–105
Investment-saving relationship, 273
Investment tax credit, 100

Involuntary unemployment, 334–341, 343, 345, 364, 367, 368, 371, 375
  adjustment from, 338–346
  definition of, 334, 336, 338
IS curve, 33, 37, 324, 342, 366–379
  derivation of, 33
  interest elasticity of, 367, 370
  slope of, 33, 36

Kaldor's model, 278
Keynes' disequilibrium model, 332–343, 379
Keynes' disequilibrium proposition, 331
Keynes-Wicksell model, 299, 311–318
"Keynesian case" multiplier, 210, 236, 239
Keynesian model, 3, 366
  assumptions in simple Keynesian model, 29
  of demand for money, 162–175, 184
  dynamic properties of, 39–42
  of investment, 105
  simple, 29, 257
Keynesian "special case," 365, 379
Keynesian view on monetary (or fiscal) policy, 377, 379

Labor:
  demand for, 43, 226
  effective demand for, 52
  potential supply of, 227
  supply of, 43, 226, 229–230
Labor demand curve, shape of, 226
Labor hoarding, 223
Labor income, 182
  in money demand function, 182–184
  in money supply function, 208
Labor-leisure choice, 230, 251
Labor market disequilibrium, 332
Labor market equilibrium, 44, 229–230, 233, 234, 270
Labor-output ratio, 270, 272
Labor share, 220, 253
Labor supply curve, shape of, 229–230
Lagged deficit, 217
  coefficient of, 217
Lagrangian function, 97
Layoff rate, 260
Leakage effect, 142
Leisure:
  as argument in consumption function, 226
  consumption of, 226
  price of, 228

Life-cycle hypothesis:
  Ando-Modigliani, 64, 80, 227
  Brumberg-Modigliani, 80
  cross-section studies of, 81, 83
  for long and short run, 82
  long-run studies of, 83
Limited-quantity hypothesis, 324–327
Linear production function, 221
Liquid assets, 161
  liquidity preference (*see* Demand for money)
Liquidity trap, 365–371, 373, 375, 379
LM curve, 324, 332, 366–379
  derivation of, 33
  flatten-out, 367
  shift in, 248
  slope of, 33, 36
Long-term capital, 143
  movement of, 143

Macro models, 4
Macroeconomics, 4
Marginal efficiency of capital (MEC), 30, 105, 106
Marginal product, 275, 291
  of capital, 99, 220, 221, 223, 286, 294
  of labor, 43, 220, 221, 223, 286, 301, 302, 331, 333
  value of (VMP), 43, 99
Marginal propensity to consume (MPC), 60, 62, 64, 76, 79, 272, 366
  long-run, 85, 87
  short-run, 86, 87
Marginal propensity to save (MPS), 270, 278
Marginal rate of return on investment, 29
Marginal rate of substitution, 281, 286, 287
Marginal tax rate, 30, 366
Marginal utility, 186
  diminishing, 187
Marshallian system, 324, 328
Maximum consumption, 275, 276, 283, 294
Measured consumption, 72
Measured income, 72
Medium of exchange, 161
Micro models, 4
Microeconomics, 4
Monetarist vs. Fiscalist, 35–36
Monetary base, 195, 210, 236, 332, 366
  adjusted, 197, 199, 200–202, 204, 205, 236
  demand for, 204, 205, 206, 208, 210
  derived demand for, 204
  equation of, 197

Monetary base:
  equilibrium, 208–210
  supply of, 200, 210
Monetary policy:
  with budget constraints, 218
  in disequilibrium, 341, 350, 373, 379
  effect on aggregate demand, 28
  effect on interest rate, 36–38
  expansionary, 310
  with a new multiplier, 204
  as shapes of IS and LM vary, 36–37
  "shift effect" of, 52
  "slope effect" of, 52
  variables for, 210
Money:
  as asset, 300
  "broad" definition of, 181
  as consumer's good, 306
  cost of holding, 30
  definition of, 159, 161, 181
  demand for, 31, 159–184
    (*See also* Demand for money)
  in growth models, 298–318
  inside, 236
  "narrow" definition of, 161
  in open economy, 147–148
  outside, 236
  per capita stock of, 308
  real, 30, 300
  stock of, 30, 45
    (*See also* Supply of money)
  supply equation of, 30
Money demand function, 161–184, 313
  "kinked," 367
Money illusion, 331, 334, 335, 338, 340
Money market:
  disequilibrium in, 364–365
  equilibrium in, 31, 233, 234
Money/output ratio, 267
Money wage rate, 252, 254, 331, 334
  rigidity of, 335
Monotonic adjustment, 359
Multiplier:
  in expanded model, 236
  fiscal, 35–36, 49, 203, 213, 216, 239
  with government budget constraints, 214
  government expenditure, 215
  government purchase, 215
  government receipt, 215
  long-run, 217
  monetary, 30, 35–36, 49, 50, 202, 203, 210, 213, 239, 332
  short-run, 217

Multisector model, 294
Mutual savings bank, 123, 183

National demand (supply), 350, 351, 360
National income, 10, 18, 346
  deficit and surplus in, 20–21
  gross, 17
  measurement of, 18
  transactions excluded from, 10
  transactions included in, 10
National income account, 10, 140
Near-money, 179, 180, 182, 184
Neoclassical model:
  assumptions for, 272
  in demand and supply, 42–46
  in economic growth, 272–277, 291, 294
  equilibrium in, 44
  in investment, 94–104
  in investment theory, 94–104
Net exports, 16
Net national product (NNP), 17, 18
New macroeconomics, 4
Non-bank public, 182, 205
Non-human wealth, 73, 79, 182, 184
Nonproperty income, 82
Non-tatonnement hypothesis, 347, 349
Normal distribution, 186

Observed quantity traded, 360
Obsolescence of capital, 289–291
Okun's law, 257
"Open economy," 142, 248
  equilibrium condition of, 142
Open market operation, 200
  defensive, 200
  offensive, 200
Opportunity cost, 99
  of holding money, 169, 305, 314
Optimum amount of investment, 105
Optimum capital stock, 95–103
Optimum monetary policy, 309
Optimum precautionary balance, 169
Optimum rate of price change, 309
Optimum transaction balance, 169
Oscillatory adjustment, 359
Output:
  definition, 8
  "demand-dominated," 27
  equilibrium, 31
  full-employment, 24, 27
  national output, 9

Output:
  real, 27
  "supply-dominated," 27
Output-capital ratio, 278, 309
Output elasticity, 224, 286, 287
  constant, 269, 289
Output-labor cost ratio, 293
Output-labor ratio, 270, 272
Outside money, 236
Overall savings effect, 206

Pareto efficiency, 349, 362
Payment pattern, 167
  in transaction demand for money, 167
Per capita consumption, 274
Per capita investment, 274
Perfect information, 324
Permanent consumption, 68
Permanent income, 67
Permanent income hypothesis, 66–71, 88
  empirical test of, 74–80
Permanent tax, 88
Perpetuity bond, 186
Personal consumption expenditure, 16
Personal exemptions, 30
Personal income, 18
  disposable, 18
Personal income tax, 212
Phelp's Golden Rule of Accumulation, 275
Phillip's curve, 254–262
  empirical, 258
  long-run, 262
  shift in, 261
  short-run, 262
  vertical portion of, 260
Physical capital, 177
  return to, 177, 183
Physical consumption, 308
Physical savings ratio, 308
Planned income, 330, 350
Planned price, 328
Planned saving, 269, 272, 315
Planned transactions, 350
Policy measures in disequilibrium, 358
Polynomial utility function, 188
Population, working age, 228
Portfolio choice model, 175
Portfolio effect on money demand, 216
Precautionary demand for money, 160–170
Present value, 96
  maximization of, 96

Price:
  "demand-dominated," 27
  in money demand function, 178
  "supply-dominated," 30
Price adjustment mechanism, 299
Price behavior, 253
Price-elasticity:
  of demand for exports, 145
  of domestic imports, 145, 146
  sum of, 142, 146
Price-hedging, 133
Price ridigity, 323
Price takers, 329
Primary forces, 346, 351, 352, 354, 357–360, 362
Probability distribution, 169, 184
  subjective, 186
Product:
  final, 11
  intermediate, 11
Production adoption coefficient, 137, 138
Production function, 43, 95, 219–231, 233, 234, 265
  CES, 221–223, 231
  Cobb-Douglas, 220–223, 225, 227, 231, 253
  fixed proportion, 222
  linear, 222
Production statement, 13
  of a firm, 13
  of all firms in the economy, 14
Productivity, 247, 252–253
  average, 253
  capital, 99, 220, 221
  effect on wages and prices, 252
  labor, 220, 221, 249, 252, 253, 256
  marginal, 251–253
Profit-equity ratio, 218
Profit maximization, 220, 253
Property tax rate, 120
"Putty-clay" model, 289, 294
"Putty-clay" production function, 104
"Putty-putty" model, 289

Quadratic utility function, 186, 191
Quantity theory of money, 300
Quasi-rent, 291, 293
Quit rate, 260

Random variable, 186
Rate of change:
  in capital, 312, 315

Rate of change:
  optimum in prices, 309
  in prices, 256, 313
  in relative excess supply of labor, 255
  in wage rate, 254, 291, 293
Rate of growth, 53
  in labor force, 270, 272, 308, 309
  in output, 265, 266
Rate of interest (*see* Interest rate)
Rate of return:
  after-tax, 99, 120, 121
  before-tax, 102, 121
  on capital, 301
    (*See also* Marginal product of capital)
  on equities, 174, 179
  on human capital, 177, 179, 183
  internal, 105
  on labor (*see* Marginal product of labor)
  on physical assets, 177, 179, 183
  on real balances, 301
  on saving shares, 207
  on time deposit, 207
Real balance-output ratio, 301, 308
Real corporate saving, 29
Real money balance, 27, 45, 235, 248, 300, 301, 377
  demand for (*see* Demand for money)
  supply of (*see* Supply of money)
Real sector model, 272
Real tax effect, 248
Realized income, 341, 346, 362
Realized transaction, 350, 351, 362
Rediscount, 200
Reduced form, 242
Regulation Q, 125
Relative income hypothesis, 64–66, 88
Rent:
  on unit of capital, 99
  U.S. interest, 99
Rental value of capital services implicit, 100
Replacement investment, 103
Required growth of capital, 275, 278, 299
Required propensity to consume, 272
Reserve, 197, 199, 200
  borrowed, 200, 205
  desired, 204, 205
  excess, 200, 205
  free, 200
  required, 200, 201, 204
  unborrowed, 200, 201
Reserve ratio:
  average, 201
  desired borrowed, 207

Reserve ratio:
  desired excess, 205, 207
  desired free, 201, 202, 210
  free, 202, 206
  required, 201
Returns to scale:
  constant, 221, 299
  decreasing, 221
  increasing, 221

Sales tax, 212
Savings:
  capitalists, 278
  ex ante, 272, 315, 340
  ex post, 279, 340
  forced, 279, 316, 318
  planned, 269, 272, 315
  workers', 278
Savings and loan associations, 123, 124
Savings rate, 267
  constant, 272
  forced, 315, 316
Scale factor, 221
Securities, 159
  demand for, 174
  desired amount of, 209
Short run, definition of, 324, 328
Short-term capital, 144
Simultaneous equation system, 41, 325
Social insurance, 212, 257
Society's total endowment, 349
Solow-neutral, 280, 284–285, 294
Special drawing right (SDR), 199
Speculation:
  role in inventory model, 133
  role in money demand, 159, 170–175, 184,
    185, 365
Speculative demand for money (*see* Demand
  for money)
Speed of adjustment, 343
Spillover effect (force), 345, 350–360, 362, 364,
  365
  macromodel with, 350
Spiraling adjustment, 359
Stability conditions, 42, 314
Stability of macro system, 40, 41
Standard deviation, 169, 187, 188
Statics, 7
Steady state, 258, 291, 292, 303, 307–309,
  316
Steady state growth rate, 269, 280, 294,
  316

Step function, 172
Stock:
  buffer, 132
  capital, 94, 234
  definition of, 3
  housing, 120, 121
Stock adjustment hypothesis, 94
Stock equilibrium, 103
Structural equation, 242, 259
  substitution effect, 190
Substitution parameter, 221
Supply of labor, 43, 223–230, 235
  shift in, 250
  wage elasticity of, 239
Supply of money, 182, 234, 248
  equation of, 195, 200–204, 210

Tatonnement, 324, 326–329, 345
Tax:
  net real tax, 30
  net tax, 20
  real tax effect, 248, 250
Tax equation (function), 212, 366
Tax rate on labor income, 229
Tax savings, 99
Taylor's theorem, 40, 314
Technical change, 240
Technical progress, 280–294
  capital-augmented, 284–285
  clay-clay type, 289, 293
  disembodied, 280–289, 294
  embodied, 270, 280, 289–293
  Harrod-neutral, 280–285, 289, 293,
    294
  Hicks-neutral, 281, 286–289, 294
  labor augmented, 281–284
  neutrality of, 280
  putty-clay type, 289–294
  putty-putty type, 289
  rate of, 283
  Solow-neutral, 280, 284–286, 294
Technology, progress in, 267
Term of maturity, 183
Time deposit ratio, 200
Time deposits, 159, 181, 207, 208
  demand for, 183, 202, 207
Time path:
  of output, 247
  of price, 247
Total transactions vs. GNP, 168
Transaction cost, 131, 168
Transactions demand for money, 162–170

Transfer payments, 10, 30, 168
Transferred demand, 351, 352
Transitory income, 69, 78–80
Treasury, 195
Treasury bills, 183
Treasury currency, 196, 213
  outstanding, 197

Uncertainty, 168, 170, 174
  and demand for money, 168, 185
Underemployment disequilibrium, 339, 365,
  367, 370–379
Unemployment:
  definition of, 23
  frictional, 24, 254, 255
  involuntary, 324
  "normal," 24
  seasonal, 334
  voluntary, 334
Unemployment rate, 254, 255, 259
  global, 254
  for married males, 259
  natural, 260, 262
  for women and teenagers, 259
Union wage demand, 251
Unionized economy, 251
Unions:
  monopoly power of, 256, 339
  wage demands of, 251
User cost of capital, 104
Utility function:
  expected, 185
  including leisure, 226
  including money, 308, 318
  intertemporal, 226, 338
  polynomial, 188
  quadratic, 186
Utility maximization rule, 329

VA loan, 124
Value-added, 219
Value of marginal product of capital, 99
Value of marginal product of labor, 43
Variable, 4
  concept of variable, 4
  endogeous variable, 4
  exogenous variable, 4

Wage:
  money, 228, 252, 254, 331, 334, 339, 345, 370
  real, 228, 252, 331, 334, 339, 345, 370
Wage bargaining, 335
Wage-price freeze, 257
Wage-price guidepost, 257
Wage-price-productivity relationship, 253, 254,
  262
Wage rigidity, 323, 335, 338, 340, 341, 345, 375
Wage stickiness, 230
Walras' Law, 365
Walrasian system, 324, 326–329
"Weak approach" to financial-sector analysis,
  195, 204–208
Wealth, 5, 60, 80, 162, 175–177, 180, 367
  definition of, 176, 235
  human, 176, 177
  nonhuman, 126, 180, 182, 184, 229, 231, 235
  potential human, 227
Wealth effect:
  on consumption, 80, 217, 248, 250
  on leisure demanded, 229
  on money demanded, 176, 215, 236
Wealth elasticity of money demand, 181
Wharton School study on consumption
  functions, 60
Wholesale price index, 21
Windfall income, 79
Work force composition, 259